STORE

BY

Nan Tillson Birmingham

G. P. PUTNAM'S SONS
NEW YORK

Library of Congress Cataloging in Publication Data

Birmingham, Nan Tillson.
  Store.
  Index
  Includes bibliography
1. Department stores—United States. I. Title.

HF5465. U4B57   1978   381   78-14204

ISBN 0-399-11899-3

PRINTED IN THE UNITED STATES OF AMERICA

CONTENTS

PART III

PART IV

DEDICATION
to
Marion Tillson Bradford
Nancy Adams Holliday
Mark, Harriet, and Carey Birmingham

and
In Memory
of
My Mother and Father
Adele and Warren Tillson

Preface and Acknowledgments

More than three years have passed since my cousin, Nancy Adams Holliday, and I reminisced about stores we had loved and shopping trips we had taken and she said, "Someone ought to write a book . . ." Since that California summer evening in 1975 I have traveled thousands of miles throughout the United States. I've toured stores, practically lived in many, attended store promotions and openings, and interviewed hundreds of people in merchandising, fashion, design, architecture, and city planning. I was fortunate enough to be able to gather further information relating to American retailing and fashion in England, France, Italy, Scandinavia, and India.

My thanks go to all the people who over these years have been informative and supportive. I want to express my appreciation in San Francisco to Jean and Carl Livingston, Jr., Cyril Magnin, Ellen Magnin Newman, Ross Anderson, Norman Wechsler, Neal Fox, John Brunnelle, Dorothy Frank MacKenzie, Mrs. Fred Bloch, George Trapp, and Edna Jager, secretary to the late Grover Magnin. I am *deeply* indebted to Elizabeth Curtis for her important contribution and for introducing me to Mrs. Grover Magnin, and to Mrs. Magnin herself, for her remembrances of her I. Magnin days and her merchant husband, and to "Our" Miss Rose French, whom I have tried unsuccessfully to locate.

9

Also in San Francisco my thanks to Philip Schlein at Macy's and Hal Haener and Susan Graham; to Henry Hopkins of the Museum of Modern Art, sculptor Ruth Asawa, and Trader Vic Bergeron for allowing me to be a part of their contest judging and to the Trader for the superb lunch. My thanks to Davey Rosenberg of Marino and Rosenberg.

I am particularly grateful to Evelyn Aleshin for providing me with "lost" information on the City of Paris, and to Earl Moss of the Victorian Alliance and architect Philip Johnson in New York for further City of Paris data; to Jim Holliday, former director of the California Historical Society, for putting me in touch with historian Dr. Abraham P. Nasatir in San Diego, who guided me to his bibliography, which led me into the Rare Book Department of the New York Public Library for papers and diaries about the Isthmus of Panama crossings and the French in California during the Gold Rush. My thanks to Wendy Wong of the University of California Oral History Department for her assistance and to Robert Hink of Berkeley for his cooperation; to my good friends Tina Cella and Andrew Delfino for introductions and hospitality and to Daulton Hatch of Carmel for his interest and encouragement.

In Southern California I want to thank Jerome Nemiro, Anne Stegner, Raymond Dexter, Helen Moore, Dorothy Roth, Virginia Florence, Louise de Vries, Bert Lara, June Parenti, Katherine Henderson, Rudy Galindo at Bullock's Wilshire, Miss Stella at I. Magnin & Co., George Allan of the Wilshire Chamber of Commerce, my aunt and uncle, Mr. and Mrs. Earl C. Adams of San Marino, California, for their memories, and Mrs. Glenn Winnett Boocock of New York and Mrs. Leslie di Carpegna of Millbrook, New York, for sharing remembrances of their father and grandfather, respectively, P. G. Winnett of Bullock's Wilshire. My thanks also in Los Angeles to my friends Dr. Richard Davis and his wife, Madelyn; to Stephen Gavin and to George Milliken, and to my son, Carey, for their hospitality; to Mary Ellis Carlton of the *Independent Press-Telegram* in Long Beach for data on Buffum's.

I am grateful to Walter Evans of Seattle for putting me in touch with Nordstrom's; in Phoenix, I want to thank Edward Jacobson, Mrs. Charles Korrick, Ed Korrick, Jerry Lewkowitz, and Harry Rosenzweig. Thanks to Redmond Largay and Catherine Wueste of Goldwaters and to Sandy Love, Mili O'Neill, Favor Hazelton Slater, Linda Kite, Dearie Karatz, Jerry and Ollie McNamara, and a special salute to my father's friend and World War I fellow officer, Frank Brophy, for giving me a picture of the early days in Arizona. Thanks to Kathleen Hite and Jane Roland in Carefree.

In Oklahoma City I am indebted to Mayor Patience Latting, Jane and Buddy Rogers, Joseph Connolly, Dannie Bea Hightower, and Frank Hightower, and my friends Nancy Berry and Chef John Bennett II.

My thanks in Dallas, Texas, to Sally Marcus, Mrs. Herbert, Jr., for introducing me to Mrs. Herbert Marcus, Sr., and Mr. Stanley Marcus; to Neiman vice-president Tom Alexander, and in Fort Worth to Tom and Ginny Barnett of Neiman's and to Martha and Elton Hyder for their kind hospitality, and Neiman's Marsha Harris.

My thanks to Dr. and Mrs. Maurice Rusoff for introducing me to Mrs. Simon Lazarus in Columbus, Ohio.

The Detroit contingent of John Coxeter and Beverly Klemola of Carl Byoir Associates and Robert Jackson of the Renaissance Center Partnership were wonderfully informative and enthusiastic; and my thanks in Atlanta, Georgia, to John Portman Associates for their cooperation; in Chicago, Arthur Osborne, president of Marshall Field & Co., Mr. Fran Foley, and Barbara Greener of *The Field Glass*, the in-house magazine, all guided me through the colorful story of Field's, but I want to say a special word for Mary Wheeler, Field's archivist, who spent long hours taking me inside and out through the store and introducing me to the personnel, along with searching her files, crates and cartons on her own time for the material about the "Men from Field's" and other delightful stories. My thanks to David Daleiden and Jason Thomas for Field's vignettes. At Water Tower Place, James Klutznick of Urban Investment and Development Corporation and Jacquelin Fridrich of the Ritz-Carlton Hotel were generous with their time and information. A special nod to Mildred Custin of Mildred Custin, Ltd., in New York for her knowledge of Water Tower Place, Renaissance Center, and retailing in general.

I appreciated Sarah Lawler's material and input on Dayton's, Minneapolis, Minnesota.

Aline Macy Clark very kindly provided me with Macy family material and the genealogy; my thanks to Lisl Dennis for putting me in touch with her Macy relatives; to Wilhelmine Waller of Bedford Hills, New York, for data that led me to Dorothy Hinitt, who had lived in Florence Macy Sutton's house, and to Miss Hinitt for her information about the house and our tour of Sutton's Corners; to Philip Murray for information about R. H. Macy and Nantucket Island.

A very special thank you to Mrs. Bernard Gimbel for sharing intimate memories of her husband and for providing me with Gimbel material. I am deeply appreciative of Bernice Fitz-Gibbon's encouragement and I thank her for continually giving me stories of her days at Wanamaker's, Macy's, and Gimbels. I'm grateful to Jeanne O'Neill, Mrs. Leslie Forester, Charlene Sutton and especially Phyllis Condon for recollecting their days with "Fabulous" Fitz.

My thanks to Helen O'Hagan, Sara Middleman, and Miss Lee at Saks (New York), and an extra word of gratitude to my good friend, Merve Retchin, at Saks White Plains, who listened endlessly and with her knowledge of retailing kept me on the right track. My thanks to former Saks executives Barry Summerfield and Milton Hofflin and to Mr. Hofflin of Copeland, Novak and Israel for introducing me to Adolph Novak, whose expertise on store architecture was invaluable. My thanks to M. Jean Bugin at Gimbels-Saks Buying Office in Paris. Mrs. Adam Gimbel was most gracious in sharing her memories of her life with the late Adam Gimbel and recollections of her fashion career as Sophie of Saks Fifth Avenue. In the the world of high fashion and design, I wish to thank Adolpho, who is a particular delight, for his contribution.

At Gucci in Rome, Florence, New York, and Beverly Hills, I want to thank Dr. Aldo Gucci, Roberto Gucci, Giorgio Gucci and his wife, Maria Pia, R. E. Kirkpatrick, Maria Elina Angelotti, and Chicki Kleiner, with a special word of appreciation to Ruby Hamra of Hamra Associates; to René Picard of the Canadian Embassy, Rome, for the story of the Italian envoy and the Queen of France; to Bruce Karatz of Kaufman & Broad, Paris, for guiding me to "La Maison sur le toit" at Le Printemps; to Richard Walker, Director of British Isles Buying Agency, Inc., formerly of Abercrombie & Fitch, London, and his wife, Crystal; Adrienne Spanier of Peter Jones, and also in London, my friend Angela Allen.

My thanks at Bergdorf Goodman to Ira Neimark, Suzanne Butterfield, and Jo Hughes; at Henri Bendel to Susan Goodman and Buster Jarrett, and to Kit Fisher, formerly of Bendel's; at B. Altman & Co., to Judy Jenney and Marion Baer.

I want to thank the former chairman of the board of Bloomingdale's, Lawrence Lachman, and the present chairman, Marvin Traub, and Mrs. Lee Traub; also Barbara D'Arcy, Peggy Healy, Richard Knapple, Candy Pratts, Ruth Eshel in New York, Lillian Moran in Stamford, Connecticut, and Nancy Rosenfield at Bloomingdale's White Plains.

At Air India my thanks to Director Peter Mahta, Chota Chudasama, and Pallavi Shah in New York and Captain Jimmy Martin in Bombay; in New Delhi to Miss V. Pai of the Department of Tourism; Allan Bradford of ABC News; and also in Bombay, to Munira and Nana Chudasama, Vilas and Mota Chudasama, Camillia Panjabi, Dr. Sarala Patel, Leybourne Callaghan, and Sheila Nixon, and my friend Shakunthala Jagannathan of the Bombay Tourist Office, for their introductions and hospitality on my trips to India and for giving me an insight into their country; to my friend "Baiji" Shobah Kanwar of Jodhpur and Her Highness the Maharani of Jodhpur, my thanks for a memorable 1977 Thanksgiving dinner at the Umaid Bhawan Palace in Jodhpur and for stories of Bloomingdale's in Rajastan.

I want to thank Leonard Sloane of *The New York Times* and the co-author of *The Great Merchants* for his encouragement and assistance in the early stages of my research; also at the *Times*, Enid Nemy and Bernadine Morris; and Bailey Morris and Joy Billington at *The Washington Star*.

There are several people who have been involved with my book either directly or indirectly and my thanks goes to Joan Glynn of Wells, Rich and Green; Bill Kummel of Bear Sterns & Co., David Ruttenberg of Wolf, Haldenstein, Adler, Freeman and Herz; Dale Remington of Kaleidoscope; Jeanne Capodilupo, Community Affairs Coordinator, Woodlawn cemetery; Margaret Thalken of *Vogue*; S. Ralph Cohen of Scandinavian Airlines, New York; and my friends Daisy Borden, Alice and Milton Greenberg of Rye, New York, and Lyn Tornabene of Greenwich, Connecticut. My thanks also to Alitalia Airlines.

In Rye, New York, my thanks to Betsy and Tom Dulick for overseeing my house and dog and to Kevin Miserocchi for keeping it all together. At the risk of being outrageously sentimental I remember fondly my sweet, old, funky dog, Zoid, who lay at my feet and gave solace during my hours at the typewriter, and who during my final chapter had the good taste not to try my emotional energies, but quietly went to sleep forever.

I want to express my appreciation over the past ten years to Vita Nelson, editor and publisher of *Westchester*. I wrote recipes and hostess advice for her magazine until she quite literally pushed me out of the kitchen and presented me with bigger challenges—which brings me to dear Frank Zachary of *Town & Country*, who had faith in me, and Dick Kagan, Jean Barkhorn, Marie Louise Doyle, Nancy Gardiner, Linda Gwinn and all the staff with whom I have had the joy of working since the spring of 1974. Information on Phoenix, Oklahoma City, the Social Register, Vernon and Irene Castle, and various aspects of fashion and home decor were gleaned while working on articles for *Town & Country*. The Gucci chapter, "Via Condotti Comes to Via Fifth," appeared in total in *Town & Country* (December 1977) titled, "Merchant Aldo Gucci."

The staffs of the various departments and the microfilm section of the New York Public Library are to be commended for digging out books, newsclips, and film; my thanks to the staff of the Rye Free Reading Room and to Lois Klein, who gave me assistance and provided her daughter, Leslie, as a researcher of musical lyrics pertaining to stores. Thanks also to the various members of the staff of the Harrison Library who helped me and the staff members of the Museum of the City of New York; *New York* Magazine; *Women's Wear Daily*; and the Metropolitan Museum Costume Institute. My thanks also to Mary and Frank Kilpatrick of the Village Book Store, Rye, for locating books.

There has been no end to the tolerance, patience, and encouragement shown me by my friend and agent Roz Cole. My thanks to John Dodds, formerly of G. P. Putnam's Sons, for believing in me, and to my editor at Putnam, Ned Chase, whose good counsel when my energy flagged was to "keep going." Ned's assistant, Charles Krinsky, whom I met on a big day for both of us—his first at Putnam, and my manuscript delivery day—has been most helpful in the final details. My thanks to Senior Editor Diane Matthews.

My sister, Marion Tillson Bradford, was helpful in recalling our growing up in Modesto, California, and was strength because she

was always there; I appreciate my brother-in-law Clarkson Bradford's memories of his uncle, David Yates of Marshall Field & Co.

My children, Mark, Harriet, and Carey Birmingham, who are
not children in the small sense, but who will always be *my children*,
I thank for their cheers from the sidelines and for much more. Miss
Harriet researched the pneumatic tube material and discovered
Roger's in Greenwich, Connecticut; Carey made a million trips to
the grocery store, copy shop, and typist and as an NYU journalism
student assisted with his editorial judgment; Mark, in faraway Colorado, was a long-distance spirit-lifter. More than anything, I
thank them for loving and caring.

And now a word about Mildred Dicker, who called after a long
absence, as if by magic, when my need was great. Mildred came
back into my life as a typist and remains forever as a friend. She
worked late hours against the time pressures, even when her husband, Sidney, was critically ill. Mildred not only typed, she tidied
up my punctuation and spelling and participated in research by putting me onto Harry Beethoven and Woodlawn Cemetery as
sources for my book. Her enthusiasm was boundless. Mildred de-
serves an extra special thank you—she is an extra special person.

My thanks to Harry Beethoven of West Palm Beach, Florida, for
his story and letters.

The one thing that almost brought this project to a total halt was
the enormity of the subject that I had undertaken to write about.
The most painful job for me was elimination of material. I alone
made the decisions about what is included in this book. I alone did
the research, with the exception of the material I have mentioned. I
am responsible. I am well aware that there are many fine stores and
dedicated merchants throughout the country that I have omitted or
only touched upon lightly—my choices were made in an effort to
create from all the components that go into making a store a com-
posite picture within these pages of a STORE. I hope all the merchants and people involved in one way or another with stores will
understand that they are in spirit what this book is about.

I have used the term *department* store to refer to both department stores as we know them today where they sell hard (appliances, furniture) and soft (fabric, clothing, accessories) goods and
specialty stores where they feature only soft goods. There is a fine
line drawn between them, but in the beginning stores grew out of

shops by adding a variety of departments, therefore they are in truth all *department* stores.

These acknowledgments have the ring of a lengthy Academy Award acceptance speech, but the appreciation and thanks come sincerely from my heart.

NAN TILLSON BIRMINGHAM

Rye, New York
July 1978

PART I

What Is a Store?

ONE

Beyond the Bottom Line

A store is a place where goods are bought and sold. It's business—profit or loss. The name of the game is buying and selling and it's the bottom line of the balance sheet, red or black, that counts. Almost half of American businesses are retail operations and the Commerce Department estimated total retail sales for the month of June, 1978, at $66.8 billion. These figures represent every kind of store imaginable, from supermarket to sex shop. The endless variety of stores includes discount houses, warehouse salesrooms, neighborhood shops, even stores that aren't stores, but mail-order catalogues. Throughout the country, however, there are stores whose influences have gone beyond their impact on our economy. These are department and specialty stores, past and present, old and new, large and small, that have in many ways gone beyond dollars and cents, beyond the bottom line.

These stores are mobile time capsules. They are reflections of our history, heritage, and regional differences. They are guideposts to what our life is, along with being tastemakers and trendsetters, showing what our life should or could be. They provide merchandise that is essential to everyday living and the stuff that dreams are made of, promising the good life—beauty, chic, comfort, and status. These stores are entertainment—show business, pageantry, and parties. They are social meeting places and sometimes community centers. They are landmarks and tourist attractions. They are three-dimensional constant-moving pictures.

Stores are born and take on life. They pulse with the energy of their management, employees, and customers. They develop personalities. They are sensuous and seductive, filled with imagination and fantasy, or they are practical and down to earth. Some are even intimidating and frightening. Stores have smells and sounds and ambience. Walter Hoving, who should know, having been executive vice-president of Macy's and Montgomery Ward, chairman of Associated Dry Goods, president of Lord & Taylor and, later, of Bonwit Teller, and chairman of Tiffany since 1955, said in an interview with *Women's Wear Daily*, "A store must have a kind of soul."

People get emotional about stores. They may be loyal and love one store so much they won't shop elsewhere. Then again, they may hate a store and vow never to set foot inside its doors. Sometimes love and hate get mixed up and a person may shop in a store he hates to buy merchandise he loves.

There are stores that grow and become impersonal and stores that grow and maintain a close relationship with their customers. There are stores that don't grow.

There are stores that stay young and swinging, others that get old and dowdy. Stores die. The death of a store is painful, for it takes with it bits and pieces of our lives. Stores are filled with associations—wedding dresses, baby clothes, furniture, toys, and stereos, and, and, and—all the trappings that rotate through our days and years. Stores are filled with memories of Christmases and shopping trips.

Stores are different things to different people. Jeannie Sakol, whose novel *New Year's Eve* has key scenes set in New York stores, says, "Stores are second homes for city people." Writer Priscilla Tucker would like to have a store for her first home and says, in an article in *New York* magazine, "I've been thinking a lot lately about where I'd like to live and decided on Macy's. It's New York's ultimate loft." Charles Kennedy, a member of the Eliot Feld Ballet, lists in his *Playbill* biography: "HOBBY: Bloomingdale's."

The *Minneapolis Star* discovered in a survey taken in the Twin Cities, Minneapolis and St. Paul, where they have a plethora of cultural institutions and sports events, that shopping was the area's number-one leisure activity. These results are no surprise to anyone who knows Dayton's, the largest retailer in the upper midwest, and one of the most promotional-and community-minded stores in the country. There are constant activities at Dayton's—an all-day Senior Citizen Prom, a banquet for the Minneapolis Girls' Track and Field Team, a three-week store-wide promotion on today's woman, themed "You've Come a Long Way," with daily seminars on women and health, careers, and life-styles. During Tradewinds Week, there were demonstrations of African headdress making, Philippine dancing, Kung Fu and Karate, along with African, Thai, Japanese, Korean, and Don the Beachcomber cooking. In January 1977, there was the "Dayton's presents the Virginia Slims Tennis Tournament" at the Met Center, with bus transportation provided from the store. But nothing has matched the furor of its 1976 Christmas creation of a chocolate factory, based on Roald Dahl's children's book *Charlie and the Chocolate Factory.* Willy Wonka, the wizard of the factory, presented magic shows and conducted tours through the fantasy in the store's 12,000-square-foot auditorium. During the five-week period, there were special shows for handicapped youngsters in institutions.

During the pre-Christmas season, over 355,000 people from five states poured through Dayton's. For people from small towns or rural areas, such shopping trips are events long to be remembered.

Another tradition is the intercity shopping trip. Nancy Rosenfield, director of community events at Bloomingdale's, White Plains, New York, recalls the highlight of each year, her trip with her mother to New York, from Boston. "We did this from the time I was a little girl until I went to college. These trips were terribly exciting. The train, the children's department at Best's. I remember when I got my first Scotch plaid cap with ribbons down the back—it was very sophisticated for Boston. My mother would shop at Bergdorf's and Jay Thorpe, and we'd take a thrilling subway ride to Brooklyn and Loehmann's. We'd visit the Metropolitan Museum and eat in restaurants and stay in a hotel. The time, the secrets, and the fun we shared have always been part of our relationship."

Caroline Kibler of Atlanta, Georgia, describes in her southern accent her anxiety when shopping in the north because, "Mama talked so funny. In New York she'd say, 'After *Burger-daw-huffs* we'll go to *Bessy's* [Best's] for my *brassy-ears.*' We were followed in Marshall Field's by a woman who finally sat by us in the tearoom and said, 'I've walked behind you because I just love to hear you talk.' Mama said, 'Honey, come join us and you can *heah awl* you want.' Years later I realized how charming Mama was, but at thirteen I wanted to die, and I hated those trips up north.''

Philadelphian Anne Foster recalls an Altman corset lady in New York, ''Mummy called her her *under-pinning* lady. I felt when she hugged me her softness would ooze out of both ends of the stiff tube that encased her—like filling when you put a fork in an eclair. I get my *under-pinnings*, pantyhose and briefs, and the kids' things at our shopping center. There's no big deal. I wonder if we haven't missed something. Those trips Mummy and I took—shopping and the matinees—they were very special.''

These city exchanges were misinterpreted by at least one store management. A former Marshall Field executive remembers their error in judgment about opening a Milwaukee branch. ''We sent a marketing man to Milwaukee to study the prospects of putting a store there, and I think he did his research at the country club. He came back and informed us that, yes, indeed, the ladies in Milwaukee loved Marshall Field's. What he didn't find out was that they loved Marshall Field, *Chicago*—it was part of their social life. Friends would get together and come down on the train. They'd spend the day in the store shopping, have lunch in the tearoom, and perhaps a few drinks in the club car on the trip home. It was a beautiful, memorable shopping experience They didn't want to get into their cars and drive a short distance to a Marshall Field in Milwaukee. We'd missed the whole point.''

Inter-country shopping trips are made for a variety of reasons. The tide of border-hopping in Europe changes with the rates of exchange. During the holiday season of 1977, Piccadilly, Bond and Regent streets were a babel of French, German, Japanese and Arabic. With the value of the pound at a low ebb, shopping in London, which is always a delight, had the added joy of being a bargain.

For the citizens of the U.S.S.R. who can move freely out of their country—diplomats, airline personnel and a handful of others—the NK Department Store in Copenhagen and Stockmann's in Helsinki are favorite shopping centers. The colorful, modern Scandinavian merchandise has a special fascination for the Soviets when compared to the drab merchandise in their government controlled G.U.M. stores.

In the north of the United States a store is, according to Merve Retchin, former Chicagoan and Salon Manager at Saks, White Plains, "a place to get out of the cold. In Chicago it's a cup of Marshall Field's cream of chicken soup. And then there's the Field Special, a piece of lettuce with turkey, ham, Swiss cheese, bacon, and a kind of catsupy Russian dressing. You've never had anything like it!"

For several generations in Hartford, Connecticut, G. Fox & Co.'s Tea Room was an important part of the shopping experience. Today the leisurely lunches and fashion shows have been replaced by a quick-service restaurant for hurried customers.

Not so at the wonder on Wilshire Boulevard in Los Angeles. What would Bullock's Wilshire be without the fashion shows at lunchtime in the elegant Tea Room? The chef has outdone the Field Special with the Wilshire Tower "Five" Sandwich. The menu reads:

Featuring Breast of Turkey, Ham, Swiss Cheese, Avocado and Sliced Eggs, Layered Between Wafer Thin Bread and Topped with Russian Caviar Dressing, Presented with Frozen Fruit Salad.

There are also mid-afternoon pick-me-ups like a Cappuccino Royale Sundae:

A Cappuccino Blend Espresso Coffee and Chocolate Fudge Layered with French Vanilla Ice Cream, Lavishly Garnished with Whipped Cream and Roasted Almonds

and the house specialty, Caffe Cappuccino:

A Blend of Four Liquors, Hot Coffee and a Scoop of Whipped Cream, Served in a Snifter—Hmmmm!

Less adventuresome, or perhaps more diet-conscious shoppers can order Scotch or a martini on the rocks.

In the southwest, a store is a place to get cool. At the Biltmore

Fashion Park on Camelback Road and Twenty-fourth Street, in Phoenix, Arizona, "It's a status thing to shop in your tennis clothes," says Sandy Love, Salon Manager at Saks Fifth Avenue. When Saks opened here fifteen years ago, it placed a hitching post in the parking lot, for customers who arrived on horseback. There is an ongoing high-fashion rally that lobs back and forth between Saks and I. Magnin & Co., the anchor stores in Fashion Park. For all the boots and breeches and jeans and sneakers, Phoenicians sparkle like the desert stars when they are not on the courts, poolside, or in the saddle. The Phoenix-Scottsdale oasis is dressy, classy, and expensive. Mindful of this twinkling and the tinkling of silver that accompanies it, across the street, down the roadway lined with topiary orange trees, in the grand old Biltmore Hotel's L'Orangerie, John Weitz, Pauline Trigère, and other luminaries of the fashion world can be seen lunching with the store people. "It's La Grenouille and Orsini's among the saguaros," says a doyen of dress design, referring to the New York Seventh Avenue crowd's favorite watering holes.

In Texas, there are air-conditioned mini-cities all under one roof, like the climate-controlled Ridgmar Mall in Fort Worth. This massive, cross-shaped shopping center is secured by Dillard's, Sears, Stripling's, J. C. Penney, and a spanking-new Neiman-Marcus. There are 120 other shops and restaurants lined up, in between, on two levels. The General Nutrition Center fights a single-handed uphill battle for health food among such food establishments as Mr. Goodcreme, Luca Pizza, Famous Ramos Hot Dogs, The Original Cookie Company, Tiffany's Bakery, and the inevitable Taco Spot. Available within the mall are pets and plants and lots of pants. There are Just Pants, Jeans West, John's Jeans, New West and County Seat. In this rarefied atmosphere, protected from the blazing sun, the eyes of Texas are just plain good business. Among the services are Dr. Richard K. Ditto, Optometrist; Pearle Vision Center; Dr. L. Porales, Optometrist; and Royal Optical. American Express and Blue Skies Travel Agency will provide an escape from this hermetically sealed consumers' total environment.

The florid prose of the Ridgmar Mall brochure and map says it all:

Where a parquet path wends its way in and out of more than 125 fine stores and restaurants . . . all under one roof.

Ridgmar offers an incomparable variety of items from jeans to jewels, from tools to toys. . . .

Here skylights let the sunshine filter in . . . to give you a feeling of the outdoors, indoors . . . rains never dampen your spirits, winds never blow and rippling waters create beautiful fountains. Here trees grow tall with benches curved beneath their branches so you can relax for leisurely shopping.

Discover Ridgmar Mall's new horizons . . . today.

Stores are a place to go when the wind comes sweeping across the plains. "Oklahoma City, not Chicago, is the windiest city in the United States," says an Oklahoman proudly, and Balliet's in Penn Square, a specialty store known for super service, is an elegant retreat from the wind. Citron-terrycloth robes are provided in each dressing room. Customers can move around between fittings and peruse jewelry, accessories, sportswear and shoes. Primarily a high-fashion store, Balliet's offers a handful of carefully selected cosmetic lines, and beautiful un-windblown women stand ready to freshen customers' makeup. A uniformed maid serves coffee, tea, or sherry. Lunch can be ordered in from nearby Pistachio's. Owner Buddy Rogers, who comes from a long line of merchants, says, "Service is another commodity we have to sell. My grandfather was a cigar salesman. He married a young lady named Baer in Arkansas, and with her brother Julius Baer, and Aaron Fuller, he opened The Boston Store. Baer and Fuller decided to go to St. Louis, where they founded Stix, Baer and Fuller. My grandfather bought them out, and stayed in Arkansas. He always said, 'Never forget you run a country store.'" Moving across thick carpeting, underneath crystal chandeliers, surrounded by exquisite store appointments and elegant merchandise, Rogers said, "Every time my head gets a little full, I remember—I run a nice little country store."

Downtown, next to the Hightower Building in a small townhouse, is Hightower's, a shop filled with Baccarat crystal, Limoges china, fine jewelry, linens, a kitchen boutique, Cook's Corner, Lady Godiva Chocolates, and a boutique with designer fashions. Hightower's is called the "Tiffany" of Oklahoma City.

Frank Hightower majored in French history at Yale and returned from the east with some highfalutin ideas. He brought luxury goods into the rough-and-tumble cattle and oil town. Fifteen years ago he opened The Cellar downstairs in the Hightower Building.

Red carpeting, white damask, fresh flowers, antiques, and excellent food and wine made it the city's first fine restaurant under the supervision of chef John Bennett.

Oklahoma City is almost dead center in the United States. It is a masculine city—in spite of Patience Latting, the mayor—a mix of midwestern wheat farmers, western cattlemen, southwestern oilmen, eastern financiers, and southern gentlemen. Barbed wire mixes with pipelines, combines, ticker tape, pecans, and magnolias. In 1935, when Joseph Connolly opened a men's apparel shop, the tough, hard-working Sooners had little interest in fashion. "When I opened Connolly's, there was a need to educate the men. You couldn't buy a pair of black shoes, they all wore brown," said silver-haired, ebon-shod Mr. Connolly, who wore oval New Zealand jade cufflinks to fasten his white French cuffs. "Now when Oklahoma City men move in and out of board rooms all over the globe, they are the best-dressed men in the world."

"Frank Hightower, Joe Connolly, and Buddy Rogers have done for Oklahoma City in the last few years what Neiman-Marcus did for Dallas in the early part of the century," says an Oklahoma businessman.

When most stores began, they relied on family—mom and pop, aunts and uncles, brothers, sisters, sons and daughters, cousins, nephews, and in-laws. A handful of stores still do today—among them Strawbridge & Clothier in Philadelphia, where fourth-generation Strawbridges sit on the board of directors. In Texas there is a third-generation Sakowitz serving as chairman of the board of Sakowitz's and a fourth-generation president. There is also a Sakowitz great-granddaughter on the board of directors. Third-generation Nordstroms operate Nordstrom Best, Inc., stores in the Pacific northwest and Alaska. Three generations of Livingstons and their wives run Livingston's, the last family-owned specialty store of its size in San Francisco. Carl Livingston, a nephew of David Livingston, who founded the store over a hundred years ago, is chairman of the board. His wife, Peggy, is the gift buyer. Carl Livingston, Jr., is president of the company, and his wife, Jean, is merchandise manager for fashion accessories. His brother, Barry, is executive vice-president, and Carl Jr.'s son, Chip, a fourth-generation Livingston, is manager of the main store. To keep it all in the family, Barry's wife, Barbara, an interior designer, has decorated Livingston's "twigs." Scattered throughout the city and down the peninsula, the "twigs" were a unique merchandising idea. The shops are smaller than full-scale branch stores, do not require a large inventory, and can be quickly supplied from the downtown parent store.

Across the Bay in Berkeley, J. F. Hink & Son occupies two-thirds of a city block on Shattuck Avenue. To East Bay residents, Hink's is as beloved as the University of California's Campanile. J. F. Hink moved the store from Woodland, California, in 1904, in an effort to find a stable market. He had suffered losses in the money panics and the crop failures that had afflicted the agricultural area around Woodland at the turn of the century. His son, Lester, was recalled to Berkeley from Eureka, California, where he worked in his brother's store and played baseball with the hope of becoming a professional. He proved to be as dynamic in the store as he had been on the ball field. One of Lester Hink's merchandising innovations was the 8½x11-inch card sent to customers to announce sales. Both sides were chock-a-block full of values and a surprise gift awaited the customer who cut out the coupon imprinted on the card and presented it to a salesperson at Hink's. There were also Lester Hink's poems.

Berkeley is not the rock-throwing, pot-smoking, rabble-rousing, radical community that the world has come to know. That is not Berkeley. That is—the University of California *at* Berkeley. Berkeley is conservative, solid, and quiet living. It's less expensive than San Francisco and has the cultural advantages of a university town. Many older and retired people live in Berkeley. It is sunny, warm, full of trees, and gardens grow like crazy. Lester Hink loved Berkeley and Berkeley loved Lester Hink. His customers looked forward to the sales announcements, the gifts, and the jingles with Mr. Hink's warm jokes, homey philosophy, and patriotism. Along with the lists of St. Valentine's Specials:

TO MY VALENTINE
Dear Valentine in nineteen-four
We opened first our Berkeley store.
And all these years we've tried our best
To place good service to the test.

With quality our constant aim
Our efforts have not proved in vain.
For patrons came from near and far
They know how sound our values are.

Where friendship and good will abound,
Where courtesy is always found,
While parking here is sure to please
For with wide aisles, you park with ease.

Oh yes, a gift awaits you dear,
It's use will help you banish drear,
Though cloudy skies may mar your day
And winter winds have right of way,

Some hours spent can still be nice
Relax, enjoy Bouquet of Spice.
And now to add just one more line
Remember, you're my Valentine.

Respectfully,

(signed)
L.W. HINK
President

Lester Hink was independent. He refused to stay open on a traditional retail sale day and informed his customers:

CLOSED WASHINGTON'S BIRTHDAY
We will respect George Washington's name
Because of his selflessness, sans glory or fame.
Our store will be closed because of his worth
Happy to honor the day of his birth.

Lester Hink took an active part in his store, working every day and writing jingles until he retired in 1976. He died less than a year later, in October 1977, when he was over ninety years old.

"There's nothing sophisticated about Hink's. It hasn't changed one whit in years and you can find anything you are looking for there, and that's what the Berkeley ladies like," says a Berkeleyite. "Lester Hink was a stickler for the basic rule of merchandising—'Know Your Customer.'"

His son, Robert Hink, is president of the company. Another son,

Lester Hink, Jr., the company secretary, is in charge of operations. Mary Hink, Robert's wife, is general manager. There are
several children, but none of them takes an active part in the store.
According to Robert Hink, "As far as the family is concerned, it
looks as if this is the last hurrah."

In February 1978 Hink's was sold to C. H. Dunlap Co. of
Modesto, California. This retail firm also has stores in San Jose and
Bakersfield. For Robert and the other Hink members who plan to
remain in the managerial positions the last family hurrah has been
shouted.

Family-owned stores are becoming a thing of the past, as sons
and daughters, unlike ballplayer Lester Hink, decline to give up
their own pursuits. Some blame retailing. "The store was my father's whole life, twenty-four hours a day, seven days a week,"
says one son. "Who can compete with the volume buying of the
big corporations?" asks another. "It's a dog-eat-dog business,"
says a third.

An exception to this is forty-year-old Robert Sakowitz, president of Sakowitz' in Houston, Texas. Like his father, Bernard,
who is chairman of the board, Robert is an innovative and imaginative merchant. He is one of a handful of fourth-generation merchants. His great-grandfather Louis Sakowitz, opened a store
before 1900, catering to the needs of the merchant seamen in
Galveston, Texas. The store was demolished in the Galveston
flood of 1900 and rebuilt in 1902 as a men's haberdashery—Sakowitz Brothers—by Louis' sons, Simon and Tobias. A Houston
store was built in 1908 and the brothers divided the mangement
chores of the two stores until the Galveston hurricane of 1915 destroyed that town's store and they moved their entire operation to
Houston. Sakowitz' continued to grow in the southwest under the
guidance of Tobias's son, Bernard. Its position as a specialty store
has been strengthened further throughout the sun belt under the
leadership of Robert Sakowitz. Robert's sister Lynn Sakowitz
Wyatt serves on the board of directors. Not only are the Sako-
witzes unique for maintaining family control of their business,
Robert and Lynn are the only brother and sister to both appear on
the Best Dressed lists.

Some stores that are no longer considered family stores but independent corporations are Carson, Pirie, Scott, in Chicago; Thal-

himer, in Richmond; and Hutzler's in Baltimore. There are a few unique ownership situations. The Mormon Church has a one-third interest in the Zion's Mercantile Institution in Salt Lake City, Utah. B. Altman & Co. is owned by the Benjamin Altman Foundation. The foundation, started by Benjamin Altman, a bachelor, prior to his death, is one of New York City's leading philanthropic organizations.

Retailing has become increasingly complex. *Bigger* has become synonymous with *better* and enormous amounts of capital are required to meet operational and expansion costs. As a result, many stores have merged, become divisions of huge corporations or subsidiaries of vast conglomerates, foreign and American. Of the great stores that have closed during the past ten years, some have gone bankrupt, others have paid their stockholders and closed up shop, giving up the fight.

Among the retailing corporations are those with recognizable store names like R. H. Macy & Co., The May Department Stores Company, Marshall Field & Company, and Dayton-Hudson Corporation. There are also corporations whose unimaginative names—Allied Stores Corporation, Associated Dry Goods Corporation, and Federated Department Stores, Inc.—give no clue to the great stores and glorious old names that are entwined in their corporate structure. Jordan Marsh, founded in Boston in 1851 by a young Yankee from Maine, Eben Jordan, is an Allied Store. So is the lyrical-sounding Bon Marché, in the northwest. Associated Dry Goods is the parent organization of such time-honored institutions as Lord & Taylor; J. W. Robinson; Stix, Baer & Fuller; and L. S. Ayers and Company. Federated, a giant among retailing giants, was founded in 1929, when Filene's, Abraham & Straus, Lazarus, and Bloomingdale's pooled assets. Along with these original stores, the Federated empire includes Bullock's Inc., and the architectural landmark, Bullock's Wilshire. This Cincinnati-based corporation controls another golden girl company of the west, I. Magnin & Co. Its latest acquisition has been the southern belle among stores, Atlanta's beloved Rich's.

Carter Hawley Hale Stores, Inc., has grown out of the retail corporation Broadway-Hale, Inc., into an international corporation. Broadway-Hale, Inc., came into being when Hale Brothers in San Francisco purchased The Emporium and the Broadway stores.

Carter Hawley Hale now owns Capwell's, the original grand old store of Oakland, and Weinstock's, formerly Weinstock, Lubin, in Sacramento. It owns Walden Book Co., Inc., a chain of 477 bookshops, and Sunset House, a gift catalogue company. The jewels in the corporate crown are Neiman-Marcus and Bergdorf Goodman, and the crown sometimes lies heavy on the head. In 1974, Carter Hawley Hale acquired 20.5 percent interest in House of Fraser Limited, the largest department store business in the United Kingdom, with eighty full-line department stores and nearly seventy smaller stores throughout England, Scotland, Wales, Eire, Northern Ireland, and Denmark. Three years later it sold its interest in House of Fraser for a rumored $80 million, leaving Holt, Renfrew, a specialty store in Canada, its only foreign company.

Reverse Anglo-American ownership is involved with Saks Fifth Avenue and Gimbels. They are owned by Brown & Williamson Industries, Inc., a subsidiary of the British-American Tobacco Company, Ltd. If tobacco seems a strange mix with department and specialty stores, take a good look at Joseph Magnin, and Rhodes department stores, all cozied up with Monterey Mushrooms, Puna Papaya, Pacific Pearl Seafoods, and Fisher Cheese, in a luau of subsidiaries of Amfac Inc., a conglomerate that also controls Columbia River Farms, Kaanapali Beach Resorts, C & H Sugar, and Hawaiian Discovery Tours, to name a few.

Then there is Buffum's in Long Beach, California, which was sold to Australians in 1974. The store was founded in downtown Long Beach in 1904 when Charles Abel Buffum and his brother, E. E. Buffum, came from Lafayette, Illinois, and purchased Schilling Brothers. The name was changed to the Mercantile Company and the store catered to the conservative population of 5,000 consisting mostly of retired middle-class midwesterners.

In 1912 a new three-story building was erected and the company was renamed Buffum's. The store continued expanding along with Long Beach and the Buffums grew rich. They became important members of the Long Beach establishment. Charles Buffum at one time served as mayor of Long Beach. His son, Harry, who became president of the company in 1934, was known as "Mr. Long Beach" as a result of his many civic activities. The company went public in 1961 but the Buffum family maintained a certain amount of control through the board of directors. With Harry Buffum's death in 1968, the family control was weakened and in 1974 the company was sold to David Jones, Ltd., the second largest department store group in Australia.

For all the influence of the Buffums—through the store, Charles's political activities, and Harry's civic affairs—it has been Charles's daughter, Dorothy Buffum, who has made an indelible mark on Southern California. In 1919, Dorothy entered Stanford University. She was caught up in the full swing of campus social life and was elected Campus Queen. She met and later married Norman Chandler, scion of the empire built on the foundation of the *Los Angeles Times.* Dorothy Buffum Chandler, known to her intimates by her nickname "Buff," became "the power broker behind the *Times,*" according to Robert Gottlieb and Irene Wolt, in their book *Thinking Big.* She was also the driving force behind the Los Angeles Music Center, which includes the Dorothy Chandler Pavilion. Gottlieb and Wolt wrote: "Dorothy Buffum Chandler's ascent to power in Los Angeles put her in position to supplant the Chandler family as the real power at the *Los Angeles Times.* Her mild appearance concealed the passion of a sharp in-fighter who would remake the city and the corporate empire in her own image."

Some of Buff's critics who felt she used heavy-handed fund-raising tactics in an effort to bring culture to Los Angeles refer to her as "La Buff-aloe," but no matter, Dorothy Buffum Chandler has come a long way from being the storekeeper's daughter in the Los Angeles outback of Long Beach. The Australian purchase of Buffum's was not nearly as heavy-handed as it was speedy. The $21-million sale was finalized in a phone call from Sydney to Long Beach.

Another merchant, while not a newspaper publisher, emulated one. In the twenties, J. J. Haggarty, a department store magnate of Los Angeles, built a palatial seaside mansion high on a promontory overlooking the Pacific Ocean at Palos Verdes. It was a somewhat smaller version of William Randolph Hearst's hilltop monument, San Simeon, 250 miles up the coast. Haggarty spent a fortune outfitting the thirty-two rooms with ceiling murals, carved railings, lavish bathroom fixtures, and other accoutrements of domestic splendor. There was a subterranean lodge, a private pier, and a tower from which one could contemplate the sea and the seven acres of gardens.

Unlike San Simeon, no one ever called it home. Mrs. Haggarty thought the estate was too far from Los Angeles, so the family remained at a town house. After Haggarty died in 1935, the mansion stood vacant for several years. Finally, a midwestern inventor and manufacturer bought it and filled it, inside and out, with life-size nude paintings and nude statues. He and his family visited his Palos Verdes nudery on rare occasions, but no one lived there. After the inventor's death, the nudes were auctioned off but there were no takers for the property and it remained empty until 1950 when the Neighborhood Church of Palos Verdes bought the Haggarty house and converted it into a thirteen-room church. Today, the chapel retains a fine painted ceiling, the work of Italian fresco artists imported during the building of the mansion. The Neighborhood Church bought all the merchant's grandeur for a psalm: $70,000.

Publishing, politics, and retailing are not such strange bedfellows. Besides Mayor Buffum, other merchants have minded the city, state, and country along with the store. The ultimate salesman turned politico was Harry Truman. With his friend Eddie Jacobson, Truman opened a haberdashery in Kansas City following World War I. The first year was a very good one, when men returning from the service needed new civilian clothing. The second year they found themselves overstocked and in 1922, the store closed. Truman refused to go into bankruptcy and for the next fifteen years he was paying off creditors. By 1934, only eleven years before he became President of the United States, he was financially in the clear.

In *Plain Speaking, an Oral Biography of Harry Truman*, Merle Miller asked:

"Mr. President, did you like being in the retail business?"

Harry Truman answered, "To tell the truth, I never had a chance to spend too much time thinking about things like that. What I did was what I had to do or thought I had to do . . . to make a living most of the time. You'll notice if you read your history, that the work of the world gets done by people who aren't bellyachers."

Mr. Miller wrote:

> I once asked Mr. Truman what he felt he had learned in the haber-
> dashery and he said, "Well, I learned, although I'd never had much
> doubt about it, never to elect a Republican as President. [Warren G.
> Harding had been elected President in 1920.] Because he'll look out
> for the rich and squeeze out the farmer and the small businessman."

Another merchant had a brush with being elected President. The
Honorable Barry M. Goldwater, former chairman of the board of
Goldwaters, an Arizona store with a long and colorful history, was
a United States Senator from Arizona at the time of his nomina-
tion. He was also a Republican. Goldwaters, now a division of Associated Dry Goods Corporation, began with Michel Goldwater,
the Senator's grandfather, driving pack animals and a buckboard
filled with merchandise to the isolated Arizona miners. By 1878,
Goldwaters was established in Prescott in the first brick building in
Arizona, and by 1885, Michel Goldwater was mayor of Prescott.
His political flair may have passed on to his grandson.

Favor Hazeltine Slater, daughter of an old-line Prescott banking
family and former society editor for the *Arizona Republic*,
shopped as a girl in the Prescott store, which to this day has a western general store atmosphere. When they came to the city, the family shopped in the Phoenix store. "Goldwaters had the finest fabrics in the state of Arizona. Mother would buy yards of fine cham-
brays and old-fashioned dotted Swiss to take to our dressmaker in
Prescott. We'd always see Barry because he was everywhere. He
was a natural merchandiser. He had very high standards and kept
track of everyone and everything in the store. He'd been pulled out
of college to work there when his father had a heart attack and I
don't think he liked it, but he always had a smile and a winning
way. Being a salesman and being a politician seemed to go hand in
hand."

Most people feel that Barry Goldwater was bored with merchandising and was anxious to get on with a political career. They cite,
for example, the time he orbited a live mouse from the basement to
the mezzanine in a pneumatic tube. The arrival turned the accounting department into a frenzy of hysterical bookkeepers.

(Pneumatic tubes are often the bane of cashiers who are unwit-
ting sitting targets for the sender's imagination. Michael Joseph,

owner of D. W. Rogers & Co., a local department store in Greenwich, Connecticut, has spent his life in retailing. He has a charming and whimsical way with his employees and customers alike. He is responsible, thoughtful, and an unlikely candidate to perform dirty tricks. And yet, one day as he left the store for lunch, he eyed a mannequin with a broken finger. He put the finger into his pocket with the intention of gluing it back when he returned. At lunch he had a better idea. When he finished his meal, he dipped his finger into catsup. He returned to work and fired the gory digit off in a tubular cylinder up to the cashier. The recipient was not amused. After near cardiac arrest, she picked up her pocketbook and without a word walked out of the store and never returned. When remembering the incident, Mr. Joseph said, "I guess business was slow that day." There are endless possibilities that can be hurled through a store to liven things up—mash notes, eggs, snakes, and snips and snails and puppy dog tails.)

You can put the salesman into the Senate, but apparently you can't take the salesman out of the senator. Sonia Adler, founder and editor of *The Washington Dossier*, the monthly social-gossip magazine of the capital, saw Senator Goldwater at a sporting event. She commented on his outlandish bright green sports jacket and he replied, "In my business, if you can't sell it, you wear it."

During World War II, many retailers who did not enter the service served their country well. Stanley Marcus of Neiman-Marcus was a dollar-a-year consultant to the clothing division of the War Production Board, heading up the women's and children's sections to develop fabric conservation programs. Marcus is generally credited with the acceptance by manufacturers, designers, and retailers of the famous order L-85, a regulation that limited fabric for covering a female figure to three and a half yards. Because of this, fabric shortages were averted.

The Straus family, who acquired full ownership of R. H. Macy & Co. in 1896, has the longest list of political credits. Isidor Straus served a term in Congress in 1894. His brother, Nathan, president of the New York Board of Health for four years, was largely responsible for pasteurized milk in this country and for putting up milk stations in the city where a glass sold for a penny and milk was given to mothers free. Nathan was also park commissioner. Another brother, Oscar, had only a brief connection with the store before becoming a public servant. He was a member of President Theodore Roosevelt's cabinet as Secretary of Commerce and Labor. He later served as United States Ambassador to Turkey. Işidor's son, Jesse, managed Macy's with his brother Percy, until 1933 when he was appointed Ambassador to France by President Franklin Roosevelt.

Edward A. Filene of Boston's Filene's was a member of the Chamber of Commerce Commission of the United States and the International Chamber of Commerce under President Roosevelt and served on a variety of peace committees after World War II.

Luther Hodges of Marshall Field & Co. was Secretary of Commerce under President Kennedy.

Ruth Farkas, Ambassador to Luxembourg under President Nixon, is a member of a retailing family. Mrs. Farkas is the wife of Alexander's founder and retired chairman of the board, George Farkas. She is the mother of a whole gaggle of the company's top brass: Alexander Farkas, president; Robin L. Farkas, senior vice-president, real estate; Bruce R. Farkas, executive vice-president, administration; and Jonathan Farkas, assistant vice-president, administration.

The late Richard Rich of Atlanta's famed Rich's, which became a division of Federated Department Stores, Inc., in 1976 after Mr. Rich's death, was a special assistant to the United States Ambassador to Brazil while serving as a major in the Air Force during World War II. His son, Michael, Rich's senior vice-president, moved into the embassy crowd indirectly in 1977 when he married Retta Taylor, daughter of Anne Cox Chambers, United States Ambassador to Belgium. Mr. Rich's mother-in-law is known as the "Katharine Graham of the south" because of her affiliation with the Cox syndicate of southern newspapers and television stations. Taken all together, the family retailing, publishing, and political power adds up to a bushelful of Brussels' clout.

Marvin Traub of New York and Bloomingdale's kicked up a storm in Washington in the spring of 1976 prior to the opening of suburban stores in Tyson's Corner, Virginia, and White Flint, Maryland. In a question-and-answer article on the front page of *The Washington Star* (May 16, 1976) Bailey Morris asked:

Question: "What would Marvin Traub like most to be were he not the president of Bloomingdale's?"

Answer: "Well, over the years we have had personal and great interest in India and have spent some time there in that country. And I have thought that if I ever should retire from retailing, it might be adventuresome—a very adventurous assignment to take on the job as Ambassador to India. But I have also decided that it might be presumptuous of me to think about it—but I've been fascinated by the country."

Although Washington is filled with ambitious people, it is accustomed to their expressing their desires in a soft-spoken double-talk and it reeled at Mr. Traub's candor. In another *Star* article (September 1976) Joy Billington asked, "Are Washington department stores going social?" There was a reference to Marvin Traub's "admitted interest in an Ambassadorial post" and the Traubs' "rumored social ambitions." A Washington hostess, apparently unaware of Macy's Strauses' diplomatic service, and forgetting her own support of Goldwater for President, sounded like Oscar Wilde's Lady Bracknell when she commented, "My dear, Mr. Traub is in trade!" There were also undercurrents of the old Washington–New York rivalry.

A saner comment came from an Indian official who worked with Mr. Traub on the spring 1978 Bloomingdale's -Air India promotion: "I think he would make a very fine Ambassador. He's an erudite, knowledgeable and organized man. He understands business and he knows my country and loves it. Why such a fuss when you have a peanut farmer in the White House?"

Quite aside from the owner-families in the store, there was a time when the store itself became the family. Management was like the parent and the staff was akin to children. It was all one big happy family. Paternalism provided more protection than heaven (or a decent wage) for the working girl. Early on, stores were considered safe and acceptable places where women could seek employment. Undoubtedly it was more pleasant to work in a store than in a sweatshop. But the hours were long and pay was abominably low. In the 1870s, salesclerks started with a salary of $3 or $4 a week with no commissions. They worked a six-day week from 7:45 A.M. to 7:00 P.M. Cash girls or boys, fourteen-year-olds who ran about answering the call for "Cash!" received $1.50 a week. By the turn of the century, salaries climbed to $8 or $10 a week. Some stores provided hot lunches at a cost of 8¢ or 9¢, but paying rent was something else. Young women who did not live at home were destined to live in dark and dreary rooming houses.

Charles B. Webster, an early Macy's partner, either mindful of the working girl's living conditions or through a fit of conscience, left $1,325,637 in his will, "to improve conditions of unmarried working women" through the establishment of a hotel for girls earning less than $35 a week. Webster House was established in 1917 on West Thirty-fourth Street to provide room and board for a nominal fee in pleasant surroundings.

P. G. Winnett, co-founder of Bullock's in Los Angeles, and one of the legendary father figures in retailing, was a small man with a pixie face, a twinkle in his eyes, and a great sense of humor. Mr. Winnett came from Canada in 1896 at the age of fifteen and worked as an errand boy at The Broadway in downtown Los Angeles. In 1907 he helped found Bullock's. He was the creative force behind Bullock's Wilshire, which opened in 1929. When the stock market crashed a month after the store opening, Bullock's Wilshire was dubbed "Winnett's Folly."

Mr. Winnett, like many fathers, was both loved and feared. He was a perfectionist and had a weekly routine touring the Bullock's stores. On each store's designated day, the entire personnel, sales staff and models, were required to be on the floor for a specific period. Mr. Winnett looked over stock, displays, and people, making notes in a little black book. If a department passed his keen-eyed inspection, he reached into his pocket and as he left, slipped the manager or buyer a cellophane-wrapped candy. It is said that the models automatically passed inspection and were rewarded with foil-wrapped chocolate kisses. These coveted awards were treasured and saved over the years by the members of his staff. In 1966, in an interview with *Women's Wear Daily*, Mr. Winnett said, "I'm a leveling influence. Women buyers need reassurances, a pat on the back. They don't live on paychecks alone."

In 1964, Winnett fought, unsuccessfully, the take-over of Bullock's by Federated Department Stores, Inc. He ceased holding any position after the merger, but held a lifetime employment contract as an advisor, visited his office every day, and made his inspection tours dispensing his sweets. He had made a morning tour on the day that he died in 1968 at the age of eighty-seven.

Jerry Nemiro, the current president of Bullock's Wilshire, said:

"The anecdotes about P. G. are endless. It was said that he was a great fanny-patter and was always pinching the girls, but that is attributed to everyone in the store business." He added quickly, "I haven't done it lately!"

Under the entreprenurial eyes, it became not only acceptable but fashionable to work in a store. In the late thirties and early forties, debutantes discovered the fun of work and the fashion-show ramp. Many of the merchant princes had Cinderellas behind the counters and society princesses parading around in their finery.

Traditionally, stores have been good to women. In the early days, however, they kept in the background. Mary Ann Magnin, the founder and power behind I. Magnin, named the store after her husband, Isaac. Margaret Getchell, a half-blind cousin of R. H. Macy, started as a cashier and became the store supervisor, which would be comparable to today's merchandise manager. She was responsible for the store's growth from a hole-in-the-wall dry-goods store into a full-fledged department store. Yet when Macy took on a partner, it was Margaret's husband, Abiel LaForge.

There are and have been hundreds of famous saleswomen and buyers—among them Jo Hughes of Bergdorf Goodman; Marvin Traub's mother, Bea Traub of Bonwit Teller; Sara Middleman, once of DePinna's and Best & Company, presently director of the Connoisseur's Suite at Saks Fifth Avenue; Elizabeth Curtis of I. Magnin, San Francisco. In top management, there have been the late Dorothy Shaver, president of Lord & Taylor; Beatrice Fox Auerbach, of Hartford's G. Fox & Co.; Ann Hodge, president of Bullock's Wilshire and Hortense Odlum of Bonwit Teller. More recently Mildred Custin of Bonwit Teller and Geraldine Stutz of Henri Bendel. There were the famous "in-store" designers: Sophie Gimbel of Saks, Stella of I. Magnin, and Irene of Bergdorf Goodman. At the moment, with the exception of Miss Stutz, women seem to be stopped at the vice-president level. There are Barbara D'Arcy and Peggy Healy of Bloomingdale's, G. G. Michelson of Macy's, and Anne Stegner of Bullock's Wilshire, to name four. Van Venneri of I. Magnin and Kay Kerr of Neiman-Marcus are among the legendary women in retailing.

Women have made their mark in advertising and public relations more often when they have left retailing and gone on their own. The great leader in advertising was "Fabulous Fitz," Bernice Fitz-

Gibbon, a Wisconsin farmgirl who started out teaching in a one-room schoolhouse and by 1941 had an annual income of $90,000 as advertising director of Gimbels. Jane Trahey started writing copy at Carson, Pirie, Scott and, after a stint at Neiman-Marcus, formed her own advertising agency. Mary Wells Lawrence, whose agency, Wells Rich Green, bills over $50 million anually, started as a copywriter at Macy's Youngstown. Joan Glynne, former Bloomingdale's vice-president, works on special projects for Wells Rich. Eleanor Lambert, of fashion fame, started doing freelance fashion artwork for L. S. Ayers in Indiana while still in high school. Ruby Hamra, of Ruby Hamra Associates, was director of promotion and public relations for Gimbels for nine years. Today she handles posh fashion accounts like Gucci with aplomb. When she spoke of her Gimbels years, she said, "If you can survive in retailing, you can survive in anything."

In her book, *Jane Trahey on Women & Power*, Jane Trahey points out that of 13,973 department and specialty store board members in the country there are only nineteen female directors. It may be that the present large corporate and conglomerate structure has closed women out of the top management positions. Jane Trahey's "today" advice: "Want power? Get thee to the Wharton School of Finance."

How much influence stores have in any region varies with the territory, the era, the merchants, and the merchandise. Occasionally, stores have been avant-garde architecturally. More often they have reflected the going style of the period—Victorian clutter, Italian Renaissance, Art Deco, functional-modern. Taken all together, they have set the tone for some of the greatest shopping streets in the world—Fifth Avenue, New York; Michigan Boulevard, Chicago; Wilshire Boulevard in Los Angeles. On a smaller scale are Rodeo Drive in Beverly Hills and Worth Avenue in Palm Beach. Union Square in San Francisco has hopes of being surrounded by elegant stores. At the moment it is flanked by I. Magnin and Macy's up-to-date Shop on the Square on one side, the St. Francis Hotel and Maison Mendessolle on another. Saks Fifth Avenue has hopes of moving into the Fitzhugh Building on another side, the home of Roos-Atkins. Neiman-Marcus has projected plans for moving into the old City of Paris building on a corner that abuts the square.

One of the most unique modern mercantile developments is Chicago's Water Tower Place, a vertical shopping center built around a seven-story mall, the Ritz-Carlton Hotel, and a soaring tower of condominium residences. Marshall Field and Lord & Taylor are both located in Water Tower Place, along with innumerable smaller shops.

Urban blight and the demise of downtown stores go hand in hand. Once the disease begins, it is almost inevitably terminal. If a store stays too long, it is doomed. If it pulls up stakes and moves, the area is most certainly left without hope. A large piece of vacant real estate attracts vandals, squatters, and arsonists. The recent decision of R. H. Macy & Co. to close its store in Jamaica, Queens, New York, one of Macy's earliest branches, came as a dreadful blow to an area fighting for survival.

Downtown Oklahoma City has taken on one of the most energetic urban renewal programs in the country. Hundreds of deteriorating buildings and stores have gone with the push of the dynamite plunger. Several modern high-rise office buildings have been completed. The Myriad, a four-square-block convention center with a mirrored façade has risen out of the rubble, and the Skirvin Hotel has been renovated. The buildings are connected by an underground Metro Concourse, carpeted tunnels for pedestrians that are lined with colorful graphics along the walls. There are already open plazas, fountains, and pocket parks, but downtown still looks like they are filming *2001* and *Hiroshima* simultaneously. There are plans for a lake and recreational area to be integrated with the business complex and a future residential area of condominiums and town houses. The Galleria is a projected enclosed, air-conditioned, multilevel shopping mall that will house four department stores, several shops and restaurants, and cover four city blocks. This ambitious plan will make Oklahoma City one of the most up-to-date cities anywhere. "In five years it will be fantastic," says Mayor Patience Latting. A cynic says, "I just hope I live long enough to see this mess cleaned up."

It is doubtful whether any store contributed as much to the tone of a city as the City of Paris. San Francisco might not be called the "Paris of the Pacific" had it not been for a ship named *La Ville de Paris* that arrived in San Francisco Bay in 1850. The merchandise had originally been loaded on a different ship, months earlier, in Le

Havre, France, for the arduous Atlantic crossing to Panama. Here the merchandise was unloaded and taken piecemeal by canoe and muleback on the treacherous journey up and over and down across the Isthmus of Panama. The luxury goods and fine wines were transferred to a chartered brig, renamed for the trip *La Ville de Paris*. When the brig arrived in San Francisco, it became the first City of Paris store. The finery was sold from her decks to avoid the crime and fires that plagued the tent and shack town. For the next 122 years, the City of Paris, and the Verdier family that owned it, contributed to San Francisco's French flavor. The store and the merchandise it sold affected not only the city's style in dress, home furnishings, and manner of entertaining, but also its taste in art, music, and architecture.

The City of Paris closed in 1972. The building was to be razed and a new building erected, one to house that star of the Lone Star State, Neiman-Marcus. But the City of Paris is still there, partially boarded up and forlorn looking, topped by a weather-beaten sign of a scaled-down Eiffel Tower draped with the tricolor flag of France. It is wrapped in yards of petitions. In the future, it may be boxed in litigation and tied with lawsuits. "It's a hideously expensive piece of land," says a Carter Hawley Hale executive, "and the meter keeps ticking." The corporation and its architect, Philip Johnson, have worked valiantly with the store's plan in an effort to save the stained glass dome and the rotunda where the famous thirty-five-foot City of Paris Christmas tree once turned slowly. San Francisco, a city that cherishes every brick that came over as ballast, will not let the City of Paris go.

Not all stores had beginnings as hazardous as those endured by the City of Paris, nor have they ended with so much drama, bitterness, and show of loyalty, but most stores have, at one time or another, been victims of catastrophes. There have been fires, floods, earthquakes, hurricanes, and tornadoes. The Civil War took a toll of stores in the south and the north, either through destruction or financial ruin, due to the blockades and an inability to obtain merchandise. Panics, depressions, and recessions have marked the end for many stores; others have weathered the disasters and survived.

The men who opened stores, and the supportive and influential women who helped them, were as diversified as the nation, when it came to temperament, personality, and background. They had in common courage, patience, and stamina.

Some stores were founded by native-born Americans—usually young sons in large families, who had to strike out on their own. Others were started by immigrants. Often there was a metamorphosis from peddler with a backpack to peddler with a horse and wagon or mule and buckboard, and finally to storekeeper. The nationalities and religions of the immigrants reflected the political, economic, and religious upheavals in Europe. There were English, Irish, Scotch, French, Swedish, and Middle European immigrants from Poland, Germany, Hungary, and Bavaria who became merchants. John G. Bullock immigrated from Canada to Los Angeles, where he founded Bullock's, Inc. Stores were started by Quakers, Jews, Presbyterians, Catholics, Lutherans, and Mormons. Most of the merchants were young, in their teens and early twenties. Youthful beginnings were not unusual in the nineteenth century when life expectancy was little more than forty years, but in 1953, it was looked upon as something of a joke when a twenty-one-year-old Italian opened a store in New York's established marketplace.

Roberto Gucci, grandson of an Italian saddlemaker, Guccio Gucci, was sent to the United States from Florence by his father, Dr. Aldo Gucci, director of Guccio Gucci, Soc. R.L., the year his grandfather died. A little leather-goods shop was opened in the Savoy Plaza Hotel, on the Fifty-eighth Street side—just a boccie ball throw from Fifth Avenue and that arbiter of fashion, Bergdorf Goodman. Neither the handsome young man nor his small boutique appeared to be any competition for the stores that were in control of Fifth Avenue and the luxury-goods trade.

The merchants' march up Fifth Avenue from the bottom of Manhattan had been long, arduous, and filled with casualties. It had taken 125 years to reach the corner of Fifty-eighth Street and Fifth Avenue and the Plaza, not far from Central Park, where the assault came to a halt. By 1950, only Lord & Taylor and Arnold Constable had gone the distance to Fifth Avenue from Catherine Street, where the earliest shops were established near the wharves at the tip of the island.

There had been a fifty-year stopover during the last half of the nineteenth century in an area called the Ladies Mile, between Eighth and Twenty-third streets, bounded on the east by Broadway

and on the west by Sixth Avenue. Lord & Taylor was nearing fifty
years of age when it moved into an ornate mercantile "palace."
There were also newcomers to this retail scene. B. Altman & Co.
moved from Third Avenue and opened "The Palace of Trade." *Palatial* and *opulent* were the words for the magnificent new structures. Cast-iron and marble facades shone white and brilliant in the
sunlight. They were trimmed with Moorish filigree and gimcrackery. The metalwork was stamped with palm fronds and pineapples.
Leafy vines were entwined among the rosettes. There were marble
columns and marble arches and marble floors. Smart striped awnings were raised and lowered to protect the glorious window tab-
leaux from the bleaching rays of the sun that flooded the wide tho-
roughfares. There were flags flying. The Ladies Mile was a grand
pastryshop filled with delicious architectural Victorian wedding
cakes.

The people were equally decorative. There were ruffles and
waistcoats. Silk top hats were tipped and parasols twirled. There
were hoop skirts and petticoats and high-button shoes. Fat, pink-
cheeked children, trimmed with ribbons and laces, were paraded
into Best & Co.'s Liliputian Bazaar on Twenty-third Street, for
sailor suits and reefers.

There were liveried coachmen and footmen and doormen and
grooms. There were brass buttons galore. Shiny carriages with
tufted leather seats and fur laprobes were drawn by sleek high-
stepping horses as they rolled up and down the avenues—Sixth
Avenue—Broadway.

Inside the imposing confections were further marvels. Luxurious steam elevators, giant carpeted boxes, lifted customers up and
down, disgorging them onto the galleries that surrounded the co-
lonnaded rotundas. Rich, heavy chords, mixed with glistening ar-
peggios, poured forth from pipe organs to resound off the Carrara,
travertine, Portor, and Italian Rose floors and walls, and the
stained-glass domes. Fountains rippled and palm fronds rustled.
There were the windy pipelines of the pneumatic tubes that slurped
and sucked and hissed and threw up the brass bullet carriers that
sent money back and forth from a central cashier's office. Speedy
transactions occasionally bogged down when suction, with the
force of a tornado, would inhale a wisp of gift ribbon. A giant spool

would unwind, sending yards of the stuff throughout the labyrinth of twisting tunnels to jam the works.

Best & Co. could be called on the telephone. (One asked the operator for "Eighteenth Street, number one-six-seven.") B. Altman & Co. could be called on *two*. ("Eighteenth Street, three-three-O" or "three-three-two.") For customers to be able to find and use a phone, while in the store, was as difficult then as it is today. The 1893 Metropolitan Telephone and Telegraph Company directory warned:

> The use of a private telephone by others is a violation of contract and a positive disadvantage to the subscriber who may be called for while line is in use. Subscribers should direct transient users to the most convenient pay station.

The telephone directory was a fair guide to the rich. Following the original telephone switchboard installation in New Haven in 1878, private, noncommercial phones were only in the homes of the wealthy.

With New York City's population increasing rapidly, so many new people with so much new money, it seemed important to know who was who.

In the early 1880s, Mrs. Charles Minton distributed, for a small fee, the addresses of her favorite shops and the addresses and visiting days of her friends. After her death, her son, Maurice, expanded the guide to include advertising and 3,500 names. It was sold as *Minton's List*, but it was no longer exlusive and personal and it died.

Philip's Elite Directory appeared in 1884. It was followed by *Uppington's Elite Directory* and *Lain's and Healy's Directory of Brooklyn*. For all their toney-sounding names, they were blatantly commercial. Manufacturers of player pianos and ladies' corsets were important advertisers, along with the grand stores in the Ladies Mile. *The Trow Metropolitan Directory of Selected Names Arranged by Streets and Suburban Towns Within 25 Miles of New York City* must have been a door-to-door salesman's dream come true.

For spectators who wanted to know the cast of characters who participated in the revelries of the period, there was the newspaper listing of Mrs. William Astor's famous "Four Hundred." This was a party list edited by society's arbiter, Ward McAllister, to accommodate the size of the Astor ballroom. The 400 names were in McAllister's head and when he finally wrote them down for the paper, there were outrageous errors in the names and spellings. When asked why 400, McAllister airily replied: "Well, as a matter of fact, there are only 400 worthwhile people in New York." It appeared that there were even fewer. McAllister's list actually contained 320 names.

It was left to an undistinguished gentleman from New Jersey, with a squeaky voice and droopy mustache, to set it all straight. In 1885, Louis Keller started a gossip sheet, *The American Queen and Town Topics*, with James B. Townsend and T. J. Oakley Rhinelander. Two years later he sold his interest, but kept the subscription list. Keller, capitalizing on Maurice Minton's idea, but avoiding advertising and lists of shops, published these subscribers in the first *Social Register* in 1887. It was an unassuming, 84-page volume that contained 881 names. The four quarterly editions cost $5.00 per annum. It was not until 1900, however, when Louis Keller included telephone numbers in the *Register* in type six points larger than the telephone directory's, that the little volume took on importance among the elite. And then the scramble was on to be included in the book that clearly answered in print the question of who was "high" society.

The end of the nineteenth century was a high old time, at least for the rich, who did not have to work long hours, in dreadful and often humiliating conditions. The country had survived a devastating war. It had weathered finanical panics. Cities were growing by leaps and bounds. Industry was burgeoning. There were the telegraph, telephone, railroads, and great "floating" palaces that crossed the Atlantic to Europe. There were champagne and caviar and turbot in lobster sauce. There were galantines and ballottines and duck terrines and grouse. There was venison. There were compotes of cherries and plums and pears. And there was that glory of glories—first presented by Escoffier at the Savoy Hotel in London in a silver bowl, nestled between the wings of a carved ice swan— vanilla ice cream, smothered in peaches and covered with a purée of fresh raspberries. *Pêche Melba!* It was created, according to the *grand chef,* to commemorate the performance of *Lohengrin,* given at Covent Garden by the *grande cantrice* of Australia, Madame Nellie Melba. It was also in appreciation of the two orchestra seats she had given him. Without the swans it was quite an acceptable dessert for the home. And there were crisp, starched young women, right off the boats, to serve it all. Certainly it was the best of all possible worlds.

At the turn of the century, the hint of the demise of the Ladies Mile was no more than a whispery swish of taffeta. Two gigantic stores appeared uptown on Broadway at Thirty-third and Thirty-fourth streets. But these were not the stores of the *haut monde;* these were family stores for the hoi polloi who rode on trolleys and the elevated train. They had little to do with the Ladies Mile. Macy's moved from Fourteenth Street and a mishmash of stores that had been linked together, and Gimbels arrived, fat and sassy, from Philadelphia. The new massive department stores around Herald Square would have little to do with the status quo.

But the decampment started. This was no retreat—it was another major advance. Swiftly, the stores that had catered to the carriage trade, the wealthy customers who rode around in carriages, folded their palatial tents on the Ladies Mile and the procession stole north, turning east on Thirty-fourth Street. Arnold Constable, B. Altman & Co., Bonwit Teller, W. & J. Sloane, Franklin Simon, and Lord & Taylor built elegant new stores here at the beginning of the east side, on Fifth Avenue.

A couple of struggling, out-of-date stores were left behind in the wake of the triumphal march, and they crumbled into decay. By the middle of the twentieth century, they were pitiful reminders of the once-fashionable, once-elegant, once-colorful Ladies Mile.

The last push north up Fifth Avenue took place during the 1920s. It was led by Gimbels-Saks Company, which built the lush Saks Fifth Avenue store between Forty-ninth and Fiftieth streets. Bonwit Teller, Bergdorf Goodman, De Pinna, Best & Co., The Tailored Woman, Peck & Peck, and Tiffany established themselves in the Fifties, along Fifth Avenue. Smaller shops like Jay Thorpe, Henri Bendel, and Milgrim settled around the corner on Fifty-seventh Street. New York's Fifth Avenue became the greatest shopping street in the world. During the 1950s, one could still write sonnets about Easter and other bonnets worn by the customers of the stores on the avenue—Fifth Avenue. What chance did a young Italian with a midget boutique have of getting into the rotogravure while all the photographers were snapping the elegant Titans?

In 1978, the Savoy Plaza Hotel is gone—replaced by the General Motors Building. Roberto Gucci is gone—returned to Florence—where he is the director of Gucci's Florence store and the company's export division. The Fifty-eighth Street Gucci boutique is gone. But Gucci remains—up and down the avenue—Fifth Avenue. It has not only succeeded along the bottom line in the tough, competitive marketplace, it has changed the picture of that marketplace. The march up Fifth Avenue had ended at Fifty-eighth Street and the Plaza. Gucci, joined by other Italians turned around, and like Roman Legions, marched *down* Fifth Avenue. They deployed into side streets, opened up stores, and gobbled up real estate like it was tortellini. Today Fifth Avenue and its cross-streets in the Fifties are a veritable antipasti of delicious Italian goods—clothing, shoes, handbags and luggage, jewelry, books, china, and linens—laid out in elegant shops named Valentino, Roberta di Camerino, Bulgari, Ferragamo, Buccellati, Rizzoli, Ginori, and—Gucci! Italians, descendants of noble merchants who, centuries ago, had the courage to roam the world and bring back new life, new spirit, new light to the darkness of Europe, have brought a new look and an old language to New York. The password along Fifth Avenue in the late 1970s is "Ciao!"

Lawrence Lachman, the former chairman of the board of Bloomingdale's, a store that did not make the march uptown but grew from humble beginnings in the outer reaches of the east side, said: "Look back and there's nothing static about retailing. It changes with management, with living habits, with the movements of population. All those things have enormous effects. Go back fifty years in New York City and stores that were household words aren't even on the scene. Which stores will continue to be strong? I wouldn't venture to guess. All we know is that it will change."

PART II

Out West in the
Indian Nations

TWO

A Memorable Shopping Experience

or

"Our" Miss Rose Turns Traitor

When I was a little girl in what, God forbid, might be called the "olden days," I had a great many relationships with stores and the people in them. I would go with my mother to Ayers' Market or Mellis Brothers when she went grocery shopping. Mr. or Mrs. Ayers was always good for a treat—an apple, a bunch of grapes, or a pomegranate, which you had to take home to eat, so you wouldn't risk getting pomegranate juice on your dress. I remember butcher shops because you could write your name with your toe in the sawdust on the floor and the butchers were very flirty with both my mother and me. Later, during World War II, it was to the family's advantage that my mother had never been snooty or thought the butchers were "fresh." She always smiled prettily and rather coyly "jollied them along." A few extra couponless lamb chops under the counter never hurt anyone.

On Wednesday, my mother's bridge club day, my father would come home from his business, which wasn't exactly a store, but a lumber company and mill. He would take me to the Central Drug Store and we'd sit at the soda fountain counter for lunch. It was very clubby and there were lots of jokes. I felt very grown up when I was with my father, and he'd let me have a Coke, which was considered by my mother and grandmothers to be on a par with drinking sulfuric acid. Favorite lunch: peanut butter and jelly sandwich,

51

grilled flat as an envelope, Coke, and ice cream with hot chocolate pudding. Afterwards, we might go to Nichol's News Stand (or was it the Nickel News Stand?) for a shoeshine. I would accompany my father on errands, perhaps to L. M. Morris Company, when he bought office supplies or dropped off an adding machine or typewriter to be repaired. Wednesday was a very special day.

I would also go shopping with my grandmothers. One favorite venture was the trip across town to Roos' Poultry Market. It was rather macabre, that big warehouse filled with crates of cackling chickens and the "buck-buck-be-awkuck"—thud. And the smell of singed pinfeathers. This was particularly exciting during the holidays when a plump turkey had to be selected.

My sister, Marion, who is five years older than I, and our friends used to play store. We'd set up carton boxes for counters and pile up orange crates for shelves. We'd fill the shelves with toys, old pots and pans and dishes, and our mothers' cast-off shoes, hats, purses, and scarves. We'd separate pennies, a few nickels, and fake money in the cups of muffin tins and we were in business. We'd buy and sell and try on, imitating our mothers, aunts, and grandmothers. We also played house, dress-up, and "movie star." One played "movie star" with "papes"—paper dolls and cars and furniture that we had cut out of magazines and glued onto cardboard. Our fathers' shirt cardboards were one of the necessities of life. We had an older neighbor, Chick Downey, who was in her teens and was very artistic. She made very glamorous papes. She also designed dresses for them that hinged with flaps over the shoulders. These were the ways in which we idled away the long hot summer afternoons in a small town in the California Central Valley during the 1930s. We didn't play hopscotch or running games until dusk and the cool of the evening.

I was born and raised in Modesto, California, which has since become famous as the home of Gallo wines and George Lucas. (Only a few years ago when Marion was in L. M. Morris Company, where George's father worked, Mr. Lucas said he rather wished George would give up all that crazy stuff he was doing in Hollywood, come home, settle down, and sell typewriters.)

George Lucas set the action for *American Graffiti* in a California valley town and although it was not filmed in or identified as Modesto every Modestan knew George had depicted his hometown. For one thing the drive-in where the carhops served on rollerskates *had* to be Modesto's unique and famous Burgee's. For another, the streets his film characters "dragged" in the 1950s in their souped-up hotrods were obviously Tenth and I streets—the main shopping streets when I was growing up. As creator, writer, and director of *Star Wars*, George Lucas has said that as a boy he watched *Flash Gordon* on television and fantasized about outer space. We all played make-believe as kids growing up in the Valley. It was too hot to do anything else.

You were allowed to go downtown to Tenth Street to shop with the adults if you *behaved yourself.* I loved going to Minnie Dunning's, where my grandmother, whom we called Avis Nana, bought her hats or had them made. Miss Dunning and the ladies would fuss over me and allow me to try on hats. I would sometimes do an imitation of one of my movie stars and everyone would laugh. I would, of course, *behave myself* and when the serious business of hat buying began, I would be put to sorting out the ribbons in the drawers that lined the walls beneath the shelves filled with hatted egg-shaped wooden heads. I also separated the feathers, flowers, and fruits that were stuffed into countless boxes. I particularly liked clumps of shiny red celluloid cherries and pink silk-petaled floppy roses.

When Avis Nana wanted to buy a gift or have a watch repaired, we would go to Shoemake's Jewelry Store. For all the glitter of polished silver, twinkly glassware, and radiance from the trays of jeweled rings, nothing in the store sparkled as much as Helen Shoemake, who appeared to wear the entire diamond stock on her fingers and wrists and pinned on the collar of her blouse. Mrs. Shoemake was a bouncy, exuberant lady who designed her own hats and gave lectures about it. I thought she was very glamorous. She had hennaed hair, which I found exotic, if not downright wicked, since there was a lot of talk about women who "touched up" their hair. My sister and her friends nicknamed Mrs. Shoemake, "Mrs. Baah—l," since that was the way she pronounced the popular present of that time, cut-glass perfume bottles. Mrs. Baah—l, talking about her wares, would send us into paroxysms of snickers which were stifled until we got outside the store. I don't think she had a glottal stop. I think it was more what my father would have called "putting on airs." Mrs. Shoemake was the only woman in town who appeared socially in a monkey fur coat. Indeed, she was the only woman in town who owned one.

Shopping with my other grandmother, Alice Nana, was more subdued since she sewed, and buying yard goods was rather tedious. Unlike hat trimmings, there wasn't much you could do with yard goods except look at it. There was some fun at Latz Dry Goods Store. For one thing, it was the headquarters for Munsingwear and the store was filled with funny-looking displays and cutouts wearing long underwear. Whoever bought *longjohns* when the temperature outside was 110 degrees, I can't imagine. The other thrill happened when a purchase was made. There were wires all over the main floor, mid-air, and when you paid the clerk, she would place your money in a little basket and ring a bell. The basket would go clickety-clickety-click up the wires and disappear through a mysterious window on the mezzanine. In a moment the basket would reappear and *swoosh*, it would come careening back down to the clerk, who would hand you your change. I wanted to be small enough to ride in one of those baskets.

These shopping trips would end at the Central or the Velvet Ice Cream Shop, where we would have a lemonade or root beer float. The girl at the ice cream shop always said "rut" beer, which was almost as side-splitting as "baah—l." If you had behaved yourself exceptionally well, keeping your socks pulled up, never whining or sitting on the floor, or blowing your breath on a glass display case so you could draw a picture with your finger in the "steam," you were allowed to order an "all-round" chocolate ice cream soda, a double treat, since it was a chocolate soda with chocolate ice cream.

For all of the thrills of these jaunts downtown, they were nothing compared to the great adventure of our shopping trips to The City. Latz' might be all right for underwear, socks, and p.j.s, but for proper clothes, it was necessary to make the three-and-a-half-hour motor trip to San Francisco and those elegant edifices, The White House, City of Paris, H. Liebes & Co., Livingston Brothers, and The Emporium, where one had to make a visit to ride on the new contraption called an escalator. Sommer & Kaufman was for shoes and I. Magnin for new dress-up clothes. My mother would write ahead to "our" Miss Rose in the children's department at Magnin's and give her the date and time of our arrival. The trips centered around Marion and me. My mother and her friends would go to The City another time to shop for suits and dresses and hats at Magnin's, Ransohoff's, or Maison Mendessolle. My mother did not agree with my grandmother about Minnie Dunning's sense of style.

We were Valley people. We lived in the San Joaquin Valley, east of San Francisco, part of the vast Central Valley. On mid-nineteenth-century maps of California that had circulated throughout the world, this area had been painted yellow and stamped with a printed overlay that read "Gold." Actually the gold ore was not in the Valley, but in the hills farther east. Gold came to the Valley later in the century and from higher up in the Sierra Nevada mountains in the form of water. It was harnessed through a series of dams and flowed through canals down into the flat desert and made the Valley bloom into one of the richest agricultural areas in the world.

My grandfathers had come into the Valley as young men—one to work as a clerk in a lumber company and the other as a school-teacher. My grandmothers were born in the nearby towns of Paradise and Coulterville. Both my parents were born in Modesto.

To Valley people, San Francisco is The City. There is no other. Valley people often identify themselves *not* by their hometowns—Lodi, Stockton, Manteca, Ripon, Salida, Modesto, Turlock, Ceres, Merced, Madera, etc.—but rather by how long it takes to get to The City. The answer to "Were do you live?" is, "I live an hour and thirty (forty, forty-five, fifty—whatever) minutes from The City." This implies that you come from north of San Francisco—Marin County—which is OK, or south—down on the Peninsula—which is also OK. It is a Valley syndrome, but in this manner you avoid remarks like "You mean people actually *live* in those hot *hell-holes* you go through to get to Yosemite and Tahoe?"

My friend, Barnaby Conrad, who was something of a professional San Franciscan, came to my sister's house for cocktails after he lectured in Modesto in the late 1960s. Eyeing the Oriental rugs, the decor, and the garden beyond the sliding glass doors, he said, "My goodness, I had no idea 'Valley people' lived like *this!*"

The Valley, to San Franciscans (if they think about it at all), is imagined as one large, rundown trailer camp, peopled by sallow migrant farm workers and wetbacks. They also have a strange concept of geography. California, to the San Franciscan, is less a state than a state of mind that is a narrow strip running north and south from Belvedere Island, on the north side of the Golden Gate Bridge, all the way south to Pebble Beach. It is bordered on the west by Maui and on the east by the San Francisco-Oakland Bay Bridge toll booths. Beyond the tolls, all the way to New York City, lies a vast wasteland, with a way station at Lake Tahoe and, more recently, Aspen.

Secretly, I must admit, a lot of Valley people wanted to be City people in those days, before cities got such bad names. But they had to accept the next best thing, which was to look like City people. "Our" Miss Rose, being a City person herself, knew exactly how nice little City girls should look. It was very important to be nice. That went hand and white-cotton-glove with behaving yourself.

Our shopping trips to The City took place several times a year—in the fall, before Christmas, and in the spring. They lasted two or three days and were filled with all the excitement The City had to offer—shopping, the theater, museums, and restaurants. They were magic days.

My grandfather, Charles Tillson, and my grandmother Avis would arrive early in the morning to pick up my mother, Marion, and me. Behind the wheel of their seven-passenger Pierce Arrow was their driver, Ronny. It might appear to be "putting on airs," to have had a Pierce Arrow limousine in a small Valley town, but it was not. It was a *necessity*, since my grandfather had some twenty years before bought an automobile and driven it directly into a tree. After that he always had a driver since he was "scared to death" of those "infernal machines." The idea of my grandfather being scared of anything was beyond belief, since he told the most hair-raising stories at Sunday dinner about coming west on foot as a boy of fourteen.

My grandfather's father was killed during the Civil War while serving in the Union Army. His widow was left raising a large family in Rochester, New York. My grandfather suffered from asthma and it was taken for granted that he would die at an early age during one of his ghastly attacks. But someone heard about a place called Denver, in *high country*, where the air was thin and one could breathe. He hired on to a surveying crew heading west, laying out the railroad. He worked as a runner, the boy who ran ahead and held the stake on which the surveyor took a fix with surveying instruments.

In Rochester, whenever my grandfather had saved a few pennies from odd jobs or selling newspapers, he had stood in the back of the gallery of the local theater and watched the traveling road companies. One of the few personal possessions in his pack, heading west, was a copy of Shakespeare's Complete Works. At night, around the campfire, he would read to his fellow laborers, many of whom were illiterate. As the months passed, the readings turned into full-scale performances, with my grandfather taking all the parts. Later, in the telling, as he stood dramatically at the head of the table at Sunday dinner, brandishing the carving knife back and forth across the steel, he would fill the oak-paneled dining room with blizzards, animals, and Indians. There were spellbinding tales of puma and mountain lion tracks that he had found in the snow around his tent. (Anyone in Modesto who had ever *seen* snow was unique.) And there were always Indians in the background ready to attack. On many occasions my grandfather had saved the lives of the railroad gang. Once the Indians who surrounded the camp were so captivated by the magical performance of the young boy leaping and bounding and shouting around the flickering flames, they joined the audience and smoked a peace pipe. That's what my grandfather told us. We would sit breathless and wide-eyed until my grandmother would say, "Charles, the meat is getting cold."

My grandfather would place the steel on the miniature cut-crystal barbell that held the carving tools up off the damask tablecloth. Holding the fork like a rapier and the carving knife like a sword, he would attack the roast or bird and "Cry, 'God for Harry! England and Saint George!'" The Swedish girl would pass the gold-banded Limoges plates which had been purchased at Gump's in San Francisco.

My grandmother Avis was indeed a little bird. She was four feet ten inches tall and would flit and fly and flutter through her day, which began early in the morning with a glass of hot water with a squeeze of lemon juice. This matutinal libation was the only water she drank throughout the day and she took great pride at dinner as she would slide her water goblet toward me and say, "I *never* drink water, you know." I always sat on my grandmother's right so she could perform this ritual—though why, I'll never know, since it was her contention that drinking water with meals gave a person "the bloat." She would say with equal pride, "I *never* eat onions," and she may have been on to something. She was six months short of one hundred years old when she died. My grandmother's favorite entree was chicken fricasee, but it was seldom served since it did not require carving, and this seriously curtailed my grandfather's theatrics and left him sullen.

Ronny was a disappointment to me. He was a driver who wore a dark suit and cap. I wanted him to be a chauffeur in maroon livery with brass buttons, puttees, and pants that ballooned at the thighs. That was the way they looked in the movies. I was in my Shirley Temple period. I wanted more than anything in the world to be Shirley's best friend and understudy. Best friend—so we could play in her much publicized playhouse. Understudy—so that I could be discovered and become famous and call a driver a chauffeur and drive up in front of Grauman's Chinese Theatre amid the searchlights. My Katherine Cornell/Joan of Arc period came later.

As we started on our shopping trips, we would drive across the flat valley in the early morning to beat the heat—or there was the season of the tulle fog, thick white blobs that would lie ahead on the road along the river. "Methinks I see my father's ghost," my grandfather would point out, and we would come to a near halt and inch our way through the patches, blindly. Ronny would open the door to follow the white line along the side of the car. Then abruptly, out of the white darkness and up into the brown foothills, through the Altamont Pass, where we would stop at the summit to let the car cool, we could relax again.

My grandfather sat in the front seat, turning occasionally to regale us with the "cougar in the tree who almost leaped down and devoured me" story, or the "rattlesnake in my sleeping bag" story, or bits of *Lear* or *Richard II*. We would play word and number games and my sister and I would take turns sitting in the jumpseat. As we twisted out of the Altamont, down the steep grade, someone inevitably told the story about the truck whose brakes gave out on this very spot and it ran away out of control. We drove across the Livermore Valley and up into more hills, green now, and sometimes wrapped in a different kind of fog, not thick and treacherous,

but wispy and soft and mysterious, down into the line at the Oakland Pier and onto the ferryboat for the trip across the Bay to—The
City.

At the Palace Hotel, we would be greeted effusively by Hughie,
the doorman. My grandfather would sweep majestically through
the lobby, the ladies of his court trailing behind. There would be
enthusiastic greetings from the desk clerk and Joe, the hatcheck
boy, who was really a very small old man, and Jimmy, the cigar
boy, who was really a very fat, middle-aged man. I suspect that my
grandfather was a big tipper. We would freshen up and, leaving my
grandparents to rest, my mother, sister, and I would be off to meet
my aunt at the glove counter at The White House.

For generations, the glove counter was the meeting place. You
had to fight your way through the crowd, midday, to buy a pair of
gloves. Buying gloves, and the ritual that went with it, was a wonderful experience!

First the saleslady would put your arm on a little pillow and place
her elbow alongside yours, as though poised for an Indian wrestle.
She would fold her hand against your hand and press against your
palm, measuring your fingers. She would turn and flip open and
close several of the hundreds of little drawers that lined the wall.
She would place neat packets on the counter and unfold the tissue
paper. Pointing out the latest fashion, a button here, a flat bow
there, a bit of embroidery on the cuff, she would take wooden
tongs that looked like curling irons and do mysterious things inside
the fingers of one glove and then slip it onto your hand. She'd work
her way down each finger with her fingers, tuck in the thumb last
and tug tight at the wrist. Then she would turn your hand over, give
it a little squeeze and a pat, and say, "There! Now doesn't that
look nice?" Gloves! Almost as much fun as hats!

In my fresh new gloves, I would take my aunt's and my mother's
hands and we would cross the street to Temple Bar for lunch. Temple Bar was not a bar but a tearoom—at least not until that day in
December 1933. I remember everyone seemed terribly excited and
nervous and the waitress said, "Would you ladies care for a—
cocktail?" My mother looked thoughtful as she removed her kid
gloves, and waving them casually in the air she said, "I'll have a
sidecar." My aunt giggled and said, "I'd like a Manhattan." The
waitress said, "How about the little lady? Would she like to try our

'Shirley Temple'?'' Everyone looked smug, and when the drinks arrived the ladies lifted their glasses and my mother said, "Here's how!" My aunt said, "Here's mud in your eye! Imagine, ordering a cocktail, just like that! Isn't it wonderful!" I didn't understand why the celebration. I wasn't even sure what a cocktail was, but imagine having the jewel-colored liquid afloat with cherries and orange slices named after you! Much better than a dessert—Apple Brown Betty, Crêpes Suzette, Charlotte Russe—all those glorious ladies immortalized in calories. A cocktail named after you—that's the cat's pajamas! Almost as good as having a pair of shoes named after you—Mary Jane—Buster Brown—only I hated Buster Brown because we had the same awful haircut. (I subsequently learned that halfway around the world I was immortalized—ask for "Nan" in Bombay or in an Indian restaurant anywhere, and you get a basket of lumpy bread.)

On the following day, Saturday, we would go to I. Magnin's for our new dress-up outfits and to Sommer & Kaufman for shoes. If time allowed, we would take a quick walk through Chinatown before lunch at the Palace Hotel and the thrill of thrills, the matinee at the Curran or Geary theater. On Sunday there would be a late breakfast at the Cliff House, a visit to the de Young Museum, the Conservatory, the Japanese Tea Garden or the Palace of the Legion of Honor before our late-afternoon trip back into the Valley.

My mother, sister, and I did not take my grandmother shopping with us if we could help it because she would slow us down by getting lost. This is not so much have to do with her being small (although that did make finding her difficult), as did the fact that she had been raised with three brothers, had a doting husband and son (my father), all of whom had guided the little lady into and out of elevators, through doors and down hallways, her entire life. Although she said, "I don't have a bump of location, you know," the truth was she had problems with left and right. If coming from her hotel room she had approached the elevator from the right, in returning to her room she would get off and go right—which was wrong. Even as children, we would take her elbow and say, "This way, Nana," and the tiny toy-doll of a lady would squeeze our hands and say, "I have no bump of location, you know."

When we arrived at Magnin's at the appointed hour, we would be greeted by "our" Miss Rose, as we stepped off the elevator.

Standing beside the mini-mannequins in pleated skirts and knee-socks, there would be hugs and Miss Rose would call us "her darling girls" and remark about how much we had grown. I considered Miss Rose to be the most beautiful woman in the world, after my mother, of course. Miss Rose had hennaed hair.

It was always the same. We would go into the fitting room and there, hanging side by side against the wall, would be new matching reefer coats. Now last year's new coat would become this year's old coat. It would be "let down" and worn to school. There would be sailor hats hanging on hooks, velours for fall and winter and leghorn straws with navy-blue grosgrain ribbons down the back for spring.

This particular Saturday, Miss Rose was more than her usual ebullient self. She bubbled, bounced, and patted my sister and said, "Just you wait until you see!" I sensed that something different was about to happen and I had a strange foreboding. I was right.

As we entered the fitting room, there on the hanger, hooked over the top of the swing-out mirror, was a single-breasted maroon coat with a velvet collar. Lying flat across the shoulder was a matching maroon Scotch cap. "A princess coat for a princess," Miss Rose said, as she whipped the coat from the hanger and held it like a royal mantle for my sister, who had flung her old coat onto a chair. Hanging on the opposite mirror was the same year-after-year, square, fat, ugly, hideous, disgusting navy-blue reefer, in a small size. I wanted to scream and cry out, "No, no—it's not fair! Maroon! My *favorite* color." I wanted to lie down and kick my feet up and down, hard, on the floor. Of course, I did not do either.

I had one recourse. I would never speak to anyone again—ever! I slid into the corner of the fitting room, folded my arms across my chest, and stood rigid and silent. My sister stood on the little wooden drum in front of the triple mirrors, which Miss Rose adjusted so she could see herself, and herself and herself, thousands of herself, front, back, and sideways—a whole monstrous chorus of maroon-coated Marions turning and twirling. She squealed and shrieked and they all hugged themselves as she looked over her shoulder and screamed, "Oh, I love it! I love it!" She generally behaved like an idiot.

I stood quietly as Miss Rose began to approach me, holding the horrible reefer by the shoulders, shaking it like a matador shaking his cape to entice a bull to humiliation and death. "And now, my darling girl, let's see how beautiful you are going to look." And another step forward, and another shake of the cape. "Come, my darling girl, let's try on your pretty new coat." But something had gone wrong. Miss Rose was not dancing and swirling with grace. Miss Rose was pawing and snorting and snarling and charging. Miss Rose was the ogre who lived under the bridge, the giant with an eye in the middle of his forehead, the wolf in grandmother's bed. I had never noticed before how big her nostrils were nor how they opened and closed, exhaling steam down over her hairy upper lip that curled and uncurled over her fanglike teeth. Miss Rose was a very ugly person!

I waited for my mother to save me. I waited for my mother to say, "Miss Rose, we want another maroon princess coat in a small size, please." But she did not. What she said was, "Put your arms in the sleeves, dear." I held my arms tighter and planted my feet firmly on the floor. "Put your arms in the sleeves," my mother repeated. My sister said, "She's jealous—look at her, she's jealous!" And it pierced back through the multitudinous Marions into the mirror's depths echoing from one to another, "Jealous—jealous—jealous—" And Miss Rose said, "Now, my darling girl, in a few years you'll be grown up and you can have a coat like the little English princesses." And my mother said, *"Put your arms in the sleeves!"*

I stood as lifeless and stiff as the plaster children all dressed up by the elevator. And then my mother took hold of my wrist and wrenched my arms apart and pulled me after her, out of the fitting room, around the miniature tables and chairs in the children's millinery, through the lingerie department, past the corsets, past the brassieres, past the maribou bed jackets, through the mirrored door, into what I had once thought was the most beautiful ladies' room in the world. She spun around and gripped my shoulders and said, "You are a very ungrateful little girl." And I supposed she was going to say something about the starving Armenians also being cold Armenians, but she did not. She reached into her purse and out came her Mason and Pearson hairbrush and she raised it, holding the flat side in my direction. "You are going to go back in there and try on that coat and behave like a lady." I whirled around and ran out past the nightgowns, past the filmy negligees, past the garter belts, past the step-ins, into the fitting room and into the *stupid* coat.

I was better prepared for the shocks at Sommer and Kaufman. When my mother described my sister's coat, the salesman said, "I have just the thing." He brought out stacks of boxes and rumpled through the tissue paper and then, like the prince holding the glass slipper, he presented a black patent-leather pump with a flat grosgrain bow and a *heel*! He straddled the bench and it occurred to me if I swung my foot very hard, I could kick him, just below the knee. He placed the shoehorn behind my sister's heel. It was tight, but he said, "Of course she'll be wearing silk hose." Not socks—*hose*! My sister strutted across the room. "It's called a Cuban heel, Madam," he said, and moving the bench in front of me, "Now, little lady, I suppose you are going to have a new pair of these?" and he unbuttoned my Mary Janes.

If I could just throw up! I could not, so I curled my toes so he wouldn't be able to get the new shoes on, but with his thumb and middle finger, he pinched me hard above the heel. Then we walked across the room and I stuck my feet into the big machine and the salesman switched the switch and we looked down through shields like the ones on my grandmothers' stereopticans, and there were my bones, all creepy and green, like fossils outlined by the soles of the shoes. There was a strange wartlike nub, free-floating over my arch—the pearl button. "Now, little lady, wiggle your toes." My feet were as motionless and petrified as paleolithic markings. "That's right, little girl, *wonderful*!" said the salesman. "They're a perfect fit, Madam." And it was over.

"She's being an awful pill, Mother," Marion said as we walked toward Chinatown. I had wished that the little animals around my mother's shoulders that were biting each others' tails would come to life and turn their beady eyes upon my mother's neck. They would spring apart and sink their sharp teeth into her throat and as the blood spurted and gushed and she screamed and writhed and pulled at the flipping, tossing bodies of the animals, I would say, quietly, "Try and behave like a lady, Mother." But now I had a better plan. As the first pagoda building along Grant Avenue came into view, I plotted:

—*I will never eat again! AHA!*
Before long we will be at lunch with my grandparents in the Gar-

den Court of the Palace Hotel and I will begin my long, vengeful and fatal fast. At first my grandmother will pat and cajole and slip me her water glass and ask, "What is it, my precious one?" I will sit motionless, hands in my lap, my legs dangling straight down—NOT crossed at the ankles—eyes straight ahead, jaws clenched. When the French pastry tray arrives, I will close my eyes, swallow hard, and shake my head. My grandfather will say, "What is the matter with our dearest little girl? I think this child is sick." And only then will I break my silence. Looking at my mother, I'll say, "She was going to hit me!" My grandfather, appalled, will pound his fists on the table and say, "Adele! How could you? You were going to strike this wonderful person? Adele, I'll have to ask you to leave the table and you will not be going to the matinee with us this afternoon."

Later, as I lie in my bed—with the cream-colored headboard decorated with the carved blue bow—dying, my mother will take from the brown and white pinstriped Magnin box, a maroon princess coat and a matching maroon Scotch cap. She will plead, "Look, darling, look, you can have anything you want, only eat something!" Too late my mother will sob and beg forgiveness. I will keep my silence, turn my face to the wall and like Beth in "Little Women," I will expire. My daddy will hate my mother for the rest of her life for what she has done to me. The French pastry business would be the hardest part of all.

As we walked into the Chinese shop, the glass wind-chimes tinkled gently. The smell of incense was everywhere and prickled my nose. We circled the counters along the narrow aisles, trying not to bump anyone with our suit and hat and shoe boxes, or tip over the cylinders filled with multicolored parasols and rolled-up kites. *Perhaps I could hide the suit box with its loathsome contents, or perhaps the small silk-kimonoed woman balanced on her wooden-block sandals would steal it. Perhaps I could start a tong war and lose the box in the chaos.*

The counters were filled with treasures, trick painted boxes with sliding parts and secret hiding places, and little dolls that opened up and there were dolls within dolls within dolls, until the only one left was the size of a pinky fingernail. There were paper flowers that exploded in bowls of water and fat Buddhas. My mother flipped open a fan decorated with blossoms, clouds, and butterflies, and waved it in front of my face. "Don't you want to pick out a souvenir?'' she asked. *Oh! No, no, no. How cruel!* I closed my eyes to shut out all the beauty and the Oriental mystery that surrounded me. And then I felt it brush my cheek. Softly at first, and warm, different from the breeze of the fan. And then, tickling, down around my collar. I opened my eyes. Over my mother's hand, like a puppet, was a white rabbit. Slippers. Bunny bedroom slippers with pointed ears, pink eyes, and a black button nose. My mother leaned close to my ear and whispered, "I think you need a new pair of these, don't you?" "Oh, *yes*," I said. "Oh, yes." And I threw my arms around her neck and kissed her in the softness below her chin and inhaled the sweet smell of Emeraude by Coty. "I love you, Mother, I love you," I said, and she held me tight.

At lunch in the Garden Court, my grandfather and I ate oysters on the half-shell, and my sister said, as she always did, "I don't see how you can *stand* those things sliding down your throat." My mother, sister, and grandmother finished their towering Garden Court salads—artichoke hearts with spires built of crabmeat and asparagus—all golden with hard-boiled egg-yolk beads on top. When the last oyster had slid down my throat, I took a few of the button-sized crackers and plunked them into the tiny cup of cocktail sauce, the way my grandfather did. I spooned in a dab of horseradish and stirred the mixture with the miniature fork. I stabbed the crisp, pungent morsels, scooping up the last drop of the fiery crimson sauce. I alternated sips of ice water from the two goblets in front of me.

Before lunch, I had modeled my glorious new coat for my grandparents in the marble foyer outside the dining room and everyone had fingered the gold insignia on the sleeve and agreed that I was very beautiful. I had taken the elastic from under my chin and tucked it into the crown of my velvety new hat, before we sat down, because there was no wind in the Garden Court.

And now my grandfather spoke of the Hamlets he had seen. Barrymore had been the finest. And he talked of Nazimova, Duse, Le Gallienne, and the upcoming treat, our afternoon matinee with the Lunts.

I reached under the table to run my fingers over the unscuffed tips of my uncracked patent-leather shoes and slipped my hand into the paper bag on my lap, to stroke the fuzzy slippers. The white-gloved waiter arrived with the pastry tray. He presented it to my sister with one hand and with a large fork and spoon, held like tongs, in the other, he indicated the chocolate beehive in the center of the scrumptious display and said, "There's only one left, Miss." Marion looked at the beehive, and glanced at me. Then she pointed to a strawberry tart and said, "I'll have *that one*, please."

My fork broke through the tissue-thin chocolate dome that covered the marshmallow beehive and eased down into the moist, black cake below. My mother and grandmother delicately spooned their yellow lemon and pink raspberry ices. My grandfather selected a cigar from the tray that rested on Jimmy's belly. Jimmy snipped the cigar with his clippers and snapped a giant torch for a flame. My grandfather rolled the cigar between his lips, and as he puffed, plump blue clouds billowed around him.

Overhead, colossal balloons, captives for the evening's gala, quivered and rolled about inside an enormous net stretched below the stained-glass dome. In the background, the string quartet played "Zigeuner."

There were gypsies and tambourines and ribbons flying—yellow, pink, and blue satin streamers floated and twined among the palm fronds. The ceiling bobbed with jujubes and gumdrops and jellybeans. There were garlands. Wrapped in the marble cyclorama of the Garden Court, filled with music, color, wonder, and love, I knew that there was not, anywhere in the world, a happier or luckier little girl than I was.

THREE

The "City"

San Francisco, California

"He taught me the world, the whole world, first hand," Mrs. Grover Magnin said, in lilting tones that bespoke her Louisiana childhood. She was speaking of her late husband, the legendary force behind I. Magnin and Company. Chiming Christmas carols were ringing in the background. Eight years had passed since Grover Magnin died, in March 1969, at the age of eighty-three.

"We started so long ago and I was so young and innocent. I knew *nothing*. He just took me over; he taught me everything," she said. "When we were buying our art collection, Impressionists, mostly—Renoir, Degas—it was always *our* collection. Never *his* or *mine*. You see, we were never separated. *We* were *we*." She paused. "I still grieve for him."

Jeanne Magnin was seated at *her table*, in the tower restaurant, the Top of the St. Francis Hotel, overlooking Union Square and the gleaming white Vermont marble I. Magnin store at Geary and Stockton streets—her husband's magnificent creation—that had replaced the old I. Magnin store, a block away at Geary Street and Grant Avenue, in 1948.

At the table were Elizabeth Curtis, Fine Dress buyer for Magnin's for forty years, and Jerry Longstreth, manager of I. Magnin & Co., Carmel. Miss Curtis, beyond her professional relationship with Magnin's, had been like a member of the family to the child-

67

less couple. "I worshipped them both," she said, her own voice showing traces of her southern upbringing in Mississippi and Tennessee. The women were chic and "I. Magnin," an elegant look that has given San Francisco women the reputation for being among the best-dressed women in the world.

Earlier, when Mrs. Magnin had entered the restaurant and stood at the top of the stairs, she looked tall—a presence wrapped in a black sable cape. Her flaxen hair shone in the winter sunlight and her enormous blue-green eyes had searched out her companions. She was slim and blessed with that attribute San Francisco women possess from walking up and down the hills—beautiful, slender legs. After she came down the stairs and stood next to the head waitress, there was the reality of how petite and delicate she was. Mrs. Grover Magnin has the look of exquisite porcelain.

"We lived in a two-story apartment on the third and fourth floors of this hotel for forty-three years," she said. "It had stained-glass windows and a great deal of hand carving. It was a beautiful apartment and everybody came there. Dior, Margot Fontaine, George Cukor, people from the worlds of opera, theater, films, fashion, and art. *Ev-er-y-body*! It was a dream come true. You see, Mr. Magnin had the finest store in the world. There was no other like it *anywhere*! Ooooh, I have the most wonderful memories! Why, we enter*tained.* Sometimes we'd have dinner parties for a hundred people." She dropped her voice to a whisper. "When this hotel was bought—by Western Hotels, I think—the manager—he was a little 'snot-nose'—could never figure out how we got better food than he did. My dears, we'd lived here since 1931, and my mother-in-law, Mrs. Isaac Magnin, had the apartment next door. She lived here from 1919 until she died in 1943, when she was ninety-four years old."

The romance of Jeanne and Grover Magnin was filled with beauty, devotion, and a dash of intrigue involving several matchmakers. The story of the founding of I. Magnin & Co. is filled with romance, beauty, devotion, and pluck. To travel from London to San Francisco in the 1870s, around the Horn with six children, took a great deal of that, but pluck, along with energy, drive, and ambition, was a quality that Grover Magnin's mother, Mary Ann Magnin, had in abundance. Her son wrote:

The business was founded under very peculiar circumstances. My parents were married in London and had six children there and two in America. One died, which left me as the youngest and only living member of the family born in the United States. They came to this country after having a small business in mirror frames and picture frames. They came directly to San Francisco and my father got himself a job with S. & G. Gump, because my father was very skillful in wood carving and laying gold leaf. In those days, the mid-Victorian period, these large mirrors with huge, full frames and painted portraits of people were always framed in this manner.

Both my mother and father came from Holland. My mother was born in Scheveningen, and my father was born in Assen. His father was a teacher of Semitic languages at Groningen University. At the age of fifteen, father left home and came to the United States and got "sucked" into the Civil War and the Union Army. After the war was over, he went back to his home town to see his father and couldn't find him. But a friend of his father's told him if he went to London and looked up a certain family by the name of Cohen, he thought they knew where he was. And when he did, he met my mother and they fell in love and got married. Father wanted to come to America and mother said she wouldn't leave London as long as my grandmother was alive.

After she passed away, they did come. They were not rich, but they did have a small amount of money. They had six children and they packed up and came directly to San Francisco, where they settled and father got his job with S. & G. Gump.

One day Mr. Gump sent for my father and said he had a promotion for him. It might have been two dollars a week.

Isaac Magnin was offered an advancement to be a painter of gold leaf ceilings, but Mrs. Magnin, fearing he might fall, leaving her widowed or caring for a crippled husband along with her large family, insisted he leave Gump's. Mrs. Magnin, an accomplished seamstress, had been making fine baby clothes, and Mr. Magnin, with a pack on his back, began selling them.

In 1876, they opened the first I. Magnin & Co., a small needle, thread, and notion shop. Mary Ann Magnin's needlework expanded to include bridal trousseaus and fancy shirtwaists. As the orders increased, she hired helpers. During the early morning, she would buy her materials at the wholesale houses. Throughout the day she sewed, took orders, and made alterations. In the evenings, she supervised the cutting of garments to be worked on the next day. She also took care of her family. Her son John had a head for business and she encouraged him in his studies of arithmetic and accounting. Grover, her youngest son, she talked to about quality, design—and she blindfolded and tested him as he felt fabrics and textures—moiré, pongee, peau de soie, linen, and laces. There was her son, Joseph, who later left the family company and founded his own business, and a son, Sam. The three daughters were taught fine handiwork.

A new store was opened on Market Street, and John Magnin entered the business. A larger store was being built at Grant Avenue and Geary Street in 1906, when it was destroyed in the April fire and earthquake. At that time, twenty-one-year-old Grover was recalled from Stanford University, where he had hopes of studying architecture or engineering. The family opened a store in their Van Ness Avenue home until they could rebuild downtown.

Mr. Magnin reported:

> Mother had practically retired from the business by 1900, although she was always most active in matters of big policy.
>
> I entered the business in April of 1906 and after an apprenticeship of over two years, having worked in every department of the store, including the receiving room and office, buying, and each department, I then became the general manager.
>
> In 1908, after which time my brother, John, moved to New York [to open a buying office], Mother used to pay a visit every day and one day after returning from New York, where she saw the beautiful white marble floor at B. Altman's, she said to me, "Why don't you put in a marble floor, on the first floor?" I told her it was very expensive, and would cost around 10 or 15 thousand dollars, in those days that was a large sum of money for Magnin's. "I know," Mother said, "but if the company can't afford it, put it in, and I'll pay for it.
>
> In about 3 weeks the marble floor was in and the company survived the expense.

Mary Ann Magnin continued her daily visits, almost until the day she died. There are personnel who remember the later years, when Mrs. Magnin's chauffeur would drive her the two and a half blocks from the St. Francis Hotel. The immaculate, regal little old lady wearing beautiful jewelry was brought into the store in her wheelchair, which Grover, with his engineering background, had had mechanized. She would be wheeled about by her devoted maid, Annie, around the counters, where she would greet everyone, then into the elevator and up to the office of her beloved son Grover. It is said that in her very last days, she came by ambulance and was brought in on a Gurney stretcher and rolled through her store.

For all her elegance and finery, plucky Mary Ann Magnin never lost having a touch of the pioneer. On Saturday nights, various male employees in the lower executive echelon were commandeered to visit Mrs. Magnin in her St. Francis Hotel apartment for an evening of what might be called *robust* poker. It is said that Mrs. Magnin inevitably came out the winner at the end of the evening. In fact, the evening didn't end until she was.

Mrs. Magnin was devoted to her daughter-in-law, Jeanne, but it is hinted that her possessiveness prevented her son from marrying the young beauty until 1931, by which time he was forty-five years old. The wedding was a gala, and the tiny, ivory-skinned, blond bride was a show-stopper, dressed in black velvet. She wore a small black velvet hat and carried a large spray of purple orchids.

Jeanne Magnin said of her mother-in-law: "She was a *won*derful woman. She always had the first kiss when Mr. Grover came home. He was so good. He was such a *good* boy." And then she rolled her giant eyes "Oooooooooooooh, if you've ever known a strong woman, she *was it!*"

Mrs. Grover Magnin's voice rose and fell like willow branches shifting in a bayou breeze. She punctuated her conversation with quiet squeals and sighs and laughter. "I came from Louisiana, father had a cotton plantation, not the biggest or most advertised. He died when I was seven. My mother had eight children. She was French—fine skin, violet-blue eyes, blue-black hair—*beautiful.* I never saw a hair out of place and she always wore white—white linen—after my father died.

"I was very young, hardly sixteen. There was this boy—oh, he was from a very fine family—from Mississippi. If I told you the name of the town you wouldn't know it—Hickory—Hickory, Mississippi. And then my mother died. I wouldn't have left before she died. Never! I was living in a dream world, 'cause when you were brought up in Louisiana in those days, you thought that a woman working was sleeping with men—a fallen woman." She gave a little hoot.

Leaning forward, confidentially, she asked, "*You want to hear how I got my job at Magnin's?*" She beckoned everyone closer with her fingers, tipped by perfect, long, rose-red fingernails. Then with a quick motion of her graceful hand, she waved everyone away. "Oh, I feel too *stu*-pid telling it. The world is so different today."

Encouraged, she continued, "I went into Magnin's to buy underwear—lingerie. And the buyer got hold of me and said that they were having a fashion show, with the new imports, and they needed me. I thought, Who ever needed *me?* I'd never seen a model. I'd never been to New York. I'd never been *anywhere.* I guess I had *something*—that was nice. I must have had something nice. This buyer took me by the hand, up to the mezzanine and filled out that thing—that thing you have to fill out to get a job. I didn't know *anything.* Do you know that I came in the wrong door for I don't know how many months." There was a squeal of laughter. "I was *scared to death* and I'd cry all night. I was so afraid being alone, with no family. I was afraid to leave Magnin's to go to my hotel. I was so *stu*-pid. They had thirty-five models. They shocked me to death. They'd tell stories. They'd say, 'damn.' I didn't drink. I didn't smoke. They were so worldly and wise, and I was just an infant. They must have had a good time laughing about me, those models. It's a wonder they liked me—but they did. All the buyers kept saying, 'Once he sees you, there'll never be anything else.' When he came home from World War I, there I was waiting. I didn't *know* I was waiting. I didn't *know* the buyers were plotting. I was so young, I didn't know my feet from my hands. When I met Mr. Magnin, I was afraid of him—of all things. I wouldn't go to his office to model. I'd cry big tears—like elephants'.

"Then there was the motion picture. One of our customers, Mrs. Walsh—her husband owned all the motion picture theaters in San Francisco—fell in love with me. She was not my size, but, my God, she had to have me model for her! She said to one of the buyers, 'This girl should be in the movies.' She introduced me to her husband and they wrote a part for me. The film was made down on the docks on one of those steamers that go to Japan. I took another model with me as a chaperone. The film was called *Straight from Paris.* Imagine *me*—in Paris! When the film came out, the other model wasn't in it. Ooooooh, I remember her name, but I won't tell it. I thought I'd be fired from Magnin's if they ever knew, but Mr. Magnin came to the opening. I couldn't *believe* it. He'd known all the time. God took care of me. And Mr. Magnin—from the moment he'd put eyes on me—and he didn't tell me about it. He was very shy. He just wanted me for his little baby.

"But am I not fortunate that he found me when I was young and inexperienced? We grew in love with each other more and more—all the time—and that's why I can't get over it now. I just can't."

Later, Mrs. Magnin moved about her spacious Nob Hill apartment. "It seems so small, after the St. Francis. I keep bumping into the walls." Most of the art collection was gone, donated to the de Young Museum and the Palace of the Legion of Honor. Some of it was sold at auction in New York, some bought by Norton Simon. But the room was a bower, filled with Jeanne Magnin's own floral paintings, bright and colorful roses, still lifes and landscapes. Mr. Magnin's paintings were in sharp contrast. They were geometric, abstract, structured, and engineered. "I painted all my life," she said. "When Mr. Magnin retired in 1951, everyone told me, 'Don't let him retire. He'll *die.*' But he had to, you see, that was the rule. When they merged with Bullock's in 1944, that was the rule—you retired at sixty-five—so he *had* to. *But I wasn't going to let him die.* He started to paint, with me running around him, being a monkey to entertain him while he learned, and not letting him think I was teaching him, 'cause he'd been so successful all his life. He'd always taught me *everything.* Now I taught him the fundamentals without his knowing it—acting like a child and laughing with him. He loved it to death. He was a born artist. You see, he wouldn't have built Magnin's otherwise. Nobody could copy him. They just didn't have the heart and soul.

"He was such an artist! He could see beauty. Do you know where he got the idea for those etched antique-mirror counters that are trimmed in bronze? From a *cigarette box* in Paris. And talent—he could see talent. He brought Henriette le Clert from New York, but she was *very* French. She did custom design in the store. And Miss Stella—she designed in Los Angeles, oh, for *so* many movie stars. She is only now retiring."

Around the room, in polished silver frames, were photographs of Dame Margot, the Duke and Duchess of Windsor, Mrs. Magnin, breathtaking, in a Dior gown.

"My husband introduced Dior to the world in 1947. Lucien Lelong had both Balmain and Dior as designers. In those days, they weren't given any credit. Then there was the young one— Givenchy—he was working for Madame Whats-her-name? Made the big shoulders? *Schiaparelli.* And Balenciaga. We knew them *all.* We traveled *every*-where. Paris, London, Vienna. We spent *days* in museums—in galleries. We spent our life in art. We collected here, there. Mr. Magnin always gave me beautiful things. The finest. So many things. The vanities—there's one with my name— Jeanne—in diamonds—*quality* diamonds. And this—" She held out a delicate coin-sized watch on a filigreed threadlike chain. "It keeps perfect time. I gave my watches away. I never liked things on my wrists—made me *nervous*—but I always had to have a timepiece. Sometimes I wore Mr. Magnin's gold watch—so many beautiful things." She caressed each memory with her mind. "That beautiful world—that we'll never get back again."

She turned toward the big picture window and her view. *The view*—the most cherished possession of so many San Franciscans.

"The lights at night," she said, "such a beautiful thing." This woman, herself a work of art, looked out across the Golden Gate, in a direction away from Union Square, the store, the St. Francis, the past. "But how I *miss that man*, dear," she said.

Around the corner from Union Square, down Stockton Street, at the corner of O'Farrell, emblazoned all the way around two sides of an old building, remodeled crisp and white, written in clean, sharp letters, is the name Joseph Magnin—Joseph Magnin—Joseph Magnin. Down the side of the building out over the sidewalk are two signs—Joseph Magnin—Joseph Magnin. At the corner of the building eight-foot-high letters on the wall read "JM." The signs, the vibrant colors in the awnings, and the snappy trim make the statement. This is Joseph Magnin; make no mistake. This is not a stringer, spinoff, hanger-on, or second- or third-rate I. Magnin. This is Joseph Magnin, and you'd better believe it.

It was not always so. There was a time when the store was meekly called J. Magnin—almost as though it hoped to catch a few customers who had made a mistake or had bad eyesight and snag them away from the classy brothers, John and Grover, at I. Magnin, around on a more fashionable corner.

When Joseph Magnin left the I. Magnin family business, he went into real estate and then into apparel and millinery. According to his son, Cyril, "My father could do more with a buck than any man I knew, but when he opened his own business, called Don-El-Factors (after two of my children, Donald and Ellen), and the store, we were kind of second-rate. I. Magnin had the big reputation and we couldn't get the first-rate merchandise."

It was not until after World War II, when Cyril Magnin realized that California was filling up with people who didn't know their *I*s from their *J*s, that he decided to make it clear that *Joseph* Magnin was the swinging Magnin, "with it" and moderately priced. And he went after the youth market with a vengeance.

"I wanted to make it very clear that we were not only *not* I. Magnin—we were not Saks, Ransohoff's, or Maison Mendesolle. Nor were we The White House, the City of Paris, or The Emporium—nor that interloper from New York—Macy's. We found new resources for merchandise, but we had to get our message across. One way was to spark up the store with color, inside and out. Another was to find talented young people to work for us.

"I ran an ad, 'Need Graphic Artist,' and two young ladies, Virginia Sisk and Tony Moran, responded together. They had been working for Roos-Atkins, a conservative old-line firm. Virginia said, 'We're expensive, five hundred dollars a week, but you get the two of us for the price of one.' I figured they couldn't make it worse. Their first ad was a big Valentine tree made with the words 'We Love You' and signed 'Joseph Magnin.' It was the talk of the country. It was a new look in advertising—bold, fun, and to the point—and those two were the best! It wasn't until much later I learned what meager salaries they were getting at Roos's and they just took a shot in the dark and blurted out five hundred dollars. But they were worth every cent and more later on. And we had Marget Larson, one of the greatest art directors in the world. They had the idea of putting *JM* on scarves and other accessories; it was a revolutionary idea—nobody had done such a thing—but they sold like crazy. It is the same with the double Gs we have on buckles and scarves and ties. We hold the Gucci franchise in fifteen of our stores. I've always tried to keep ahead of the game. People have stolen from me, but by the time they copy my ideas, I've been off and running with something else, something new."

Mr. Magnin, at seventy-eight years old, is chairman of the board of Joseph Magnin, now a subsidiary of Amfac, Inc., which has its corporate headquarters in Honolulu, Hawaii. The Joseph Magnin headquarters on Spear and Harrison streets, near the Embarcadero, houses a computer center for the main and branch stores that rivals Mission Control. A walk down the halls leading to Mr. Magnin's office is a wild trip through vivid purple, yellow, orange, aqua, green, red, and blue graphics painted on the walls. Mr. Magnin's office has a superb view of the docks and the Bay Bridge; it is filled with pre-Columbian and abstract art, and the decor is as modern as a spaceship.

Cyril Magnin is Chief of Protocol for San Francisco. A former president of the Port Commission and the Chamber of Commerce, he is known as Mr. San Francisco. He has an eclectic art collection—modern, Oriental, African, and pre-Columbian. He's given the Jade Room to the de Young Museum, more than a quarter of a million dollars to the Opera and brought the American Conservatory Theatre to the City. He recently turned actor himself, playing a part in the film *Foul Play*. His love of theater and opera came from his father who knew "every aria in every opera ever written."

Like many another San Franciscan, when his view was destroyed, Mr. Magnin moved. A longtime resident of the Fairmont Hotel, he settled across the street at the Mark Hopkins Hotel when the building of the Fairmont Towers interfered with his picture of the Bay and bridges.

Except for that, he said, "I have been very lucky in my life." One bit of luck came when he stopped in New York on his way to Europe in the mid-1920s and called on Ben Herschel in an effort to match some fabric from that company. Anna Smithline, the young head designer, sold him two yards of the needed fabric. A few days later on board *The Leviathan* ("In New York they called it the *Levi Nathan*," he said, chuckling, "because of all the manufacturers that took it to Europe"), he met Miss Smithline again, with her sister, the famous designer Adele Simpson. He made arrangements with the purser to move the young ladies to a larger stateroom since they were unhappy with their below-deck accommodations. The purser, much to everyone's delight, provided the Smithline sisters with an unoccupied suite for the same price as their original fare. The threesome toured Europe, and by the time they returned on the *Queen Mary*, Anna and Cyril were engaged.

"We were married at my grandmother, Mary Ann Magnin's apartment in the St. Francis Hotel. I was kind of her pet among the grandchildren and she gave us a beautiful wedding. The table was centered with a huge sunken arrangement of flowers and they got out the gold royal china. It was something—as only my grandmother could do." Mr. Magnin added, "We never carried Adele Simpson, my sister-in-law's line. She was involved exclusively with I. Magnin, and after all, business is business."

Mr. Magnin's daughter, Ellen Magnin Newman, said, "The growth of Joseph Magnin came after World War II. My father turned to young people, not only as customers, but also as employees. He has many great attributes, but most important, my father was never threatened by young people. He had great faith in their talent. He listened to them and was willing to relinquish authority and responsibility, which is rare among executives, but this was what made Joseph Magnin something special." Mrs. Newman, at one time creative merchandising director for Joseph Magnin, was one of the young creative talents her father had faith in. Today, she is president of her own firm, Ellen Newman Associates, consumer consultants. She is also a member of the board of directors of Amfac, Inc. This retail, real estate, hospitality, food and agricultural conglomerate had a gross revenue of over $1.25 billion in 1976.

Ellen Newman is smart and snappy, like her white and chrome-trimmed office which is filled with plants. The office is located across the street from the St. Francis Hotel. She is businesslike and describes her company as "interpreting consumer moves to corporations." She uses expressions like "eye-balling the world," words like "viable," and refers to things like "congeneric diversified service corporation." These are a long way from thimbles, needles, and thread, and it is doubtful that Mary Ann Magnin would have the slightest idea of what her great-granddaughter was talking about, but surely it all must bring a smile to the plucky, peppery little lady in that great big workroom up there.

It is very difficult for newcomers to understand what dates like "nought-six," the year of the earthquake and fire, and words like "pioneer" and things like "the view" mean to San Franciscans. But woe betides the merchant who fails to understand this fierce pride in tradition and sense of loyalty to the past. No one learned this lesson harder than Macy's when it came from New York to establish a store in the forties and inherited the location of one of the most conservative old-line stores in San Francisco—O'Connor and Moffatt. Willick Bingham, Ernie Molloy, and John Garling, New York hotshot managers, arrived with New York whoopla techniques—huge promotions with low-priced merchandise. Former O'Connor-Moffatt customers, along with White House and City of Paris customers, snubbed the newcomer, switched their loyalties to The Emporium on Market Street, and stayed away in droves. "Face it, they just plain didn't like anything from New York," said Hal Haener, one-time employee of The White House and a Macy's San Francisco executive for twenty-four years.

Years of long-range planning, upgrading stock, and imaginative merchandising have gone into washing the Herald Square image out of Macy's hair. One of the first moves to get San Franciscans into the store was Willick Bingham's creation, the Macy's Flower Show. How could a city that had flower stands on virtually every downtown corner resist? People flocked into the glorious display. But looking was one thing and buying was something else again. Gradually, Macy's captured a share of the housewares and home-furnishings market by courting the newcomers in California's post-war population boom and the branches prospered in the suburbs, but little inroad was made on the fashion scene.

In the mid 1950s it stopped fighting for the old guard natives and went after their teenage children, youngsters who were inclined to be more loyal to their peers than to their conservative parents. They established the Macy's Hi-Set Club and built up a membership of over 50,000. Hi-Set had representatives in the high schools who held coveted Saturday jobs in the store. There were makeup clinics, TV fashion shows, a teenage magazine, and a gala fashion show in the grand ballroom of the beloved Palace Hotel. Since you couldn't get more San Francisco than that, even parents were wooed. These young customers eventually became older customers, young marrieds, and parents, and by that time Macy's was "their store," but it was a long, slow seduction. For all the marketing research, graphs, projections, and statistics, there is one basic that Macy's knows—time passes. If teenagers grow into adults with buying power, then it follows that kiddies grow into teenagers, so get them while they're young.

The Thanksgiving Day Parade has been an annual event at Macy's since 1927, with the exception of three years during the war. But it was a very *New York* Macy's Parade—a point made clear by Erica Jong, in the beginning of her book *How to Save Your Own Life:*

> . . . As a little girl, I was allowed to stay up all night on Thanksgiving Eve to watch the trucks carrying the helium cylinders arrive and the great wrinkled latex balloons begin to take shape under their sandbagged cages of netting. . . . Mickey Mouse, Donald Duck, Superman, the panda and the dinosaur would be spread out on the black asphalt of the street.
>
> . . . We felt we *owned* the parade, and we would go downstairs and chummily feed sugar cubes to the policemen's horses, thinking ourselves the luckiest kids in New York City—special, singled out, rare.

Even with the parade on television, how does all that New York whoop-de-do get kids to drag their parents down to Union Square or into any other California Macy's? *The Macy's TV Parade Contest*—that's how!

The rules:

1. (Easiest rule) Watch Macy's Thanksgiving Day Parade at 1:30 P.M. Thursday, on KRON-4
2. Draw a picture of something you specially liked in the Parade— like a float, a balloon, a dancer.
3. Make your drawing no smaller than 8½ x 11" and no bigger than 11 x 14".
4. Print your name, address, age and birthdate clearly. (Grown-ups can help in this part only, if necessary!)
5. Bring your drawing to any Macy's Toy Department before Store Closing Time, 9:30 P.M. on Wednesday, December 1.
6. Prizes will be given in three age groups: under 6, 6 to 9, 9 to 12 (and ages will be verified).
7. Judges in the contest will be Mr. Henry Hopkins, Director of the San Francisco Museum of Modern Art, sculptor Ruth Asawa and bon vivant Trader Vic Bergeron.

* * *

Here are the 63 wonderful prizes:

FIRST PRIZE: $50.00 Macy's Gift Certificate for
each age category.

SECOND PRIZE: $25.00 Macy's Gift Certificate,
10 for each category.

THIRD PRIZE: $10.00 Macy's Gift Certificate,
10 each age category.

On Wednesday, December 8, the judges arrived promptly at Macy's before 10 o'clock. The large oval table in the board room was cleared; coffee and Danish were on a stand in the corner. Cartons upon cartons filled with the drawings were wheeled in on dollies. There were *thousands* of pictures. Mr. Hopkins and Miss Asawa, stalwarts of the art world, and Trader Vic, the king of San Francisco hospitality and a painter himself, are busy people. They are sought after and their time is precious. It might be assumed that they would toss the cartons' contents into the air and choose the ones that landed right side up, or, blindfolded, someone would reach into a box for a winner. Not so! The judging was painstaking, time-consuming, and serious. The pictures were laid out on the table. They were perused, eliminated, and perused again. There were comments on composition, technique, and imagination. The clock ticked on. There were arguments and compromises, and finally, the sixty-three winning pictures were selected from the masses of entries.

At 1:15, after three hours of judging, the Trader said, "Let's all go over to my saloon for a drink and lunch. I think we deserve it." And they did.

Philip Schlein, the forty-two-year-old president of Macy's California, said: "To make shopping an attractive experience, I think everybody concerned has to have a good time in a pleasant atmosphere. For the personnel, the customers, anyone who has anything to do with the store—it has to be fun." If the contest-judging was any example, he was right, 'cause everybody had a ball.

The evolution of Macy's San Francisco has continued, and with the recent opening of the Shop on the Square fashion department, Macy's now has a facade on Union Square, cheek by jowl with I. Magnin & Co. "We're the new 'Old Kid' on the block," said Susan

Graham, director of publicity. The new "Old Kid" was also the testing ground for The Cellar, the masterful revitalization of the old Macy's bargain basement into a gourmet cookery, housewares, and book mall, with a reproduction of Mama's, a favorite restaurant of San Franciscans. This renovation took place under the guidance of Ed Finkelstein, the then head of Macy's San Francisco, the now president of Macy's New York. Mr. Finkelstein has brought The Cellar to New York and turned Macy's old dowdy, dusty basement into the "most exciting street in New York," which is one of the major reasons writer Priscilla Tucker wanted to live in Macy's. New York Macy's has a replica of P. J. Clarke's that is open nightly until eleven, and it and The Cellar are "the place" to be seen on Sunday and for brunch. Unlike the original San Francisco Flower Show lookers-on, these are customers and the buying is as frenzied as it was in the old days at a bargain-basement blouse table.

Publicity director and former New Yorker Susan Graham, mindful of what tradition means to San Franciscans, pointed out the cracks in the brick walls above the modern chrome-trimmed clothing racks in the Shop on the Square. "This was Blum's Candy Store. When we remodeled it into The Shop and stripped down the plaster, we found those places where the bricks had shifted. These walls withstood the *1906 earthquake!*" Spoken like a native!

As the doors to the street opened and closed with customers coming and going, there was the *dink-a-dink-dink* of the cable cars in the background, as they glided along the Powell Street side of the Square. Over the past thirty years, San Francisco has slowly, and sometimes reluctantly, opened her Golden Gates and now Macy's belongs, like cable cars and flower stalls and Trader Vic.

Like all city downtowns, San Francisco has had its share of change. There are some things, however, that remain the same— like Gump's. There are still the concave (or is it convex?) windows that give the illusion that one can reach in and touch the Oriental treasures: the Imari porcelains, lacquered boxes, evening bags made from old obi brocade; the jade jewelry, desk sets, and carved horses; the iron shi shi dogs, replicas of the fierce lionlike animals that guard Japanese temples, that protect the ivory birds and snuff bottles. "It's a mixing of the Occident and the Orient," a taxi driver said while passing and pointing to Gump's. In San Francisco, it's a time-honored tradition that, real or phony, inside every taxi driver lives a little bit of Saroyan.

Ransohoff's, across the street from Gump's, is gone; it moved into the old I. Magnin building at Grant Avenue and Geary, but now it is gone from there. Davis-Schoenwasser, famous for baby clothes, school uniforms, bridal and debutante gowns, is gone. H. Liebes & Co. is gone.

The White House and its glove counter are gone—a victim of miscalculations and bad judgment. After the war, The White House management purchased the steel parts for an escalator and leased a building next door to house it, thinking that there would be a postwar depression and the price of labor to install it would go down. While the storage building sapped off working capital for rent, labor prices soared. In addition, the management made several merchandising errors. One was their failure to understand the mystical power and the real profit in cosmetics and perfume that has turned virtually every main floor of every store into a makeup parlor and smelly paradise. They buried these departments in hard-to-find corners. Then, The White House, a middle- and upper-middle-class department store, made a belated move to expand into the suburbs. It built a branch store in a primarily low-income, predominantly black neighborhood in Oakland, and the beloved White House, pioneered by the French Raphael Weill family, submerged into the red.

Today, Saks Fifth Avenue remains on Grant Avenue. Saks, in spite of being New York, understood San Francisco very well. When it prepared to open in 1952, it placed in charge, as manager, a very young, very attractive bachelor, James Ludwig. Mr. Ludwig became involved in San Francisco's community and social life. He was sought after and the toast of the opera, symphony, and debutante crowds. By the time Saks opened, the Fifth Avenue connection was overlooked by the San Francisco customers, since the manager, James Ludwig, was one of them.

Livingston's is still an old-line family store, run by an old-line retailing family. Spruced up, it is nevertheless cozy and friendly and home to its customers. Elsewhere in the city, Livingston's "twigs" provide a boutique-y ambience for younger customers.

Across the street from Livingston's, on the corner of Grant and

Geary, the *old* I. Magnin building looked shabby and down-at-the-heels. This was where "our" Miss Rose ruled the children's department and we shopped with my mother until 1948, when the new I. Magnin store, wrapped in marble and elegance, opened a block away on Union Square. During the 1976 Christmas season, the little old lady of a building sported shabby pink awnings. They had the look of a soiled seventeenth-century ruff, gone limp, around a faded aristocrat's neck. The giant *R*s on the awnings were reminders that Ransohoff's had moved its prestigious Post Street specialty shop into these premises in an attempt to survive. During this holiday season, raucous laughter blared from hidden speakers, and in the corner display window, "Laughing Sal," a gigantic mechanical fat lady, with stringy red curls bobbing and papier-mâché eyes rolling, chortled and shook with electric paroxysms. "Sal" had graced the entrance to the Fun House at Playland-at-the-Beach Amusement Park from 1940 until its demolition in 1970. She had once lured fun-seekers in to view themselves in mirrored distortion and suffer indignities of electric shocks from the prods of mischievous clowns, and the embarrassment of skirts blown high with wind jets. Now here she was in all her vulgarity in the old Magnin-Ransohoff's window, hustling for the Great American Christmas, a craft fair.

Inside, the Street People, San Francisco's name for its hippy population, mingled around the booths containing macrame, hand-tooled leather, sheepskin coats, and pottery. The ghosts of slim socialite models, who had once paraded through the aisles in Nettie Rosenstein gowns and Hattie Carnegie and Lilly Daché hats had fled, trailing with them their misty scents of Chanel No. 5 and Guerlain's Shalimar. The air was filled with the smells of hot dogs, cider, and espresso coffee. A hand fell on my shoulder as I walked through the door onto Mary Ann Magnin's white marble floor, copied from B. Altman. "That'll be a dollar." "For what?" I asked. "I'm only looking." "For looking—there's an entrance fee. Pay the buck and then you can look."

I stepped back out onto the street and bumped into what might have been Big Foot or the Yeti in overalls. "Excuse me," I said. A hand raised from the elbow, poised like he was going to try on gloves, only he did not hold up five fingers—only one—the middle one.

I walked quickly up Geary Street toward Union Square. Past the gray-painted-over windows of the City of Paris, past the smell of gardenias at the mini-cable-car flowerstand, past the white marble of Magnin's and on beyond Macy's Shop on the Square. At the corner of Powell Street, I stepped gingerly across the cable car tracks and the open slots with the cables running beneath, terrible booby traps in the days of spike heels. I moved up the steps and into the lobby of the St. Francis Hotel, leaving the once chic old lady of a building and the electronic guffawing of "Laughing Sal," a mockery of more genteel days, far behind.

I went up the stairs into the cocktail lounge—no longer called the Patent Leather Bar—and thought I'd sit down and have a Bloody Mary. When the waitress came, I changed my mind. "I'd like—a Margarita," I said. Somehow that seemed more appropriate in California.

FOUR

The City of Paris

San Francisco, California

GOLD! That word that turns sane men mad! GOLD! For a handful it means riches and power. For most it means only adventure, hazards, and hardships. For many it means death. GOLD! In Egypt, in India, and in the Orient, centuries ago, men turned greedy for the gleaming metal. In 1200 B.C. Armenian miners who washed the metal from the sand in their sheepskins were attacked by a band of Greeks. The story became the myth of the Argonauts who were led by Jason in the search for the Golden Fleece.

In the west, the Spanish did not mine gold. They plundered, robbed, and murdered for it in Mexico and South America and became the richest country in the world. The English lay in wait on the high seas and plundered, robbed, and murdered the Spanish. Sir Walter Raleigh made two trips to South America and sailed up the Orinoco River in search of El Dorado, the land of gold.

In 1848, the Mexican War was over. The treaty was signed and Mexico was paid $15 million for the ceded Southwest Territory and California. This was Manifest Destiny, a thing clearly intended from the beginning of the world. The Stars and Stripes of the Union now stretched from sea to shining sea.

That same year, James Marshall was building a sawmill, when he picked a nugget out of the millrace. His housekeeper boiled it all day in lye to see if it was the precious metal, and he took it to Fort

Sutter in Sacramento for testing. It was *gold*! As the secret leaked out, a new disease with more epidemic proportions than the plagues swept the world—*Gold Fever*!

The greatest migration America has ever known began. Farmers left crops to rot. Ministers deserted their flocks. Classrooms were closed and tools were thrown down. Eastern coastal communities were deprived of their more ambitious and industrious young men. New England towns and the islands of Nantucket and Martha's Vineyard, hard hit by the decline of the whaling industry, were emptied of almost 90 percent of their male population. Men, young and old, who had easy access to the sailing ships headed south for the Isthmus of Panama or the trip around the Horn. In San Francisco, officers and crews quite literally *ran* for them thar' hills and the ships were left rotting. The United States Navy refused to put into the port, knowing this was the only way to avoid desertion by its sailors.

All the routes to California were perilous. The tempest-tossed trip around the Horn took five months. Crossing the plague-infested Isthmus or bandit-ridden Mexico held other terrors. Great covered wagon trains were organized to make the painful journey across the continent. Ahead lay Indians, thirst, hunger, heat, cold, and exhaustion. There was the Oregon Trail and the mountains by the way of the Great Salt Lake, and the horrors of the alkaline desert on the Santa Fe Trail. Thousands went down on ships without a trace. Thousands of nameless graves line the trails across the deserts, the plains, and the swamps of the Isthmus.

European newspapers began to carry fantastic stories of fortunes made overnight and more thousands left their native lands, braving the Atlantic crossing before the nightmarish trip west to strike it rich.

France was suffering from an economic crisis following the Revolution of 1848 and the establishment of the Second French Republic. The government organized and sponsored the *Société des L'Ingots d'Or* (pronounced delicately in French *lang-go door*) to send impoverished Frenchmen to California. To attract purchasers of shares and raise money, a lottery was held. The grand prize was a gold ingot worth 400,000 francs. Alexandre Dumas *fils* was hired to write the brochure and tickets were sold all over Europe. Although the plan was to raise 7 million francs to send 5,000 poor

Frenchmen to California, free of charge, only 3,885 went. These few may have regretted accepting the free passage for they were harassed and called *the Lingots* (pronounced harshly in English *the ling-guts*) which was to become an ethnic slur for several generations of French descendants.

How could the foremost silk-hosiery manufacturer of France, Felix Verdier, hearing of the fortunes being dug from the ground, share in the bonanza? What did a Parisian merchant know of picks, shovels, buckets, sluices, and gold pans? *Rien!* But—*D'accord! D'accord! Boff! Boff!*—what of men's souls? Their spirits? Their stomachs? Surely a gentleman walking on streets paved with gold would do so in soft leather shoes, wearing a finely cut suit, ruffled shirt, and silk cravat! *Ah oui!* And a *petit-point* vest! The hand that tipped *le chapeau haut de forme* would be covered with a kid glove. And on his arm—*Mon Dieu!*—a delicious-smelling lady would move her silk-covered legs beneath her skirts. Skirts of *le calicot? La mousseline? Qu'est-ce que c'est? Mais non!* Skirts of *peau de soie* and swoosh-swoosh—the tantalizing music of rustling taffeta petticoats! *Mais certainement*—they would be surrounded by art and velvet *portières*. They would be seated on carved furniture and they would drink champagne from crystal goblets—*n'est-ce pas? Ooh-la-la!* In 1850 Felix Verdier's brother, Emile, set sail to bring Paris to San Francisco. *Alors!*

The arrival of the brig *La Ville de Paris—The City of Paris*—in San Francisco harbor, with her cargo of French luxuries, had a profound influence on this tent and shack, rough and tumble town. That, and the fact that the Lingots did not take to the reckless, hard-drinking, quick-on-the-trigger, rugged life in camps and settlements like Slumgullion or Jackass Gulch or Roaring Camp. They retreated to San Francisco, which was only slightly less hazardous. They lived together in groups the life they had lived in France. They did not become citizens because they considered Americans savage and ignorant. They did not learn English. They glorified French. They established themselves in occupations more suited to their past experience and delicate natures. They became the proprietors and employees of the restaurants, hotels, and gambling parlors. All of this, in time, would affect the character of San Francisco; the city would become famous for fine food, beautifully dressed women, and a unique style in home decor and entertaining.

Later, the French influence would be permanently stamped on San Francisco by two American architects, John Bakewell and Arthur Brown, Jr., trained at L'Ecole des Beaux-Arts in Paris. With the assistance of a Frenchman, Louis Bourgeois, another L'Ecole graduate, they would create the City of Paris store with its Louis XVI interior. The firm of Bakewell & Brown would design the City Hall, the War Memorial Opera House, and the Veterans Building—a little bit of Paris in the Civic Center complex.

Farther out by the Pacific Ocean, an exact replica of the Palais de la Legion d'Honneur in Paris would be built and given to the city by Alma de Bretteville Spreckles in memory of the California men who lost their lives in World War I. In front of this graceful museum, filled with paintings, tapestries, and sculpture, surrounded by gnarled, windswept cypress trees, a large statue of a young woman in armor, on horseback, with her sword raised toward God—Jeanne d'Arc in a gesture of defiance—would challenge all who threatened the Paris by the Golden Gate.

The love of beauty, art, and music, the sense of grace and gaiety that make up San Francisco's love of elegance are due, in part, to Felix Verdier's harebrained scheme—considering the distance and dangers—of outfitting a ship with a paradise of silks and satins in her hold, to sail to El Dorado.

While Felix sold his hosiery mills to finance this adventure and assembled assorted goods, Madame Verdier selected dresses, bonnets, lingerie, Persian scarves, and the finest fabrics and laces to accompany the casks of rare wines, barrels of ports and brandies, and cases of champagne.

When the ship was loaded, Emile set off with the merchandise from Le Havre, across the Atlantic Ocean and the Gulf of Mexico to Puertobello on the Caribbean side of the Isthmus of Panama. There was very little that was beautiful about the port that had once been the chief ornament of Spain's colonial empire. It had thrived as the shipping center for sending the rich booty of Central America back to the Old World. But in 1671 it had been captured, sacked, and laid waste by the freebooter Henry Morgan. For 180 years it had returned to the jungle until the California gold rush revived it. Situated at the mouth of the Chagres River, which was the first upstream leg of the Isthmus crossing, the town was, according to Hubert Bancroft, a traveler of that time:

. . . surrounded by heaps of filthy offal, the greasy, stagnant pool bordered with blue mud—nearly bound by the foliage that skirted the town. There were fifty bamboo huts with thatched roofs and bare floors and no windows. It was a pestilential town. . . .

No one wanted to stay for long and the Indians kept their *bungos*, dugout canoes that would carry ten to twelve passengers and/or baggage upstream to the village of Gorgona, a fair distance from the ships. The Indians, roused from their sluggish village life by the hordes passing through, quickly came to realize what their *bungos* and the trip upstream meant to the exhausted, eager, gold-seekers and their prices soared. The fifty-mile journey across the Isthmus of Panama became one of the most traveled routes in the world, in spite of the minimum $750 one-way fare from New York and the number of bribes required. Thirty thousand people a year were passing over this spit of land until 1869, when the transcontinental railroad was completed. By 1855 the Panama Railroad was finished and although the trip was shortened, and some of the discomforts were eliminated, the cutthroat bands of brigands that raided and looted the trains and massacred the passengers and trainmen added a new terror.

The earliest travelers were men, and while there were many adventurers, gamblers, and roughnecks among them, most were well-meaning farmers, teachers, and merchants like my great-grandfather Isaac Perkins, from Ipswich, Massachusetts, or Charles and Rowland H. Macy, from the Boston area. In the race to California, time was of the essence. It was believed that the gold was gushing from the streams and, like a faucet, would slow to a trickle and then turn off. Few were equipped or knowledgeable about the journey. They wore hot and heavy clothing. Their shoes were inadequate for slogging through the jungle mud. They were armed with an incredible array of weapons, pistols, swords, and clubs. Everyone wore a "Bowie" knife strapped to his leg or tucked into his belt.

Soon the women followed—"professional" women from New Orleans and eastern coastal cities. Groups were organized and "chaperoned" by a madam.

Later, wives and children were sent for and lengthy courtships were carried on through the slow mail routes as the lonely men in the west wrote to the lonely women in the east, often filling their letters with the glories of the good life in California and minimizing the dangers of the passage. Gradually the home-town girls, knowing where the boys were, packed their belongings and headed west. In 1857 my great-grandmother was a member of the packet set. A New England spinster nearing forty years of age, she sailed from Massachusetts to Panama, crossed the Isthmus, and sailed to San Francisco on the steamship *Golden Age*, one of the crowded filthy ships that plied the coast. She traveled inland to Sacramento, ostensibly, according to a family album, to "visit" an Aunt Florence. Since "nice" women were in short supply, her motive must have been more than social. She met and married Isaac Perkins, a hardware salesman from her home town of Ipswich and in her middle years gave birth to three sons and one daughter, Avis, my grandmother.

The promise of the rewards, in love or money, for making this journey must have outweighed the risks and hardships. While taking care of one's person and belongings was difficult enough, the problems and logistics accompanying Emile Verdier and an entire shipload of goods would seem insurmountable.

Once the price was agreed upon, the merchandise and passengers were transferred to the *bungos* and the grueling three-day trip up the river would begin. Being en route, however, was no guarantee that the natives wouldn't demand further bribes along the way. It was a firm belief, perhaps perpetrated by the Indians, that alcohol was a deterrent to tropical diseases, malaria, cholera, dysentery, and the dreaded Panama Fever. More often than not, a keg was tapped and natives and passengers alike paddled upstream through the luxuriant jungle vegetation filled with bright-hued birds and monkeys, singing and shouting drunkenly. Occasionally someone fell overboard. Alligators slithered into the water from the hot riverbanks. *The Letters of Etienne Derbec, A French Journalist in the California Gold Rush*, told of ". . . gigantic lilies, mangos, zapote with fruit the size of a man's head."

Gorgona was an odorous swamp. There were no accommodations and for many who had fallen ill on the crossing or the trip up the river, it was the end of the journey. For others, the two- or three-day trip by mule down the treacherous trail to Panama City lay ahead. Parts of the trail, once the main route of the Conquistadors for transporting the gold from Central America to the mouth of the Chagres River, were worn down over the centuries as deep as thirty feet. Often goods and passengers riding in the deep, narrow canyons were washed away in torrential tropical storms that turned the trail into a flash-flooded violent river. Vultures circled overhead.

In 1851, traveler Henry Sturdevent wrote:

> After being jolted to almost paralytic unconsciousness on the mules, alternately burned by the tropic sun and soaked by the tropic showers and liberally bespotted by the mosquitoes and other nameless visitors of the previous 3 nights, the Argonauts hailed Panama (City) with delight.

At Panama City, Emile again transferred his goods, this time to the chartered brig renamed *La Ville de Paris*, and set sail for San Francisco. A sailing ship, unlike the overcrowded steamers, did not go north up the coast of Mexico and California. It headed northwest and sailed almost to the Hawaiian Islands to catch the wind to deliver it down into San Francisco Bay. The voyage could take from thirty to ninety days, depending on the winds. There was reputedly a crest on the ship with the motto "Fluctuat nec Mergitur"—"It may rock but never sinks." This bit of bravado may have been reassuring to Emile Verdier, but what the rocking and exposure to salt air and tropical rains and heat had done to the rare wines and fine champagnes is questionable. *Mais peu import.* The liquors (or what was left of them) were not for the discerning palates of Frenchmen, but rather for the ruffians back from the gold fields and the rag, tag, and bobtail of the Barbary Coast with gold dust in their pockets to pay—a factor that eliminated problems with rates of exchange.

The luxury goods were sold at sky-high inflationary prices, directly from shipboard, not only to avoid paying high rent, but also to protect the merchandise from thieves and the fires that plagued the tinderbox buildings of the city. When his cargo was gone and his decks were trimmed with gold, Emile Verdier hoisted anchor and started the return journey to France—no mean feat, considering the difficulties in obtaining a crew. Emile made his second trip in 1854. Arriving with more merchandise, this time he sold his goods from a store on Kearney Street.

There is a great deal of conflict about the early history of the City of Paris. Various partners were taken into the firm, presumably to keep the operation going with less exotic goods, while Verdier returned to Paris. There were also several changes of location. While making his third delivery trip in 1860, Emile died in Panama, probably from the dreaded yellow fever or one of the other tropical diseases that haunted the travelers. The irony is that by this time he must have been making the trip on the Panama Railroad—surely a welcome luxury to a man who had survived four of the ghastly crossings by *bungo* and muleback. The four- and five-year gaps between the arrivals of new merchandise from France could hardly be regarded as a fast turnover, but each round must have been highly profitable. Over the next years, a Mr. Kaindler became the Paris representative; G. Moreau became a partner and buyer with a New York office; and L. Scellier and A. Lelievre conducted the business in San Francisco.

My great-grandmother never suffered any ill effects from this arduous journey until she received word from Ipswich that she had been excommunicated (or whatever the equivalent would be—my other, Catholic, grandmother always said "excommunicated") from the Quaker church for traveling alone as a single woman. Judging from pictures of this stern woman and details heard of her dour personality, this was surely as unjust as the Massachusetts witch burnings. The shock of this news was so great that she never again left her house, except years after my great-grandfather's death when she moved into my grandmother and grandfather's house. She never left this house either until she died at the age of ninety-four, according to the story we were told. But she must have stepped out of her own house at least out of personal necessity, since my great-grandfather Perkins died as a result of a bite inflicted on him in the outhouse by a black widow spider. This *corpus delicti* was savored by members on my mother's side of my family who apparently regarded Mr. and Mrs. Perkins as haughty Yankees. This impression may have come from my great-grandmother's isolation and long-life mourning for her church. Then again, perhaps the poor woman, after the Panama crossing and its accompanying terrors, suffered from agoraphobia, the fear of open spaces. At any rate, it was always said that the Perkinses had no reason to be so uppity, since "they didn't even have indoor plumbing like the rest of us."

Felix Verdier died in 1869, never having seen the city upon which he had imposed an element of his good taste and style. His twenty-year-old son, Gaston, was sent to San Francisco as president of the City of Paris and once again the store changed location. On May 10, 1869, Gaston wrote his mother a letter. Quite coincidentally, a ceremony took place on that day that put an end to the dreaded trek across the Isthmus. Henceforth, freight and passengers would move from coast to coast on the transcontinental railroad, for on that May 10, 1869, the tracks being built from the east met the tracks being built from the west, at Promontory, Utah. The last tie was cut from native mahogany or laurel, and bound with silver. On a silver plate, set in it, were engraved the words "The Last Tie on the Pacific Railroad" and the date, followed by the names of the railroad officers and directors. The spikes for the last rails were of gold from California and silver from Nevada—the west was open!

Gaston made no mention of this momentous occasion to his mother. Like his father, he was interested in the aesthetics to feed men's souls and the food to feed his own stomach:

May 10, 1869

My dear Mama,

On Saturday and Sunday we made changes in the arrangement of goods and also devoted the two days to fixing up the windows for we needed beautiful displays for the opening.

On that Sunday evening, Mr. Scellier invited all to dinner and we certainly deserved it. We were served a magnificent repast and surely enjoyed it. Naturally, we drank several toasts to your good health. Let's hope they will come true, and I am grateful to Mr. Scellier for proposing them.

The following year, Gaston and his friend Leon Weill, brother of Raphael Weill of The White House, returned to France to serve in the army during the 1870 Franco-Prussian War. Paris, even in wartime, must have been a welcome relief after a year in boisterous, rip-roaring, treacherous San Francisco. The town's main streets, where the merchants sold their goods, were filled, along with the mud and slop and horse droppings, with the flotsam and jetsam of humanity. There were cutthroats, blackguards, and adventurers from every race and nation. There were Chinese, Mexicans, Germans, Italians, and South Americans who fought and danced in Little Chili. The old wealthy aristrocratic Spanish families kept themselves barricaded in the Spanish quarter, isolated from the invaders. Along the wharves, the "Sydney Ducks" from the penal colony in Australia lived by robbery and there were professional gamblers and ladies of the evening, afternoon, or morning from everywhere, including the islands of the South Pacific. Decent women were hard to find, my great-grandmother and her Aunt Florence notwithstanding. Everyone carried pistols and Bowie knives. Drunken brawls and shootings were everyday and everynight occurrences.

The lure of Paris must have proved too much for the sensitive Gaston Verdier, who, the year before, had signed his letter to "My dear Mama" with the closing "I kiss you with all my heart." He stayed on in France and re-created the Verdier Hosiery Mills and did not return to San Francisco for twenty-six years.

In spite of the fact that a M. Gallois, who was sent from Paris to manage the store, defected to Raphael Weill, and a M. Fusenot, sent to Los Angeles to open a branch, simply resigned, formed his own company, and took over the Los Angeles business, the Verdiers—Gaston and his mother, Mme. Felix—must have been doing something right with their laissez-faire management. When Gaston returned to San Francisco in 1896, taking with him his fourteen-year-old son, Paul, it was to supervise the construction of the City of Paris building on a 50-vara lot. The *vara* was a system of land measure left over from the Spanish. A 50-vara lot was one that measured a square of 133⅓ feet. The structure, one of the first steelframe buildings constructed by the Spring Valley Water Company, was located on the corner of Geary and Stockton streets. It was considered sheer folly by the other merchants to build a store so far out in the sand dunes where there was little more than a blacksmith shop and a scruffy park called Union Square.

Paul worked as a cashboy until, being a patriotic Frenchman, he returned to France for his military duty. He came back to America and spent a year and a half as an apprentice in McCreery's, a New

York department store. Shortly after he arrived in San Francisco, the general manager died and twenty-four-year-old Paul found himself in charge of the store. The year was 1906—only weeks before April 18.

Paul Verdier later wrote about that fateful day and often spoke about it. His accounts were always poetic and heartbreaking. There are some discrepancies which may have been due to shock or tricks of memory, but certainly his activities on the first of the days in hell that began with the earthquake and ended with the holocaust that destroyed four-fifths of the city were superhuman. He wrote:

I had an apartment on the thirteenth floor of the Alexandria Hotel on Geary Street. I was awakened by the falling of a large wardrobe and first thought that my room had been entered by burglars, but I soon realized that I was experiencing my first earthquake—and a long one at that. [In another report, ". . . the building cracked and quaked for 55 seconds. 55 seconds is a long time!"] I said to myself—"You poor boy, you will find yourself on the sidewalk much quicker than you want to. How can this building so tall and so narrow resist the horrible sways of the earthquake?" It made a noise like you hear in a forest in a big windstorm when the trees crack, only here the pillars and beams were not of wood but of steel.

Paul dressed, ran downstairs and the few blocks to the store, where he found the wax figures in the show windows lying flat and, with the exception of a wall from a neighboring building that had collapsed through the skylight, "little damage." He later went to the roof, where he described the fire as it spread up Market Street:

In the afternoon both the Palace Hotel and Call Building were on fire and it was a tragic but most colorful sight, the yellow flames of the Palace Hotel, built of wood mingling with the blue flames of the Call Building, built of steel with white and black smoke rising into the blue California sky.

He went out to Van Ness Avenue with his horse, Denis, and a buggy, to the Hotel St. Dunstan, where his father, Gaston, his mother, and his sister, Suzanne, were staying, having arrived from Paris two weeks earlier for a vacation. The hotel was a wreck and his family was sitting on the opposite side of Van Ness. They were unharmed, but shaken, since a wall had fallen in on Suzanne's room. Paul and his father returned downtown and loaded four of the store's delivery wagons with the most valuable merchandise. After the wagons were loaded, they realized that there was no place to take them where they would not be in danger of being mobbed and looted and that the goods out of the store would not be covered by insurance. They unloaded the wagons and returned the merchandise to the store. And then, as incredible as it may seem, considering the shambles around them, they ran true to form, being Frenchmen, and:

> We all went to luncheon at Marchand's. It was a delicious luncheon and the last that this oldest and most celebrated of the French restaurants of San Francisco was to serve.

Later, accompanied by one of the delivery wagons, which contained the store's books and papers and $4,000, they picked up Mme. Gaston and Suzanne and their luggage. Whether they had been left sitting on the sidewalk on Van Ness Avenue while the gentlemen dined is not clear. The family then went out to Golden Gate Park, which was fast turning into a tent city with the refugees from the stricken areas. Paul wrote with annoyance that "the rooms at the Casino had all been taken by demi-mondaines of San Francisco."

He found a friend, Captain Dillon, the director of his riding school, who provided them with rooms. Paul would sleep in the stable with Denis. Paul wrote that Captain Dillon would be "remembered for his golden heart."

With the problems of lodgings settled, the Verdiers were willing to mix with the demi-mondaines of San Francisco when absolutely necessary. Paul Verdier wrote: "We dined that night at the Casino."

After dinner, Paul took Denis and drove back downtown toward the store, where:

> Cinders and papers were flying through the air. As I crossed Van Ness Avenue, a half burnt paper fell into my buggy. I was terribly disconcerted when I saw the coat of arms which was imprinted on a bill from the City of Paris.

At Mason Street, he was stopped by a cordon of police and he asked for permission to walk to the store:

"The City of Paris!," the police answered, "nothing left of it. It burned an hour ago." I broke down and cried like a baby.

The Verdiers moved quickly to establish new headquarters, pending reconstruction. Van Ness Avenue, the broad street that had stopped the westward sweep of the fire, became the new shopping center. Paul Verdier wrote:

The City of Paris was the first store to move there and was fortunate in securing the spacious Hobart mansion at the corner of Van Ness and Washington. Older San Franciscans will remember the appropriateness of the arrangement of the departments. Linens were sold in the dining room, books in the library and dainty French lingerie in the bedrooms.

Ten department heads were dispatched to New York with instructions to rush goods to the new store by express. Paul Verdier had his office on the second floor, overlooking the swimming pool that had been built by Aimee Crocker. A tea garden was opened in a vacant lot next door, but it was not successful because of the proximity of a church which prevented them from obtaining a license to serve wine or liquor. For a time, the City of Paris operated automobile buses to bring customers to the store.

In the spring of 1909 the new City of Paris, built on the old site by Bakewell & Brown with the assistance of the French architect Louis Bourgeois, was completed. The French atmosphere made the City of Paris unique among American stores. The oval rotunda in the style of Louis XVI was surrounded by galleries with ornamental grilles and supported by white and gold fluted pilasters. Floating above it all was an exquisite dome of stained glass representing the good ship *La Ville de Paris* under full sail and bearing the motto "Fluctuat nec Mergitur." A large sign announced: CITY OF PARIS COMES HOME AGAIN. On a bright May morning, sightseers and well-wishers streamed through the doors to offer congratulations, look at the marvel, and drink toasts in vintage champagne.

In the basement below the City of Paris, a mini-Paris was created in Normandy Lane. There was a bookshop reminiscent of the stalls along the quays, a restaurant with a champagne bar, a fine cigar store, the Patisserie with breads and pastries, and the Verdier Wine Cellars. At the famed Rotisserie, a pioneer take-out food department, golden browned chickens turned on spits and the smells of fine foods cooking drifted upstairs and mixed with a potpourri of French perfumes in a heady, sensuous combination. At Christmastime, the famous tree filled the rotunda, turning slowly.

Paul Verdier was a great San Francisco gentleman, a patron of the arts, and one-time president of the Legion of Honor. He was also a frugal Frenchman. Sheila Moore Rathbun of Washington, D.C., and Middleburg, Virginia, worked in the Art in Action department, where weavers and potters and other craftsmen displayed their talents. Mrs. Rathbun recalls: "We were inundated by poodle fur from Mr. Verdier's French poodles' clippings. This was spun and then the weaving lady wove it into an afghan."

When Paul Verdier died in 1966, his sister, Comtesse de Tessan (Suzanne Verdier), became the chief executive until the store closed its doors on March 31, 1972. The City of Paris did not go bankrupt, but it was losing money, so it paid off all outstanding debts and Vice President Paul Chauvin, nephew of Comtesse de Tessan, announced in a letter to the *San Francisco Chronicle*: "We shall . . . bow out in a dignified and honorable manner befitting our San Francisco tradition. . . ."

Liberty House, the British firm famed for Liberty scarves and small-floral-print English challis, moved into the premises. The gilt in the fluted pilasters supporting the dome was painted over with white in an attempt to update the look of the store. A half-page ad with a picture of the dome appeared in the newspapers on April 2, 1972:

FRANKLY, IT'S LEFT US SPEECHLESS

It's not easy to inherit 122 years of tradition. Especially in San Francisco. First, thank you. Your warm response has overwhelmed us. And just in case you haven't heard yet—the dome is staying. The tree is staying, and so are the croissants, brioche and Verdier champagne. But what about the dozens of other things that have made The City of Paris "La grande dame"? We want you to tell us about them. So that we may combine the fine old traditions with our fresh Liberty House excitement. Write us.

But alas, this was not Agincourt with England triumphant. This was San Francisco. Not only was it "not easy" for British conservative taste to inherit 122 years of French style and tradition—it was impossible. Liberty House retreated.

But lo! Fresh troops were rallying in the Alamo as the eyes of Texas turned upon California. Carter Hawley Hale Stores, Inc., the California retail conglomerate that owned the property occupied by the City of Paris building, had plans for its demolition and the construction of a modern store which would utilize the vast square footage lost in the rotunda—an aesthetic luxury no retail operation can afford in the late 1970s. This modern building would be occupied by a Carter Hawley Hale division—Neiman-Marcus.

Hola! A new champion appeared from within the ranks. Mrs. Evelyn Aleshin had managed the City of Paris Rotunda Gallery, where a great seventeenth-century Gobelin tapestry, purchased from the Hermitage Museum in Russia, had graced one wall. A soft-spoken woman, Mrs. Aleshin, had moved quietly among the superb antiques in the department that was a favorite of Comtesse de Tessan, and now she threw down the gauntlet and holding a fistful of papers with thousands of signatures, she stormed the bastions of the Landmarks Board. Hadn't San Francisco saved the cable cars? Ghiradelli's Chocolate Factory? The Garden Court of the Palace Hotel? Why not the City of Paris? The cudgels were taken up by the Victorian Alliance, and the Battle of the Dome was on!

Earl Moss of the Alliance explained what actions had been taken to save the building: "The Victorian Alliance actually established and funded the Citizens of the City of Paris Committee. Then recruited the eighteen or nineteen other neighborhood organizations which provided little old ladies to sit at card tables and collect signatures on the petitions. We collected some 66,000 signatures of people who wanted the building preserved in its present state. Those signatures were presented to the Board of Supervisors when it came before the Board. They declined to declare it a city landmark. After that it became a state landmark and a national landmark on the national registry, but that gives us no protection of any kind."

In the fall of 1977 Mr. Moss said: "I don't know where we are right now. Some plans have been presented and nothing much seems to be happening. Neiman-Marcus presented the plans and nobody that we know seems to be happy with them. They've made no attempt to apply for a demolition permit or whatever. We intend to go through the EIR, the environmental impact report, exhaustibly, which has to be made whenever demolition is applied for with a building. Nothing of that sort has been done to trigger any legal action. There won't be until they apply for a demolition permit and then we will sue to get an EIR which could tie them up for three or four years in the future going through the legality. Activists can get involved and pressure the planning commission to decide that an EIR is required and then it can nit-pick at every little detail.

"Liberty House, which is Amfac, is in the adjoining building. They occupied the City of Paris and claimed they didn't make much of a success because of the inadequacies of the building per se. They built their own modern, scientifically designed building, designed for modern merchandising, next door and they're doing worse than they did before, which proves that it is not the fault of the building it's the fault of the merchandiser."

John Carl Warnecke, the architect originally hired by Carter Hawley Hale, is no longer involved with the project and the task of saving the dome has fallen on the shoulders of architect Philip Johnson. Mr. Johnson makes it clear: "We are saving more than the dome. We are saving the whole room. It was very hard to do, but I think it's worth it because the dome itself without the room wouldn't make any sense.

"The building itself can't be kept and there is disagreement out there, as you've probably heard. It is impossible to bring it up to present-day earthquake standards and our engineers refuse to work on it if it isn't brought up. The original metal frame was built in the eighteen-nineties, the building burned in the earthquake and fire, then the beautiful interior was put in after 1906. We feel very strongly about keeping the beauty of the 1907 architecture and the tradition of the Christmas tree; we don't feel the same about the original frame of the building done by another architect ten years earlier.

"We have taken the whole room, totally preserved and glazed it in at the corner. I think it works very well, it's a fantastic engineering feat. The room can be seen through the enormous glass windows and the Christmas tree will practically be out in Union Square.

"We wouldn't tamper with tradition, in fact we wouldn't change the building at all if we didn't have to, but we want to save what's great. We think that's what tradition is—that room—we don't want to call it the dome, it's the *room and the dome*—they're what we want to save."

The side entrance of the boarded-up building is open to the public. Inside an area is screened off from the rotunda with nailed-up sheets and tarps. Racks and tables around this section contain marked-down merchandise from the Joseph Magnin store farther down the street. People milling around and pawing through the shirts, dresses, blouses and skirts give the once-elegant City of Paris the air of a dowdy bargain basement. The building seems to be falling victim to time, vandals, and graffiti, while the battle of the dome goes on. If there can be no compromise while the clock keeps ticking perhaps only time will win.

Behind the screening high atop the center of the building the sun moves overhead and beams down through the stained glass—brilliant yellows, greens, and blues—Matisse colors, kaleidoscope in changing patterns around the empty rotunda. *La Ville de Paris* with its prophetic motto sails on, silhouetted against the California sky. It never sinks—or does it?

FIVE

La Belle Dame de Wilshire Boulevard

Los Angeles, California

Paris, Ontario, Canada *and* Paris, France, for different reasons, were influencial in the creation of the wonder on Wilshire Boulevard, Bullock's Wilshire, in Los Angeles, California.

John Gillespie Bullock was born to Scottish parents in Paris, Ontario, in 1871. He left school when he was eleven years old and went to work delivering groceries for $2 a week in an effort to help his widowed mother support the family. Then came the proud day in his boyhood life when he was given a delivery wagon to use on his rounds. In later years he remarked, "It was my ambition while driving that wagon to have, some day, as big a store as Rheder's." By the time he was twenty-five, he had been promoted to the position of clerk in the town's largest store but his salary was too meager to support the girl he wanted to marry. His fantasy was turning into an impossible dream in that Canadian village. Paris could hardly offer the hardworking, ambitious young man any hope for a dazzling future. According to the 1961 Canadian census, one hundred years after John Bullock's birth the town had a total population of 6,271.

When word came from an uncle that there were golden opportunities in the golden state of California, John borrowed money for a ticket south and $150 from his mother. His sister packed enough food for the journey, and in 1896 he headed for the City of Angels.

Los Angeles in 1896 was not Lotus Land, Tinseltown, or the Home of the Stars. Hollywood was an orange grove; Beverly Hills was solid with bean fields; and Los Angeles was little more than a pueblo, in spite of real estate promotor H. Gaylord Wilshire. In 1895, he made the prophetic statement "Wilshire Boulevard will unquestionably be the fashionable concourse and driveway of the city of Los Angeles."

Neither the future *fashionable concourse* nor any other street was paved with gold when John arrived in town. Only after weeks of intensive searching did he land a $12-a-week job in a small store at Broadway and Fourth Street—The Broadway Department Store.

Six months after Bullock was employed, the store's owner, Arthur Letts, hired another Canadian boy as a $1-a-week cashboy. Fifteen-year-old Percy Glenn Winnett and his family had moved from Winnipeg to Victoria and emigrated to Southern California. His father, John William Winnett, had a furniture shop in a rooming house located at Seventh and Broadway. From an early age, Percy was a spirited individual. Named John William after his father and called Jack, he renamed himself Percy, after a boyhood hero. "I don't know where the Glenn came from," his daughter, Glenn Winnett Boocock, said. "I suppose he liked the sound of Percy Glenn, but he was called 'P. G.' which was more memorable than Jack—except for my grandmother, of course, she always called him Jack."

The teenage boy, dressed in short pants, went for a job interview at The Broadway and he was warned by his father not to mention Canada. He did as he was told. When Arthur Letts asked P.G. where he came from, he answered, "Puget Sound."

Over the next ten years, Bullock advanced to men's furnishings buyer and a $75-a-month salary. Although this was less than double his starting wage, it made it possible for him to marry his Canadian fiancée. In a short time, Bullock was promoted to superintendent and Winnett, who had moved up to the position of clerk, took over the responsibilities as menswear buyer.

At this time, a store was being built three blocks away in the nether reaches of the shopping area, near the site of the rooming house where P. G.'s father had his shop at Broadway and Seventh. Work came to a halt when a partner in the enterprise died. Letts, fearful that his lease might not be renewed when it expired, took over the building and gave John Bullock $250,000 to establish a store in order to fill the space until the time might come when it would be needed by The Broadway. They agreed to give the store a short name. It was called Bullock's in the fashion of a successful New York store, Macy's. Thirty-five-year-old John Bullock was president. Twenty-five-year-old P. G. Winnett was vice-president and general manager.

The party held on the night of March 2, 1907, prior to the official opening, was a forerunner of the "in-store" gala openings, promotions, and benefits that have reached extravaganza proportions in the 1970s. Tom Mahoney and Leonard Sloane describe the event in *The Great Merchants*:

> Thousands crowded through the brightly lit buildings to listen to bands play on the lower floor and to see a pony show in the roof garden. In later years, Easter services were conducted in this roof garden.
> But rain, something of a rarity in Los Angeles, fell when the store opened for business on March 4 and customers were few. "You could shoot a cannon through the aisles without hitting anyone," Winnett recalled. Those who came found a beautiful store, singing canaries and violets. Bullock's gave away violets every March 4 for many years.

The Bullock's opening was followed six months later by the panic of 1907. As other stores failed, Bullock's struggled for survival by putting on a show of success. Shelves were stocked with empty cartons. One floor was completely closed and six delivery wagons, empty for the most part and with no place to go, were driven around town with a business-as-usual flair. The ruse worked and when people did shop, they shopped at Bullock's. The first year's sales were $1,310,725. Twenty-two years later the prestigious and elegant Bullock's Wilshire opened its doors on September 29, 1929, less than a month before Black Thursday, October 23, and the Wall Street crash. "My father always said that he never opened a store unless there was a national financial disaster," Mrs. Boocock recalls. In 1929 a new practice was put into effect in an effort to keep Bullock's Wilshire open. Buyers and sales personnel kept books on their customers and telephoned to advise them of the arrival of new merchandise that would suit the customers' fashion needs. Over the years, this personal attention from the sales staff would become one of the outstanding features of the store's service.

In September 1927, two years before the opening of Bullock's Wilshire, an announcement was made that staggered the Los Angeles financial community. Bullock's had formed a corporation to take over the interest held in Bullock's by the estate of the late Arthur Letts. Preparations were made to sell stocks and bonds worth $8.5 million. This was the biggest piece of mercantile financing ever attempted locally and many believed it was too large an offering for Los Angeles. In October, $4 million in Bullock's 6 percent secured sinking fund gold bonds were placed on the market and oversubscribed in less than one hour. Two days later, $4.5 million in shares of Bullock's 7 percent preferred stock were subscribed in a shorter space of time. In less than two hours after the books were opened to the public, $8.5 million in Bullock's securities were sold. The sale of stocks and bonds to create Bullock's, Inc., was epochal in California financial circles at that time.

John Bullock, the millionaire merchant and Southern California business and civic leader, returned briefly to Paris, Ontario, in 1930. He was feted by his former employer, Henry Rheder, and the town fathers at a dinner given in his honor. He was presented with a commemorative plaque. It was a triumphant event and one of the happiest days of Bullock's life. When he died suddenly three years later, in 1933, his home-town paper, *The Paris Star*, wrote:

> Nowhere was the news of the sudden passing of John G. Bullock, of Los Angeles, California, received with greater regret than among those associated with him during his youthful days. With all the multitudinous duties with which he was burdened he did not neglect his church or the precepts instilled in him by a mother whom he cherished while she lived, and who shared in his success when it came to him.

Along with being one of America's merchant princes, John Bullock was a dominant figure in the tremendous growth of Los Angeles. He worked continuously on one of the major necessities for this growth—the availability of water. The *Los Angeles Times* wrote:

When the waters of the Colorado River are poured through the aqueduct to supply the needs of thousands in Southern California, among the names most honored as promotors of this mighty enterprise will stand the name of John G. Bullock, the indefatigable worker in and for the Metropolitan Water District.

Bullock had a vision of what water could do for California and as chairman of the board of directors of the water district he had headed a Los Angeles committee which had obtained passage of a $220 million bond issue.

When John Bullock had arrived in Los Angeles as a young man, he had deposited his $150 in the Citizens' National Bank. He made his withdrawals from the bank a week apart in one-and two-dollar amounts while he was looking for work. Later on in his career, this same bank financed store expansion to the extent of $6 million. He left a personal estate in excess $2.5 million, most of it in Bullock's, Inc., stock. His lifelong friend and business associate P. G. Winnett succeeded him as president of Bullock's.

Winnett carried on his former partner's involvement in civic affairs and the dream of a great store. As Bullock had foreseen the need for water, Winnett sensed the area's reliance on the automobile. He organized the Citizens Transportation Committee, which conducted the first survey for a Los Angeles freeway system. "My father had a vision of Los Angeles superhighways with no tolls. He said, 'Tolls delay movement and the point of highways is to *move* traffic, not slow it,'" his daughter explained. He also pioneered the Greater Los Angeles Plans in an effort to rally the community to be ready for the massive population growth he knew would come after World War II. Thousands of servicemen had passed through the city and P. G. knew they had tasted the sunshine and relaxed living. He also knew they would return with their families to live in the area's casual manner that today is called the California life-style.

Under Winnett's leadership, Bullock's, Inc., would reach new heights. His first vision to become a reality was the creation of the miracle on Wilshire Boulevard—elegant, avant-garde Bullock's Wilshire.

In the 1920s, when Bullock's made the decision to expand beyond the downtown shopping area, the barren site selected on Wilshire Boulevard was in the suburbs. Wilshire Boulevard was wide, gracious, and lined with magnificent houses, palm trees, and a handful of lavish apartment buildings and apartment hotels for "winter people." The luxurious Ambassador Hotel, built in 1921, was set back from the boulevard. The Spanish hacienda-style hotel and cottages were surrounded by twenty-one lush acres, graced by camphor, magnolia, and palm trees. A movie-set variety of palm trees was created indoors. The hotel's famous Cocoanut Grove nightclub was a papier-mâché jungle where artificial fronds and ensuing generations of romantics would sway to airy tunes played by music makers like Freddy Martin and his orchestra. Today, this manicured acreage around the hotel is prime real estate or, according to George Allan of the Wilshire Chamber of Commerce, "the world's most expensive lawn."

Across from the Ambassador was the original Brown Derby, built in the shape to match its name and painted brown. The restaurant drew Hollywood's early stars and star-gazers from around the world to Wilshire Boulevard. It was a forerunner of the nonsense architecture and fakery that are considered indigenous to Southern California.

The route Wilshire Boulevard followed from downtown Los Angeles to the Pacific Ocean had been in use for centuries. Long before Europeans arrived in California, Shoshone Indians traveled along the path from their village, Yang-na (located around the Civic Center area), to the inky boglike hunting grounds where animals, lured by a film of shining water, would be trapped by the viscous tar that lay beneath. The tar (asphaltum, or *brea*, in Spanish) was used by the Indians to seal treasure boxes and to caulk canoes. Spanish settlers followed the Indian trail and used the tar to roof their adobes. They named the trail El Camino Viejo, "the old road." In 1828, José Antonio Carillo, the *alcalde* of the Pueblo de Los Angeles, granted the area to Antonio José Rocha, a prosperous Portuguese blacksmith with the proviso that all inhabitants of the Pueblo be allowed free access to the tar pits.

The Hancock family acquired Rancho La Brea from Rocha's heirs in 1860. In 1901, geologist William Orcutt discovered skeletons of such animals as the imperial mammoth, ancient bison, the giant sloth, and sabre-tooth cats preserved in the tar. The find is considered to be the most important single collection of fossil remains from the Pleistocene Age in the world. Others considered the black blobs a petrified thorn in the side of the Glamour Capital

of the World. The La Brea Tar Pits have been fodder for gags since
the heyday of radio comedians like Jack Benny, Fred Allen, and
early Bob Hope. The tradition of "tar pit" jokes was revitalized
when television hosts like Johnny Carson and Merv Griffin moved
their programs from New York to Los Angeles. Millions of years
after the primordial ooze first gurgled its way to the earth's sur-
face, it traps the unsuspecting. The La Brea Tar Pits are kept alive
and bubbling with laughter on the networks.

From the beginning, Bullock's Wilshire was planned to cater to a
new carriage trade in a new kind of carriage—the automobile. Winnett had faith that the customers would come not only from the
fashionable houses that lined the boulevard and sprawled over up-
per-class neighborhoods like nearby Hancock Park, but also from
well-heeled, far-off Pasadena and Santa Monica as well. Bullock's
Wilshire was one of the first businesses to envision the full meaning of the automobile to Southern California. A vast parking lot for
595 cars was included in the plans. The main entrance to the store
was at the rear through a gate along a drive under a porte-cochere,
graciously called the Motor Court.

After the opening, the *Los Angeles Times* of November 2, 1929,
described this innovation:

> Into this court the patron may drive her car to the entrance that
> gives on the elevators, have the car taken care of in the great area at
> the back and returned to her by a call system similar to opera first
> nights. The system also provides that her packages will all be stowed
> in the car when it arrives for its passengers.

The original plans for the store combined up-to-date conve-
niences with elegance and traditional design. Los Angelenos,
mindful of their heritage, were accustomed to Spanish and Mediterranean architecture—graceful archways, white and pink stucco
walls, terra cotta floors, and tiled roofs. The area was also filled
with solid square-framed brick and shingle houses. They had covered front porches and second floors that perched like oversized
dormers. Small versions of this style were called "airplane bunga-
lows"; larger ones might have been dubbed "midwestern-sturdy"
architecture. The flamboyant movie stars in the growing film industry built their palaces in Italian Renaissance, English Tudor, or

French château styles. Architectural taste in Southern California was, for the most part, conservative.

What happened as Bullock's Wilshire evolved at 3050 Wilshire Boulevard was beyond even Hollywood's wildest imagination. The architectural marvel that began to take shape on the barren corner had passers-by agog. The flights of fancy in the use of space, building materials, and design were unknown in Los Angeles.

Not everyone was impressed or pleased as the massive structure unfolded with its soaring 241-foot tower, bronze ornamental facings, and decorative trim. The woman who lived across the side street feared that a prison was being built and ordered her gardener to plant more trees on her property to screen her from the "monstrosity." There is no record of the woman's reaction to the finished store. It could hardly have been complimentary, nor could her plantings have saved her from the presence of the Bullock's Tower, which was illuminated by 88 floodlights, a total of 39,000 watts, and the "Blue Light" on top, a group of four mercury vapor tubes.

Nearly everyone else considered the exterior of Bullock's Wilshire to be magnificent. What awaited the public on the inside was mind-boggling. When the store opened, customers and gapers discovered a "modern" interior of stark opulence and creative artworks unlike any other in their city. Bullock's Wilshire has since become an architectural landmark. In 1969 it was declared "Historical Cultural Monument #56" by the Municipal Arts Department of the Cultural Heritage Board of the City of Los Angeles. Bullock's Wilshire might have been another run-of-the-mill structure, however, had it not been for the fact that in the mid-1920s, with the building plans on the drawing boards, P. G. Winnett took a trip to Paris—Paris, France.

France is generally credited with the development of the first department store—an ironic contradiction to Napoleon Bonaparte's gibe that England was the "nation of shopkeepers."

In 1852, Madame and Monsieur Astride Bouçicaut, a couple with unparalleled retailing vision for their time, opened a small shop on the unfashionable Parisian Left Bank. They first sold standard lengths of fabric, more commonly known as piece-goods. They added an early type of ready-to-wear—loose-fitting coats and mantles—to their stock. This was followed by sections where shoes, millinery and underwear were sold. It had taken merchants generations to move from open-air market stalls indoors to individual shops, but within a span of eight years, the Bouçicauts' store, Bon Marché, incorporated a myriad of shops under one roof. By 1860— *et voilà*—the department store!

The mid-nineteenth-century department store was little more than four or more separate departments. Fabrics for clothing and household uses were the backbone of the merchandise—gloves, parasols, hosiery, and reticules (small purses of metal mesh or fabric) were introduced.

In the 1850s, the Bouçicauts' business practices were as innovative as their store was. The first unusual feature was that customers were welcomed inside the shop to move about and peruse the goods. Displays were developed and used as enticements to buy. Prior to the opening of Bon Marché, a shop was regarded as (and generally was) the home of the shopkeeper. Shopping was a serious and rather dour business. Entering a shop was an invasion of privacy and one was obliged to buy. Shopkeepers were indifferent, haughty, and often rude. An attitude of reluctance to part with their wares prevailed.

The Bouçicauts also introduced the unheard-of practice of marking goods with fixed prices. This put an end to the haggling which had created an air of animosity between buyer and seller. They instigated a policy for exchanging and returning merchandise. Daily deliveries were made from their store throughout Paris by van or foot-porters. And they put into operation a practice that struck at the very core of shopkeeping—the sale. Periodically they made goods available at bargain prices. Piece-goods were traditionally sold with high markups, which enabled the merchant to remain aloof from his customers' dickering and bickering. A slow turnover of merchandise was of little importance when profits were large. Bon Marché's revolutionary methods brought it a flurry of business, a fast turnover, and permitted it to lower prices. Less profit was made up in more volume.

In the beginning, competitors sneered at the Bouçicauts' new merchandising psychology. It was called "du romantisme en boutique" and regarded as sheer folly. But as their success became evident, others followed their lead and developed new methods of salesmanship, sales techniques, and service. Bon Marché was soon copied in Paris. The original Le Printemps department store opened in 1865. La Belle Jardinière opened the following year. In 1876, a magnificent new Magasin au Bon Marché was built in the rue de Sèvres, designed by L. C. Boileau and the great French engineer Gustave Eiffel. The golden Age of the department store began.

Not everyone agrees with the theory that Bon Marché was the first department store, nor that it was responsible for many of the merchandising methods we know today. British social historian of shopping Alison Adburgham, in a spirit of oneupsmandship, writes in her book, *Shops and Shopping, 1800–1914, Where and in What Manner, the Well-Dressed Englishwoman Bought Her Clothes:*

> The French, who sneered at the English as "a nation of shopkeepers," have been given the palm for pioneering modern methods of retail trading. Yet the innovations which Monsieur and Madame Boucicaut introduced to Parisian shopkeeping in the 1850's would not have been new in London. And there were provincial English shops which developed into department stores long before the Bon Marché first opened selling piece-goods only.

She cites the example of Kendal Milne in Manchester, a shop established in 1831 and originally called The Bazaar, which maintained a policy that *"Price shall be marked on all the goods, from which no abatement shall be made."* The shop also encouraged people to walk around among the counters and look, without feeling obligated to buy. With a touch of British hauteur, Miss Adburgham adds:

> The explanation may be that American businessmen "discovered" the Bon Marché, wrote about it, and based their own great stores upon its methods. Few travellers from the New World will have visited Bainbridge's of Newcastle nor Kendal Milne & Faulkner of Manchester before 1850.

Miss Adburgham's pride is admirable considering the nineteenth-century Englishman's snobbish attitude toward "trade" and anyone connected with it. But the argument over who should be credited with "firsts" is a tempest in a Crown Derby teapot since it was British and American inventions that made the department store possible.

The basics of retailing—merchandise to sell and customers to buy it—developed slowly as a result of late eighteenth-century and early-nineteenth-century inventions. In 1765, a Scott named James Watt invented the first steam engine. At the same time, James Hargreaves, an Englishman, was working out a machine, called the "spinning jenny," which could spin several threads at the same time. In 1785, Edmund Cartwright, an English clergyman, made the first loom that ran by mechanical power. These three great inventions began to change England's rural way of life. Factories sprang up and towns and cities mushroomed. In addition, steel was needed to make the machines that would make the cloth, and coal was needed to power them.

Political forces accompanied the industrial developments. In 1846 the British Corn Laws—laws that levied a heavy tax on foreign grain—were repealed. Before the repeal, the high prices demanded for domestic grain meant high prices for bread and imposed a hardship on factory workers and city dwellers. The repeal of these taxes was a victory for the industrialists over the landowners and farmers. As other taxes on goods from abroad were done away with, a policy of free trade developed. The country became less agricultural and more industrial, less rural and more urban, and the power shifted from the landowners and farmers into the hands of the men who ran her factories and whirring mills. London became the wealthiest city on earth. England became the workshop of the world. When England displayed her industrial wealth in London at the Great Exhibition of 1851, it was clear that the industrial revolution was moving ahead under full steam.

There were contributions to the growing machine age from other countries. In the United States, a New Englander named Eli Whitney invented the cotton gin in 1793. This contrivance could pick the seeds from raw cotton three hundred times faster than they could be picked by hand. The cotton crop increased from 2 million pounds in 1791 to 177 million pounds in 1821. In France, a tailor named Barthélemy Thimonnier invented a primitive sewing machine in 1830. A Boston mechanic, Elias Howe, made improvements on it and another Bostonian, Isaac Merrit Singer, improved on Howe's model. In 1851, Singer patented and introduced the first sewing machine that was practical for housewives as well as clothing manufacturers. John Barran of Leeds, men's tailoring manufacturers, introduced the new sewing machine in Britain in 1856. Symington's of Market Harborough, corset manufacturers, installed three Singer machines in its workroom. Early factory production developed mainly in men's clothing, which was more standardized and less apt to change than women's costumes. Early women's ready-to-wear was produced largely in cheaper grades, except for underwear and loose cloaks, capes, and coats, where fit was not important. Some children's clothes could be made by machine.

Mass production of fashionable women's clothing was impossible because of the intricate construction and detail involved. Women wore elaborately shaped bodices. Skirts were fitted over hoops, then bustles. In 1900, elegant Edwardian women reached new heights in body distortion as they donned and laced up the S-shaped corset. Dressmaking was an exercise in engineering.

The highborn and very rich were dressed by court dressmakers and couturier houses. Others patronized "a little dressmaker." Many households employed one or more seamstresses on a regular basis and the importance of the "sewing room" in some nineteenth-century houses was only a step below that of the kitchen or the nursery.

As they expanded in size, department stores became an important source for women's clothing. Blouse, skirt, and dress models were displayed and made-to-measure outfits were contracted out to workshops and homes or were sewn in the store's workrooms. As a store became a manufacturer, workrooms expanded to take up entire floors and as many as fifty to a hundred garment workers were employed. While machines could be used for linings and certain seams, most of the work was highly specialized and done by hand. In the work areas, there would be a bodice room, skirt room, sleeve room, boning room, and tailor's room.

As merchandise was manufactured to sell, there developed a new breed of customer to buy it—mill, mine, and foundry owners, shippers, bankers, and railroad owners—a middle class with immense buying power and a desire to flaunt the symbols of their new prosperity. The simple dresses of the opening years of the nineteenth century gave way to the enormous crinolines decorated with every imaginable kind of trim—lace, braid, ruffles, tassels, pompoms, and swags. Massive taffeta skirts rustling over innumerable petticoats sounded like the crackling of crisp new bills, but the message was more genteel. Women's clothes became an ostentatious show of family wealth.

Interior decoration was another means for displaying one's riches and possessions, and stores introduced home-furnishing departments. A man's home became an overstuffed castle filled with heavy furniture, curtains and voluminous draperies, tufted ottomans, bric-a-brac, and lots of children. Large families, no longer the necessity they had been on farms, were another show of affluence. Children were dressed up from birth, bedizened with ribbons and frills. Babies were paraded about in elaborate baby carriages or prams and older children were surfeited with fancy toys. Stores were only too happy to provide these luxuries.

Although the machines for manufacturing the products to show off wealth had been invented, the machines for maintaining them had not. Staffs of servants were required to keep the households dustfree and polished; the acres of fabric laundered, pressed, and repaired; and the children fed, dressed, entertained, and educated. Household staffs required uniforms, which department stores made available in their ever-growing number of departments.

A market for lower-priced merchandise also developed. Servants skimped and saved in order to emulate the latest modes of their masters and mistresses. Even the grossly underpaid factory workers had a limited buying power. Stores created their own customers with the employment of women. As stores began to dress women from the inside out, starting with their corsets, female clerks became a necessity. Along with the shopgirl, another young woman was emerging in offices and schoolrooms—the middle-class working girl whose job required a proper wardrobe. Edna Wollman Chase, the legendary editor of *Vogue*, was employed at the age of nineteen in that magazine's circulation department. She recaptured her feelings as an 1895 working girl in her book, *Always in Vogue*:

> With my new job I was becoming very clothes-conscious and wanted to be like all those other girls who, looking older than their years in the mature fashions, but looking, too, somehow frail and appealing under the sheer weight of yard goods, smiled shyly across

the café tables at the young men with the plastered-down hair and high, stiff collars and coats buttoned tight across their chests.

Store services expanded. Medical science, like household machinery, had not kept pace with the times and death became a commodity. An elaborate funeral, like everything else elaborate, was an indication of the size of one's bank account. Funerals and the required clothing that went with them became important business for the growing stores. The mourning room and adjacent departments for mourning skirts, gloves, and hosiery took up more space in the ground plan of Marshall & Snelgrove, built on Oxford Street in 1876, than the combined departments for cloaks, haberdashery, carpets, and costumes. Harrods to this day boasts, "We have the last circulating library in London, and customers may buy their theatre tickets, arrange their travel and bury their grandmothers by using the services we have to offer."

France, caught up in the on-again-off-again republics and empires that followed the French Revolution in 1789, was torn by political strife and exhausted by the Napoleonic wars. She had neither the time nor the energy to be a major participant or contributor to the industrial revolution that was taking place across the channel in England and across the Atlantic in America—a fact that did not go unnoticed by English manufacturers. When Wellington and his armies were bracing themselves for the Battle of Waterloo, British blockade-runners were delivering British-made uniforms and boots to Napoleon's armies across the channel.

During the last half of the nineteenth century and the beginning of the twentieth, everything except women's tightly cinched waistlines expanded. America spread west. Queen Victoria's England spread throughout the world. The middle and upper classes swelled. They were glutted with abundance—belching factories and bulging pocketbooks. They built massive houses and stuffed them with portly furniture, plump pillows and pudgy children. Fat capons graced their groaning sideboards. But something was missing from British and American life. The French had it. They had had it for a long time and they never lost it through war and chaos or the rise and fall of the nobility and political upheavel. They have it today. It is called style.

Style is elusive, but it affects architecture, arts, manners, and fashion. More than likely it was the Bouçicauts' *style*—an artistic panache combined with financial daring that captured other merchants' imaginations. While England went about the heady business of empire building and the United States—staggered by the Civil War—began reconstruction, France, after the years of turmoil, looked everywhere for light and discovered a new brilliance. Artists moved from their studios to the out-of-doors. Manet, Renoir, Monet, Cézanne, Van Gogh, and Seurat found the splendor of full sunlight and the cool mystery of dawn or twilight and flooded their canvases with color. Gauguin's vibrant reds, yellows, and blues exploded under the Tahitian sun.

Architects brought the sunlight indoors. Giant stained-glass ceilings floated over the galleries of the new stores, supported by marble, carved wood, and iron columns. Iron moldings, ceilings, and struts were twisted and shaped into lilies, poppies, and vines, and gigantic metal gardens bloomed in the sunshine that poured into the new structures. Designers and builders followed the lead of Belgian architect Baron Victor Horta, the master of Art Nouveau. His stores and shops were masterpieces of structural and decorative elegance. In addition to letting in light, glazed and decorated façades created showcases and provided a new sport—window shopping. The emission of daylight permitted customers to inspect goods in a natural light. With light and opulent surroundings, stores created an aura of elegance and respectability. According to Alexandra Artley in *The Golden Age of Shop Design, European Shop Interiors 1880–1939*:

> A building fabric that was all too visibly above suspicion was one way in which the proprietors of department stores could make it plain that however commercially novel their establishments, they were not overheated dens of vice into which society women used, in polite theory at least, to a circuit of escorted visits to opera houses, race meetings and private *soirées*, need fear to trust themselves.

France may have been the front-runner in store design, display techniques, and merchandising methods, but as more stores appeared or expanded throughout Europe and the United States, there were variations and innovations everywhere. Tearooms were installed to further the atmosphere of gentility and provide an area for relaxation and sociability. String orchestras and pipe organs created a mood in much the same manner as Muzak did in later years and taped rock-and-roll and disco music do today.

Lifts, powered by human, animal, or water power from the first century, were operated by steam in England by 1800. But they were treacherous and unreliable. In 1853, an American, Elisha Graves Otis, invented a safety device which made the passenger elevator a reality. In 1898, Harrods installed the first escalator. The experience of riding on the moving staircase was considered so harrowing that the store stationed two attendants at the top to assist the terrified customers and revive them with cognac and *sal volatile* if necessary. Apparently,Americans were less prone to attacks of the "vapors" when the first escalator was installed in the United States at Gimbel Brothers in Philadelphia. It was quite literally taken in stride.

Although other countries made technological advances to improve the efficiency and comfort in the new mercantile establishments, France held trump cards—her supremacy in fashion and quality merchandise. No other country in the world took fashion as seriously as France. Paris had been the artistic center of France from the end of the seventeenth century when Louis XIV concentrated the political, intellectual, artistic, and social life around him at Versailles. Prior to this time, fashion varied from country to country and city to city but the brilliant splendor of the Sun King's magnificent court set the tone for the rest of Europe. Court fashion changes were conveyed to other countries by fashion dolls dressed in the manner and materials of the real-life originals.

By the last quarter of the eighteenth century, the idea of a publication devoted to fashion developed and the *Collection des Habillements modernes et galants* was distributed. During the 1800s, the *Journal des Dames et des Modes* used engravings of doll-like figures to provide fashion information. *La Mésangère* was the first magazine to show a model in a lifelike situation. It also related fashion to sex. A picture of a young girl poised while her cavalier kisses her hand had the caption "A ce soir." With the publication of the *Gazette du Bon Ton* in 1912, fashion art reached new heights. Paul Iribe, Georges Lepape, Erté, and other French artists became respected and influential fashion illustrators. They were sought after by the new American fashion magazines, *Harper's*

Bazaar and *Vogue* (which merged with *Bon Ton* in 1925), and the French fashion message was carried to an ever-widening audience. Many of these artists sold their talents to the growing business of advertising art.

During the *fin de siècle* the influence of the courts and aristocrats began to wane and the new, affluent "high society" became the dictators of fashion. Fashion as a class-conscious spectacle entered a heyday and Paris was the mecca of fashion for all the world. The "King of Fashion" was an Englishman, Charles Frederick Worth, who was born in Lincolnshire in 1825. He set up his dress workrooms in Paris in 1858 and by 1864 the House of Worth employed a thousand workers. He was a favorite dressmaker of Empress Eugénie of France and Queen Alexandra of England—the last of the royal fashion leaders. The rich from Europe and, more increasingly, America, poured into his salon as Worth's originality and flair for elegance reached dazzling heights. The famous, too, became fashion-setters. The great ladies of the stage—Sarah Bernhardt, Eleanora Duse, Maxine Elliot, and Lillie Langtry—were showcases for the great Parisian couturiers—Doucet, Callot, Mme. Paquin, Redfern (a former London tailor), and, of course, Worth. While there have been film stars, socialites, and celebrities that have been well dressed and fashionable, the last great fashion leader in the true sense was Jacqueline Kennedy Onassis during her brief reign as First Lady.

As long as the influences on fashion were centered in Paris, it mattered little to the French from whom or where they came. In 1909, when Serge Diaghilev's Ballets Russes arrived in Paris, the impact was instant and overwhelming. The impression made by the ballet *Schéhérazade*, in particular, was overwhelming. The daring, sensuous colors in Léon Bakst's costumes and decor, the exciting music of Rimsky-Korsakov, the passionate abandon of Michel Fokine's choreography, and the dazzling technique of Nijinsky swept Paris off its feet. Twenty years later, a London critic, S. P. Dobbs, wrote: "The first performance of *Schéhérazade* was an important evening for the theatre, for dressmakers, for interior decorators, for jewellers and for all branches of decoration. It is difficult today to realize the metamorphosis which transformed the decorative arts."

Art Deco with its Oriental motifs, splashes of brilliant color, and sweeping curves, became the rage. A leading couturier of La Belle Epoque, Paul Poiret, embraced the Eastern influences and turned his respectable clients into harem girls. Chic women donned loose kimonos and *jupes-culottes*, or trouser skirts, in kaleidoscopic colors and richly textured fabrics. They wore turbans crowned with upstanding aigrettes and endless ropes of pearls. Poiret also loosened the constricted waist on the corset and straightened the S-shape, which permitted women to stand erect rather than pitched forward as they had been for years.

The new Arabian Nights fantasy of fashion required heady scents. Products with sultry names like Maharadjah, L'Ambre de Delhi, and Guerlain's still popular Mitsuoko were created to replace the bland, flower essences of the previous era. The famous fashion artists designed exotic Art Deco perfume bottles that were made by Lalique and Baccarat.

Although the new fashions began to spell the demise of the corset, the constrictions needed further unlacing and that came with a different form of dance than the ballet, and a new kind of woman, a young American girl.

In 1912, two Americans in Paris on their honeymoon ran out of funds and took a job as a dance team in the Café de Paris. These unemployed actors, Vernon and Irene Castle, gliding gracefully, free, and together in their unadorned, uncomplicated clothes, became the rage. First in Paris, then everywhere in Europe and America, young people tried to capture the Castles' spirit and style. Diana Vreeland, consultant to the Costume Institute of the Metropolitan Museum of Art in New York, included Irene Castle in the museum's exhibition of the ten most influential "American Women of Style."

Irene Castle bobbed her hair and wore a simple little Dutch cap in contrast to the enormous plumed, blooming, feathered heaps that women had fastened with épée-length hatpins to their mountains of hair. She shortened her skirt in order to dip and slide to the sensuous rhythms of the tango. She moved with a freedom unknown to those dressed in the fashionable hobble skirts. But most important of all, Irene Castle took off her corset. For women, at last, the twentieth century could begin.

Time, reporting on the spring Paris opening on February 6, 1978, said:

"Fashion is a reflection of the times. We all need a little calm,"
proclaimed French Designer Jean-Louis Scherrer last week.

Change *calm* to read *splendor, elegance, excitement, respectability,
comfort, freedom, madness,* or *drama,* and you have a three-hun-
dred-year-long parade of fashion.

P. G. Winnett found in the mid-1920s a Paris where everything
was happening. A Paris that, according to art and culture maven
Gertrude Stein, "was where the twentieth century was. . . ." The
City of Light was the rendezvous for everyone from everywhere.

Gertrude Stein was most certainly there holding court for established and aspiring artists and writers. Her friend, Alice B. Toklas,
was busy cooking up batches of hashish cookies. Pablo Picasso,
Georges Braque, and Joan Miró were there, along with Diego Ri-
vera, the Mexican, and Amedeo Modigliani, the Italian. Ezra
Pound could be seen hurrying about. Almost everyone was in the
cafés. Michael Arlen might be seen at the Dôme, along with Kay
Boyle, Ernest Hemingway, e.e. cummings, Janet Flanner, John
Dos Passos, and F. Scott Fitzgerald. Stravinsky was hardly seen
anywhere. He had too much work to do. So did James Joyce, who
was finishing his monumental *Ulysses.* But he occasionally
dropped by Sylvia Beach's famous bookstore, Shakespeare and
Company, where almost everyone could be found when not in the
cafés. American composers Aaron Copland, Roy Harris, and Vir-
gil Thomson were about. So were the French—Jean Cocteau and
André Gide.

Les Deux Magots, the Rotonde, and the Sélect were also filled
with the talented or the would-be talented hangers-on or thirsty
American tourists in search of good gin, a decent wine, and a
chance to rub elbows with *la vie Bohême.*

Paris had been determined through World War I not to lose her
role as arbiter and absolute dictator of fashion and, rather amazing-
ly, had kept the fashion industry afloat. Clothes became looser and
simpler. Skirts rose about the ankle and then to mid-calf as women
led active wartime lives. Elegance was not overlooked, however.
The *Gazette du Bon Ton* recommended elaborate costumes for attending concerts in hospitals because, "we must make ourselves as

beautiful as we can for the wounded . . . we must strike a contrast with the grim, depressing surroundings of the hospital wards." *C'est la guerre.*

A young woman arrived on the Paris scene in 1920. She had had a shop in Deauville and during wartime had adapted sailors' jackets and men's pullovers for women's wear. She started a new fashion trend. In Paris, Gabrielle Chanel declared: "I make fashions women can live in, breathe in, feel comfortable in, and look younger in." It was the antithesis of what high fashion had meant. Chanel simplified everything. The gimcrackery, ruffles, and bows were left behind. So were feather boas and parasols. Accessories were few and simple. Scarves, a strand of fake pearls, or an artificial gardenia became the trademarks of the well-dressed woman whether she was well-heeled or not. "Coco" Chanel introduced a new musky, unflowery scent. The matter-of-fact exquisite smell of Chanel No. 5 wafted over Europe and across the ocean to the United States. It was named after her "lucky" day, her birthday, August 5. Understated elegance became a new fashion phrase, and the Chanel suit was born.

Something else was born. The postwar offspring resulted from the marriage of wartime technology and the new fashion look. After the wartime gestation period, mass-produced ready-to-wear was delivered. Fashion, even copies of the finest designers, would be available to everyone in every price range. The stores became the mass purveyors of this mass production and catered to customers in every size, shape, age bracket, and income level. *Haute couture* remained. But the bread and butter was in the copies.

Chanel retired in 1939 for fifteen years. When she returned to the fashion scene with fanfare in 1954, Paris was appalled that she had not made sweeping changes. The production of copies and volume buying by the great American stores saved her from disaster. She was snubbed in her own country but was a smash hit in America.

In the Broadway musical hit *Coco*, starring Katharine Hepburn as the legendary Chanel, this triumph was expressed succinctly in the lyric:

> Paris hates the fashions
> Gave them all the ax,

But everything's fine
Right down the line
At Orbach's, Bloomingdale's, Best's and Sak's.

P. G. Winnett discovered something else in Paris besides new
and vital fashions and an ambience of musical, literary, and artistic
creativity. The Bauhaus group was exhibiting at a Paris exposition.
The Bauhaus, architects and crafts people who lived, studied, and
worked together in Germany, displayed no romanticism or Art
Deco fantasy in their work. It was pure line, design, and function.
It was "modern" in every sense of the word.

Starting with architecture, Bauhaus founder Walter Gropius extended his interests into the whole field of the arts. The Bauhaus
proclamation, "Architects, sculptors, painters, we must all turn to
the crafts," included weavers, metalworkers, potters, workers in
wall painting and stained glass and lighting and furniture design.
The names of those involved are as impressive as those of the international habitués of the Left Bank cafés. Along with Gropius,
there were Miës van der Rohe, Marcel Breuer, Paul Klée, Josef
Albers, and Wassily Kandinsky. Anni Albers' woven rugs, wall
coverings, and fabric brought a new dimension to the weavers'
craft. Laszlo Moholy-Nagy revolutionized the concept of space
and light. The Bauhaus artists moved about in the various fields of
art. The final aim of all the arts and their massive contributions was
the complete building.

P. G. Winnett returned to Los Angeles filled with the spirit of
Paris and the ideas of the Bauhaus. He destroyed the drawing
board plans for Bullock's Wilshire and worked closely with architects John and Donald Parkinson to create a concept of contem-
porary-art-in-business that was a radical departure for retailing. "It
was so 'modern,' so new, particularly for southern California,"
said Glenn Boocock, "that I don't think those architects had the
faintest idea what they were doing."

The guiding light through the project was designer Eleanor Le
Maire, a close friend who had encouraged Mr. Winnett to go to
Paris. Along with the architects, thirteen artists, famous and unknown, were commissioned to integrate the interiors and decor
with the building. Copper, nickel, bronze, and brass combined with
masonry, marble, cork, glass, and wood. Woven textures for walls
and floors along with lighting fixtures were carefully designed.

The ceiling of the marquee at the Motor Court entrance was covered by a giant fresco-secco mural by Herman Sachs. The winged figure of Mercury was surrounded by automobiles, airplanes, a gigantic ocean liner, the Santa Fe Chief, and the Graf Zeppelin. It was called "Spirit of Transportation."

The wide central foyer, extending from the Motor Court to the Wilshire Boulevard entrance, had walls of St. Genevieve rose marble quarried in Missouri. Vertical light panels cast a soft glow of opaque light over the rosewood cases.

Another Herman Sachs triumph was the painted glass ceiling in the fifth-floor Desert Lounge. The sun filtered through green and gold desert motifs, and abstract cacti were repeated in the grill-work ornamenting the windows. Touches of color in shades of the desert sunset were incorporated in the decor. In the larger Lounge Room, lacquered wall panels depicted California animals—the work of French designer Maurice Jallot. The floor of the Lounge was covered by a 30 x 60-foot hand-woven chenille rug.

The indefatigable Walter Hoving, whom P. G. Winnett had called "the greatest merchant in the world," had told him that around every corner of a store there should be a surprise, and Bullock's Wilshire was filled with surprises. There were both artistic and merchandising treats. The *Los Angeles Times* reported on the new store with headlines: "Bullock's Wilshire—An Adventure in Modernism." The paper reported one of the surprises:

> A gem of a "little smoking room" (for women) in reds and black and silver is rather informally tucked into one corner where low, deep chairs and softly upholstered stools offer relaxation. Here are telephones, distinctly modern smoking equipment, distinctive mirrors.

There seemed to be no limit to the imaginative use of materials. The paneling in the Women's Shoe Salon was lathed from a single tree—the only one of its color and grain ever found in Central America. The walls of the Fur Atelier were lined with varying shades of cork.

A horse owner and enthusiast, P. G. Winnett had the same vision about the meaning of sports to Southern California that he had about the automobile. Along the gallery leading to the Sportswear Room hung a giant tapestry, "Le Soleil," by French artist Jean

Lurcat. An abstract mural by Gjura Stojani depicting the "Spirit of Sports" was constructed of silvered plaster relief, thin strips of wood veneer, and flat fresco and graced one wall of the Sportswear Room. Directly off this room was the Saddle Shop. The wall cases were made of dark red oak. The floor was covered with vermilion tile and a hand-woven rug in deep browns and orange-red. The deep tones set off the bas-relief wall sculpture by Eugene Maier-Krieg that suggested a hunt scene and a carefree canter over hill and dale. In the shop's corner was a stall where "Bullock's Barney" stood impervious to his elegant surroundings. The life-sized plaster horse was an accommodating mount for the equestrian who wished to check the fit of his or her breeches. Everywhere in the store, the California sunshine and the life that was lived in it were celebrated. There was a Play Deck, filled with "play" clothes, "sun" suits, "sunback" dresses, "beach" pajamas, and "poolside" costumes. P. G. Winnett's interest in sports and fashion and Bullock's merchandising techniques and buying power were instrumental in the development and growth of California's fledgling sportswear industry.

There were departments where P. G. Winnett deemed modern design inappropriate. The high-fashion salons were a suite of eighteenth-century rooms located on the second floor. The Directoire Room resembled a private drawing room of that period and provided a background for formal and evening wear. There was a Louis XVI Room for afternoon dresses and coats and a Louis XV Room for fine accessories. Off of the suite, which was commonly referred to as the "French Rooms," was a "retiring room" fashioned after Josephine's bathroom at Malmaison.

As a result of face-liftings over the years, these rooms have changed. Through some scheme for merchandising travel clothes, the delicate Louis XV Room was redecorated to capture the mood of a safari. The walls were covered with fake leopard patterns and African ceremonial masks. The current president of Bullock's Wilshire, Jerome Nemiro, endeared himself to his old-guard personnel when he discovered the original chinoiserie wall coverings stored away in the Tower and with the assistance of display director Raymond Dexter restored the room to its original elegance.

When the store first opened, steps were taken to make the employees aware that this was no ordinary store. This was a special place. A particular vocabulary was developed. There were no *customers*, only *patrons*. A *clerk* was a *salesperson* and an elevator or telephone *operator* was an elevator or telephone *attendant*. A Mrs. Beardslee was brought in to conduct classes in etiquette. Female salespersons were required to wear hats and gloves when entering and leaving the store. Patrons were to be treated with the courtesy one would show a guest in one's own home. Courtesy and service were raised to an art form, which prompted a longtime employee to say, "We pampered our patrons like lap dogs."

Helen Moore, who retired after forty years as gift buyer and an expert on the famous Marghab linens from the isle of Madeira said, "This was Mr. Winnett's baby. We'd introduced the store to Southern California and we'd do anything that could be done for our patrons, our store, or our Mr. Winnett."

Changes have occurred over the years in things other than the decor. Katherine Henderson, matron in the "retiring room" for over twenty years, misses her black uniform with its starched white collar, cap, and apron. Today, she says with disdain, "We wear blue jersey uniforms now—drip dry. Mr. Winnett kept everything to a higher point."

There was no end to the pride and devotion the employees had for their store and their employer. "I think Bud St. John slept in the receiving room during Christmas," Dorothy Roth, stationery buyer for over thirty years, recalled. "He worked the clock around." And yet, when Lavona Kohl, Bullock's Wilshire's world-famous toy buyer, discovered her Santa Claus suffering from a disease that often afflicts Santa Clauses, she called the receiving room. "He's drunk," she fumed. Within minutes, Bud St. John was suited up and "Ho, ho, hoing" for the *little* patrons in the Toy Department. "Of course, then he didn't get any sleep in the receiving room or anywhere else. He had to catch up on his own work through the night," Mrs. Roth added.

Christmas for department stores and most departments begins months before December. The late Margaret Mayer, handkerchief buyer, began in July working at home in the evenings, lining her Christmas boxes with paper lace and filling them with handkerchiefs folded in her secret fold.

No one had a more unusual Christmas job than engineer Rudy Galindo, who brushes off his longtime employment by saying, "I

was left at the store's door in a basket." He started working for
Bullock's Wilshire thirty-eight years ago. He was a "route" boy—
one of the boys who delivered the packages from various departments to the Motor Court. This service, along with valet parking,
has gone the way of the formal maid's uniforms. So has the drive-
through porte-cochere, which is now closed. In the days of Bullock's Wilshire's famous white ostrich-plume Christmas tree,
Rudy and the other "route" boys would be pressed into service to
assist Mary Goodholme, of the Tabery Design Corporation, in
readying the tree. "We started in August handwashing each plume
in soap and water. There were *thousands*. The washing wasn't so
bad. It was the drying! We had to blow each one dry. While we'd
sit there and puff, Miss Goodholme would shout, 'FLUFF! BOYS!
FLUFF!' *The tree* was that woman's life. They gave it up after she
died. Where else would they find anyone who would work that
hard on a bunch of ostrich feathers?

"You want to know how things change? I can remember when
Miss Ann Hodge was store president and discovered a route boy
with a crew cut. She sent him off the floors where patrons could see
him, down to a basement job, until his hair grew—*long*! How about
that?"

Not everything has changed. The Porcelain Room is much the
same. Manager Virginia Florence, an employee for over twenty
years, regards her department as "the most spacious and beautiful
porcelain gallery in the United States." She and buyer Katherine
Choate cherish their Dorothy Doughty birds, Doris Linder horses,
Boehm *objets d'art*, Bernard Winskill's Royal Worchester military
figures, and Ronald Van Ruykevelt's game fish and game birds.
The gallery is an aviary—a greenhouse filled with limited edition
china *aves* and delicate ceramic flowers—orchids, water lilies, peo-
nies, camellias, and cacti. It is known throughout the world to col-
lectors, who pay from $25 for a small figurine up to $35,000—the
price for the Boehm Studio's life-sized porcelain "Eagle of Freedom" executed for the Bicentennial. One year and 178 integral
handmade mold parts were involved in making this majestic American Bald Eagle. Thirteen of these eagles were offered to the public
in honor of the original American colonies. A fourteenth was presented to President Gerald Ford for the White House Bicentennial
Collection.

In spite of the architecture and interiors, the fashions and sportswear, superb gifts, porcelains, rare books, antiques, and exquisite stationery, to generations of Southern Californians, Bullock's Wilshire is the Tea Room. Daily fashion shows take place along the ramps that are set on the carpet strewn with cabbage roses. Fresh flowers grace each table. Crystal chandeliers sparkle over the bower lined with lattice and cockatoo-figured wallpaper. The food is above the average "tearoom" fare, thanks to the direction of Louise de Vries, a newcomer who arrived on the job six years ago. What exactly is the charm and mystique of the Tea Room? Miss de Vries credits her staff, saying, "So many have been here for over twenty-five years." June Parenti, a waitress for thirty-three years, is one example, dressed in her immaculate pink and white uniform. A crisp white linen handkerchief explodes from her breast pocket. She whirls about efficiently and cheerfully and would appear to know everyone who steps into the Tea Room.

Bert Lara is an ebullient man who dances and sings on television in his off hours and has performed his songs in Spanish, Italian, and French at the famous Cocoanut Grove farther down the boulevard. Bert started working at Bullock's Wilshire "ages ago" as an elevator attendant, moved to "wigs for men," and has been the maître d'hotel at the Tea Room for six years. He is famous for kissing his older patrons. "I try to make them happy," he says. "I fuss over them. Heaven help us if I'm busy and they don't get a hug and kiss. The ladies get very hurt."

My cousin, Nancy Holliday, and her mother, my aunt Ilse Adams, are Bullock's Wilshire Tea Room buffs—par excellence. Nancy explains: "It's just that *nothing* has changed. Oh, the fashions on the ramp, of course, and the booze. They didn't always serve booze. I've gone to that Tea Room with my mother since I was a little kid. It wasn't easy since it was located on the fifth floor. You see, after the thirties earthquake, I overheard my Dad tell Mother that "downtown some of the stores ran out of *juice!*" It was a befuddling thought for a young person. I knew it wasn't *orange* juice or *tomato* juice—but I got a red zone—something was wrong. The next time we went shopping, I decided it was *elevator* juice. I didn't ride in them for a long time. Hell's bells! I know every staircase in Bullock's Wilshire. And another thing—I think those waitresses' handkerchiefs are made of plaster of Paris. They haven't changed one fold in forty years."

Recently Bert Lara fussed a great deal over one of "his ladies" when she celebrated her birthday in the Tea Room. She and her friends were having such a good time that no one bothered to count the 103 candles on the cake.

It has been more than fifty years since P. G. Winnett created the gracious "modern" ambience of Bullock's Wilshire. He was a handsome man and, according to his daughter, "He was not a man of many words, but he had a lovely sense of humor. He loved his horses that he kept at his Rancho San Vincente—his little adobe house there and his garden. On Mondays he would bring baskets of fruit and pomegranates to the employees. He loved his family and was a wonderful father. He didn't have any great interest in or understanding of art—what he had was vision."

A widower for many years, Mr. Winnett never remarried and led a quiet social life. He adored his daughters—Glenn, who married Kenyon Boocock and moved to New York, and "Sporty," who married Walter Candy from St. Louis—and his son, John, who died as a young man. In his later years, Mr. Winnett kept up a weekly and and intimate correspondence with his many grandchildren.

The Boococks' daughter, Leslie di Carpegna, had a particular affection for him. "We took him with us on our honeymoon," she said. "He gave us a trip to Hawaii, and we insisted that he join us. You can't imagine what fun he was! *Everybody* loved my grandfather."

None of Mr. Winnett's heirs has entered retailing nor have they shared his love for merchandising. They have, however, inherited his love of sports. His grandson, John Winnett, captained the U.S. Equestrian Team at the Montreal and Munich Olympic Games. Glenn Candy Cooper, a granddaughter, lives in Idaho, is married to Sun Valley entrepreneur William Janss, and is an avid skier. Her brother, Walter Candy, Jr., lives in nearby Ketcham and shares the Jansses' enthusiasm for the sport. A great-granddaughter, Cristian Cooper, is a seventeen-year-old ski champion who recently competed in the World Cup Races in Europe and is a promising hope for the U.S. Olympic Ski Team.

In 1933, P. G. Winnett became president of Bullock's, Inc., with John Bullock's death. In January 1944, two weeks after the death of Mary Ann Magnin, at the age of ninety-four, an event took place that could never have happened during her lifetime. I. Magnin became a subsidiary of Bullock's, Inc. Seven years later, Grover Magnin was forced to give up his store at the age of sixty-five, under Bullock's mandatory retirement rule. At this time, P. G. Winnett was chairman of the board, and the president of the firm was his son-in-law, Walter Candy.

One of the fiercest proxy fights in retailing took place in 1964 when Federated Department Stores, Inc., proposed merging Bullock's Magnin into their growing retailing corporation. P. G. Winnett violently opposed the merger. Leading the opposition to him was Walter Candy. Prior to joining Bullock's Wilshire as merchandise manager in 1933, Walter Candy had been affiliated with the Busy Bee Candy Company in St. Louis, Missouri.

It was a pitched battle and the bitter fight raged between P. G. Winnett, the largest individual stockholder, and his son -in-law, for control of the board of directors.

"It was a terrible thing for our family," Mrs. Boocock recalls. "It put my sister in a dreadful situation between her father, whom she adored, and her husband, Walter Candy. There was also a very determined vice-president, Philip Somebody-or-other [Philip Corrin, vice-president and vice-chairman of the board]. I have chosen to forget his name. He was on Walter's side. My father was in his eighties. They were *his* stores. It was *his* company. He had started it *all* as a very young man. How could anyone want to take that away from him? Eventually, they did. The younger men won and it left terrible scars." In 1964, "Winnett's Folly" and Bullock's Magnin, pioneers of California taste, the California look, and California elegance, became a division of Federated Department Stores, Inc., with headquarters in Cincinnati, Ohio.

Perhaps mindful of the empty, unproductive years that Grover Magnin endured, P. G. Winnett held a lifetime contract as an advisor to Bullock's, Inc. He kept his office in the corporate building downtown and continued his visits to the stores. On the morning of July 18, 1968, he toured Bullock's Wilshire, passing out his sour balls and chocolate kisses. In the afternoon, he died in his home. He was eighty-three.

Former employee Helen Moore said: "I came from North Dakota, taught school in Iowa, and ended up in Los Angeles. I can honestly say that everything wonderful that has happened in my life, I owe to Bullock's Wilshire. It may sound corny, but I've kept the last candy Mr. Winnett gave me. It's still wrapped in its cellophane. Mr. Winnett was a short man—in stature. In everything else he was ten feet tall."

My cousin Nancy, a Bullock's Wilshire patron who now lives in Northern California, put it this way: "It's simple—there's just something *very special* about Bullock's Wilshire."

Nancy and I were sitting by a roaring fire in her house high up in the Contra Costa County hills, sipping after-dinner cognacs and reminiscing about growing up in Southern and Northern California. We talked about our mothers and shopping and the stores we remembered. Nancy said: "I even walked up *all those stairs* at Bullock's Downtown when I went to a personal appearance of Uncle Whoabill. Remember him? Maybe he was only in Los Angeles— very big on the radio—an early-day Captain Kangaroo. You were supposed to say 'Whoabill' when you were under duress, and then not cry. I tried it once when I hit my finger with a hammer—it didn't work. Like this, you said WHOOOOAAAA—BILL." She burst into song and to the tune of "School Days":

"Whoabill—Whoabill—Dear old Uncle Whoabill,
Piggy and Tommy and Ticky Bear—
Dum da dee—Dum da dee—Dum tee dum—"

"I remember Uncle Whoabill was a *very* big disappointment. And then there was Robinson's Blue Fairy and a smelly, drunken Santa Claus. Now *that* was a real put-up job. The Blue Fairy would ask you what you wanted for Christmas, then skip ahead and tell Santa. My brother and I figured that one out because the poor old Santa was so plotzed he'd get it all mixed up. Oh, my God, all those crazy times growing up. But what *fun!* You know," she added, "somebody ought to write a book about it."

We laughed and had another cognac.

SIX

The Korrick Boys and The Goldwater Boys

Arizona

Charlie and Abe Korrick were co-owners of Korricks, a department store in downtown Phoenix for over sixty years. "The Boys," as they were called by almost everyone who knew them, were the "they-don't-make-'em-like-that-anymore" breed of merchants. They knew what business was all about. "Give me de volume and I'll show you de profit!" bantam-sized Abe would shout and he'd pound a table, desk, or counter with his fist. "The Boys" had followed their older brother, Sam, from Poland when they were teenagers at the turn of the century. They never lost their immigrant-boy image or their Jewish accents.

Being a Jew was not always easy in Phoenix, a city where posh winter resorts and country clubs maintained hard-line *restrictions*. There were situations such as the one when the town's leading citizen and prominent merchant was playing golf as a guest at a resort club. An assistant manager was sent out to the fairway to inform him, "I'm sorry, sir, but you can't play here. This club is restricted and you are a Jew." The golfer said, "Hell, son, I'm not a Jew—I'm a pioneer!" The young man looked embarrassed and confused and the player added, "You go and tell them I'll only play nine holes. I'm half Jewish."

Sam, the oldest Korrick, had emigrated to El Paso, Texas, where he worked and lived in the back of Diamond's store until he saved enough money to go on his own. He moved to Phoenix—population under 5,000 in 1895.

Arizona was not a hospitable place. It was plagued by drought and floods, arrows and bullets, and the heat was unbearable.

A Union officer returning to Washington from the Apache wars that ended with the capture of Geronimo, when questioned about the Territory, said, "It's a great place, Arizona. A trifle warm, but all they need is water and *good society.*"

His commander replied, *"That, sir, is all they need in hell!"*

Good society had been even more scarce in 1860 when two other brothers, Michel and Joseph Goldwater, came to Arizona from California to peddle their wares in the gold fields from a buckboard and mule backs. The Goldwaters hauled goods over treacherous roads like the Trail of Graves and delivered to companies like the Vulture Mine. Joe was wounded in an Indian ambush. The bullet was removed at a makeshift Army outpost hospital and he wore it on his watch fob for the rest of his life. Mike was robbed by bandits at gunpoint.

In 1872, the Goldwaters opened a store in Phoenix. The first house had been constructed on the present Phoenix townsite only a year before and customers were scarce. When the store failed, they moved northward to the mining town of Prescott. In 1880, Joe sold out his interest to Mike and moved to Bisbee, where he went into partnership with Miguel Castenada in the Copper Queen Mine area. This tough town proved to be even less friendly than the rest of Arizona.

On December 8, 1883, five masked gunmen of the Red Sample Gang forced Joe Goldwater to open the safe at Castenada and Goldwater–General Merchandise. A local citizen about to sound an alarm was shot and the ensuing Bisbee Massacre, second only to the Fight at O.K. Corral in the annals of Arizona gunfighting lore, began. When the bandits were captured, an old Spanish coin with Mr. Castenada's initials was found in their possession. Five members of the gang were tried and sentenced to hang. A sixth member was sentenced to the territorial prison for twenty years. The citizens, enraged at the leniency, obtained a rope from Goldwaters, took the prisoner from jail, and meted out their own justice. The coroner's report read: "The deceased died of emphysema of the lungs, which might have been caused by strangulation, self-inflicted or otherwise."

After serving as mayor of Prescott, Mike turned the business over to his sons, Baron and Morris, and returned to San Francisco. Morris became Prescott's mayor in 1895.

Baron wanted to move the store back to Phoenix so they settled their disagreement in western-movie fashion by playing a few hands of casino. Baron won and the store relocated in Phoenix. As Arizona grew, so did Goldwaters'. They became the agents for Singer sewing machines. They sold steam engines and mining equipment along with plows, fencing, barley, bacon, and ribbons and laces. They imported rococo furniture from Vienna and made purchases from fine stores. Old ledgers show shipments received from Marshall Field & Co., in Chicago; Lord & Taylor and Arnold Constable in New York; Strawbridge and Clothier in Philadelphia, and Raphael Weill (later The White House) in San Francisco. Morris originated the store slogan, "The Best Always." He also brought the first telegraph line into Phoenix, became the first operator, and sent the first message: "Get the hell off the line."

Eventually, Baron's sons, Barry and Robert, took over the store management. The young men proved to be creative merchants. They promoted designs with characteristics of the Southwest. They had fabric hand-screened with authentic Arizona cattle brand designs and the material was ordered from all over the world. Over a period of years, more than a million yards were sold. Sterling silver swizzle sticks in the form of branding irons were another exclusive, and they originated the famed Antsy Pants, white cotton undershorts printed with giant red ants. These sold in the thousands. Barry Goldwater was elected to the United States Senate in 1953 and in 1964. Only a shade more than a hundred years from the time Michel Goldwater had struggled through the hostile desert frontier, his grandson was a candidate for the office of President of the United States.

Sam Korrick arrived in Phoenix at about the same time the Goldwaters came down from Prescott. He rented a 25x40-foot building on East Washington Street, a rutted dirt road lined with wooden plank sidewalks. He sent east for merchandise and, using the shipping crates for counters and display tables, he sold work pants and shirts, calico and muslin, hats and boots, buckram, and whalebone stays in The New York Store. The name was meant to add glamour to the dingy, gas-lit surroundings in the rugged town, but the banners over the doorway were down-to-earth *hard sell*: "The Cheapest Goods in the City," "Doing a Strictly Cash Business," and "No Trouble to Show Goods."

Sam prospered, expanded, and sent for his brother Charles, age seventeen. Together, they began to organize the merchandise. Cowboy goods were set up in one area, miners' wares in another. Gentlemen's ruffled shirt fronts and fancy vests were in another section. High-laced shoes, corsets, and bustles were placed where women could have privacy. The New York Store became a *department* store and the name was changed to Korricks'.

In 1902, an ad in the *Daily Republican* announced: "One Day Extraordinary Bargain Giving." Six-cent lawn, muslin, and calico were marked down to 3¢. Ladies' summer corsets were sold at half-price for 35¢. A dozen pearl buttons cost 3¢. Sales became such a tradition that a Phoenician said: "There were Saturday sales, first-of-the-month sales, end-of-the-month sales, first-of-the-week sales, middle-of-the-week sales, three-day sales. You *never* bought anything at Korricks' that wasn't on sale."

In 1903, Sam died and nineteen-year-old Charles, too young to sign contracts, operated the store under the guardianship of Simon Overfelder of the First National Bank. Charles sent back to Poland for his fourteen-year-old brother Abe.

For the next sixty years, Charles was president of Korricks' and Abe was merchandising manager. A longtime employee described the store's operation: "Saturday mornings before the store opened, everyone gathered and The Boys stood behind a long table covered with samples of the day's sale merchandise. Mr. Korrick—Charles—greeted us. He was mild-mannered and polite and he always ended his brief opening by saying, 'And now I'd like to introduce my little brudder, Abe.' Abe would give his sales pitch for the day's specials with the enthusiasm of a football coach."

Abe Korrick never walked. He always ran. His office was a shambles. Bills of lading and invoices from thirty years were buried in the debris, but nothing was lost. He carried every sales figure and business transaction in his head. It was easier than sifting through papers to find them. He spoke the language of Broadway and Seventh Avenue and his whole world was "making the buy."

Abe Korrick was a legend in New York and Los Angeles buying offices, where he'd cry and moan and carry on with histrionics until he had worn sellers down to their bottom price. After he had closed the merchandise deal—just when everyone was catching his breath from the exhausting bargaining—he'd start over to wheedle down the price of freight. When Abe was out of town, he'd telephone the store every night to get the day's figures. His life was making the buy, advertising it, selling it, and going back for more.

In 1913, the Korricks made an unprecedented move in a town of less than 10,000. They built a three-story department store at Fifth and Washington streets with an elevator and cooling system. More unprecedented than the building was their financing it through an Arizona bank. Phoenix banks in 1913, only one year after Arizona became the forty-eighth state, were considered risky and most people went to California to borrow large sums of money. Not the Korricks! They were local merchants and they would do business with their own customers—the local bankers. They borrowed $70,000. This faith in their community where they had prospered would affect The Boys' attitude toward expansion and change and have a longtime influence on the growth of the store.

The new store did a flourishing business, but within a few months, the loan was called. A rumor had spread through Phoenix like a sagebrush fire—"The Korricks are going broke." It was generally felt that local merchants—Goldwaters included—envious of the beautiful store, had started the gossip to teach The Boys a lesson for having fancy ideas. The Korricks struggled to cover the loan, replacing it from a St. Louis bank. But they vowed never, ever, ever, to borrow money again—a difficult feat in a business that operates on credit.

During the postwar forties and early fifties, when Phoenix boomed and sprawled over the Valley of the Sun, Charles's son, Ed, a member of the firm, pushed for expansion into the burgeoning shopping centers. Charlie and Abe, paralyzed by the thought of debt, delayed until 1957, when they built a branch in Christown. "The move came too late," said Ed Korrick. "The branch cost several million dollars and at the same time they refused to let go downtown, where everything was beginning to decay. Dad was seventy-eight years old and Uncle Abe was seventy-four. They couldn't see how business had changed and yet they refused to give those of us who were younger any authority. They finally decided to find a buyer."

Ed Korrick accompanies the boys to St. Louis to see their old friends Arthur Baer and Leo Fuller of Stix, Baer and Fuller. There was an offer of $2 million for the stores and before the deal was closed, the four men went into the next room, leaving young Korrick in the outer office.

"When Charlie and Abe came back out, they were white and shaken," Ed recalls. "I thought the negotiations had gone well and couldn't imagine what had happened.

"On the train back to Phoenix they were sullen and silent, until Charlie said, 'We don't want to sell to Stix, Baer and Fuller.' And that was that.

"Later, I learned what had happened behind those closed doors. Arthur and Leo tried to soften the blow and started a pitch, 'This will be wonderful for you boys. You've worked hard in that store all your lives. You're both in your seventies and now you can retire with all this money.' It had never occurred to Charlie and Abe that if they sold the store they wouldn't stay on to run it."

It was impossible for the employees (or the customers, for that matter) to imagine Korricks' without Charlie and Abe. They were all one big family. There had been all those morning meetings and the competitions for sales, and picnics and songs. There had been the time when Charlie, at age seventy-five, had been convinced to take a vacation and had gone with his wife, Blanche, to Hawaii. When he returned, he wanted to share his holiday with his employees on Saturday morning. Standing in a flowered Hawaiian shirt, he opened the meeting with "Aloha," pronouncing it with the guttural sounds in "chutzpah." His mementoes were laid out on the table and he held each one up for all to see—a cocktail napkin from the airplane, a matchbook from a hotel, a menu from a restaurant—as he described the trip from the moment they had left Phoenix. He told in detail what they'd had to eat and drink. "It probably sounds corny," said an employee, "but it was really very touching. All his life, from the time he was a kid, he'd been minding the store." Finally his time was up and he would have to continue the travelogue the following Saturday because here with the merchandise was "my little brudder, Abe."

What would Korricks' be without Abe running, all five feet three of him, through the aisles? He kept his elbows tucked in and his arms flung out in front. It was said that when he hung his coat on a hanger it stayed in the same position—the sleeves jutting out straight.

At a testimonial dinner in 1957 honoring Abe for his fifty years with the store, the employees gave him a swivel chair. Jerry Lewkowitz made the presentation, "The chair is symbolic. We know you're never going to sit on it unless it's Sunday. But one thing is sure, your name is on it so you can't put it in the stock and sell it."

Senator Barry Goldwater, a third-generation member of a pioneer merchant family, spoke to the first-generation pioneer merchant. The Korricks and the Goldwaters had been competitors for over sixty years. The Senator said: "If anybody'd told me thirty years ago that I would stand up and try and say something nice about Abe Korrick, I'd have thrown him the hell out.

"I'll never forget, about a year after I went to work in our store, I tried to make a little money on the outside at night selling oil burners and radios, and they [Korricks] got hold of the same table radio I had. I was doing all right—selling it for $59.50—and he [Abe] started selling it for $49.50. It cost $35.00 and the day that I got to $17—I was selling it at that—I called Abe out into the alley, which was our favorite meeting place, and I said, 'Now, damn it, Abe, this has gone far enough! Let's get back to making some money!' "

Charlie Korrick, who had been honored at a fifty-year service dinner a few years earlier, spoke, showering Abe with accolades. He ended his speech with, "I'm happy and proud of my kid brudder Abe's achievements."

Phoenix Mayor Jack Williams spoke. Letters were read from Arizona Governor Ernest W. MacFarland, senior Senator Carl Hayden, and New York manufacturers. A plaque and gold watch were presented along with glowing tributes from the employees. Charlie and Abe had a strong affection for their employees. Early on they had developed a profit-sharing plan. They were repaid by loyalty and the over-twenty-five-year service list of employees grew each year.

Not everyone felt affection for The Boys—Abe in particular. A woman recalls being in the store and passing Abe who, without looking up, bellowed, "You're fired!" The astounded woman said, "But Mr. Korrick, I don't even work here." "I don't care," he yelled, shaking a piece of merchandise in her face. "You're fired anyway!"

Then there was the Rosenzweig Jewelers incident. Charlie went to Isaac Rosenzweig, Phoenix's leading jeweler, to have some pearls strung, as a gift for his wife. He had bought them wholesale and preferred not going to his "in-store" jeweler. The pearls were strung and knotted. When he picked them up, Mr. Rosenzweig said, "That'll be three dollars, Charlie."

"*Three dollars?*" Korrick howled. "For *string! That's* no way to do business, Ike!"

Isaac Rosenzweig poured the pearls out of the felt bag, laid them out flat, took shears from his desk drawer, and snip, snip, snip.

No Korrick entered Rosenzweig's again. No Rosenzweig ever again shopped at Korricks'.

On Friday, May 11, 1962, the following news appeared in the *Arizona Republic*:

CALIFORNIA CHAIN BUYING
CONTROL OF KORRICKS STORES

Broadway-Hale, Inc., a 21-store retail group, will acquire control of Korricks stores in Phoenix under terms of an agreement involving the exchange of stock worth about $4 million.

Edward W. Carter, president of Broadway-Hale, said in Los Angeles that Korricks will continue to operate under its present name as a subsidiary of the West Coast group with no change in management or personnel. Abe and Charles Korrick will remain as the active operators of the business here.

The Boys, Charlie and Abe, were nearing eighty years of age and they were each given a five-year, $80,000-a-year contract, an office, and a secretary. "But of course, there was nothing for them to do," said an employee.

In 1966, after the death of both brothers, Korricks' name was changed to The Broadway. Charles's widow, Blanche, protested the change to Edward Carter.

Mrs. Korrick presently lives quietly in a house on the grounds of the Mountain Shadow Club. She had been studying music in the north when she met Charles and after moving to Phoenix, she gave recitals and musicales in the culture-starved desert town. Since then she has been active in supporting the Phoenix Symphony and enjoys the concerts. "He was such a wonderful man," she said. "He let me go north for the Opera and he gave me everything I ever wanted." She paused. "Why do you suppose they would change the name to The Broadway? *That* doesn't mean anything in Phoenix—but Korricks' does. And besides—they *promised.*"

The days of the Korricks' Prosperity Dinner for their employees, like the one in 1916 when the menu announced "Canape a la Char les" and "Young Chicken Fricasse a la A B," were over. So were promotions like the first letter to be sent into Arizona across the Atlantic Ocean and the United States via airmail. The letter, written by D. Roditi & Sons, of Germany, to the Korricks, triggered the banner headlines "Korricks' Organization, World Wide, Seizes Opportunity and Sends Letter by Giant Graf Zeppelin."

There would never be another Korricks' annual sales contest chicken and beans dinner where the winners ate chicken and the losers ate beans and everyone sang songs like "God Bless America"—and, to the tune of "Smiles":

It takes smiles to swell the bonus
It takes smiles to run a book
If we smile we see the pesky shopper
Who has just "come in the store to look."
Then along comes summer's paid vacations
And our Christmas gift checks in great style
All in all, the smiles we give for Korricks'
Are the smiles that make life worthwhile.

The simple little things were over. *Good society* had come to Arizona.

SEVEN

Everybody Loves a Party—
Everybody Loves a Show
Texas and Other Countries

It is almost impossible to pinpoint how and at what point one becomes enamored with and loyal to a particular store. In the past, shopping habits were passed from mother to daughter, from father to son. Trust and friendliness were factors. People shopped where they were known, could find their way around with ease, and were familiar with the merchandise.

As cities grew, transportation was important in the development of clienteles. In Los Angeles, because of the trolley cars that went by The Broadway Store, Arthur Letts's first slogan was "All cars transfer to Fourth and Broadway." In New York City in 1902, the phrase "All cars transfer to Bloomingdale's" was launched by the grandest publicity campaign ever created at that time. Songs, slogans, umbrellas, and pictorial extravaganzas made the phrase known to virtually every New Yorker and visitor to the city. This penchant for promotional razzmatazz is a major part of Bloomingdale's "personality." On any Saturday the White Plains, New York, store looks like a medieval street fair. There are jugglers, clowns, food and cooking equipment demonstrators, and pretty girls wandering around modeling pretty clothes. It is fun for all and there are enough gourmet samples available to alleviate hunger or to provide for an entire free lunch. During the week in the Stamford, Connecticut, store, special events director Lillian Moran has a vast number of morning programs that go far beyond clothes and *kinder* and *küchen*. In one March week her diversified programs included: The New York Cosmos Soccer Team; Easter Egg Decoration—Ukrainian Style; Nineteenth Century Art and Architecture; Tablesettings by Tableware Editor Molly Siple, of *House Beautiful;* Arlene Francis (and her autobiography); and Exercise the Natural-Action Way. There were also "Special" special events like the Junior Tennis Clinic and Pre-Natal Clinics.

The ultimate Bloomingdale's promotion, India—The Ultimate Fantasy, took place in the spring of 1978. Every department in all fourteen stores participated. Plans for the "Ultimate Fantasy" were in the making for twelve years. Over $10 million, thousands of miles of travel, innumerable personnel, and Air India were involved.

To capture the customer, advertising campaigns in the various media have reached a high level of sophistication. Banners for the "best" ads bounce around like Pele's kicks and passes. So do the art directors, graphics artists, fashion illustrators, layout experts, and copywriters who create them and are lured (or stolen) from store to store. "Fabulous Fitz," Bernice Fitz-Gibbon, put phrases and slogans into the American vernacular as she moved from Wanamaker's to Macy's to Gimbels. Wherever Fitz reigned, the ads were literate, witty, and became required reading for the general public. They also sold—*anything*—from black chiffon nightgowns, to bird houses, to manure. In *Minding the Store*, Stanley Marcus writes that he "discovered" Virginia Sisk in San Francisco and "took a chance on her." Actually, she was creating the award-winning ads for Joseph Magnin when she was "discovered." At the moment, the accolades for the snappiest ads in New York are going to B. Altman & Co. but should the department be raided, who knows where the zippy copy might show up next.

Window displays have been going through a revolution during the past few years. Except for Christmas windows, which often took a year of planning and execution in many stores, most displays were random shows of heaps of merchandise or lifeless figures in "real-life" situations—attending a party, waiting for a bus in simulated rain, back-to-school in a classroom. Today, with the use of electronics, *near* porn, surrealism, and humor, window displays have become exciting "street theater." They use violence, sex, and fantasy, and touch on heretofore unvisual themes, such as murder, suicide, and homosexuality. The windows are sometimes shocking, often confusing, and occasionally vulgar. They are talked about, stir up controversy, create masses of publicity, and draw crowds. They also sell merchandise.

Robert Currie, former director of visual planning for Henri Bendel, is generally credited with starting the new trend. The *enfant terrible* of displays, according to Michael Emory's book *Windows*, is Candy Pratts, display director at Bloomingdale's. Twenty-seven-year-old Miss Pratts studied merchandising at the Fashion Institute of Technology. She spent four years creating displays at Charles Jourdan Shoes, before joining Bloomingdale's two years ago. She is, says Emory, "a tough, aggressive New Yorker, and her windows reflect her brashness, her daring and her finely honed sense of irony."

Candy Pratts is also extremely professional. When questioned about her talent and enormous creative energies, she said: "I work within my own scope. These are my fantasies, my dreams, my desires. I have no plans. If I feel like being all red—red walls, red floors, everything red, then that's what we do that day. I'm not making any political statement. My windows aren't political. There are forty of them that rotate and change every two weeks. Four new windows a day. There are eight floors of interior store displays to worry about. It's like throwing a party for ten or ten thousand. Except I only throw a party if I *feel* like it. I'm not into fine line. It's like the red—it's what I feel. Display encompasses all the arts, in a salaried situation. I'm given creative license. If I weren't, I wouldn't be here. This is all a process of much work. It's trendy and it only lives its moment—but when that moment comes, I am way ahead and on to something else." This young Puerto Rican woman with her "Chore Girl" hair style and hip manner is not only "today"—she is "tomorrow."

Victor Hugo's windows for Halston are the most irreverent in New York. Gene Moore's displays at Tiffany & Co. are exquisite gems of creation as stunning and eye-catching as the jewels he is displaying. Colin Birch, visual display director at Bonwit Teller, leans toward space and sparseness. He often leaves a window empty. In the total concept exhibited in a bank of windows, the empty space is part of the design.

As "new-wave" window design spreads throughout the country, the question "What kind of art is it?" is hotly debated in some circles. It is called "immediate" art, "popular" art, "decorative" and "disposable" art. More than anything else, it is entertainment and the art controversy matters little as long as it attracts an audience. Show business and retailing have gone hand in hand for many years.

Whether it is merchandising, advertising, promotions, displays, or personnel, the competition is fierce to find and hang on to that vague element and combination of elements that make a store a "must." The efforts are kept top secret—"Does Macy's Tell Gimbels?"

Stores go in and out of fashion like clothes go in and out of fashion. In the 1940s, during the heyday of store president Dorothy Shaver, if you didn't buy something at Lord & Taylor—forget it— you hadn't been to New York. Macy's was once a tourist attraction on a par with the Empire State Building and the Statue of Liberty, then slipped from the top limelight for several years. Macy's is once again in the running and coming up fast on the west side. Bloomingdale's still holds the lead. Good Lord, look at what happened when Queen Elizabeth and Prince Philip came to New York in 1976! Someone turned bloomin' Lexington Avenue around just because *the Queen wanted to go to Bloomingdale's*, and what with protocol and all that jazz, Her Royal Highness *had* to alight from the right side of her limousine.

No one knows where or when the name "Bloomie's" originated. It is generally believed to have been a neighborhood expression—a convenient shortening of Bloomingdale's. As Bloomingdale's gathered momentum during the 1960s as the "in" store, the name was used to convey familiarity among the chic young east side New Yorkers who had arrived in the area. The staffs of the advertising, publicity, and public relations departments tuned in their sharp ears and realized that "Bloomie's" was in the lingo as an affectionate nickname in New Yorkese and they began to promote it along with a palsy-walsy, kid-next-door image.

In preparing for the store's centennial celebration in 1972, a new type was created for the logo by artist Massimo Vignelli with vice-president of advertising Joan Glynn and Bill Berta. They used lower case *b*. The l along with an overlay of the *double o's* formed a subtle 100 out of the l-o-o. The design was youthful and informal but sophisticated. Not surprisingly the type was named Blooming-type. To carry the fun friend image a step further BLOOMIE'S is printed on underpants and T-shirts so that customers can wear the proof of their favoritism emblazoned across their BOOBS and BUMS—you can't get more intimate than *that*! The idea that one can get "addicted" to Bloomingdale's and turn into a BLOOMIE'S "junkie" is the result of a serious campaign aimed at the youth market and their drug-oriented jargon. The message is that Bloom-ingdale's 106-year-old store is young and swinging. BLOOMIE'S un-derstands kids. To an age group that is strongly influenced by peer pressure BLOOMIE'S is a *peer*. It is a fine line to tread in order not to offend or lose young-marrieds, middle-class, middle-aged house-wives and other regular customers. But Bloomingdale's manages to tread softly and carry a big stock—and wear many hats.

These young customers are called "Saturday's Generation." Bloomie's lets it be known that it is "with *it*," where *"it's* at," and where *"it's* gonna be." "We can spin on a dime," says Peggy Healy, vice-president–public relations, as she explains how Bloomingdale's keeps abreast with the fast-changing fads and fan-cies of fickle youth. She defines Bloomingdale's further by adding, "We're the sizzle on the steak." Whatever they are and whatever it is—it works.

One evening I was seated next to a young woman on an uptown Madison Avenue bus. She was in her early twenties, but she wig-gled and fidgeted like a three-year-old. We were caught in the traffic.

"Do you have the time?" she asked.

"It's five-fifteen," I said, checking my watch.

"Oh, damn!" she said. "I'll never make it. I knew I should have taken the subway."

"Meeting someone?" I asked.

"No, but I've *got* to get to Bloomie's before it closes."

"Picking up something?"

"No, no, no," she whispered with a touch of secrecy and hys-teria. "I'm a Bloomie's addict. I'm not into drugs, but I s'pose it's like needing a fix. If I don't get to Bloomie's at least once a week, I get sick. I mean *physically* sick. I throw up."

I tried to shift away and wished there would be a break in the traffic for both our sakes.

She made statements come out like questions. "I read in *The Wall Street Journal* about this poor girl whose husband got transferred to Los Angeles? They bought a cute house and everything, but she was off the wall being that far away from Bloomie's. She left her husband and came back to New York."

"That seems a bit extreme," I said.

"*The Wall Street Journal* wouldn't lie! I can understand it. Look at me! I'm a basket case. I really got screwed this week. I couldn't get up there on my lunch hour and I can't make it tomorrow. That's the best time—Saturday. *Everybody* cruises Bloomie's on Saturday."

"Couldn't you try a withdrawal? Go to Saks or Bonwit's once in a while?"

"You don't understand. I'm *hooked.* I suppose to you a store is just a store—a place to shop? Bloomie's is a part of my life! It's like a good friend or family. It means a lot to me. It's kind of like church. Only I don't go anymore. Or my shrink. I can be all uptight. Then I get to Bloomie's and I begin to get it all together. It's a security blanket maybe? You know, there's so much crap around and everything changes so fast—it makes me feel good just to go there. It gives me a sense of—of—" She groped for a word.

"Continuity?" I asked.

"That's it! Continuity. The whole bloody world will probably be blown to bits, but Bloomie's will always be there. It always *has* been there. I love that place. There's never been another store like it anywhere. I mean a store that people were involved with emotionally, that they really *cared* about."

She was wrong. But then she was very young.

"There's a real mystique about the place. It's a phenomenon— it's almost as if it were alive."

She had bought the whole package. The whole ball of wax, so to speak. But perhaps having faith in Bloomie's was better than having no faith at all.

The bus came to a halt and she looked at the street sign. "Oh, my God, if I run, I think I'll make it. See ya."

When the door opened, she leaped to the curb in one long stride and was off and running. Running toward clothes and food, and furniture and friends. Running toward church and home and peace of mind. In the big, lost, lonely, alienating city of New York, the young girl was running toward hope, toward love, toward Bloomie's.

There is with any kind of fanaticism the danger of backlash. Recently a new superstar was being interviewed about her phenomenal success and the attributes and attitudes that were responsible for it. After listing talent, good looks, hard work, free thinking, and individuality, she added, "*and* I wouldn't be caught *dead* in Bloomingdale's."

In Texas, a visit to Neiman-Marcus is as *de rigueur* as visits to the Vatican, the Louvre, and the Tower of London are in Europe. While "visiting" a store is not the same as being attached to it, it is a beginning.

I went to Neiman-Marcus in Dallas when I was on a lecture tour in the southwest a few years ago and I can honestly say that I was *not* hooked. I had read somewhere that "Neiman-Marcus is a state of mind. Almost a state of grace." It may have been my own state of mind or the pressure of time that caused me to miss something. I had been on the road for a week. I was jet-laggy, frumpy, and frazzled and I had an upcoming dinner date at the Petroleum Club with an "old beau" I hadn't seen since college. He was driving up from Waco—you get the picture? I quite literally crawled into Neiman-Marcus's beauty salon and whimpered, "Help me." They certainly did go to work putting me together. Shampoo, set, manicure, pedicure, facial, makeup—the whole *enchalada*. They pampered me and when I left, everyone said, "Hurry on back now, ya heah?" It was all very pleasant and revitalizing, but no bells rang. No colored lights flashed. Maybe I expected too much. The magic of Neiman-Marcus didn't *grab* me at that time, but it did a few years later when I met a delightful member of the Marcus family. A series of very unusual events led up to that meeting. It didn't happen in Texas either. It happened in Nepal—of all places!

One evening in 1973, I was sitting in the Yin and Yang Hash House in Katmandu, Nepal, smoking a joint, when the Baroness

Garnett Stackelberg said to me, "Nan, do you know where the
powder room is?"

"*Powder* room?" I gasped and choked and exhaled the sweet-
tasting smoke. I had been holding my breath. I'd heard that was
proper grass-smoking form and I was trying to be blasé.

"Yes," she answered. "The powder room. The *ladies'* room."
She looked uncomfortable, but then all our party did in the ambience of this low-ceilinged dive. People appeared to be one-dimen-
sional. Colored lights fluttered and the scene jerked and flickered
like a silent movie. The music was unbearably loud. The banquette
around our low table was hard and constructed for small people
with more flexible limbs than ours. The air was as thick as an inver-
sion and as pungent as an herbal tea. I knew that somewhere in a
corner Sidney Greenstreet and Peter Lorre were sitting in rumpled
white suits in peacock chairs, being sinister. The atmosphere was
heavy with *sinister.*

We were six who had originally been on a press junket with other
journalists and several celebrities to India, for the inauguration of
the Oberoi-Sheraton Hotel in Bombay. There had been additional
Oberoi galas in Delhi. Then we few had come up to Nepal. Besides
myself and the Baroness, a travel and society columnist from
Washington, D.C., there were peppy, outspoken Millie Considine,
whose husband, Bob Considine, had returned to the States; Dale
Remington, president of the New York Travel Writers' Association and Kaleidoscope, Inc., a radio and television producing company; the young wife of the manager of the Sheraton-Kuwait; and
a freelance writer on assignment for *The Christian Science Monitor!* We were a far cry from your run-of-the-mill potheads. So
much so that after ordering beers from the sinister waiter, we had
stared naively at the stash of flimsy, rolled cigarettes and strange
brown lumps he had left in the middle of the table. Suddenly Millie
had squealed, "Ah, chocolates!" and popped a piece of raw hashish into her mouth and gobbled it like it was a Lady Godiva bon-
bon, before anyone could stop her. As for myself, the way things
were shaping up, I decided this was as good a time and place as any
to try marijuana. And I lit up.

Above the amplified rock and roll, again Garnett yelled, "Nan,
where is the ladies' room?"

Garnett Stackelberg is an American married to a Middle European baron. She is a pretty, feminine woman, given to a frothy kind
of elegance. While most of us were in jeans or dressed casually for
this hash house caper, Garnett was wearing an immaculate white
linen sheath, sprinkled with pink and yellow flowers. It was topped
by a flowing coat, the color of tea roses. Her ash-blond hair was
wrapped in acres of tulle and looked like a strawberry soufflé. She
wore pink silk pumps, which she absolutely refused to remove and
leave on the pile of *chappals* (flat, water buffalo-hide sandals) that
were stacked up by the entrance. (I couldn't say that I blamed her
for *that*.)

Garnett is used to garden parties and drawing-room receptions.
She is very much at home in embassies—both foreign and American. As a matter of fact, this particular afternoon, we had had tea
with our United States Ambassador, Carol Laise, at the American
Embassy, thanks to Garnett's connections. She had high hopes of
paying a call on King Birendra and his wife at the palace. Here in
the din and clang of the Yin and Yang, she was not only *not* comfortable, she was downright *miserable*.

"Garnett," I said gently, choosing my words with care. "This is
not Washington and the White House. This is Katmandu and a
hash house. A dope den," I added, trying to sound sinister. "I
would suggest that you ask the guide to take you back to the Soaltee Hotel."

"*Where is the ladies' room?*" she persisted.

I gave up. "It would be my guess," I said, taking intermittent
puffs, "that it is through those cretonne curtains." It was a fair
shot since the curtained doorway was the only exit, other than the
entrance.

Before I could move, the Baroness had climbed up onto the banquette seat, placed her hand on my head for balance, and was
walking over me. As I was enveloped by her coat, it was like being
immersed in a mass of pink cotton candy. I shielded the joint to
keep from setting her on fire. A stiletto heel gouged deep into my
thigh. Jumping down, she turned and pleaded, "Will you *please*
come with me?"

I glanced toward the frayed curtains, inhaled deeply, and answered, "*No way!*" She stalked off through the doorway.

Within seconds, she was back. Her face was ashen. The pink

pumps were wet and stained. Like a kid leaping into a swimming hole, she clutched her hand over her nose and mouth. *"Where is that guide?"* Her muffled shout carried over the electronic cacophony.

Meanwhile—back at the banquette—Millie Considine was beginning to richochet off the den walls. *The Christian Science Monitor* person was falling into his beer. Yvonne Hunnold seemed to have drifted off to far-away Kuwait. Dale Remington, in slow motion, was going somewhere to find the guide. I was stoned. It was a memorable Katmandu experience!

The next day, I flew into the bush to spend a few days at the Tiger Tops Hotel and take an elephant safari through the jungle. When I returned to the Soaltee Hotel, everyone had left except Dale. We met in the bar for a drink. Suddenly, the elephant-riding or the Nepalese martinis, or both, caught up with me as we talked about the past few days. Loud, raucous laughter came in fits and starts. "Oh, my God! Didn't Garnett *know* about Nepalese plumbing? Or the lack of it?" I asked. "But why *me?* I must either look like I'm in discomfort or like I'm terribly relieved. All my life I've been asked about the location of the ladies' room. How am *I* supposed to know? There *must* be something about me. But the powder room in a Katmandu hash house—that has got to take the cake!" We whooped and laughed until the tears came.

A voice called from behind us. "You two sound like you're having fun. Where are you folks from?"

We collected ourselves and answered, "We're from New York."

"We're from Texas. Would you like to join us?"

We stepped back to the adjoining booth and sat down with two attractive, very chic women. One said, "I'm Sally Marcus from Dallas, and this is my sister, Mildred Buckingham, from Fort Worth." We introduced ourselves and I asked, subtly, "Sally *Marcus?* From *Dallas?*" Implying a question she had probably been asked more times than I had been asked about ladies' rooms. "Yes," she answered, smiling, "Marcus. Mrs. Herbert, *junior.* From Dallas. We have a little shop down there."

Sally Marcus and her sister, Mildred Buckingham, and I crossed paths several times while touring India. Through our shared experiences we became friends. In the fall of 1976, I was met by Sally Marcus at the Dallas-Fort Worth Airport. We whisked downtown, into the Republic Bank Building, up in an elevator to a high floor and through a door marked Stanley Marcus—Vice-president Carter Hawley Hale Stores, Inc. Consultant. As I was about to meet the personage, the "legend," as Stanley Marcus is often called, I had a mad moment wishing I had worn my old Balenciaga suit. Then he might have started the conversation with "Ah, I see you are wearing a Balenciaga." This would immediately establish me as a woman of fashion and good taste. I would answer, "Yes." Unfortunately, although the suit has held up well, my waistline hasn't. So it hangs in the back of my closet. I decided not to say, "I *own* a Balenciaga suit."

The offices were a fantasy of plants and eclectic art. There were paintings, portraits, sculpture, and objets d'art. There were African masks, shields, and fertility figures. Mr. Marcus, or "Mr. Stanley" as he is called in the retailing tradition of adding Mr. to the first name, is charming and erudite. Aside from being a man of great taste who knows fashion, he is a master salesman, merchandiser, executive, and a superb showman. The surroundings were flamboyant and theatrical.

We talked about his book. He signed my copy of *Minding the Store.* We talked about my book. We talked about his store and he gave me names of people to see. I tried to gather something of the essence that makes the Neiman-Marcus magic. He said, "I have the simplest tastes. I am easily satisfied with the best." It was a remark his Aunt Carrie Neiman *and* Oscar Wilde had made before him.

We returned to Sally's to lunch in a bright, sunny room with a garden of flower-upholstered furniture and masses of hanging ferns. The room was as cheery as Sally Marcus. We talked of India and Nepal and our chance meeting there.

In the afternoon we called on Sally's mother-in-law, Mrs. Herbert Marcus, Senior. Off of her living room was a greenhouse, a mass of blossoms and vegetation. Mrs. Marcus holds the title of vice-president in charge of horticulture with the responsibility of plant maintenance supervision in all stores. Mrs. Marcus was in her nineties. She was very chic. She was very sharp as she spoke of "her boys," Stanley, Larry, Eddie, and Sally's late husband, Herbert, Junior. (Edward Marcus died in Apirl 1977, at the age of sixty-seven.) She was a bit annoyed with Stanley in particular.

Mrs. Marcus had a companion who usually accompanied her when she went on errands, but this morning she had a small chore at the bank and it was unnecessary for the woman to go. Her chauffeur drove her to the Republic Bank and escorted her inside. She conducted her business, went into the main building, took the elevator, and went up to see Stanley. The secretary was amazed when she walked in alone. Stanley was distressed. The chauffeur was to blame. "Nonsense," Mrs. Marcus said. They all implied she had done something sneaky and said, "Now, Mrs. Marcus—" "Now, Mother—" Who did they think they were—telling *her* where to go and when and with whom?

Those boys should have known their mother. They should have known that you don't mess with a Texas pioneer. You don't mess with Minnie Marcus. She had, after all, seen it all.

Minnie Marcus was born Minnie Lichtenstein, in Dallas, in 1882. Her parents had immigrated from Russia. Growing up, Minnie had a joyous time as one of the most popular Jewish girls in Dallas. She met Herbert Marcus, but she was a belle and saw no reason to get married. Also, her family objected to Herbert's German background and although he was working in Sanger's Department Store, he hardly had a penny to his name—and what he had, he spent on his elegant clothes. But Minnie had met a will as strong as her own. In 1902 she and Herbert married. They borrowed money for a honeymoon.

The couple lived with Minnie's family and then moved into a boarding house. When Minnie was pregnant with Stanley, Herbert Marcus applied for a raise. It was granted—$1.87½ a month. He rejected it, quit the job, and joined his brother-in-law, Al Neiman, and his sister, Carrie, in a sales promotion venture in Atlanta. Carrie Marcus had been working in A. Harris department store when she had met and married Al.

By 1907, the Atlanta operation was so successful that they were offered two alternatives. They could swap the advertising agency for stock and a Missouri franchise in the fledgling Coca-Cola company or sell for $25,000 cash. They took the cash. In the light of

what happened with Coca-Cola over the years, Stanley Marcus remarks that Neiman-Marcus was founded on "bad business judgment."

The threesome, averaging twenty-six years of age, returned to
Dallas determined to open their own quality store. Dallas was a
boisterous, wide-open cotton and railroad town. The oil boom had
not yet happened. Fort Worth was the Cow Town, so called after
Chicago meat packers opened the slaughterhouses there. Fort
Worth is amused by this moniker today as residents point out the
cultural attributes—the Amon Carter Art Museum, the Kimbell
Museum, and the Van Cliburn Piano Competitions.

With the $25,000 and additional borrowed money, the intrepid
trio rented a two-story building at the corner of Elm and Murphy.
They spent $12,000 remodeling it with mahogany paneling, deep
carpets, and fine fixtures. Al and Carrie set off for New York with
$17,000 to buy fashionable merchandise. Dallas in 1907 had a popu-
lation of 86,000. There were 222 saloons and nobody counted the
other "commercial" establishments. The tough, drab cotton town,
filled with tough, hard-driving people, seemed an unlikely market
for their finery.

There is the story of a traveling salesman from New York who
blew into town on opening day and saw the crowd around the
store. He saw dresses in the windows that he had seen on Fifth
Avenue and furs from Revillon Frères. "What the hell is this?" he
asked. "This is Neiman-Marcus," someone answered. "It'll never
last!" the drummer barked and walked away. He wasn't alone with
these feelings.

The store did last. It struggled through the economic panics and
grew steadily until the spring of 1913 when a fire destroyed the entire building and all its contents.

A new store was constructed on the present Dallas downtown
Neiman-Marcus site at Main and Ervay streets. There was another
crisis in 1928. Al and Carrie Neiman were divorced. Al's interest
was bought by his former brother-in-law and he left for New York.
This storm was weathered for the most part because Carrie Neiman, who was a beautiful woman, was a brilliant buyer with an uncanny instinct for fashion. She never remarried and devoted the
rest of her life to the store. She became the taste and fashion arbiter of Dallas. She died in 1952.

Since the Marcuses could not afford a maid, Minnie took her young son with her when she went down to the store. While she shopped, she left Stanley playing with spools and thread on the floor of the alterations department. Mr. Marcus has said he began his store experience at the age of two years. With the new store and with Al Neiman gone, it was a piece of luck that Stanley, who had graduated from Harvard Business School by that time, joined the firm and his genius began to bloom. In the meantime, Minnie had done her job well. She had produced exactly what every growing retail store needed—she gave birth to three more sons.

In 1968, Neiman-Marcus became a subsidiary of Carter Hawley Hale Stores, Inc. With new capital available, Neiman-Marcus stores have been sprouting up around the country faster than mung beans. Richard Marcus, Stanley's son, was appointed president of Neiman-Marcus in 1973. Stanley Marcus became executive vice-president of Carter Hawley Hale, Inc. Recently, at the age of seventy-two, he retired from that position. With fifty years of retailing expertise behind him, Stanley Marcus became a consultant. One of his major clients is Leber Katz Partners, the Neiman-Marcus advertising agency.

Stanley Marcus, having tasted literary success with the publication of *Minding the Store* in 1974, is working on another book. The subject is the best of the best. Recently in New York he interviewed Dr. Aldo Gucci on the subject. The meeting of these flamboyant merchants, both in their seventies, was akin to a summit conference. Both gentlemen have imposed their superb taste, fashion expertise, respect for quality, and their showmanship on several generations of shoppers throughout the world. They are men of international fame, monumental charm, humor, and ego. Neiman-Marcus, however, the purveyor of "the best," does not handle Gucci merchandise. In the southwest it is sold through Frost Brothers. A fashion authority in Rome for the "Alta Moda Italiana" fashion week explained, "Some years ago Dr. Aldo and Mr. Stanley had a little spat." In view of these particulars and the personalities of these retailing giants, the meeting can be considered *historical*. It will be duly reported in Stanley Marcus's new book which is expected to be ready for publication in 1979.

In view of the *spat*, it was amusing when an executive at the Fort Worth opening, pointing out to the crowd the flags flying over the

new store, said, "We have the flags of the United States—Texas—
Fort Worth and—Gucci!—the only flag he ever designed." An assistant whispered in his ear. The man corrected himself, "Er—I
mean—*Pucci!*" Dr. Aldo, himself a lover of flags, would have been
delighted.

Many ingredients have gone into creating the Neiman-Marcus
mystique. The fine fashions, the exquisite china, linens, and gift-
wares, and the imaginative gift wraps are all part of the package.
But what makes Neiman-Marcus uniquely different from stores in
California, Chicago, and New York are the innate qualities of
friendliness, humor, and exuberance in Texans, both sales personnel and customers. You are rather apt to find yourself if not exactly
disclosing your life story, at least giving your reasons for being in
Texas when you make a purchase at Neiman-Marcus. It has something to do with the sound of your voice. Speak to a salesman or
woman and more than likely they will ask, "You visitin'?" After
you've gotten it all straight about where you are from and why,
they will probably say, "Well, I hope you are havin' fuh-n." Fun
holds a very high priority in Texas.

For many of the country's rich, famous, and beautiful, Neiman-
Marcus is The Greenhouse, the beauty resort operated in conjunc-
tion with Charles of the Ritz and the Great Southwest Corporation
in Arlington, Texas, between Dallas and Fort Worth. For most
guests, a visit to the beauty and health center is serious business,
but occasionally there is a native guest who keeps it all in perspective.

I have a Texas friend who spent a week at the spa, but requests
anonymity. "I'm persona non grata at the Greenhouse," she said,
with pride. "I gave a party. Everyone gets so self-involved, I decided it ought to be more friendly, so my last night there I had a
party. Everybody loves a party! I had glasses, lime, and tonic sent
to my room. I had one *tiny* bottle of vodka, one, mind you, from
the airplane. I was going to dole drops out with an eyedropper to
twenty people. A staff member came in and raised hell, 'No alcohol!' So I emptied the vodka down the basin right in front of her
and filled the bottle with water. Then I taped invitations to everybody's door and in the late afternoon, they all came to my room.

"I had the Inn of the Six Flags, the motel in Arlington, send over
the band. Well, the party got goin' pretty good. The band was

playin' their banjos and jumpin' up and down on the bed. Some of the ladies got squiffy on that water—just seein' that little vodka bottle. And we danced and yelled and hollered and whooped—Texas style! We had a baw—ll! Goddamnit, honey, I'd been so bored and—do you think that for two thousand dollars a week, I was gonna be *bored*?''

The Neiman-Marcus Christmas Catalogue has spread the mystique throughout the country. The publication is read by thousands nationally. The "His" and "Hers" gifts have become symbols of Texas wealth, humor, pizazz, and exuberance throughout the world. Over the past fifty years, these gifts have included matching airplanes, producing oil wells, registered Herefords, a matched set of Kohinoor diamonds, a year's maid and butler service from the Duke and Duchess of Windsor, an archeological safari in search of the remains of Allocaurus in Utah, a 48×36×18-inch $3,500 N-Bar-M king-sized Mouse Ranch with round-up tweezers and a branding iron with indelible ink, matching Greek kraters (double-handled urns) dating from the fourth century B.C. and, in 1977, in keeping with the times, matching power-producing windmills for $16,000 each, exclusive of installation, to name a few.

To honor the fiftieth anniversary of the Christmas book, in 1977, a Lear jet carrying two Neiman-Marcus executives, traveled more than 8,000 miles in three days delivering leather-bound personalized copies to selected members of the press in cities where Neiman-Marcus had stores, as well as New York, Los Angeles, and San Francisco. This kind of extravaganza should reassure some of the old-guard customers who have feared changes under the Carter Hawley Hale regime. There are still enough Marci (the popular plural of Marcus—like Lazari is plural for more than one member of the Lazarus family of Lazarus, Shillito, and Federated Department Stores in Ohio). Richard Marcus is in Dallas; Lawrence and his son, Cary, are in Houston, and Mr. Stanley is nearby. Neither *the state of mind, the state of grace*, the hoopla, nor the fun of shopping, gift giving, and gifts themselves are likely to diminish. On the contrary, with the new store openings, Neiman-Marcus, like everything else in Texas, will just be *big*.

The International Fortnight promotions conducted in cooperation with foreign countries and industries are a Neiman-Marcus institution which originated in 1957. England, Denmark, Switzerland, Austria, South America, Italy, and the Far East have been honored with representative decor and merchandise throughout the store. Organizations in the city have participated with concerts, art exhibits, film festivals, theatrical events, and many other special activities during the two-week events.

A gala benefit serves as a kick-off for the Fortnight. This event raises in the neighborhood of $100,000 for Dallas charitable and cultural organizations. The theme for the 1977 Fortnight was "La France Inconnue"—the France no ones knows. It was the fourth time France had been honored by a Fortnight. Old Love Field was transformed for the occasion, including the installation of Regine's, the world-famous discotheque. There was paté and can-can girls, gendarmes and champagne. The Duc and Duchesse d'Orleans and Ambassador Jacques Kosciusko-Morizet and his wife were there. And, of course, Régine!

Past highlights of Fortnights have been the presentation of Sophia Loren at the World Trade Center when the event celebrated Italy and a Guinness Pub that was created in the Junior Department during the Irish Fortnight. "That was a *combination*—the Irish and the Texans!" an executive commented. "The Pub was the swingin'est place in town. We went through more than a hundred kegs of Guinness and ended up serving Schlitz. Some people just stayed all day."

Production of the twenty-one Fortnights has laid the groundwork for the seven store openings since 1971. Tom Alexander, senior vice-president—marketing and sales promotion—remarked: "I'm beginning to feel like Pearl Mesta. Everybody loves a party. There's no question about that. But stores have to be careful. It can be self-defeating. This business of store parties is getting to be some kind of competition. You can bet that the fellow who wins two years in a row is going to be out of business. Everybody keeps asking if we are going to give a better party than Bloomingdale's gave in Washington. I don't know. It may be better. It may be worse. We're business, not the social whirl. We're going to have a party the way Neiman-Marcus has a party." And to give a regional paraphrase to the famous old "Nobody but Nobody" Gimbels slogan—"Nadie pero Nadie" can throw a better fiesta than Neiman-Marcus.

A week before the November 1977 opening of the Washington

store, Mrs. Herbert Marcus celebrated her ninety-fifth birthday. The family suggested that she be checked by her doctor after all the excitement, and have his confirmation that she could attend the opening. She agreed to do so.

The doctor pronounced her in good health but suggested that she take it easy for a while in light of the birthday celebration.

Minnie Marcus looked him straight in the eye and announced, "I'm going to Washington."

"Now wait a minute," the doctor said.

"I'm going to open the new store."

"On whose orders?" the doctor asked.

"Mine!" Minnie Marcus replied.

She has never missed a store opening in seventy years. And she wasn't about to now, just because of some birthday. Like I said, you don't want to mess around with Texans.

At the opening of Neiman-Marcus in the Mazza Gallerie in Washington, Minnie Marcus was seated near the entrance. She looked exquisite in a purple silk Oscar de la Renta gown. She wore a brilliant green satin stole and a perfectly matched strand of pearls. "I wore this last week to my ninety-fifth birthday party," she announced proudly to well-wishers. She was surrounded by her sons Stanley and Lawrence, their wives, and her grandchildren.

The party was a benefit for the National Symphony Orchestra and a large contingent of that group played appropriate music like "I Could Have Danced All Night" in the Gallerie.

The $35 million building had been delayed for four years by a zoning fight which cost an estimated $48 million in lost sales. But there was little evidence of the dispute as diplomats and Washington socialites and nearly a thousand guests toured the store and perused the merchandise. There were six bars, innumerable buffets, and a dance orchestra and dance floor on the third floor. The floor had been permanently installed for future occasions.

There were Texas touches but they were subdued. A masked pair of sequined cowboys mimed and held signs directing guests to "branch water" and the "dance hall." There were ten-gallon hats on a hatstand in the men's department. Blue jeans in junior wear had the map of Texas sewn on the seat. One bar was stocked solely with Lone Star beer. A chef mixed a barrel full of fresh raw beef into steak tartar—a large cannister of chili powder was used with discretion. "Corn dogs"—frankfurters fried in a cornmeal coating and served on a stick—were tried and often discreetly deposited in ashtrays. There were masses of yellow balloons and yellow roses. My son Carey, who escorted me to this blast, went off on a tour in pursuit of the beautiful young women who seemed to be everywhere.

He returned with the information that they were Texas girls indeed, and "Security." They were carrying walkie-talkies in the folds of their beautiful gowns. He wasn't sure about shootin' irons. He had also found the Neiman-Marcus definitive statement—the dessert. On a third-floor buffet table in a six-foot-long clear plastic container was a Texas landscape—shredded chocolate covered a rich fruity pudding, "English trifle." In the center was a raspberry lake of sauce. Surrounding it and pumping the pink liquid were four twelve-inch-high oil derricks. A distinguished government servant sounded like a Longhorn rooter as he stood transfixed by the circulating raspberry liquid and said, "Well, I'll be goddamned!"

On Monday morning, Minnie Marcus was at her place to officially open the store. There was nothing so prosaic as ribbon cutting for the occasion. "Ribbon cutting isn't Neiman-Marcus," Tom Alexander explained. Neiman-Marcus has a sixteen-foot-high oil derrick it uses for these openings and a liquid, symbolic of the area, is pumped through a clear plexiglass pipe. In Bal Harbour they pumped orange juice. "Actually, it was Tang with a lot of extra coloring," Tom Alexander said. "Orange juice turned out to be the wrong color." In Atlanta, they pumped Coca-Cola, and in St. Louis, Budweiser beer spewed forth. "In Chicago we couldn't find an appropriate liquid, so neon butterflies, the Neiman-Marcus trademark, fluttered up the tube." A Neiman-Marcus fragrance, Wildcat II, was struck and pumped from the well when the Fort Worth store was opened. A shifting wind on that still, 90-degree morning was blamed for drenching the guest of honor, Princess Romanoff, with the scent. "Maybe it was a little heavy for nine A.M., but we figured if it was good enough for Neiman-Marcus, it was good enough for the Princess," said one executive.

Neiman-Marcus has had problems with its *own brand* perfumes. Herbert Marcus, Senior, was blind in his later years. His son, Herbert, Junior, served as his eyes. One morning when they arrived in the store, the elder Mr. Marcus put his nose in the air, sniffed, and asked, "What the hell is *that*?" "It's our Neiman-Marcus fragrance," his son answered. "No it's not! *Get it out of here!*" Mr. Marcus bellowed. That time the perfume did not go up. It went *down* the tube, along with thousands of dollars of development money.

On the crisp November morning in Washington, Mrs. Herbert Marcus pressed the button to activate the oil well, and up through the pipe, exploding like a blowout, came red tape. "I liked Florida," Mrs. Marcus said. "I liked the orange juice the best."

Even the 100-degree August weather couldn't subdue the Fort Worth opening. It was a real folderol, a no-holds-barred-pull-out-all-the-stops Texas *hoedown* from beginning to end. Part of the excitement was generated by the traditional Dallas-Fort Worth rivalry. Some of it came from the store's staff who, in spite of all the work, were thrilled to move the mile and a half from the small Preston Center store to the beautiful 120,000-square-foot store in Ridgmar Mall.

"Tom Barnett," Mr. Alexander explained, "besides being the manager, is a cheerleader, minister, and revivalist. His store's *esprit de corps* is incredible. The staff and customers would follow him to the ends of the earth."

Barnett would not agree. He credits his personnel with the store's success and expansion. "For example, I've got three drivers—the best PR people in the world. If a package is ticketed with the wrong address, that package will get to the right person. Those drivers know everyone's correct address. *And* they'll chew out the salesperson who made the mistake."

Way back, Tom decided Christmas Eve was tough on the drivers. They didn't finish delivering the last packages until midnight and after. "They have families too, you know," Barnett said, "and there is *nothing* lonelier or colder than a closed store." The Barnetts came to the store late in the evening. Ginny Barnett brought her famous shrimp dip. Tom set up a bar and when the drivers came in, they had a party. Since then, other employees have joined them and it has become a tradition to be on hand to cheer in the late-working drivers. "It's a lot of fun!" Barnett said. Ginny agreed. "Everybody loves a party!"

It was not always fun. Barnett remembers when he was put in charge of the little Preston Center store over twenty years ago with no managerial experience. "I didn't know anything—not even where the bathroom was. Mr. Stanley came, looked, liked what he saw. But we weren't doing any business and he wanted to know why. *I* didn't know, but I thought of something I had heard buyers say on slow days. I said, 'Mr. Stanley, the people are coming in, but they just *aren't buying*.' He looked at me and that was when I learned what retailing was. He said, 'Tom, until you see 'em walk in here *naked*, they're buying clothes somewhere.' "

A few years ago, Fort Worth had six or eight inches of snow. About fifteen employees made it to work, but business was slow. Mid-morning Mr. Barnett received a call from a reporter, who said, "I hear you have a million-dollar 'snow lady' in your parking lot." He went to look. "So help me Hannah," Tom said, "there she was—the staff had used real diamonds for eyes and a nose. Covered her with paper and dressed her in a $16,000 mink coat."

His assistant said at that moment, "Tom, you didn't think we'd dress her up like Secondhand Rose, did you?"

The story reached the wire services and the Neiman-Marcus Fort Worth "snow lady" was pictured in newspapers and news magazines all over the country.

I flew into Fort Worth for the August pre-store-opening weekend. I rented a car and drove to the Green Oaks Inn located at Camp Bowie Boulevard and Highway 80, directly across from the Ridgmar Mall and the new Neiman-Marcus. The motel's giant highway sign read: "NEIMAN WHO? THERE GOES THE NEIGHBORHOOD!" It set the friendly, folksy tone for the two days of parties. Waiting for me was an invitation to the store gala, themed "A Lot of Night Music" and benefiting the Van Cliburn International Quadrennial Piano Competition. There was also a mimeographed sheet which said: "*Hi!* And welcome to Fort Worth and an exciting weekend." There was an invitation to pre-gala cocktails at the home of Martha and Elton Hyder, hosted by the Hyders and Marsland and Dick Moncrief. There was an invitation to Sunday lunch at the home of Mr. and Mrs. William Fuller. There were maps and a schedule for "our fabulous museums!" At the Kimbell Art Museum was the Tokugawa Collection of No Robes and Masks at the Fort Worth Art Museum, "America 1976"; at the

We Tillson girls, Marion and I, ready for shopping in the "City." Our hats, coats and gloves matched until "Our" Miss Rose at I. Magnin turned traitor.

The Vermont marble facade of the new Magnin's on Union Square completed 1948. One block from Miss Rose's store on Grant and Geary. (*Courtesy I. Magnin & Co.*)

Dispatcher with signaling castenet and uniformed operators at Livingston Bros., the last family-owned store of its size in San Francisco—1935. (*Courtesy Livingston's*)

"The Ville de Paris" in San Francisco Bay — 1850

The brig *La Ville de Paris* in San Francisco Bay in 1850, from a painting by Marius Herbert Roberts. The ship served as the store and goods were sold directly from the deck.

Bullock's Wilshire and Wilshire Boulevard, Los Angeles, at the time of the 1929 opening of the "modern" art-filled store, known as *Winett's Folly*. (*Credit: Beck Studio*)

Charles La Salle painting *Bisbee Massacre*, the incident perpetrated in 1883 at Castaneda and Goldwater. A gift to the store from Senator and Mrs. Barry M. Goldwater. (*Courtesy Goldwater's—Credit: Douglas K. Jones Assoc.*)

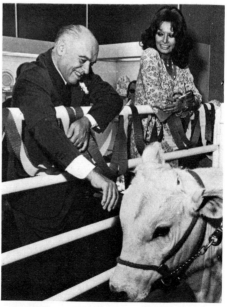

Sophia Loren, star of Neiman-Marcus' Italian Fortnight—1975—and her husband, Carlo Ponti, inspecting the "Bull in the China Shop." (*Courtesy Neiman-Marcus*)

Marshall Field's opening day 1907. The aisle and rotunda decorated as a "Temple of Mercury." (*Courtesy Marshall Field & Co.*)

Interior view of the eight-story atrium Renaissance Center, Detroit. The mega-structure contains a seventy-three-story hotel, office buildings, and a vertical shopping center, The World of Shops. (*Courtesy: Renaissance Center Partnership*)

The first store of Lord & Taylor, 47 Catherine Street. Founded 1826

The first store of Lord & Taylor founded in 1826 at 47 Catherine Street, New York. (*Courtesy Lord & Taylor*)

B. Altman & Co. April 17, 1877. The "New Palace of Trade" corner of Sixth Avenue and Eighteenth Street in the heart of New York's "Ladies Mile." (*Courtesy B. Altman & Co.*)

Hound Dog balloon floating past the "World's Largest Store," during Macy's world-famous Thanksgiving Day Parade. (*Courtesy R.H. Macy*)

Store founder Adam Gimbel's male descendants, five sons, ten grandsons, 1923. Front row from left: Louis, Charles, J. Oscar (grandson), Isaac, Daniel, Ellis, Bernard (grandson). Standing, from left: grandsons Louis, Ellis, Jr., Lee Adam, Richard, Frederick, Nathan Hamerburger, Jr., son of adopted "eighth Gimbel Brother," Adam, and Benedict, Jr. (*Courtesy Gimbel Bros., Milwaukee, Wisconsin*)

Gimbel tearoom waitresses in king-sized hairbows, black dresses and voluminous aprons with hostess and manager, 1904. Many were employed for twenty-five to forty years. (*Courtesy Gimbel Bros. Milwaukee*)

City of Paris Fashion display, 1923, featuring high-fashion hobble-skirt of post-WW I. Flowers were changed daily.

Stark I. Magnin window post-WW II, featuring Nettie Rosenstein high-fashion "New Look" of the 1940s. Roses were changed daily. (*Courtesy I. Magnin & Co.*)

Provocative "street-theater" window of the 1970s, created by Bloomingdale's *enfant terrible* of display, Candy Pratts, visual merchandising director. (*Credit: Jerry P. Melmed*)

At their Florence villa, turn of the century, straw merchant Gabriele Bucci, his wife, Elina, and son, Guccio, saddlemaker and founder of Guccio Gucci Soc. R.L., and father of present chairman Dr. Aldo Gucci. (*Courtesy Hamra Associates*)

"Buster" Jarrett, Bendel Doorman for over sixty years, and store president, Geraldine Stutz. (*Courtesy Henri Bendel*)

Saks Fifth Avenue 1978 high-fashion look. Karl Lagerfeld's black tulip dress for Chloe. (*Courtesy Saks Fifth Avenue*)

Bergdorf Goodman Fendi Fur benefit fashion show. Famous model Pat Cleveland on runway at B-G on the Plaza. (*Photo: Rose Hartman*)

Amon Carter Museum of Western Art, "Photographic Journey
Along Canadian Border." And a reminder, "Don't miss the Fort
Worth Water Gardens. *Have a Wonderful Weekend!*"

I had been joined by my friend Nancy Berry from Oklahoma
City. We dressed and went to the Hyders'. The indomitable Martha Hyder is the chairman and moving spirit behind the piano competition. Her husband Elton is an attorney. He was described by a
friend, lovingly, as *"somethin' else!"* Mrs. Moncrief was the ball
chairman.

The Hyders' house was *"somethin' else!"* Set back off the street
along a curved driveway, it was remodeled with entertaining in
mind. In the rear, the grounds filled with splendid oaks, ran down to
the Trinity River. Inside the house was a combination of periods
and styles and the multiple collections of the well-traveled Hyders.
There were superb paneled walls and magnificent Oriental rugs,
Impressionist and contemporary paintings—a Miró here, a Paul
Jenkins watercolor there. Tables were covered with malachite *objets d'art* and lapis lazuli bibelots. Couches were covered with hundreds of cushions—needlepoint, tufted, square, round, and oblong
ones. There were marble columns in the living room and African
sculpture and a French seventeenth-century Christ figure in the
dining room. There was a large Victorian birdcage with birds and a
painted leather chinoiserie screen. There were immense cachepots
with immense growing trees and there were immense bouquets of
flowers everywhere. There were porcelains and antique silver
pieces and ancient firearms. Elton picked up an aboriginal head and
said, "Look at what Martha did to some blonde she caught me
with!" Elton was a jovial man with a deep hearty laugh. "Have
you seen Martha's stoa?" he asked. "That's what we call it—a
stoa. Come on now. That's where all the fun is." And out we went,
through the French doors that led from a glassed-in sun room onto
the stoa—a large columned terrace overlooking the sweeping vista
of the river with the grounds of the River Crest Country Club in the
distance. The mariachis were playing and Elton stepped a few
steps of a Mexican hat dance and said, "Here's where the *fun* is!"

Nancy Berry knew Martha and Elton and everybody else in the
southwest. I knew Enid Nemy of *The New York Times* and Peter
Duchin of the Orchestra. Enid said there was a frenzy downtown
at the Hilton. A rhythm and blues group, the O'Jays, had arrived in

town. And the hotel manager had been chewing out the reception-
ist, "Goddamnit! You got a bunch of O'Jays up there with a bunch
of Van Cliburns!"

It didn't matter if you didn't know anybody when you went into
the Hyders' 'cause you sure got acquainted fast down there. The
big, handsome macho men gave you a little squeeze and said,
"Where you from, honey?" and "Who let this little Yankee in
here?" They'd fetch drinks and flip solid gold cigarette lighters. It
occurred to me that Texas men love to "take care of" women, and
if ever there were women who didn't need "taking care of," it was
Texas women. But it was all part of the game and everybody
played it well. Hell, honey, that was part of the *fun!*

There were huge silver bowls filled with huge flesh-pink
shrimp—over $400 worth. There were tiny stuffed tomatos and
miniature meatballs and glorious crab fingers. It was some party!
And then it was time to be off to the gala.

You can get away with *almost* anything in Texas. Hell, you can
drive to the supermarket, or even Neiman's, in a Volks, a Honda,
or a pickup truck. But for a party, an honest-to-God party—there is
an unwritten rule—*you get out the big stuff!* The flowing gowns, the
massive jewels, the gigantic cars. This is a *pahty,* darlin'. This isn't
some tacky affair.

As Nancy and I stood by the Hyders' circular drive, the gloved
parking attendants zoomed up in first one automobile and then
another, calling out as they stepped briskly, "Green Lincoln Continental! Gray Mercedes! White Coupe de Ville! Cadillac, beige!
Cadillac, brown!" The beautiful bejeweled people moved toward
the machines, calling out, "See ya over there, ya hear?" "Great
pahty, Elton!" "Martha, honey, you've *done it again!*"

A boy drove up, jumped out, and said, almost inaudibly, "Blue
Gremlin?" We stepped over to the car as the crowd watched.
Nancy stood beside the car, raised her hand over her head, pointed
to the roof of the car and announced, "Ren . . . ted!"

As we drove into the mall, we faced another battery of gloved attendants. This time in white tie and tails! Nancy said, pointing,
"Look, over there! There's a place! Why don't we just park it ourselves?" We did. Nancy knew the rules. Nancy knew the territory.

We stepped lively toward the store to the snappy beat of "The
Eyes of Texas" being played at the entrance by the Hardin-Sim-

mons Marching Band in their purple and gold cowboy outfits. With that kind of rouser, you knew it was sure goin' to be a hell of a pahty!

As we passed one of the car valets, he said, "Have a real good time in there now, ya hear?"

Inside, an employee dressed like a Bombay traffic policeman stood on a pedestal and directed the traffic. There was a carnival atmosphere. There were carts with cotton candy and bags of peanuts. There were balloons and butterflies and Japanese dolls covered with flowers. One did not have to go far to find one of the eleven bars. And there *was* a *lot* of night music.

In Men's Wear, mariachis set the beat. On the second floor, a banjo group, the Bear Cats, played Dixieland. In the store's restaurant, The Hedges, Don Edwards and his Country and Western Band accompanied foot-stomping and hand-clapping with fiddle-playing. Designer gowns of chiffon and silk swirled around the room in dos-a-dos, alemandes, and promenades. A jazz band was swinging in "lingerie." On the main floor of the mall, Peter Duchin and his orchestra played snappy, sophisticated tunes. And just so no one would get bored, periodically a troop of bagpipers marched through the store.

Everyone seemed to be there. The Clements had flown in from the King Ranch, 600 miles to the south. Lupe Murchison was there wearing emerald and diamond earrings and a crystal and diamond bracelet. Charles Tandy of Tandy Corporation and Radio Shacks was wearing a ring with a sapphire bigger than his thumbnail. Merchandise manager Walter Richardson, whom I'd met at a party given by Fendi in Rome, was busy showing his European couture collection, which prompted a woman next to me to advise, "If you don't want to see yourself coming and going in Texas—buy something cheap!" Designer Adele Simpson was somewhere among the crowd of 1,600. So were Julie Newman and the Romanoffs, Prince and Princess.

Great slices of roast beef were sliced with precision by the chefs and served with Yorkshire pudding from the groaning buffet tables. Wines and champagnes were poured. It was indeed *some pahty!*

As we came out the door, the young parking attendant said, "You ladies have a good time?" We said that, yes, we had and started walking toward the car. The boy followed us, "Excuse me, ma'am, but what kind of car *is that*?'' he asked. Nancy turned and snarled, *"Rented!"*

The next morning, the sign at the motel had changed. It read: "WELCOME TOM BARNETT—THE NEW KID ON THE BLOCK!"

We went on to the luncheon and ate creamed crabmeat and grits and then Nancy had to leave. Although I said I would drive her to the airport, she looked relieved when someone offered his limousine.

After she left, I heard gales of laughter coming from the library and looked in. "Come on in. Henry's telling stories," said a man who turned out to be Winston Le Jeune from Amarillo. His pretty wife, Francie, was there and so were Henry and Mary Sue Koontz, who had come up from south Texas where Henry's family has been raising Brahma cattle for a hundred years and Mary Sue said they have to drive twenty-five miles for a loaf of bread. They had come up for the parties, but Henry had plans to do a little business the next day. It seems he had made a mistake one day about a stranger who appeared on the ranch. He thought he was from the IRS. So he had gone off to hide. The gentleman went over to see Emily, Henry's sister. As it turned out, he was from *Cattleman's Magazine*, wanting to do a story on the family, the ranch, and their hundredth anniversary. "Now I know Emily too well," Henry said. "She'll look like she inherited the whole herd and we're the poor relatives. So tomorrow I'm goin' over to that magazine man and I fully intend to rewrite the history and I've brought pictures of my son. You see, the only way to have a good place in history— Texas history—is to write it yourself. You have to make it a little better than it really is."

I thought of those Irishmen and the Texans in the Neiman-Marcus Pub and wondered who had topped whom.

The Koontz family were isolated on their ranches near the Mexican border until some people came to make some oil leases and the Koontzes wouldn't agree until they got a telephone. They got several—on a party line. "Every time the phone rang, we all listened," Henry said. "It was better than a newspaper. There was my Aunt Emma and Aunt Betty who'd been married to Uncle John, and she always thought she was going to get the ranches away from us. Aunt Betty's the one who had all her fine jewelry insured against radio activity. I think the premiums were very low.

"This one time I did catch a great call. Old Katie Welder from the adjoining ranch called up Aunt Betty and said, "Oh, there's the keenest jewelry man just arrived, name of Julius Cohen. He's got the biggest diamonds I've ever seen.'

"Aunt Betty said, 'How big?'

" 'Well, I'll tell you, he's got one that's a little yellow and Pat won't buy it for me, but it's about 60 carats.'

"Aunt Betty said, 'Hell, you know I don't know any more about that carat business than you do—how *big is it*?'

" 'Hell, it's about *knuckle to knuckle.*'

"And Aunt Betty said, 'Now, by God, you're talkin' my language—send him over!' ' "

We all went on to another party that night and I was introduced to a Gotcha-Gotcha. Now I betcha don't know what a Gotcha-Gotcha is. It's beer in a salt-rimmed mug with a couple of shots of vodka! And I lived to tell about it. And we ate barbecued ribs and chili and pecan and lemon pie, and did we have fun! Elton was there in boots, chaps, ten-gallon hat, and shootin' irons—just to give you some idea.

The next day, we all said goodbye and agreed that it certainly had been fun. But Winston said, "You think this has been fun? You hurry on down to Amarillo. That's where we really have fun!"

I was sorry that Sally and Mildred were out of town but had gathered that August is not usually the social time in Texas. I went over to Sally's shop at the mall and bought a gift to take home. Before I knew it, I was deep into a conversation, telling them about my friend Sally Marcus. The saleswoman said, "I don't know her, but—" and she called to another saleswoman, "Elizabeth, did you know Mrs. Sally Marcus when you were in the Dallas store?" Elizabeth joined us. "I certainly did. Why she is a darlin'." "This lady is a friend of hers." "Really? How nice. She's a lovely person."

"I met her a few years ago in Nepal, of all places!" I said. "In the hotel bar. The cocktail lounge, actually. I've been down here to visit her."

"Really," Elizabeth said, "you came all the way down here from New York? How nice." She didn't blink an eye about Nepal. I think she figured it was like Lubbock or Sweetwater or Tyler.

"No, this time I came down for the store opening."

Then Elizabeth said, "I have a good friend like that—that I met like that. She lives in Abilene and when we get together, we have a ball. I met her in a bar over in Snyder during the blue quail season."

We chatted on and finally I left. "Hurry on back now, ya hear?"

Hurry back! I never wanted to leave. On the plane to New York, I glanced at the sales slip. Across the face, handwritten, it said "Thank you" and was signed Janet Lawton.

A few weeks later I received a beige postcard imprinted with a large butterfly and a small *Neiman-Marcus*. There was a message written in a neat hand:

Dear Mrs. Birmingham:
   Just a note to say thank you for shopping with me at Neimans. Hope you enjoyed your Famous Amos cookies, and had fun at the store opening. I will be looking forward to your book.
                                             Sincerely,
                                             JANET LAWTON

Good Lord! Had I told them about that? It was a long circuitous route, halfway around the world and back again, to Neiman-Marcus and Texas and Texans, but I was *hooked*!

PART III

In the Middle U.S.A.

EIGHT

Where There's No Place to Go But Up

Detroit, Michigan

There is something very reassuring about the good old middle west. In the balance of the United States, the middle west is like the fulcrum on a teeter-totter—it has great strength. It can also, from this vantage point, seesaw north, south, east, and west for ideas, talent, and financing.

Renaissance Center in Detroit and Water Tower Place in Chicago, recently constructed urban developments, are two examples of that strength and regional diversification.

"The eyes of the entire country are on them," said Mildred Custin, president of Mildred Custin, Ltd., New York, the eastern retail and fashion consultant who served as advisor to The World of Shops, which is located on two and a half levels of the 14-acre podium of the Renaissance Center complex, and to The Atrium Mall, eight levels of stores and shops, including Marshall Field & Company and Lord & Taylor, within Water Tower Place. The *eyes* she spoke of belong to retailers, fashion designers, manufacturers, real estate developers, architects, urban planners, bankers, hotel operators, city fathers, shoppers, and anyone who cares about the survival of American cities.

"Renaissance Center is exactly what its name implies—rebirth," Miss Custin said. "The Renaissance has brought downtown Detroit back to being a living, breathing metropolis again." Miss Custin is a living, breathing phenomenon in the male-dominated world of retailing executives. She has chalked up enough firsts to be recognized as America's "First Lady" of retailing. This former president and chairman of the board of Bonwit Teller was consultant to the Center and Tower managements in finding the kind of merchants they needed, establishing the contacts, and placing the stores within the complexes.

"Water Tower, on the other hand, is not urban renewal. It is a complex built in an elegant shopping area along the 'magnificent mile' of Chicago's North Michigan Avenue. Water Tower was the country's first vertical shopping mall and the idea was so new, so innovative, that there were problems of how to merchandise it, how to give it magnetism on a daily basis."

Although the needs of each city were different, both developments were designed to be total environments for living, working, entertainment, and shopping within a city. Both developments were privately financed. Both developments faced almost insurmountable obstacles.

Today Renaissance Center and Water Tower Place grace the Detroit and Chicago skylines. They are living proof of the strength, courage, imagination, and tenacity of the good old middle west. They are living proof that there is after all something new under the sun in which they shine. They are very reassuring.

Detroit, like many other cities around the country, was going down the tubes, up the spouts, and under the rainbow—and the tubes were corroded, the spouts were clogged, and the rainbow was lost in smog and pollution. During the past twenty-five years, cities, which once held the promise of the American dream for immigrants, people from farms and small towns, and city dwellers, began to wake up screaming in nightmares of violence, arson, riots, and decay. *City* became a four-letter word meaning dirty, dangerous, and doomed.

Some cities, too long asleep, became snake pits writhing in political red tape and snarls of traffic. As many businesses hacked their way out of downtown jungles and relocated outside cities in spacious corporate parks, department and specialty stores and shops followed into suburban shopping centers. So did people and money. Some cities did nothing but bemoan their fate as they discovered upon examination that their sicknesses were terminal. Downtowns became hosts for porn movie houses, sleazy massage parlors, brothels, and cheap hotels—victims of the parasites that sucked the last blood from the bleeding areas. Vultures moved in to pick the bones and cremate the remains.

Some cities woke up and cried out, hoping for advice from urban strategists and planners and financial aid from state and federal governments before all was lost.

Detroit, Michigan, of all places, seemed an unlikely candidate for urban survival. If other cities were snake pits and jungles, Detroit was pictured by the national press as a vicious cannibal devouring its own innards. Detroit became symbolic of urban North America—fading, deteriorating, racially torn apart, rotting, and murderous. Anyway, who cared about Detroit? After all, Detroit wasn't exactly New Orleans or San Francisco or Boston. The nationwide public image of Detroit was strictly "yeccht!"

Not surprisingly, Henry Ford II cared about Detroit. Most important, he cared enough to do something about it. In automotive parlance, Henry Ford became the spark plug who revved up the city and put it into high gear. On November 24, 1971, Mr. Ford said: "This revitalization is a task for the business community here. There are more than enough resources, human and financial, to undertake a job of this kind and what we have been lacking is a solid first step to get something started. The size of the development is such that no single company can handle it by itself. We want and will need the participation of other companies to bring the plan to reality."

Detroit, a tough, sturdy city in the middle west, not given to whimpering, did not turn to the federal or state governments. It rolled up its sleeves, went to work, and came up with a plan to revitalize its own downtown. The magnitude of the plan was staggering. It would cost $350 million. It would be one of the largest privately financed urban development projects in United States history. The plan was nothing short of *fan*-tastic!

"What was needed was a high profile. If Detroit was such a potent symbol of urban decay, and *it* could turn around, then Detroit could be a symbol of renewal and hope for the entire country," said John Coxeter of the Renaissance Center Partnership. The Partnership was formed by a group of businessmen to secure the necessary financial backing. "The decision was made to concentrate in one place and to dramatically transform Detroit's skyline. Even a vast sum like $350 million scattered around downtown would have been a drop in the bucket and the impact would have been lost. A 33-acre deteriorating riverfront site was selected. After 271 years Detroit is finally taking the river, its best natural asset, and doing something with it."

Located in the area were warehouses, unpaved parking lots, an old flour mill, and a railroad yard. Fortunately, there were no residences in the area, which might have meant long and drawn-out battles for acquisition and the problem of relocation of people. Time was of the essence if the project was to uplift the city and spur other downtown rehabilitations and face-lifts. The deterioration of the area also made it possible to put together a real estate package at a price of less than $10 per square foot for the property. The total purchase price of $12.3 million was a fraction of the usual cost of prime downtown land in a major metropolitan market.

Detroit went south to Atlanta, Georgia, to hire architect John Portman, the genius behind Atlanta's Peachtree Center and San Francisco's Embarcadero Center, to design Renaissance Center. John Portman is an architect who is not intimidated by the size of a project either in terms of space or the money involved. He is not afraid of innovative design and technological developments available to builders. And yet at the core of his architectural philosophy there is something very small when compared with the enormity of his buildings—man.

In his book, *The Architect as Developer*, written with urban designer Jonathan Barnett, he explains:

> Every city is the result of a great many individual decisions, most of them made by government and businesses for their own institutional or corporate reasons. It is incredible how little is done for the good of ordinary people. Every city has to go back and say: "OK, this whole thing is for that little guy who is walking around down there." How can we have this huge mass of density and profit and all the rest of it and still create a livable environment?

In his sleek Peachtree Center office, soft-spoken John Portman said, "The *little guy* will walk seven to ten minutes before he looks for wheels. This time-space factor provides a large radius in which his needs—living, shopping, employment, entertainment—can be met. We call this a *coordinate unit*. In American cities people are shoved aside by mechanical monsters. We try and reorder things to make a city viable for human habitation. We've built a city within a city. When we arrived there was a sign in Detroit—'Last person leaving please turn out the lights.' We've kept the lights on. Renaissance Center is a mini-World's Fair. The credit goes to Henry Ford. He laid everything on the line for this project and it was gargantuan!''

Light, water, nature, and color are brought into the massive structures along with levels, textures, art, and movement to accomplish this humanization. All of these elements would be for naught and the centers would be as cold, empty, lonely, and lifeless as the Super Bowl on the day after the game, if the little guy or big guy and his wife, mother, sister, cousins, kids, and friends weren't passing up, down, over, through, under, and around. Then there must be seating in case the little guy gets tired and escalators and elevators should he begin to look for some form of transport. People become an integral part of Portman's constructions—living mobiles and stabiles—that enhance the architecture.

People watching is part of the experience at the Portman centers. It takes various forms. It is sometimes akin to "standing on corner watching all the girls go by" or sitting on a park bench "piping the flight," or it may have the nonchalance of relaxing in a European sidewalk café. It can go a step further to become people watching people—*people watching*.

In his book, John Portman explains his feelings and the reasons for providing such extensive lounging areas:

> We don't have a tradition of sitting in public places in the United States. Everyone runs up and down the sidewalks like rats. But when Americans go to Europe they gravitate to the sidewalk cafes. I don't believe in mimicking the historic European cities (or anything else for that matter), but I think we can create opportunities for the same kinds of experiences.

Unlike the Peachtree and the Embarcadero centers, which were built piecemeal, one building at a time, to be connected later into a master coordinate unit, Renaissance Center was a coordinate unit on an enormous scale to be constructed all at once. This created problems that did not exist in Atlanta or San Francisco. According to Portman, "If anything were to be done in Detroit, it needed to be done in a hurry. The city did not have fifteen years to build up a coordinate unit step by step as we had done in Georgia and California. We were counteracting weakness not building on strength. The first stage had to be large enough to justify its own existence. Some 30,000 to 40,000 people move through the Center every day and now we are adding two more office buildings."

The Renaissance Center consists of five glass-encased towers rising from a four-level, 14-acre podium structure. The center tower contains the 73-story, 1,400-room Detroit Plaza Hotel. There is an eight-story lobby atrium that interconnects with four surrounding 39-story office buildings. At the base of the lobby is a half-acre lake and it has been discovered that while people are watching, they are also wishing. During each monthly cleaning of the lake, over $1,500 in coins is retrieved and donated to various Detroit charities.

The Renaissance seems to bring out a certain frivolity and extravagance in people. Hanging down from the skylight on stainless steel cables and rods is a specially woven fabric sculpture. The 64-foot-high artwork was created by Gerhardt Knodel, a faculty member at the nearby Cranbrook Academy of Art. Glittering among the folds and swags of the metallic-threaded fabrics are hundreds of nickels, dimes, quarters, and pennies. As the enormous sculpture sways and shifts and sparkles in the sunlight, the coins seem to be an integral part of the work.

John Portman found the Tivoli Gardens in Copenhagen to be a "revelation." "When you walk through Tivoli, you see that almost everyone is smiling," he explained. While Renaissance inspires awe, wonder, and admiration, there is something giddy and playful—something of the gaiety of Tivoli—in the atmosphere. The Renaissance Center radiates with joy!

There are five levels of aerial walkways across the atrium, which is canopied by an enormous skylight. The area is filled with sculptures, hanging tapestries, hanging gardens, and suspended trees. There are sixteen escalators that serve the hotel levels in the podium structure, and from various vantage points in the lounges scattered throughout the lobby and from the Pods (the banquettes that hang out over the lake), people on the escalators appear to be floating and drifting up and down through the massive structure. Electric trolley bars, piloted by pretty barmaids, are maneuvered through the promenades to provide drink service.

There are thirteen restaurants within the hotel and one of the most popular for dining and sightseeing is the Summit, located on the hotel's 71st, 72nd, and 73rd floors. This restaurant/cocktail lounge is reached by one of the two exterior glass elevators which travels at a speed of 1,000 feet per minute. The trip is a tummy-tickling, breath-holding, heady thrill like a roller-coaster ride. First-timers are apt to cling to the inside door looking like George Willig did when he scaled the World Trade Center.

The upper and lower levels of the rooftop counter rotate. The view from the darkened, moving cocktail lounge is spectacular and constantly changing. Often from this height one sees a plane or helicopter flying below. There is some consternation among newcomers to the service staff. The service area in the center of the lounge is stationary and the stations where the customers are located are continually moving. "Some people get totally disoriented surrounded by all this space and with the movement. They just can't handle it," said a young waiter. "But if you can hang in, you get used to it. You learn to relate differently in order to keep track of your tables, even in the daik." The movement, however, necessitates paying for each drink when it is served.

Several of the bars throughout the hotel are tended by the ABC, Automatic Beverage Control computer system. The ABC is a console made up of buttons picturing a wide variety of glasses and symbols. A waiter approaches the machine and calls his order. The programmer puts the appropriate glass in place, inserts a ticket into the machine, punches the waiter's code and the key or combination of keys—e.g., one for martini, two for bourbon and soda. The machine blips and rat-a-tats its computer noises and the liquid pours forth from heaven-knows-how-many-miles-away. Advice from the Summit waiter was to avoid mixed and complicated concoctions when the bartender is a computer. Although the computer keeps an inventory and automatically switches when various liquors and mixes have been depleted, people who have ordered sticky, sweet drinks have been known to get a glass of straight grenadine. "Stick

to a brand whiskey and water or soda when a machine is mixing,"
the waiter said as he flipped on his small flashlight and illuminated
the tab. "The ABC does everything but tip," he added politely.

There is also, of course, the possibility of human error.

"One Rob Roy," a waitress called behind the scenes of the first-
floor Las Vegas restaurant nightclub. She wore a strapless, red satin mini-costume. Black net stockings covered her long legs.

"What the hell is *that*?" the keypunch operator asked as he studied his keyboard.

"Punch Manhattan and Scotch," she said.

"No, bourbon," someone yelled.

The mixer punched all three buttons and the liquid gurgled into
the stemmed glass. He plunked in an orange slice and topped it
with a maraschino cherry. "Oh, what-the-hell!" he said and placed
the drink on her tray.

The central kitchen of the hotel, if stripped of its cooking equipment, could easily serve as a practice field for the Detroit Lions.
The main food preparations for the restaurants are made in this
arena and spun off to the various restaurants' satellite kitchens for
the finishing touches. This space-age cuisine is the cause of some
complaints about the similarity and quality of the food. One guest
of several days described the food in the various restaurants as
"high-class airline." The exception is Mikado, an exquisite Japanese restaurant where the food is prepared at hibachi tables.

Located on one of the podium levels is an indoor glass-domed
swimming pool, snack bar, and Health Club. Nearby is the elegant
Standard Club of Detroit, which is reached by a private elevator
and boasts a showcase ladies' room completely tiled in bronze mirror mosaics. Recently the female members who have returned
downtown to lunch and shop have found themselves assaulted in
their beautiful glass dining room by a new urban offense. Members
of the Health Club on their lunchtime workouts have discovered
the terraced roof that surrounds the Standard Club. Detroiters, like
the rest of the country, have taken up the running and jogging
craze and the path around the Standard Club makes an ideal track.
"It's not so bad in the cold weather," said one Standard Club
member, "but on sunny days, all those sweaty, hairy chests racing
by are most unappetizing."

While the fleeting glimpse of huffing, puffing jocks may be an annoyance for some of the luncheon crowd, it has been outweighed by the excitement offered in the World of Shops, the 350,000-square-foot podium area which will eventually contain 80 to 100 retail operations.

"Shopping has to be fun," said consultant Mildred Custin. "I'm very pleased with the response of Detroit to the Renaissance shops. It was scary at first. I'd been in the suburbs and heard people say, 'I haven't been downtown in ten years.' We had to have merchandise that wasn't readily available in the outlying shopping centers. This was one reason we selected a handful of internationally known fashion names for the boutiques—Courrèges, Lanvin, Halston, Valentino, and Charles Jourdan. Another reason was that these small shops can offer the personal attention customers don't get in larger stores anymore."

There are other luxury shops besides the fashion boutiques—Godiva Chocolatier, FAO Schwarz, Mark Cross leather goods, and Leonard of London Beauty Salon. " 'Les must de Cartier' at the Center is one of the most beautiful Cartier shops in the world," Miss Custin said.

"But a shopping center of this size can't exist on luxury shops alone. There has to be a mix. I learned that when I was working on the Water Tower Place. When I was planning that, I realized I was a retail snob. When you have twenty-five to thirty thousand people per day moving through an area, as you do in these larger urban centers, you have to cater to a wide range of consumer needs and incomes. But you can't go the other way and have only chain stores. It becomes a question of mixing quality merchandise with popular demand and coming out with style."

There are two midwestern stores—Winkelman's and Gantos—located in the Center, along with jeans, T-shirt, and shoe stores. There are banks, tobacconists, bakeries, florists, and record and office supply stores. There are three movie theaters and a variety of restaurants. There is Nemo's Saloon, a replica of a famous Detroit turn-of-the-century Irish pub, where a live jazz band plays in the afternoons and evenings. There is a health food center, a crêperie, and a Chinese restaurant. There are Olga's Kitchen, featuring Olga's famous souvlaki and the Koney Island Inn, featuring the famous Michigan "hot," a hot dog with chili, and there are La Fontaine, an exclusive French gourmet restaurant, and a Big Boy and a

McDonald's. The restaurants, like the World of Shops, are diversified. There is something for everybody.

"There's a cosmopolitan mix here in the Center," John Coxeter said. "When we were building it there were those who said it would be a white bastion. That's proven not to be true. There have been good racial relations here in the Center and I think it has helped the tension in the city to subside. The Renaissance has given the Detroiter something to feel good about. Early on we discovered that the local taxi drivers felt this was a place for the swells and were making sarcastic remarks about it to their passengers. We had a party for all the cab drivers and gave them a tour of the Center. Now they not only tout the Center to their customers, they also bring their families here on their days off."

"We have very little vandalism," Bob Jackson, a Partnership executives said. "People seem to dress better and behave better here than they might on the street. They respect the Center. I suppose you could say we are upgrading people. That's a basic marketing practice in the automotive industry. It's a theory that came from Mr. Sloane at General Motors—more car per car. The idea being that once a person has moved up to a higher-priced car with power brakes, power steering, and other improvements, he isn't satisfied with anything less. There's a lot of purchasing power in Detroit. The automobile industry workers are among the best paid in the country. If people are comfortable moving around the shops with high-quality goods, they'll eventually try them. It's the same idea."

"People find it is fun to shop here," Miss Custin said. "It isn't a question of knowing who your customer is. It's finding who your new customer will be and going out and getting him. The carriage trade is in its last gasp."

"The Renaissance World of Shops is the only place I know of where you can sit in a McDonald's eating a Big Mac and look into an elegant Lanvin shop ten feet away," Mr. Coxeter said.

"Opening day, when simply hordes of people started pouring through the Center, I was sitting in the lobby with John Portman. As the thousands moved around, awestruck, and threw their coins into the lake and reached down to dip their fingers into the water, as they smelled the flowers and reached out to touch the tapestries—there is a strong kinesthetic response to all the textures around—John Portman leaned back, laced his fingers together across his chest, and a big grin spread across his face. He had been determined from the beginning that Renaissance Center would be a 'people place.' On opening day, he knew that that was what he had created."

The decision to use the hotel as the anchor for the Renaissance was made because of the area's proximity to Detroit's central business district and to Cobo Hall, the city's convention center, the second largest exhibition hall in the country. The Center looked to the west for hotel management. Western International Hotels, a subsidiary of United Air Lines, Inc., the parent company of United Air Lines, operates the hotel. The company headquarters are located in Seattle, Washington. A main priority of the Center was to get people accustomed to coming downtown again and to make the area safe and attractive for shopping and active for entertainment. A later phase of the complex includes the building of condominiums along the riverfront.

"Detroit has never had a lot of people living downtown like New York and Chicago," Bob Jackson said. "It is a commuter city and being the automobile capital, almost everyone drives. We have an excellent expressway system. I live on a lake thirty-five miles from here and even in rush hour it takes less than an hour to get home. There are a few buses and a couple of trains that come down from Pontiac every morning. The trains sit in the station all day. The train crews drive back home and return in the late afternoon to take the trains back to Pontiac. It's rather a unique situation. What most people don't realize is that the Michigan countryside is beautiful. There are over five hundred lakes within an hour's drive of this city."

"For all our bad press, Detroit is really an attractive town," John Coxeter added, "but it's had such a terrible image that people come here and expect to find a dried-up kernel of a downtown surrounded by ghettos. When you get up in one of these buildings you can see that it's a green city. There's a lot of vegetation. And there's the river traffic. It's fascinating. Everyone around the Center has a Stack and Flag chart on his office wall to identify the passing ships. In the summer there are the Bob-lo boats that go down the river to an amusement park on the Canadian Island, Bob-lo. Down below is the Ford Auditorium, where the Detroit Symphony plays. And the Philhart Plaza, named for the late Senator, and the Noguchi computerized fountain, donated by the Dodges. And there'll be a sports arena, ice rink, and open-air amphitheater. There are the colorful little Portuguese trolleys that take people short distances. We call them our people-moving system. Detoit, as a city, has a lot going for it. One of the biggest things is right over there." He pointed across the river. "That's a *foreign* country! You're looking *south* into Canada. It's a quirk of geography and it's the only place in the United States you can do that. There are great little French restaurants over there."

This proximity to Canada and the city of Windsor and the entrance to the Detroit-Windsor Tunnel under the Detroit River presented a major problem during the land acquisition for the Center. A number of streets leading to the tunnel had to be taken over and the access routes to the tunnel changed. This became extremely complex under the agreements with which the tunnel authority operated. Eventually a plan was formalized whereby the Renaissance Center developers acquired all the tunnel property and the United States' half of the tunnel and then leased it back to the tunnel authority.

There is a certain envy among Americans for the Canadian view of the Renaissance. Detroiters take visitors across the river to look back at their new pride and glory. "The best view of Renaissance is from the second floor of the Windsor City Market," Mrs. Noel Buckner of Orchard Lake, Michigan, said. "Upstairs on the second floor, through the window behind the place where you get the good bacon." One can only assume that she meant Canadian bacon.

After the tunnel complications there was the Grand Trunk railroad yard and passenger station to be moved, which required the railroad's approval and that of both the state and federal regulatory agencies. There were the landing slips for the barges that ferried the railroad cars across the river to be moved and a 96-inch sewer line that ran the length of the property to be moved and 18 buildings to be razed. But all these activities seemed minor when compared to what the human resources accomplished in order to "get something started."

The package that was put together to provide the financial backing for the project seems unbelievable. The speed with which it was put together seems impossible.

The Ford Motor Land Development Corporation (FMLDC), a subsidiary of the Ford Motor Company, was instrumental in conceiving the project as a real estate development, not only to increase the city's tax base, but as a dramatic attraction to downtown Detroit for businesses, conventions, tourists, and suburban shoppers that could be profitable. The Detroit Downtown Development Corporation (DDDC) was organized as a subsidiary of the subsidiary (FMLDC) to act as the managing partner in the development of the Renaissance Center Partnership. Fifty other firms joined as limited partners. One should be so lucky to have such a portfolio, beginning with Allied Chemical Corporation and ending with Western International Michigan, Inc. In between on the list are American Motors, Chrysler Realty, DDDC (the Ford subsidiary subsidiary), and Riverfront Development (a General Motors subsidiary). Tire companies batted almost 100 percent participation with Firestone, General, Goodrich, Goodyear, and Uniroyal. Among the partners are banking, insurance, electronic, newspaper publishing, oil corporations, and conglomerates. The Renaissance Partnership at a quick glance looks something like a little Big Board. There was no altruism. Detroit was not a charity case. Every partner looked upon Renaissance as a sound business investment that would yield a return. The Partnership was organized in five months.

A consortium of five companies was put together for a $200 million first mortgage loan that consisted of the John Hancock Mutual Life Insurance Company, $60 million; Aetna Life Insurance Company, $50 million; The Equitable Life Assurance Society of the United States, $50 million; The Travelers Insurance Company, $30 million; and Ford Motor Credit Company, $10 million.

Next, a bank group was organized to provide the construction loan. Led by the National Bank of Detroit, which provided $27,050,000 toward the total, six other Detroit banks participated. Altogether twenty-eight banks throughout the country were involved, including six from New York City, four from Philadelphia, three from Chicago, seven from California, and one from Seattle.

On May 22, 1973, two days short of one and a half years—only eighteen months—from the day that Henry Ford II had said that they ought to *do* something, they had—and construction began.

Four years later, on April 15, 1977, the mirrored midwestern si-los filled with hope—the dazzler on the Detroit River—the symbol of a city's rebirth and pride—the Renaissance Center was dedi-cated.

It goes to show that in the middle west when the chips are down, when the fat is in the fire, even when the heat is on, it's never too hot for good old reliable Detroit.

NINE

Chicago, Chicago

Marshall Field's and Water Tower Place

Marshall Field & Company, one of the world's great department stores, is as legendary to Chicago and the good old middle west as Mrs. O'Leary's cow. It's as sturdy as the tracks on the Loop, as timeless as the Lake, and almost as vast as the westward prairie. It is said that Marshall Field's *is* Chicago.

For the genteel store to epitomize a city that Carl Sandburg called the "Hog Butcher of the World" is one of the many contradictions that make Chicago Chicago. For a store founded on manners, morals, and good taste to symbolize a city where the late Mayor Richard Daley told reporters publicly that they could kiss his ass is only one of the city's many anomalies. It's hard to get a handle on the "Nation's Freight Handler."

The *Marshall Field & Company Idea*, the store creed, first appeared in 1905:

> To do the right thing at the right time, in the right way; to do some things better than they were ever done before; to eliminate errors; to know both sides of the question; to be courteous; to be an example; to love our work; to anticipate requirements; to develop resources; to recognize no impediments; to master circumstances; to act for reason rather than rule; to be satisfied with nothing short of perfection.

This in the city that was the scene of the St. Valentine's Day Massacre and the trial of the Chicago Seven.

The wonder of Chicago is that there seems to be room for the city's many diversified personalities to coexist. The city is tough and tender, raucous and refined, bawdy and elegant. Sandburg's hardworking city—the "Stacker of Wheat"—has been called a free and easy town, a brassy and breezy town. The "Player with Railroads" is filled with rass-ma-tazz and all that jazz. *Chicago* was a recent bouncy Broadway musical starring Gwen Verdon. "Chicago" is the name of a pop-rock group. It's no mistake that Chicago is immortalized in music. The beat came up to Chicago from the south during the early part of the century and names like King Joe Oliver, Bix Beiderbecke, Hoagy Carmichael, and Bessie Smith, to name a few, became part of the Chicago legacy. State Street, that great street, was at one time lined with cafés and theaters where jazz bands played at the Dreamland, the Panama, the Edelweiss, and the Vendome and Lincoln Theaters. Later came the giant movie houses—the State Lake, the Palace, the Roosevelt, and the most beautiful theater in the midwest, the Chicago. These were the homes for first-run films and the Big Bands played on their stages.

Today State Street has fallen onto sorry times. The Roosevelt Theater heralds a class D movie across the marquee:

"ARMED WITH THE MOST GRUESOME WEAPON EVER THE MASTER OF THE FLYING GUILLOTINE CHALLENGES INVADERS FROM BEYOND TIME!" There's a cut-rate record shop, a store called Cheap Willies, and a vacant lot. "A vacant lot!" said a Chicagoan. "Can you imagine a vacant lot across from the main entrance to Marshall Field's on State Street, on what used to be the most valuable real estate in the world?"

On the east side of State Street, Marshall Field's covers a full city block. The store was described in 1907 in a national magazine as "more than a store. It was an exposition, a school of courtesy, a museum of modern commerce."

Beyond the Grecian columns flanking the main entrance, the customer is always right and the rule is to "give the lady what she wants." Inside the vaulted rotundas is a surety of purity. Outside across State Street to the west the area is mendacious and salacious and the ladies give what someone else wants—for a price.

In the past social leaders, visitors from farming communities, presidents, royalty, the high-class hostesses from the famous and infamous Everleigh Club, and Frankie Wright and Vic Shaw, the leading madams from the Levee, moved through Field's wide aisles brushing shoulders and were treated with equal politeness. The carriage and the carnal trades have long lived side by side in Chicago.

So have the more masculine trades. The male shoulders of the "City of the Big Shoulders" are draped with pinstriped suits, blue denim workshirts, cotton T-shirts, and Oxford cloth button-downs labeled THE STORE FOR MEN —MARSHALL FIELD & COMPANY. In the Men's Store, located in the Annex on Washington Street, there are times when Lake Shore Drive stockbrokers and Oakbrook bankers hobnob with hod carriers, bricklayers, and stackers of wheat.

A young politician who has moved up through the "back of the yards" to a position of importance in the South Side's Eleventh Ward said: "You might think that Marshall Field's would be too hoity-toity for the South Side. Most of the time the Men's Store is so refined you could throw a bomb and someone might say gently, 'I thought I heard a noise'—*except* for the Box Sale. I don't think there's anything like it anywhere in the world. It's the damnedest thing you've ever seen. It's like a fire sale—'woo-woo.' Every man in Chicago is there. If you stumbled you'd be trampled to death. Everything is sold by the box—a box of socks, a box of handkerchiefs, boxes of shorts, T-shirts, undershirts. Men go crazy. There are fellows who've got so many boxes, they can't carry them out of the store.

"I have a friend who bought *nineteen* pairs of gloves. Two boxes—one with half a dozen and one with a dozen. How come nineteen? Well, one box with six and another box with a dozen. At Field's that's a baker's dozen—thirteen. I should talk! I got so carried away once that I bought two boxes—three to a box—of short-sleeved yellow shirts. Six goddamn shirts. I don't wear short sleeves and I hate yellow! People go nuts! And you should see the trauma when some man thinks he's got a box of blue shirts and discovers there's *one* white in the box. He freaks out.

"Chicago is the ballsiest city in the United States. The people are tough—in both the good and bad sense of the word. But let me tell you that for some of those guys on the South Side the Box Sale is the biggest event in their lives. Do you know what the sexiest thing in this town is? It's not some guy's biceps or pectorals. It's not his beard or tattoo or snazzy car. It's a *label!* If a guy can pull down his collar in the back and its says THE STORE FOR MEN—MAR-SHALL FIELD & COMPANY—well. After the Box Sale you see it in bars all over town. A giant ape of a guy with his head down, holding back his collar and some chick looking down the back of his neck. That guy's got it made'cause that broad's thinking, This guy's got class."

The Annex was not planned to house The Store for Men. It was put there out of consideration for the ladies' sensibilities. The twenty-one-story building built in 1914 at Washington and Wabash, across the street from the main building, was originally meant to have six selling floors for china, glassware, and upholstery. The remaining floors were to be offices.

One morning John Shedd, the store president after the death of Marshall Field, was taking the elevator to his office when a man puffing a giant cigar stepped inside. As the smoke filled the elevator both president Shedd and the women present coughed and glared. When he reached his office, he called his managers and announced: "I've made up my mind to get the men out of this store! We'll put all the men's departments in the new building!" The Chicago ladies would no longer be the victims of the crude habits and manners of the Chicago male.

Marshall Field's, however, is much more than class. It's tradition, sentiment, quality merchandise, and outstanding service. But beyond that exists a loyalty and intimacy between the customers and the store that are unique in the world of retailing. *Business Week* (April 11, 1977) reported that a visitor being escorted through the store by the late Joseph A. Burnham, the then president of Chicago's Field's, commented that it might be easier for shoppers to find their way around the 2.2 million square feet of store if floor plans were displayed on each level. In the seventy years since the store was built, it had been asumed that the customers knew their way around. If they did not, there were always polite salesclerks or floorwalkers to point or even guide them in the right direction. Today, there are floor plans. They are inconspicuous. They are little help to the outsider. The small dot and fine print—"you are here"—places one in the middle of the maze. There are few clues on how to get out.

The store is a block square (not including the Annex). But it is difficult for newcomers to orient themselves because the store was built in different sections over the years. The buildings have been connected by walk-throughs. There are various rotundas or light-wells within the store.

The original "marble palace" on State Street was rented to Marshall Field and his partner, Levi Leiter, by their former partner, Potter Palmer, in 1868. The store burned in the Great Chicago Fire in 1871. A new store built on the same location burned in 1877. A third store was built and opened in 1879. In 1881 Mr. Leiter retired and Field and Leiter & Company became Marshall Field & Company. A second building on Washington and Wabash was completed in time for the Chicago Columbian Exposition in 1893. This is the oldest area of the store still standing. Located on South Wabash, the main floor houses the fine jewelry department where the exquisite merchandise is displayed in the original polished mahogany cases. The middle and north State Street stores were opened in 1902.

At the turn of the century, John Shedd, whom Field himself had called "the greatest merchant in the United States," pressed Field to tear down the original 1879 State Street store, build a new one, and connect the units into one grand establishment. Field agreed before he died, in 1906, and the new wonder of a store was completed in 1907. The highlight of the new store with thirty-five acres of selling space was the fabulous Tiffany Dome. The multicolored Favrile glass mosaic covers 6,000 square feet with some 1,600,000 pieces of iridescent glass. People still gasp with wonder looking at the blue and gold marvel six stories above. It was said by one art critic at the opening to be in a class with the nave of St. Peter's in Rome.

The store included the latest technological developments. It connected directly with Chicago's unique underground freight tunnels. Within the store were pneumatic tubes and conveyor belts, seventy-six passenger elevators, and an ice machine in fur storage.

Mr. Shedd, who frowned on cigarettes as well as cigars, and was a fervent believer in the temperance movement, gave every phase of the designs and construction his personal attention. Buyers were dispatched to the four corners of the globe with orders to return with the finest glassware, china, carpets, fabrics, and laces. The store was dedicated to the Field's theme—refinement, gentility, courteous and efficient service, stability, and elegance. There was to be no hawking of wares or noisy advertising of the store. On opening day, September 30, 1907, the newspapers carried reproductions of original drawings by fine artists along with the dignified text:

> We announce the formal opening of our completed retail store. The entire public is invited to see the world's greatest store at its best. Marshall Field & Company.

During the opening week, over a half million people passed through the store, awestruck by the mahogany cabinets, the Tiffany Dome, and the glorious, exotic merchandise.

Today the store consists of the South Wabash store, built in 1893: the middle and north State Street stores, which opened in 1902: south State, in 1907; middle Wabash, in 1907: north Wabash, in 1914; and the Annex, in 1914. For a non-Chicagoan the safest means of orienting oneself is to go outside the building and walk around the block until one of the two Field's clocks appears. These landmarks are high on the side of the building at State Street—one on the corner of Randolph, the other at the Washington corner. Once oriented, a visitor can reenter the store hopeful that he can keep a grip on his whereabouts.

"Everything about Marshall Field's is a big secret," said a Fieldophile. "Take sales, for instance. There's the Box Sale and there are White Sales, but for the most part, they are called 'selling.' Sometimes they say, 'once-a-year' selling. There aren't any banner headlines or large signs—no drum beating. Field's has one of the greatest silver departments in the world and when they have a sale, the values are fantastic. It's the same with antiques, but unless you're into these things or a Field's regular, you'd *never* know about them."

The windows along Washington Street recently were filled with "one-of-a-kind" new and antique silver pieces. A discreet sign in the window corner read SPECIAL SELLING.

"They don't tell what the markdown is. Field's would not be that crass. They expect their customers to trust them—and they do."

"One of the best kept secrets in Field's happened some years ago when Estée Lauder introduced the 'gift-with-purchase' into the business," said a Chicago cosmetics distributor. "This policy has become the backbone of the industry. But in the beginning, it was revolutionary, exciting, and every store was ballyhooing Estée's free gift. Do you know what they did at Field's? They *hid* it. The gift was under the counter. No clerk offered it. There was no advertising. No sign. A customer had to ask. If a woman mentioned that she could get an extra cologne or lipstick at Carson, Pirie, then the clerk would look around, duck down, and surreptitiously slip the free merchandise into the package—like it was *hot*. The idea of *give-aways* was considered so tacky by Field's that they didn't know how to handle it."

Marshall Field & Company is as incongruous as Chicago. "The contrasts are incredible," explained a Field's devotee. "For a store that was founded on the carriage trade, luxury goods, and elegance, Field's basement is better than any discount house. It has the longest continuous selling aisle in the world. It starts and runs through the Annex, goes under Washington Street, and runs the full block to Randolph. It's called the Budget Department. Field's would never use words like 'bargain,' 'cheap,' or 'cut-rate.' You almost get the feeling that Field's wishes it weren't there— except for the amount of money it makes. There isn't a department store in the country that wouldn't be grateful just to be Field's basement."

Field's executives are reticent about the basement. They are quick to point out the length of the aisle. Beyond that they speak of the department as "trustworthy." The merchandise, they explain, is "less expensive but reliable."

The massive no-nonsense Budget Department is only one of the many faces of Field's. The 28 Shop on the sixth floor is another. On September 30, 1941, the Shop was opened and became one of the ultra-posh fashion departments in the country. At the time, Field's renowned fashion catalogue, *Fashions of the Hour*, said: "The 28 Shop is its own statement—the expression of Marshall Field's credo of taste and clothes."

The Shop was named for the address of the private elevator alongside the carriage entrance at 28 East Washington Street. The concept was to create a fashion department that would be the ultimate in elegance. The elevator was paneled, lined with velvet upholstered benches. It silently rose to deposit customers into an oval foyer with pink beige, hand-rubbed oak walls. Here they were greeted by a hostess and guided into the dazzling main salon. The circular room was broken by alcoves with hand-woven beige and turquoise draperies. The rug too was beige—loomed and dyed in the Field's mills.

There were twenty-eight individually decorated fitting rooms. Some had walls lined with bamboo paneling. Others were lined with café-au-lait pigskin, mirrors, or frosted glass. The rooms had tufted velvet banquettes and were decorated in various color combinations—rose and pale green, black and peach, apricot and rose. The ceiling of one fitting room was lined with imported lace. A mammoth crystal chandelier illuminated the main salon.

The 28 Shop was designed by Joseph Platt, a Hollywood designer who was famous for his *Gone With the Wind* sets before he joined Field's manufacturing division. Platt had been told to create a shop that would outshine any other fashion salon in the world—Paris, London, New York, or San Francisco. It was a different challenge from building Tara and creating Atlanta but Mr. Platt came through with flying colors.

For the 28 Shop opening, engraved invitations were sent to five hundred of the midwest's elite. The evening had all the glamour, excitement, and curiosity of a Hollywood premiere. When the limousines converged there were searchlights and cordons of police to keep traffic moving. All of Chicago seemed to line the sidewalks in order to watch the pageantry and to glimpse the celebrities and swells. Guests were announced by a major domo, resplendent in a green and gold uniform. There was orchestra music. Alec Templeton gave a special performance. Fashions by Adrian, Norell, Jo Copeland, Nettie Rosenstein, and Hattie Carnegie, the American stars of design who had stolen much of the fashion spotlight from Paris during the war years, were paraded on beautiful women. There were lights and cameras and there was a radio broadcast from the event. For the first time in the history of Marshall Field & Company, alcohol was allowed in the store. Butlers glided through the crowd pouring champagne. The 28 Shop was an instant success and within three years its annual sales averaged over $1 million.

The 28 Shop has been remodeled in recent years. The walls are covered with pleated fabric in mustard color with blue-gray figures. The once stark salon with its few understated displays now has the look of an elegant boutique. Brass vitrines and étagères are loaded with exquisite merchandise bearing Geoffrey Beene, Dior, Trigère, Mollie Parnis, Ungaro, and Adele Simpson labels, to name a few. The practice of live models displaying clothes for individual customers has gone out of fashion (with the exception of special arrangements made for *very* VIPs). So has the practice of keeping fine merchandise behind the scenes. When jet travel exposed American women to European shops, where high rents demanded using every inch of space from floor to ceiling for display and storage, the shoppers discovered the excitement of having accessories, scarves, handbags, belts, sweaters, and blouses readily available. The boutique concept translated easily to American merchandising. It is colorful, cozy, and informal. Shopping is less time-consuming and more in pace with today's life-styles. The 28 Shop is still elegant, conservative, and expensive—but with a difference.

Off of the oval salon, in what was once several of the glamorous fitting rooms, is the Zandra Rhodes boutique, decorated by the London designer herself. The designs and the talented young woman, whose hair is green and who often wears one eyebrow penciled across her forehead, would undoubtedly baffle the store's founding fathers. In recent years, Marshall Field's has been livening up its ultra-conservative image and the presence of zany Zandra in the 28 Shop is beguiling and adds another dimension to the unique personality of Marshall Field's.

It is also unique that at a time when many stores have closed their tearooms or converted them into fast-service snack bars, Marshall Field's operates eleven restaurants within the State Street store. The Budget Dinette in the basement serves a different hot plate each day: meat loaf, potatoes and vegetable, stuffed cabbage, or tuna à la king. The lunch costs $1.50. Elsewhere there is the Bowl and Basket quick lunch. The Crystal Palace, the newly installed ice cream parlor decorated in the style of the Gay Nineties, serves an assortment of "Chicago Landmark Sundaes"—The Clock, The Tower, The Avenue, The Great Street, The Lakefront—gooey concoctions made from combinations of the 80 Marshall Field-manufactured ice creams, sherbets and ice milks. The waitresses in red and white striped uniforms and jaunty straw hats are quick to tout the high butterfat content of Field's dairy products, a surprising selling point in these calorie-cholesterol conscious times. Judging from the lines outside the Crystal Palace, it is effective merchandising.

The seventh floor at Field's is designated as the tearoom floor. There are the Narcissus Room, the English Room, the Crystal Buffet, the Veranda, and the Walnut Room. In view of the Field's adage of giving the lady what she wants, in Chicago it would seem that, more than anything, she wants to eat. The best-known tearoom is the Walnut Room with its famed center fountain, massive columns, and gleaming walnut paneling. At Christmastime, the famous Field's Great Tree rises from a pedestal covering the fountain up to the top of the three-floor rotunda. Because of recent fire regulations, the tree is now artificial. In the past, however, with the advent of spring, lumberjacks in northern Michigan were notified to be on the lookout for the right tree. In the fall, the selected evergreen giant, usually weighing one and a half tons, was cut. The branches were wrapped and it was loaded onto a truck for the trip to Chicago's Loop. How the tree got to the seventh floor was one of Chicago's mysteries. It was also an engineering feat.

1. The tree arrived at the Randolph Street entrance. It was cut in height to fit the Walnut Room. The doors of the entrance were removed and the tree was brought inside.

2. The tree was rigged and hauled up the north State wall. The rigging was attached to the thirteenth floor.

3. When the base of the tree reached the seventh floor, it was hauled inside.

4. It was then moved from the north State to the south State building and from there it was rigged in the Walnut Room.

Christmas at Field's is spectacular. Plans begin in February and work continues through the year until the November weekend when, in a 36-hour period, the store is transformed into a fantasy. Homer Sharp, in charge of design for Field stores and for window and interior displays, has said that because of the size of the store "it's like trimming the Grand Canyon."

From the opening throughout the holidays there are crushes around the windows that tell automated stories. "The Night Before Christmas" has been presented twice. In 1976, the window theme was "Chicago" and included the tree in Civic Center with Mayor Daley in miniature, lighting it. With the death of Mayor Daley on December 20th, there was a great deal of soul searching and it was finally decided to remove his miniature figure from the display.

The 1977 Christmas windows presented a courtship and wedding of Marsha Housemouse and Frederick Fieldmouse. The traditionalists who objected to the windows on the grounds that it was a "made-up story" were comforted by a visit to Santa Claus in the traditional Cozy Cloud Cottage.

The eating at Field's, like many other traditions, grew out of someone's ingenuity. A young clerk in the millinery department in the late 1880s, in an effort to keep the customers from leaving the store at noontime to go home for lunch, simply had her mother bake a batch of chicken pies. She rode to work on the trolley with the pies balanced on her lap. She spread the word to her customers and served the repasts at tables behind the potted palms. Soon her lunch was in great demand until talk of her innovation reached Marshall Field and this master of supply and demand expanded on the young lady's idea.

On April 15, 1890, a long procession of elegant carriages lined up along Washington Street. The fashionable "First Ladies" of Chicago, with names like Swift, Cudahy, MacCormick, and Ryerson, stepped forth. They had been invited by Mr. Field to open the first tearoom. The early menu cards were covered with pure linen and edged with imported lace. The finest white linen was used at table and the china bore a gold leaf border. The silver service was heavy and ornate; chafing dishes and special casseroles were used for service. The cooking was done miles away in a suburban bungalow. One of the menu's staples was, and is today, the famous chicken pot pie. Tea served between 3:00 and 5:00 became popular. It also became the custom during late afternoon hours to serve a cup of steaming bouillon to all "female clerks"—on the personal instructions from Marshall Field. "It builds strength and preserves good health," stated an executive memo.

There was a special "Hygienic menu" compiled by one Dr. E. N. Davies of the College of Surgeons. It described dishes "best suited for those of frail or delicate health."

While it would seem that Field's was perhaps ahead of the times serving "health" food, there were areas where the Quaker and Calvinist strict principles stood firm. Cocktail service was not introduced into the tearooms until a few years ago. "We have never rushed into anything that might offend any of our customers," Arthur E. Osborne, president of Field's Chicago division, explained. In this same temporal spirit Fields belatedly (compared to other department stores) opened a spirits shop. In true Field's tradition, however, it quickly became known for its fine liquors and superb wines.

Field's take-out food services include breads and pastries, ice cream, various foods served in the restaurants such as shrimp de Jonghe, bouillabaisse, a variety of quiches, and the beloved chicken pies. A line of frozen foods is available. Food products, like other Field's merchandise, meet a standard of high quality.

The food factories are located on the eighth floor of the State Street store. To have full-scale manufacturing of baked goods, ice cream, and candy taking place above the 28 Shop and the tearooms, and below the Trend House model rooms and the home furnishings and paint departments, is but another facet of the fabulous Field's operation and personality.

A tour of the candy kitchen reveals a study in chiaroscuro. White uniforms, caps, and aprons are highlighted by blobs and streaks of black—bittersweet and semi-sweet chocolate — and brown—milk chocolate—in pots and tubs and vats. Lightning flashes of black and brown dart across the canvas of the workroom as nimble fingers swirl and dip nougat and fondant nodules and lace the tops with delicate lines. letters, and peaks—symbols that are clues to the flavors and fillings beneath the shiny chocolate veneer. The confections are dropped onto a tray etched with small signatures. The molds daintily imprint "Fields" on the bottom of the bonbons. Hands, elbow-deep in the semi-liquid goo that oozes over the white marble slabs, continuously knead the mud-colored masses into the desired consistency. The swift movements are like a black and white kinetoscopic show. "Hand-dipping chocolates is a dying art," the kitchen's production manager explained.

Elsewhere in the room are cauldrons of bubbling brown sugars. Boiling oils spit and pop—roasting and toasting the mixed abstract-shaped, nut-brown nuts. Sheets of toffee crunch spread out on tables resemble edible Jackson Pollock canvases and make up a gallery of munchy, textured landscapes.

Caramels move along a conveyor belt through a machine that resembles a mini-carwash, but there are no jets of suds, hot wax, or warm air. A liquid chocolate dribbles down over the chewy lumps. The excess passes through a screen and is pumped up again to continuously coat the moving line of goodies. A glorious lip-smacking fantasy of driving a kiddie car through the machine comes to mind—eat your heart out, Charlie, in *your* chocolate factory? The machine is called an enrober.

The sweet pungent smell of peppermint fills the air. Other hands move in rhythm from chocolates to pleated paper cups to moving boxes. Any temptation—one quick hand to mouth movement, or a slip of the lip, so to speak—could gum up the works. These boxes contain the Marshall Field's "Setays," chocolates named (although no one seems to know exactly why) after the beloved general manager and executive vice-president, David M. Yates. "Setay" is Yates spelled backwards.

The charm of David Yates was legend. His nephew, Clarkson Bradford, recalled a swift, unbroken early-morning ride down State Street during the 1930s in his uncle's limousine as policemen held back traffic along the route. It was said that only at Christmastime did the limousine stop. Then the gracious Mr. Yates greeted each officer and handed out his Christmas cards. What else the envelopes might have contained no one knows. There was also the story of the gentlemanly Mr. Yates becoming indignant with an interior decorator who planned to cover the mahogany-paneled women's wear Grand Salon with fabric. "You can't cover that with drapes!" Mr. Yates snapped. The decorator, Mrs. Clara Wilson, replied, "There is positive worship of mahogany in this place. It seems to be one of the great articles of faith in the religion of this store." Mr. Yates was not amused. "Mrs. Wilson," he said, "that is *solid* mahogany!"

The most famous of all the Field's candies are the "Frangos" (patent registered). This deep, rich chocolate combined with a hint of mint is the base of the famous Frango Mint pie, Frango Mint ice cream, Frango Mint sauce, and paper-thin Frango Thin Mints. The genesis of this name came from the Seattle-based Frederick and Nelson Co. when the store was acquired in 1929 by Marshall Field

& Company. Originally the chocolates were named "Franco," an aggregate of the letters in the firm's name, FR-A-N-CO. While changing the name of the candy could hardly have been called a strong political statement, "There came a time," president Osborne explained, "when the name Franco for something as delicious as our chocolates was deemed inappropriate." Hence— FR...A...N...*GO*.

It is necessary for the candy kitchen, like the display department, to get a jump on the yuletide season. "We begin our preparations for Christmas in the middle of the year," the manager said. "Many of our products can be stored but not frozen. Proper temperatures are the most important element in keeping our confections fresh. Fortunately, by the time our cold storage is full, the weather has turned. As Field customers prepare for the winter, we are able to place thousands of our candies and chocolate mints in the cold fur vaults as they become empty." Given the vaults' contents and the margin for human error, an order-form typo requesting delivery of 1,000 chocolate-covered *minks* would seem to be a frightening possibility. "Highly unlikely," commented an executive. Then, contemplating such a disaster with amusement, he added, "Certainly *not* at Marshall Field's."

"Take him away, John Field, he's no good. Your son will never be a merchant. Put him back on the farm," said Gilbert Davis, known as "Deacon" and the proprietor of the largest general store in Pittsfield, Massachusetts. He spoke of fourteen-year-old Marshall, who had come the twenty-five miles from his home in Conway to work for Deacon Davis. While the boy put in long hours and was meticulous about every detail, his painful shyness eliminated any hope for success as a salesman. Over the years, however, the ladies began to admire the quiet attention paid to them by the young clerk and they demanded that he wait on them. By 1856, at the age of twenty-two, Marshall Field felt he had outgrown the small-town store. He moved on to the frontier city of Chicago and took a job as a clerk in a pioneer mercantile firm, Cooley, Wadsworth and Company.

Ten years later the young Quaker joined with a Dutch Calvinist accountant, Levi Leiter, in buying an interest in the Potter Palmer Dry Goods store, which had opened at 137 Lake Street in 1852.

The firm became Field, Palmer & Leiter. Two years later Mr. Palmer dropped out of the partnership and Field, Leiter and Co. was formed. In 1881 Leiter retired and Marshall Field & Company was the sole possession of the man who had *not* gone back to the farm in his youth. At the time of his death in 1906, Marshall Field was one of the richest men in the world. His son, Marshall Field II, had died a few months earlier from a gunshot wound thought to be self-inflicted but termed accidental. The tragic death was clouded in mystery. No member of the Field family ran the store after the founder's death, although a nephew, Stanley Field, was on the board of directors until he died in 1964. Field's grandson and great-grandson also served on the board. In 1966, after the death of Marshall Field IV, 126,000 of his 177,000 shares in the firm were sold on the Midwest Stock Exchange for $6,498,000. Marshall Field V, publisher of the *Chicago Sun-Times*, is not involved in the store management, nor is he a member of the board.

Marshall Field's State Street is, along with Macy's New York and J. L. Hudson, Detroit, one of the largest stores in the country. Marshall Field & Company, with thirty-one stores, including Frederick & Nelson and the Crescent stores in the Pacific northwest and Halle's in Ohio, was the leader among the independent department stores in 1976 with a volume of $611 million. It was followed by Carson Pirie Scott, Woodward & Lathrop, Strawbridge & Clothier, John Wanamaker, B. Altman, and Higbee. In the same year, Field's Chicago division, with a volume of $420 million in five stores, ranked seventh below Macy's (New York), Hudson's (Detroit), Broadway (Los Angeles), May Co. (California), Abraham & Straus (Brooklyn), and Bamberger's (New Jersey). Early in 1978, after Carter Hawley Hale Stores, Inc., of California withdrew as a threatening takeover, Marshall Field & Company acquired five Liberty House department stores in Oregon and Washington from Amfac, Inc., for $14 million in cash. "We, Marshall Field & Company," said president Osborne, "are positioned in our retailing career to become a national retail operation. We have stores almost coast to coast and we now have a southwest division. We have had to reorganize some of the traditional Field's management policies. We've brought in people from the outside, something that was very rare in the past, but we are creating a team. We will still be able to pass the baton of management along."

The State Street store and older suburban stores are in the throes of a $15.1 million remodeling job. Many of the changes are painful. The "worship of mahogany," even *solid* mahogany, has had to go. Not to be replaced by cheap materials, however, but by costly, lighter, more modern pecan wood. "A 'cheap' substitute just wouldn't be Field's," said an executive.

While change may be difficult for management, there is one segment of the State Street customers for whom the changes are traumatic. These are the famous "Field's Ladies," little old lady shoppers who are unique to Field's. Field's Ladies cut across every social, economic, and racial boundary. They have a classic look—sensible shoes, a loose-fitting coat, a hat, and an ever-present shopping bag. "I think that the shopping bags are surgically attached," said a Field's Ladies observer. "If somebody tries to swipe one of those bags in this town, he gets the little old lady with it."

There are Basement Ladies and Tea Room Ladies. They seldom cross over, one into another's territory. They both avoid the Main Floor, except to meet friends at the Randolph Street entrance. There is too much activity on the Main Floor and they are fearful of being knocked down in the rush. Basement Field's Ladies wear squirrel or muskrat fur pieces or collars and wool knit caps. Their shopping bags are string or plastic. Tea Room Ladies wear mink or broadtail and a variety of chapeaux and carry the green Marshall Field & Co. shopping bag. Some bring their grandchildren to see the decorations at Christmas and Easter; others fill their loneliness in conversations with the courteous clerks. Some Field's Ladies can be seen lunching or shopping with their daughters. The daughters wear classic-cut belted raincoats and by the year 2000 will more than likely be Field's Ladies themselves. Field's Ladies come from Roger's Park and they come from Lake Forest. They do not go to suburban or Michigan Avenue stores. Their store is State Street. They come by public transportation and they come by limousine. They have the $1.50 hot lunch in the basement dinette or a cocktail or tea in the Walnut Room. They are militant about the changes and voice their objections to clerks, managers, other Field's Ladies, and anyone who will listen, all the way up to top executives. These Ladies need no signs or maps to guide them through Field's. They know every square foot of the enormous acreage of "their store"—or did.

There are other changes that the Field's Ladies must cope with. "Occasionally there are confrontations," said a Field's Ladies watcher. "The china and glassware departments are favorite haunts. There is always something on sale or they might find a piece to match their wedding china from 1918. For a while, their presence in these departments was being challenged by the gays and you could see them hassling over the same bowl or clutching the same bread-and-butter plate. Of course the Field's Ladies would win. After all, they have been around here before there was such a thing as *gays*. The gays have pretty much retreated up to Michigan Avenue."

Field's Ladies, whether they are buying a 59¢ washcloth in the Budget Department or a gown in the 28 Shop, share an undying loyalty to the store. Aren't they the very *ladies* that Mr. Field said should be given what they wanted? There are Ladies who can remember coming to the store as little girls on opening day in 1907—no one is going to take *their* store away from them. When word of the possible California corporation take-over reached the papers, the Ladies were in a rage and near panic. "Sell Field's? Why that's ridiculous," a Field's Lady remarked. "They might as well drain the Lake *and* burn the city to the ground again. Marshall Field's is the only civilized place in this town. Take that away and what have you got? Just the old muddy swamp. Marshall Field's, you see, *is* Chicago."

In spite of the staid, solid, conservative image of Marshall Field & Company, it has not been inured to change. There has been constant change, although at times it was slow in coming during the store's 125-year history. There were the early physical changes necessitated by the disastrous fires that leveled the store in 1871 and again in 1877 when the store had to relocate temporarily and rebuild. There were changes in the company structure from its founding in 1852 as P. Palmer & Co. (written thus because the sign painter charged by the letter) to the partnership of Field, Palmer & Leiter, to Field, Leiter & Company, to Marshall Field & Company in 1881. There were innovations during the 1890s—the tearooms, large display windows, and the installation of the Big Clocks.

There were changes in the famous Marshall Field Wholesale Division, which once sent hundreds of "whizbangs"—energetic, smooth salesmen—throughout the country, like Roland Marks, who did $2 million a year in black cotton and silk stockings and who wore flashing diamond rings and had a string of actress girl-friends. It was these colorful drummers who made Marshall Field a household word throughout the country for fifty years until the wholesale business began to fall off in the 1920s. In an effort to re-vitalize the business, Marshall Field & Company built the massive Merchandise Mart, which continued to be a drain on the company through the Depression until it was sold to a combine headed by Jo-seph P. Kennedy in 1945. The Wholesale Division was liquidated in 1935.

There were changes in the manufacturing empire that began with the purchase of a textile mill in North Carolina and spread through the south and Indiana and Illinois. The cottons, woolens, laces, and knits were eventually consolidated under the Fieldcrest label. The last of the mills, originally meant to be a source of supply for the Wholesale Division, was sold in 1953.

If Marshall Field salesmen spread the company name throughout the United States, it was Marshall Field buyers who carried it throughout the world.

A 1927 full-page institutional ad in the *Chicago Tribune* head-lined, "How Do You Get Those Curious and Beautiful Things?," explained: "One answer is that our buyers travel annually 3,500,000 miles for them or 140 times the distance around the earth." Field's buyers scoured the five continents for the best, the unusual, and the exotic. As late as 1932, Field's had a handkerchief factory and resident representative in Swatow, China, 200 miles east of Canton. The cloth that was used came from Europe, princi-pally Ireland. In Swatow it was cut into strips and stamped with de-signs. The strips were contracted out to the villagers. Each district made part of the work—drawn work, embroidery, hand roll, petit point, and hemming. The handkerchiefs were returned to the fac-tory to be washed, ironed, inspected, and shipped. In the States, they were boxed and made ready for sale.

The biggest risks were faced by the Oriental rug buyers, who traveled into the remote regions of Persia, Baluchistan, Tibet, In-dia, Indochina, Siam, China, and Japan—often by donkey or cam-el, often accompanied by rifle-carrying tribesmen who protected them from bandits. They were subjected to monsoon floods and typhoons and cholera and plague epidemics. In 1931, Mr. Hinske wrote of his adventures:

> Leaving Peking, I took the train for Tsinanfu. About an hour away from Tsinanfu, I was informed that it was absolutely unsafe to go on at night, due to the bandits in the vicinity, so I got off the train at Techow and spent the night lying on a kong fully dressed with the brief case for a pillow. Early in the morning I took a jinrikisha to the Yellow River and ferried across with a load of hogs and sheep. I found Tsinanfu a barricaded city. On every principal corner were sandbag barricades, with machine guns placed so that they could sweep in either direction.

This excerpt from an article, "Mr. Hinske Goes to China," appeared in 1931 in the Field's house magazine, *The Shield*. It might well have been written by a breed that was yet to come—the war correspondent—rather than an Oriental rug buyer.

World War II put an end to such adventuresome buying trips. Then Iron and Bamboo Curtains were drawn across many exotic marketplaces. Postwar air travel, rental cars, Telexes, and the expansion of foreign buying offices marked the end of journeys like an itinerary described in a full-page Field's ad headlined "The Quest" for the two buyers who traveled over 40,000 miles in ten months:

> It was a stupendous task, entailing incessant labor, great hardships and risks—no doubt one of the most rigorous and dangerous adventures in the story of modern merchandising. Only the objective of securing surpassing collections of fine and rare rugs would have justified such an undertaking.

The "Man from Field's" in boots and breeches with pith helmet, squinting into the sunset from the deck of a river steamer heading into the interior—buying, has joined the shadowy figure of the "Man from Field's" who had moved by train, sled, horseback, or wagon through the Dakotas, Nebraska, Arizona, and along the Pacific Coast, with his sample trunks and order books, staging concerts, prayer meetings, country socials—selling. Although these buyers and sellers faded into the past and were as outmoded in a world of Kleenex as embroidered linen handkerchiefs, they were part of the background, the strength, and the color in the intricately woven tapestry of merchandising that was Field's.

There has been wear and tear on the fabric of the store over the years—fires, panics, depressions, the death of the founder and other great personnel, and financial ups and downs. There have been the changes in the dominant patterns of the company—from wholesale to retail and the elimination of manufacturing. But like the store's beautiful Tabriz, Kurdistan, and Blue Bokhara Orientals, rugs that take on a patina with age and use, Marshall Field & Company has worn well.

In 1970, plans for Water Tower Place, an urban center on Chicago's North Michigan Avenue, were announced. The $160 million structure was a co-venture of Urban Investment and Development Co., a subsidiary of Aetna Life & Casualty, and Mafco, Inc., a subsidiary of Marshall Field & Company, under the corporate name of Marban. The 74-story multi-use complex would cover a full city block and be anchored at the base by Marshall Field & Company and Lord & Taylor stores. The high-rise would include an eight-level shopping mall, a stage theater, four movie theaters, a bank, corporate and professional offices, restaurants, a hotel, condominium residences, and parking.

Water Tower Place takes its name from the Old Chicago Water Tower located at Chicago and Michigan. The Tower once stood along the shoreline before landfill left it stranded several blocks inland from the Lake. This beloved landmark had survived the Great Fire of 1871 which devastated a great portion of the city, including $2.5 million worth of stock and the "marble palace" that had been the Field and Leiter store. The Old Water Tower, described as "castellated Gothic" in style, had long been a symbol of the city's determination to rebuild and to grow. Oscar Wilde on a visit to Chicago called the Tower "a monstrosity with pepper boxes stuck all over it." He was confounded that "people could so abuse Gothic art and make a structure look not like a water tower, but like a tower of a medieval castle." The Tower is defended and venerated by Chicagoans. When a plan was afoot to tear it down to make room for the widening of Michigan Avenue, there was such a clamor that the city planners were forced to angle Michigan Avenue rather than drive it through the Water Tower.

North Michigan Avenue stretches from the Michigan Avenue Bridge to Oak Street. It was once lined with the mansions of the rich. Today it is lined with elegant shops like Tiffany, Gucci, Elizabeth Arden, Saks Fifth Avenue, I. Magnin, Bonwit Teller and most recently Field's and Lord & Taylor, filled with merchandise for the rich and not-so-rich. There are elegant boutiques, fur salons, jewelry shops, shoe stores, and galleries. The avenue, known as the "Magnificent Mile," is the main shopping area for tourists and shoppers from outlying communities and the residents of Chicago's Gold Coast, a favorite neighborhood of the well-heeled since the 1890s. It lies along the shores of Michi-Guma, as the Alongonquins called the Great Water—Lake Michigan.

The original plans for Water Tower Place were not necessarily grandiose. They were conceived as a Marshall Field store with rental apartments and perhaps a few offices.

For years buyers had been eyeing a vacant area along North Michigan Avenue that contained nothing but a couple of billboards. The property was owned by Seagram, the massive liquor corporation, which, despite abandonment of its own plans to build on the property, had turned down all offers for the prime real estate. Philip M. Klutznick (the retired former chairman of the board of Urban Investment and Development) succeeded where others had failed and acquired the Michigan Avenue parcel. Mr. Klutznick and the late Samuel Bronfman of Seagram had had a longstanding friendship and association through their work with Jewish philanthropies. With the frontage on Michigan Avenue secured, Mr. Klutznick and the others associated with the project began to expand their thinking.

"Gradually a plan evolved to do more and more to justify the use of the land," explained James Klutznick, Philip Klutznick's son and executive vice-president of UIDC Management, Inc., the management and leasing arm of Urban Investment and Development. The scope of the project necessitated further land acquisition, which in turn affected the scope of the project. A parcel on Chestnut Street was owned by John Hancock insurance people and any construction on the site was limited to a height of 559 feet, according to a deed restriction that would protect the view of Hancock Center apartment dwellers. The old Pearson Hotel was purchased and demolished. Parcel by parcel, the entire block was pieced together and plans for a city within a city became a reality.

Viewed from the South Side, Water Tower Place resembles a high, white squared-off boot with the toe of the twelve-story foot pointing toward Michigan Avenue. Behind this simple-looking silhouette lie 3.1 million square feet of the most complicated building in Chicago.

The low-rise portion of Water Tower Place comprises four below-ground parking levels, the eight-level Atrium Mall, the 1,300-seat Drury Lane Theater, the Mezzanine, a restaurant complex adjoining the theater, comprised of three distinct facilities that include a cocktail lounge, The Courtyard, a gardenlike area dotted with serving kiosks, and The Pearson Room for formal dining. The four motion picture theaters on the second floor each hold 250 people in seats "designed under the supervision of an orthopedic surgeon."

Marshall Field & Company and Lord and Taylor share the "Magnificent Mile" frontage on the ground floor and mezzanine. By the second-floor level, Lord & Taylor has shifted to an area along the north side and northeast corner of the building over the Drury Lane Theater. The second floor area that opens onto the Atrium (which in a traditional up-and-down building would have been occupied by Lord & Taylor) is filled with shops. By the third floor, the space that had been Lord & Taylor on the ground and mezzanine levels, and shops on the second level, is now occupied by Marshall Field's. At the third level, Lord & Taylor occupies the entire area across the back of the building. In other words, Lord & Taylor, which at ground level occupies the *northwest* corner, has moved by the third level to occupy the whole *northeast* and *southeast* corners of the building. Since the building is solid, except for the ground-floor display windows, and the customer moves through intricate escalator and elevator systems, both within the individual stores (Field's and Lord & Taylor), within the Atrium Mall, and within the center well of the building, he is unaware that by the time he is shopping on the third, fourth, fifth, sixth, or seventh floor of Lord & Taylor, he is a full city block away from where he started out at the Michigan Avenue entrance.

It should be pointed out that Chicagoans think differently from the rest of the world about space and directions. They do not think up and down, left and right, and 1-2-3-4. City streets are named rather than numbered. Unless one has memorized the streets in sequence, the only point of reference is Lake Michigan, which is "*always* on the east" one is told, as though that simplifies anything.

Chicago, which grew out of a marshy portage point, "Checagou" (known to the Indians as the place where the wild onions grew in abundance), has a long heritage of making space adapt to the city rather than the city adapting to space.

By the 1850s, the mud and muck on which the city was built had rendered the streets all but impassable. In 1855 the city council decided to lift the city out of the quagmire, and for the next twenty years, one of the most unusual projects in the history of city building took place. The *raising of Chicago* was one of the great wonders of the nineteenth century. Buildings were jacked up anywhere from a height of four to fourteen feet. New drainage and fill were placed underneath. New foundations were laid. At the same time, streets were raised with fill, then regraded and paved with a unique mixture called Nicholson pavement, consisting of boulder stone, block limestone, macadam, and cinders. There was a business-as-usual attitude as this bizarre project took place. A guest who stayed in the Tremont House over a period of time realized that the building was being lifted when he became aware that the front steps became steeper each day. Streets were widened and buildings were also moved around like so many children's playing blocks. In an era of horse, mule, and manpower, what would seem impossible was not unusual. Whole blocks of buildings were lifted and moved back to allow for the widening of streets or taken blocks away to a new location. Often, the owner of a three- or four-story building could be seen sitting casually by his shop on top of a platform that was being laboriously dragged by mule teams through and over the mud. All this effort to make the city livable only heightened the tragedy of the 1871 Great Fire. The twentieth-century Water Tower Place special adaptations seem minor in view of the "raising" feat.

"The complicated arrangement of the Lord & Taylor space was necessitated by the fact that both our major stores wanted frontage on Michigan Avenue. Once this was accomplished, Field's, being a partner in the venture, had a say in the use of the space above the street level," James Klutznick explained. The masterful plan was the joint venture of architects and engineers Loebl, Schlossman & Hackl and C. F. Murphy Associates. Warren Platner Associates were architectural consultants. "One of our biggest problems was convincing other retailers that our malls from the mezzanine through the seventh floor were like streets themselves. Shopkeepers at first had difficulty in comprehending what a vertical mall was. They all wanted entrances on Michigan Avenue or at least the side streets."

Much of the credit for turning retailers' street-access thinking around is given to the indomitable Mildred Custin. "Mildred knew Michigan Avenue from her association with Bonwit Teller. She put on her hard hat and after climbing around the construction, through all the chaos, she could envision an interior Bond Street or Rue St. Honoré. She knew we had a good thing going that would make desirable locations for fashion boutiques," he added.

The third level emerged as the high-fashion floor housing Courreges, Halston, and Rodier of Paris along with Matthews, Jaeger, and Tennis Lady. There is a Vidal Sassoon Beauty Salon and Georgette Klinger Skin Care Salon.

Throughout the other levels, there are mixes of shops, services, and restaurants. Once Water Tower Place went into operation, proximity to the ground floor seemed to have little bearing on business. "Our highest producer of income per square foot is located on the seventh floor. It is a very *special* specialty shop, Joy's Clock Shop."

Another superstar attraction in Water Tower Place, D. B. Kaplan's Delicatessen, uses its seventh-floor location to advantage. The three-foot menu, a 1977 winner of the National Restaurant Association Great Menu Award, notes: "Never before has a restaurant delicatessen risen to such great heights (7th floor, Water Tower Place). Nowhere on earth will you find a sandwich more mountainous than at . . . D. B. Kaplan's." The breezy menu lists 152 kinds of sandwiches such as: #7 A Brisket, A Basket; #8 Tongue Fu; #9 Studs Turkey; #49 is a Lana Tuna and #96 a Vidal Sardine. Among the seafood offerings are Lox, Stock & Bagel, Lox-A-Luck, Chicago White Lox, Lox & Brentano's, and Fish Shtik, along with Hickory Dickory Lox, and the ultimate—the Lox Ness

Monster. The menu notes that there are no charges for toasting, extra topping such as lettuce, onions, or sauerkraut, nor for condiments. There are charges for extra cheese—35¢, and for "Too much grief and aggravation to the waitress—25¢." It is fortunate that such lively reading material is at hand, since the waiting lines usually extend out into the mall.

Offices and professional suites for doctors, dentists, and businesses are located on the eighth and ninth floors.

On the twelfth floor, or roughly the ankle of the boot, the lobby, public rooms, and restaurants of the lavish Ritz-Carlton Hotel are located. There is also the exclusive Carlton Club and swimming pool and health club. The hotel rooms occupy twenty-one floors above the lobby.

The Chicago Ritz-Carlton is the second Ritz-Carlton in the United States—the other being the Boston Ritz, which was built in 1927. The six other Ritz hotels are located in Paris, London, Madrid, Montreal, Lisbon, and Barcelona. Originally Cabot, Cabot & Forbes, a real estate development company in Boston and owner of that city's Ritz, had a 50 percent investment in the Chicago Ritz. The other half was owned by Marban, the combine of the Urban Development Corporation and Mafco, the Marshall Field & Co. subsidiary. Before the hotel's 1975 opening, Cabot, Cabot & Forbes sold its holdings to Marban. In the fall of 1977, Four Seasons Ltd., a hotel firm based in Toronto, Canada, took over the management and became a partner. Marshall Field & Co. has relinquished part of its ownership and the Ritz-Chicago is now owned by Urban Development—70 percent; Four Seasons, Ltd.—25 percent; and Field's—5 percent. It was questioned whether Field's belonged in the hotel business. The various corporate entities had several conflicting ideas, among them the plans for the interiors. The public rooms were designed by Fred Schmid Associates, the bedrooms and suites were decorated by Field's.

The main lobby of the hotel is vast and luxurious and decorated by a central fountain and giant bronze bird sculpture, with a decorative skylight above. The Greenhouse, an area that extends along the side of the lobby, has Italian mosaic tiled floors and masses of trees, plants, and wicker furnishings. A sloping glass ceiling and glass walls offer a magnificent view of the Chicago skyline. Lunch and cocktails are served in this cool, fresh setting. Other public rooms are quite simply The Bar, The Dining Room, The Cafe, The Terrace, and The Ballroom. If the names are understatedly elegant, the rooms themselves are deliciously extravagant with French pinewood paneling, beveled mirrors, Louis XV chairs, Louis XIII chandeliers, and exquisite carpeting. The ambiance is sophisticated and urbane.

The guest rooms are spacious and were decorated in a traditional manner by Marshall Field & Company. Attention has been given to details such as AM/FM clock radios, color television, electric blankets, closet rods high enough for evening gowns, windows that open, and an electric call button to summon the floor waiter. There is a pantry on every floor, which is a concept of service in Ritz hotels throughout the world. One complaint about the hotel has been that the room decor is too conservative. A gentleman in town for a convention said, "When you come to Chicago, you want to swing a little. If you've been out on the town and come back to your room at the Ritz, it's so genteel you half expect to find your mother waiting up for you—if you know what I mean." There is a world of travelers, it would seem, who have become too accustomed to hotel plastic and the ice machine down the hall. Plans are afoot to "jazz up" the guest accommodations, according to a Ritz executive. *Swingers* have not been completely overlooked, however. There are suites with oversized double marble bathtubs, but the price for a sudsy romp would be costly. Suite rates start at $220 per day. "And besides," said the conventioneer, "they're called *Anniversary* Suites. Who comes to Chicago for a guilt trip?"

Above the hotel, in the calf of the boot, are forty floors of condominium residences. They are reached by a private entrance on Pearson Street. The apartments offer spectacular views of the Lake, the Gold Coast, and the city. They are the ultimate in luxurious city living. The large rooms have nine-foot ceilings. There are his and her bath and dressing rooms equipped with tubs, showers, and a bidet. Some models include a sauna.

Other amenities go with living in the Water Tower: the convenience of the shops and services in the nearby Atrium Mall and the proximity of doctors and dentists and restaurants and entertainment. Memberships are available in The Spa, the health club, and pool in the Ritz-Carlton. The hotel will provide maid, secretarial, and catering services. Chauffeured limousines are available. It is, in short, a joyous way to live in the middle of a city. The apartments range in price from $240,000 to $500,000, depending on size and floor location.

Looking down from a Water Tower Condominium, one becomes aware of the beauty of Chicago—the Lake, the wide boulevards, and the numerous parks and trees—one of the benefits of the city's high water table. "It is just about an ideal way of living. The only thing missing is a golf course," my host said. "I was raised in Rockford. My father had a little hardware store and we all lived over it. I have to say that moving in here and being able to pay a quarter of a million dollars for an apartment made me finally realize that I wasn't a small-town boy anymore. It's funny how things change."

"Not so much," his wife said. "If you stop and think about it, darling, you *still* live over the store."

"Yes," he said, "but the store is Marshall Field's, and that's class!"

PART IV

New York, New York
1823–1978

TEN

The Ladies Mile and Beyond

Broadway and Sixth Avenue

The humble dry-goods shops located along the wharves of lower Manhattan in the early nineteenth century were the genesis of several New York department and specialty stores. The mercantile trek north from the tip of the island to the fringes of Central Park at Fifth Avenue spanned more than a hundred years. There were stopovers. Shopping districts flourished, then moved on. With any migration there are casualties. The weak are passed by, they grow weaker and succumb. In such a manner, unprofitable or outmoded stores foundered and collapsed by the wayside. The vigorous ones moved ahead, jumping over one another and leaping blocks of real estate like they were playing a game of giant checkers.

One of the earliest New York stores was A. T. Stewart's. It was founded in 1823 by twenty-two-year-old Alexander Turney Stewart, who had been born in Belfast, Ireland, and educated at Trinity College, Dublin. Stewart's had a modest beginning as a dry-goods shop on Chambers Street. When it expanded in 1862 to Broadway and Tenth Street, it was the first store to be built along the Ladies Mile—the area between Eighth and Twenty-third streets and Broadway and Sixth Avenue that was to become New York's main shopping district during the latter half of the nineteenth century. This mercantile palace, the world's largest department store at that time, had a central rotunda, double staircase, and continuous organ music. The store made Alexander Stewart a millionaire. When he died in 1876, Stewart was reputed to be the richest man in America.

The oldest *specialty* store in New York was the outgrowth of a dry-goods shop opened in 1826 by an immigrant from the Isle of Wight, Aaron Arnold. The store became Arnold Constable when Mr. Arnold's son-in-law, James Constable, was accepted as a partner. Arnold Constable joined the march up the Ladies Mile in 1868 by building at Broadway and Nineteenth Street. The store's Broadway facade was white marble, while the Nineteenth Street facade was cast in iron—the architectural rage of the period. Cast-iron pieces could be molded into the decorative designs of Art Nouveau. The intricate Moorish filigree and iron trellises could be bolted together to form the fanciful façades that were the fashion of the Victorian era. The pieces were molded into ornamental staircases with elaborate grilled railings. A few of the buildings were constructed with primitive iron frameworks. These early forerunners of steel skyscrapers were half-hearted attempts to fortify buildings against fire, a major threat to all city structures. Arnold Constable followed the move east to Fifth Avenue in the area around the Thirties at the turn of the century. The store flourished for over fifty years. When Arnold Constable closed its doors Lord & Taylor became the sole surviving early dockside shop.

Lord & Taylor was nearly fifty years old when it moved onto the Ladies Mile in 1872. The building at Broadway and Twentieth Street was called a "French Second Empire Extravaganza." This was the firm's fifth location since its 1826 opening at 49 Catherine Street, near the Catherine Slip where the sailing vessels berthed and the "horse ferry" arrived and departed for Brooklyn.

Samuel Lord had been the youngest of nine Lord children who were orphaned in Saddleworth in the West Riding County of York, England. He spent his childhood in poverty, misery, and hard work. As a young boy, he apprenticed as an iron molder and eventually became a master in a foundry in Marsden, England. At the age of twenty-one, he married the boss's daughter, Mary Taylor, and the young couple set off for the New World. He worked briefly in Pennsylvania and New Jersey as an iron molder and then with a thousand dollars borrowed from his wife's uncle, John Taylor, he opened a dry-goods store on Catherine Street. He was twenty-three. Within the year, he took his wife's cousin, George Washington Taylor, into partnership. Whether Mr. John Taylor loaned the money with the proviso that his son came with it, or whether he sent his son to protect his interest is not recorded. Not only was the partnership successful, the men became close friends. Mr. Lord named his oldest son John Taylor Lord after his mentor. He named his second son George Washington Taylor Lord after his partner. His third son was named Samuel Lord, Junior. Mr. Taylor retired to Manchester, England, in 1852 but the name Lord & Taylor remained.

Catherine Street, the site of the first Lord & Taylor, was a lively, noisy, bustling market and the center of New York's commerce. A custom of the street was the hiring of "pullers in," persistent youths who aggressively and often forcibly hustled customers into shops. Mr. Lord and Mr. Taylor refused to follow this custom. Shoppers were free of this harassment along the street in front of Lord & Taylor. Perhaps as a gesture of gratitude, the customers flocked into the little shop. Within six years Lord & Taylor moved along Catherine Street into a four-story building.

During the 1840s the partners opened a store in New Orleans. This was too far away to be considered a branch, but a hundred years later, Lord & Taylor was a leader in the development of branch stores in New York's suburbs. The first branch of Lord & Taylor was opened in Manhasset, Long Island, in 1941. This kind of expansion came to a halt with the curtailment of building during World War II. It started again in the late forties and reached boom proportions. It was a trend that would revolutionize retaiiing.

The move to the suburbs and expansion into various cities called for huge amounts of capital, the accuracy of a diamond-cutter in pinpointing a site, the timing of a gymnast and—a lot of luck. Any mistake could be disastrous. Some stores moved too fast into certain suburbs only to find the developments had turned in another direction and not followed. Others delayed and found themselves being abandoned in decaying downtowns. Stores merged to survive. Others were sold to giant retail corporations or huge conglomerates—American and foreign—to raise capital. Before a store expands, the efforts to follow the old drummer's adage, "You gotta know the territory," are monumental. Experts are hired and masses of information are fed into computers. Intimate and comprehensive details about the area and the people in it are broken down into statistics, charts, and maps to be studied and collated. If, however, that mysterious, fickle, unpredictable ingredient—the customer—doesn't respond, no amount of marketing research, traffic surveys, population studies, and promotional hoopla will serve as "pullers in."

Today many luxury stores are becoming national stores spread throughout the country, not unlike the chain stores, Sears, Penney's, and Montgomery Ward. For example, demographic and family-income studies have turned Washington into a boom town for luxury buyers and sellers. In 1976, Bloomingdale's opened stores in the Washington suburbs of Tyson's Corner, Virginia and White Flint, Maryland. There is talk of a possible third store in the area. Neiman-Marcus opened the Mazza Gallerie store in Chevy Chase in 1977 near the old Washington standbys Woodward & Lathrop and Hecht's. Lord & Taylor arrived on the capital scene fifteen years ago, followed by Saks Fifth Avenue five years later. Chairman of the board of Saks, Allen Johnson, has said they are giving thought to another store in the Washington neighborhood. I. Magnin will open a White Flint store. According to _The New York Times_ (January 2, 1978) in an article titled "Washington Spending Spree Makes Retail Business Boom":

> Marjory Segal, director of public relations for Lord & Taylor, the first New York store to move into the Washington area, said, "I think other retailers have finally gotten the message. I'm a native Washingtonian and I've seen the growth in the metropolitan area. We've finally arrived. The money is here. The power is here. And the customer is here and sales have been steadily increasing. People used to run up to New York to shop, but I'm wondering if New York isn't coming to us now."
>
> Even if Washington doesn't have the elan of New York, it certainly, as Page Lee Hufty, the socialite, said at the Washington opening of Bloomingdale's, is "no longer hicksville."

"Expansion has led to the death of exclusivity," said Neiman vice-president Tom Alexander. "That is one of the reasons we work so hard to keep our _Texas-ish-ness_, for want of a better word. The next generation should be mining the ore out of the mine already sunk. You can't go running around adding 150,000 square feet of store every year—you'll run out of geography." The "expand or die" philosophy prompted another executive to remark: "Where will it all end? Perhaps the United States will become one enormous shopping mall, anchored on the west by I. Magnin, in the east by Saks Fifth, the north by Marshall Field, and the south by Neiman-Marcus. Already we're all falling all over each other." Another merchant suggested: "Maybe we should just put a dome over the whole country and turn it into one great big, air-conditioned Bloomingdale's."

Back in the simpler days, Mr. Lord and Mr. Taylor retired their profitable New Orleans store in the 1850s in order to have funds to move with New York's flow of business north to Grand and Chrystie streets. They opened in 1853. Most important, this move took them out of the south. Money and merchandise tied up and blockaded during the Civil War was a calamity for many merchants and one from which most of them didn't recover.

Prior to the outbreak of war in 1861, Lord & Taylor moved again, into a 100x100-foot store at Grand and Broadway. Mr. Taylor had retired to England and Mr. Lord was joined by his son John Taylor Lord as a partner. When the supply of cotton from the south was cut off, anyone with manufactured goods on hand could demand and get fabulous prices. The wartime profits made it possible for the Lords to retire when the conflict was over. Samuel Lord returned to Oakleigh, Ashton-on-Mersey, in Cheshire, England, a wealthy man and lived out his days not far from Saddleworth, the scene of his childhood miseries.

The store management passed to Mr. Lord's younger sons, George Washington Taylor Lord and Samuel Lord, Jr. The five-story iron-frame store the brothers built on the Ladies Mile and moved into in 1872 was considered an architectural masterpiece. It was an elegant showcase for their finery and was called a "Fashion Emporium." A thrilling new contraption was built into the store—a steam elevator—complete with tufted divan, carpeted floor, and gas chandeliers. The car was described as being as "luxurious as the grand salon of the first-class steamboats" and "a saving of strength in shopping altogether incalculable to anyone outside of a city, in which altitude, rather than ground space, is the principal architectural consideration."

The store held the promise of new heights of success, but the panic of 1873 brought it to the brink of ruin. Edward P. Hatch, who had been a successful newspaper publisher in New Jersey, and promoter of the Wilcox and Gibbs sewing machine, was brought in to help solve the firm's financial problems. In the ensuing years, he purchased the interests of Samuel Lord and John Taylor Lord. George Washington Taylor Lord's interest ceased in 1885 and Samuel Jr.'s in 1895, leaving Mr. Hatch the sole owner of Lord & Taylor. In 1904 he incorporated the business as a stock company and became the president. Mr. Hatch died in 1909 and his estate sold part of its interest to the United Dry Goods Company. The management of the store was entrusted to Mr. Hatch's grandson, Wilson Hatch Tucker.

Edward Hatch had been blessed with the same foresight or good luck that Mr. Taylor and Mr. Lord seemed to have. Prior to his death, he felt that another retail migration was about to take place—this time to the north and east. He had set his grandson, Mr. Tucker, to studying their operation and making notes and plans for a new store. The negotiations for the property at Fifth Avenue and Thirty-eighth Street were concluded in 1912. An announcement was made in the florid language of the period:

> The Honorable Career of the House of Lord & Taylor since its establishment in 1826 has engendered a wide and deep seated respect everywhere for this name. Speculation has been rife ever since the upward movement as to what Lord & Taylor would do, and why they would not move. Many "wise acres" shook their heads in protest against the delay. We were not unmindful of the criticism of our deeply interested friends, and we were diligent in our efforts to settle the question satisfactorily to all and commensurate with the continuation on a broad and dignified scale for the perpetuation of the commercial honor and standing of Lord & Taylor.
>
> We have always clung steadfastly to the belief that it is the duty of the merchant or the house to protect to the fullest extent its customers and to win their confidence through well-deserved merit and now as we are upon the threshold of a New Era, we can say that, "A Good name is better than great Riches."

Lord & Taylor opened on Fifth Avenue in 1914. The ten-story building had a granite and limestone exterior. The design was Italian Renaissance. The store was filled with up-to-date engineering marvels: a vacuum heating system, a highly efficient ventilating system, a complete vacuum cleaning system, a sophisticated arrangement for fire prevention, a cold-storage plant, and novel devices and methods for package handling and shipping. The delay and careful planning paid off. It has served as the company's parent or flagship store, as it is commonly called today, for sixty-four years.

In 1921, a twenty-eight-year-old woman from Little Rock, Arkansas, arrived on the New York scene. Dorothy Shaver was promoting a family of dolls—"Five Little Shavers"—created by her sister, Elsie. She was given full support by Lord & Taylor and the sisters prospered. In 1924, she joined the store as head of the comparative shopping bureau. After several months she felt that the customer was more important than the competitor and the concept of a personal shopping service was born. She became a member of the board of directors in 1927, was appointed vice-president in 1931 and first vice-president in 1937. In 1945, she was elected store president.

The excitement of shopping Lord & Taylor that had taken on new meaning under president Walter Hoving reached new heights with Dorothy Shaver's creative merchandising and innovations. She discovered and introduced a new generation of American designers: Claire McCardell, Bonnie Cashin, Clare Potter, Sally Victor, Tom Brigance, Luis Estevez, and Vera Maxwell.

A golden era of expansion was begun, first into the suburbs, then throughout the east and south. In the last ten years, Lord & Taylor has expanded into Texas and Illinois.

Dorothy Shaver developed special departments for small women, collegians, and teenagers. The store became the citadel for sporty femininity. A graceful hand-written Lord & Taylor logo and a bright red rose became symbols of the enduring beauty and quality available at Lord & Taylor. Joseph E. Brooks, chairman and chief executive officer since 1975, renamed the Lord & Taylor rose in honor of Miss Shaver.

The Lord & Taylor policy of finding and launching new talent has continued. Among the designers it has showcased are Rose Marie Reid, Anne Fogarty, John Weitz, Rudi Gernreich, Lilly Pulitzer, Tina Leser, Ellen Brooke, Kasper, Donald Brooks, Margaret Jerrold, and Pauline Trigère. They brought Sybil Connolly from

Ireland and she became an international figure overnight. Valentino was introduced through the store, and Emilio Pucci's silk jersey prints that became a symbol of style and good taste throughout the fashionable world made their debut in Lord & Taylor's windows.

On September 22, 1976, over six hundred people attended a store gala. These were definitely not " 'wise acres' shaking their heads in protest." These were celebrities, politicians, fashion designers, and beautiful people nodding approval of the $5-million-dollar renovation and celebrating Lord & Taylor's 150th birthday.

It is doubtful whether many of the fashionable guests who sipped cocktails and ate hors d'oeuvres were aware of a little party that had been given by a remarkable woman two hundred years before on the very same spot.

On September 15, 1776, General Washington and his Continental Army were defeated at Brooklyn Heights after continuous attacks by General Howe and the British army. During the night, Washington and his collapsing troops escaped across the river to lower Manhattan. The General went on ahead north to prepare a battleground on Harlem Heights. The troops were to follow. The next day, Howe and the British were in pursuit across the river. They landed at Kip's Bay, at the eastern end of what is now Thirty-fourth Street. There they intercepted the northbound Colonials and attempted to cut off their movement with heavy artillery barrages. The confused soldiers retreated to the nearest high ground, which was to the west atop Murray Hill on the Murray estate—the present site of Lord & Taylor.

When Washington heard the cannonading, he galloped south. He rallied his troops and prepared to retreat north to Harlem Heights. The British, slowed by their artillery, were in pursuit. All the General needed was time.

The Colonials left only minutes before the British arrived on Murray Hill. Mrs. Murray beseeched the exhausted English General and his staff to rest before they charged after the battered Americans. She served tea, wine, and sweetcakes in the cool of her garden. The British relaxed beneath the trees and it is reported that "Mrs. Murray entertained them with *sprightly* conversation." The time slipped away and so did the Continental Army. Washington and his company slogged through the swamps that lay north of the present-day New York City Public Library and Forty-second Street. They proceeded through the farms and wilderness that lay along what is now Fifth Avenue to the safety of Harlem Heights far beyond.

There would be a later march up Fifth Avenue by retail merchants. But for Lord & Taylor, the area of the Murray farm at Thirty-eighth Street and Fifth Avenue remains home.

Lord & Taylor is presently owned by Associated Dry Goods Corporation, one of the country's leading retail companies. In 1976, Associated operated 16 headquarters department stores and 123 branch stores, which included many of the prestigious names in retailing in 23 states and the District of Columbia—J. W. Robinson Co., Stix, Baer & Fuller, L. A. Ayers and Company, and Goldwaters, to name a few. The stores occupy approximately 25 million square feet of floor space and have almost 57,500 employees. The projected expansion is to have more than 180 department stores in operation by 1980.

In the language of 1977 business, the Associated Dry Goods Annual Report said:

> Sales in fiscal 1976 increased 10.6% to a record of $1,539 billion while earnings declined 5.75 to $3.01 per share. Dividends were increased during the year to an annual rate of $1.50.
>
> Sales increased strongly during the first quarter but fell below expectations in the second and third quarters as consumer confidence and spending declined. The rate of sales growth continued below expectations until the month of September, when sales returned to planned levels.
>
> However, fourth quarter results were adversely affected by an increase in the LIFO (last in, first out), inventory reserve. While the actual LIFO charge was in line with the accrual rate used throughout the year, the charge compared unfavorably with the credit in the fourth quarter last year.

On opening day in 1826, in his 20x50-foot store, roughly 1,000 square feet, Samuel Lord had meticulously recorded his first sale—a bolt of cloth purchased by Ann Fernover Price.

The original Bonwit Teller store was founded by Paul J. Bonwit in 1895 at Sixth Avenue and Eighteenth Street. It was a specialty shop devoted to women's apparel. Mr. Bonwit opened another store the following year at Twenty-second Street and Sixth Avenue in partnership with a Mr. Rothschild. When this business failed, he bought out Rothschild and took Edmund D. Teller in as a partner. The two Bonwit shops merged and the new Bonwit Teller opened in 1898 at Twenty-third Street, east of Sixth Avenue.

Bonwit Teller followed B. Altman & Co. to Fifth Avenue and was a jump ahead of Lord & Taylor on an adjacent corner on Thirty-eighth Street. In the 1930s, Bonwit Teller made the move up Fifth Avenue to Fifty-sixth Street. Two five-story dwellings on the location were razed. The mansions had been built on the site of the John Kemp Farm at the turn of the century by William Waldorf Astor. The cost to build each Fifth Avenue structure had been $25,000. Bonwit Teller's move, along with the collapse of Arnold Constable, Franklin Simon, and Russek's, has left Lord & Taylor and B. Altman & Co. the *grandes dames* of retailing on lower Fifth Avenue.

B. Altman & Co. jumped on the eastbound Thirty-fourth Street trolley and got off at Fifth Avenue in 1906, moving into a block-square building that was not to be completed until 1910. B. Altman took both altitude *and* ground space into consideration. Fifth Avenue residents were so enraged with their area "going commercial," Benjamin Altman sought to placate them by hiding his large store behind a Florentine facade and not placing a name on the outside. There was another consideration that was advanced for the time and fifty years later was unique in the entire city of New York. The Thirty-fourth Street store contained an engine room that could produce all the electricity the store needed at the time it was built. In subsequent years, additional power was provided by Consolidated Edison. Thought was being given to abandoning the outmoded installation when all of New York was blacked out on the night of November 9, 1965—except for B. Altman. The company has reconsidered the idea of giving up the old ways. Also, as the price of energy has gone up, B. Altman has found it is economically viable to maintain the private power plant. B. Altman & Co. shines like a beacon when the lights go out all over the town.

Benjamin Altman was unique among the early merchants in many ways. Little is known of his background. His father, Philip, had a millinery shop and at one time, prior to the Civil War, Benjamin was employed as a clerk in a small dry-goods store, Bettlebeck & Co. in Newark, New Jersey. He and his brother, Morris, opened a dry-goods store on Third Avenue between Ninth and Tenth streets. The lease, signed in 1865, with Amos Brown, read that the property was "to be occupied as a Dry-goods and Fancy Store, with privilege in the Wood-house."

Another store was opened on Sixth Avenue between Twenty-first and Twenty-second streets. In April 1877, a store described as "The Palace of Trade" was opened on Sixth Avenue between Eighteenth and Nineteenth streets. This was a magnificent cast-iron building rising six floors around a glass-domed court. The rotunda was *de rigueur* during this period, having been copied from France's great Bon Marché. There was a workroom on the fourth floor where suits and underwear were manufactured.

Dry goods and the suit department could be called on the telephone.

Benjamin Altman was a bachelor. Since founding a mercantile dynasty went hand in hand with founding a store, this was an unusual situation. Altman was a stickler for details and precise about time. He scheduled appointments for 12:07 or 2:13, and was strict about keeping them to the exact minute. He had a sense of elegance and a fine eye for art. When he died in 1913, his estate was valued at $45 million. His art collection, valued at some $15 million, was bequeathed to the Metropolitan Museum of Art. He is believed to have had the finest Chinese porcelains in the world. The collection also included tapestries and rugs, a Cellini cup, and thirteen Rembrandts.

B. Altman was incorporated in 1909; in 1913, prior to his death and because he had no heir, Benjamin Altman established the Altman Foundation, chartered by an act of the legislature of the State of New York. Its purpose was, and is, as the Charter states, "to the use and benefit of charitable or educational institutions within the state of New York, by such agencies and means as from time to time shall be appropriate therefor." Benjamin Altman bequeathed his holdings in B. Altman & Co. to the Altman Foundation, which accounts for the unique situation of ownership of B. Altman & Co. by the Altman Foundation. Over the years, millions of dollars have been given to medical, educational, cultural, and welfare institutions. B. Altman & Co. has endeared itself to the city of New York through the quality of goods in the store and its philanthropies.

In the early days nothing endeared Altman's to its customers more than the Altman delivery service. Starting with one horse and wagon, it is said that by the time the "Palace of Trade" was built in 1877, the stables to the west of the store held 500 sleek steeds, each carefully selected personally by Mr. Altman. These fine animals were hitched in pairs to the shining fleet of maroon delivery wagons. The horse-drawn delivery service extended throughout the city and into Westchester County. In the summertime, horses and wagons and smartly uniformed drivers were dispatched and kept at such resorts as Saratoga and the Hamptons. When the trains arrived with merchandise, it was picked up and quickly delivered in the snappy maroon B. Altman & Co wagons to the vacationing customers.

Customers came to the "Palace of Trade" from New Jersey by the Twenty-third Street ferry or from up and down Sixth Avenue on the wooden-track elevated trains. But when Benjamin Altman heard the clang-clang-clang of the trolley, the ding-ding-ding of the bell, and the chug-chug-chug of the motors carrying the carriage trade east to Fifth Avenue, he knew the time had come to move on.

Today, only a handful of the cast-iron façades of the once fashionable stores remain along the Ladies Mile. The area is seedy and the rustle of elegant petticoats and the clip-clop of horses' hooves are as lost in time and traffic noises as the sound of General Howe's artillery.

Some stores arrived on the Ladies Mile too late to stem the tide. Others stayed too long. Siegel-Cooper and Company opened in 1896. The store was as richly decorated outside as it was inside. Opening day attracted 150,000 people. There was a magnificent columned entrance and, on beyond, a fountain. In the center of the fountain was a reproduction of Daniel Chester French's sculpture "Republic," which had been made for the Chicago World Trade Fair of 1893. The stylish password of the day was "Meet me at the fountain," which of course meant Siegel's. It would have been unthinkable to imagine a time when there would not be Siegel's or the Beaux Arts Adams Dry Goods Store that catered to the rich, or the Hugh O'Neil store that catered to the working-class poor, or Stern

Brothers Department Store that catered to both. A day when there would be no great James McCreery and Company? Best & Co.? Nonsense! Impossible! But the time did come when the only customers were the spirits of shopping trips past. The once-thriving, bustling emporiums swirled and shifted like autumn leaves being blown about in a storm. Some drifted in the winds. Others were lifted up, carried off, and settled elsewhere. Some disappeared. Only Stern Brothers went on, and on, and on like a great battered iron hulk of a ship, foundering and rusting, buffeted by the seas and tides and winds of change until she sank.

ELEVEN

And Remember Them on Herald/Greeley Square

Macy's and Gimbels

Herald Square at the turn of the century was the *scene of the action*, the *heart of the tenderloin*. It was a nickel's throw in distance from the elegant Ladies Mile but in spirit, style, class, it was farther removed than Catherine Street. The expression "tenderloin" was attributed to a police captain, one "Clubber" Williams. When he was transferred into the high-living precinct where the payoffs were as high as the living, he remarked, "I've been having chuck steak ever since I've been on the force and now I'm going to have a bit of the *tenderloin*." This rough, tough neighborhood at Broadway and Thirty-fourth Street seemed an unlikely area for family-oriented, middle-class stores to encamp.

The Herald building was on the square and during the day, there was the bustle that accompanies any metropolitan newspaper district. But the newspaper offices were surrounded by high-class brothels, music halls, and saloons. At night the square came to life when the whores and sports figures and ruffians mixed with the "swells" who had come for a vaudeville show or boxing match or to see Anna Held in a Florenz Ziegfeld production at the Herald Square Theater, or to enjoy the favors of the "ladies of the evening."

It was said that Hetty Green, known as the "Witch of Wall Street," lived in one room in the old Herald Square Hotel, existing on graham crackers, which she purchased wholesale in barrel lots. The miser millionairess had cornered the Rock Island Railroad for the price of $1,365,000 along with her other high-powered acquisitions. She was called "The Witch" as much for her appearance as for her business tactics. Hetty often strolled out of her disreputable neighborhood and plied the Ladies Mile in a shabby black dress, carrying a raveled umbrella, to paw through the contents of the trash cans.

Edward Hatch, president of Lord & Taylor, saw the old crone scrounging one day and took heart. He told her if she would come by the store at some time, he would give her a new black veil. When the disheveled woman appeared and demanded her veil, she created a ruckus with the Lord & Taylor staff. Mr. Hatch was summoned to quiet the woman and remove her from the premises, but to the clerks' amazement, Mr. Hatch gifted her with the promised veil. "The Witch" then asked if there were any damaged skirts that she might have at bargain prices and Mr. Hatch graciously sold her several at fifty cents each. The boys on Wall Street were somewhat shocked when the filthy hag would announce proudly that she was outfitted by Lord & Taylor.

Virtually every merchant in the area had some experience with Hetty Green. She was a character, a celebrity of her day, and thought by many to be the richest woman in the country. There is an uncorroborated story about Benjamin Altman and Hetty Green. She is said to have bought a dress length of fabric at Altman's. She returned it for flaws. Accepting returned merchandise was not the practice of the day, but Mr. Altman, not even knowing who the lady was, but more than likely anxious to get her out of the store, accepted the fabric and returned her money. "Witch" Green was so impressed that she supposedly took Benjamin Altman to her bankers, introduced him, and informed them that if ever Mr. Altman needed credit, they were to make the arrangements and she would guarantee the loan. The story is questionable because it was known that bankers and financiers made every effort to hide in mens' rooms or under their desks when they saw or heard the "Witch" was in the neighborhood. It is also doubtful that a man as meticulous and elegant as Mr. Altman would have been seen in the "Witch's" company.

One of the earliest merchants to bring retailing into this pictur-

esque area at Herald Square was Andrew Saks. He had been born
in Virginia and raised in Lockhaven, Pennsylvania, where his family moved during the Civil War. At the age of fourteen, Andrew left
home and went to Washington D.C., where he peddled newspapers
and took on odd jobs. In 1867, at the age of nineteen, he opened a
menswear shop in that city. Six years later he was enjoying enough
success to turn the store over to his brother, Isador, and move on
to open a store in Richmond and another in Indianapolis. These
stores were left in the hands of his brother Joseph when Andrew
went to New York in 1892 and bought into a clothing manufacturing company on lower Broadway. But Andrew Saks was more a
merchant than a manufacturer and he soon felt the pull to go back
into retailing. When he opened Saks & Company on Herald Square
in 1902, he had expanded into a specialty store selling top-quality
goods. Andrew died ten years later and his brother Isador became
the president. His son Horace, who had left Princeton to join the
firm when the New York store opened, became the secretary. Horace Saks would live in the shadow of the two retailing giants who
came to Herald Square—Macy's and Gimbels. But on the east
side, the name Saks would become synonymous with luxury and
high fashion, and his store on Fifth Avenue would be known
throughout the country and throughout the world. Horace Saks
would make Fifth Avenue one of the greatest shopping streets in
the world in 1924 when he opened the grand, the eloquent, the *Very
Saks Fifth Avenue.*

When R. H. Macy & Co. opened a colossus of a store on Herald
Square that same year, the character of the neighborhood began to
change. Macy's, by 1902, had expanded into a hodgepodge of
buildings along Fourteenth Street and Sixth Avenue. Macy's had a
working-class and middle-class clientele and made no bones about
it. Macy's customers did not arrive in smart victorias, broughams,
or landaus pulled by spirited carriage horses. Macy's customers arrived on foot or by public transportation.

When Macy's made the move from Fourteenth Street, it chose
to bypass the upper reaches of the Ladies Mile and land full-grown
and enormous at Thirty-fourth and Broadway, where there was a
Sixth Avenue elevated station and the crosstown trolley. Shortly
after the land was obtained, the Pennsylvania Railroad announced
the construction of a vast new passenger station a few blocks away
at Seventh and Ninth avenues, between Thirty-first and Thirty-

third streets. If this move didn't put Macy's dead center in the hub of twentieth-century transportation, an announcement made the same year Macy's opened, did. The Rapid Transit Commission disclosed its plan for a subway extension from Forty-second Street down Broadway to Fourteenth Street. There would be a subway station at Macy's.

On a cold December morning in 1909, the arrival of new kids on the block must have been a forbidding sight. Eight Gimbels—six brothers and two of their sons—arrived in funereal attire. They wore somber black capes and coats, top hats, and bowlers for the laying of the cornerstone on Gimbels' massive New York construction site on Greeley Square. This show of solid strength must have been unnerving for even the *biggest* kid on the block—R. H. Macy & Co. Macy's was the biggest store in the world. This historical moment would mark the beginning of the Macy's-Gimbels rivalry that has been touted in vaudeville, radio, and television routines, the rivalry that has been prompted by both stores' publicity, promotion, and advertising campaigns. The Macy's-Gimbels competition is one of the best known in the world. It has also resulted in tough, competitive merchandising.

The Gimbel entourage came to New York with more than a solid front. They had money in their pockets and a fifty-year heritage of retailing that began when their father, Adam Gimbel, came to America.

Adam Gimbel was born in the village of Rhein-Pfaltz in the Bavarian Highlands in 1817. There was no united Germany at that time and the area was ruled by the Austrian Empire and its "iron chancellor," Prince Metternich. Life in this wine district was one of semi-serfdom. It was hard and it was short. A young man had little future beyond the endless toil in the vineyards, except for seven brutal years in the army. Strong, hardy young men were broken and old by the age of thirty-five. Many of the young men, and particularly Jews, for whom life was even more torturous, were going to America, and seventeen-year-old Adam joined the exodus. With half of the passage money in his pocket, he walked to Bremerhaven, a North Sea port, and haunted the docks until he found a captain who would accept what he had for fare and allow him to work off the balance in passage. The small square-rigger sailed for New Orleans.

Arriving with no money, young Adam could go no farther than

the wharf. He found work on the dock. He learned English working and listening to the tales of the frontier to the north from rivermen and itinerant peddlers who came to New Orleans to restock their inventories. After two years of frugal living and hard work, Adam was able to stock one of the enormous packs the peddlers carried on their backs. With a long-barreled rifle he carried for hunting and protection, he set off on foot, north along the Mississippi.

By 1842 Adam Gimbel had a horse and wagon and made enough profit to allow himself the luxury of a night's lodging at an inn during foul weather. Adam had longed to bring his family to America but his father had died about the time he took to the road and several years later his mother got as far as Bremerhaven, where she fell ill and died. The peddler's life was lonely, dangerous, and full of discomfort. He was constantly exposed to the elements and burdened by the heavy weight of his pack. He was easy prey for thieves. Often a peddler would be joined by a fellow traveler on the road, only to awaken in the morning and discover that his companion had stolen away during the night and that his merchandise was gone. The American Dream for these wandering merchants was to settle down with a little store and raise a family. This dream became a reality for Adam Gimbel when a dentist, Dr. Henry Fish, in Vincennes, Indiana, from whom he rented rooms to store his merchandise, retired and left the town of 1,700 population. Adam rented the entire building for $58 a year, converted it into a store, and named it, rather pretentiously, the Palace of Trade.

Adam Gimbel's reputation for honesty was far-flung. He traveled miles to refund money if he was overpaid. There is a story of the Bishop of Vincennes, whose diocese covered much of Indiana and Illinois, who was a friend of Adam's and held him in high esteem. It is said that the Bishop once left a bag of gold with the young merchant saying, "I haven't counted it. Why should I bother to count money given to Adam Gimbel?" And Gimbel supposedly replied, "A good name is better than riches." This must have been one of the most overworked expressions in retailing. Today it would make the bottom-line retail corporate executives ulcerous.

Five years after he opened his store, he met a young German-Jewish girl on a buying trip to Philadelphia. He married seventeen-year-old Fridolyn Kahnweiler and over the next twenty-four years, the couple had fourteen children. Eleven survived. Seven of them were to become the formidable Gimbel Brothers: Jacob, Ellis, Isaac, Charles, Louis, Daniel, and Benedict. In later years when he was asked the secret of his success, Adam Gimbel replied: "Others may have had their paid helpers and assistants. I had my seven sons."

There were several immediate reasons why male offspring were important to retailing. They went beyond dynastic dreams and property transference. Family could be trusted. Also father and son or brothers, or, in the case of Neiman-Marcus, a sister, together in business allowed for the necessary flexibility. One could mind the store while the other went off to the marketplace. Progeny also made expansion possible. By the third generation, however, it has become not only a question of having heirs, but also a question of "How you gonna keep 'em down in the store?" Among them, Adam's seven sons had eight sons but only two made any mark as merchants—Isaac's son Bernard and Charles's son Adam. In most cases the odds on the fourth generation staying in the family business get even lower. Adam's grandson Adam was childless. While Bernard Gimbel had three sons, only his oldest, Bruce A. Gimbel, followed in his father's footsteps. Bruce Gimbel eventually rose to the position of chairman and chief executive of Gimbels. Mr. Gimbel remained in this executive position after Brown & Williamson Industries, Inc., a subsidiary of the British-American Tobacco Company, Ltd., purchased the chain in 1973 until his retirement in 1975.

Bernard and Alva Gimbel also had two sets of twins. The first set was girls, Helen and Caral. Twin sons, David and Peter, were born to the Gimbels late in life. They worked in Gimbel's training programs only briefly before turning to careers on Wall Street. David Gimbel died at the age of twenty-nine. Peter R. Gimbel (*R* for Robin) abandoned Wall Street to become an explorer and filmmaker. He is a skindiver, shark hunter, and photographer. He dove to the depths to film the sunken *Andrea Doria*. His full-length feature film *Blue Water, White Death* was greeted with rave reviews when it opened in 1971. Peter Gimbel finds, much to his annoyance, that no matter what his accomplishments, the store won't go away. In an interview with writer Lyn Tornabene he said, "Some day, somebody is going to write my name without putting 'department store heir' after it. What the hell does that mean? You know the headline they ran in South Africa when I was there? 'Department Store Hair Finds Shark.' That about says it, doesn't it?''

On September 24, 1977, Robin Suffern Gimbel was married to Enrique Senior in St. Dominic's Roman Catholic Chapel in Oyster Bay, New York. Mrs. Senior is the daughter of Fern Tailer Gimbel Denney and the late David Alva Gimbel. She is the granddaughter of the late Bernard Gimbel and Mrs. Bernard F. Gimbel of Greenwich, Connecticut, and New York. She is the great-great-granddaughter of the founder of the Gimbel stores, Adam Gimbel. Mrs. Senior was graduated from the Esmond Guerre-Lavigne School of Fashion Design in Paris. *The New York Times* (September 24, 1977), reporting the wedding, wrote: "Mrs. Senior is an associate buyer in the junior coat and suit department at Bonwit Teller in New York." Alva Gimbel, her grandmother and Bernard Gimbel's widow, explained: "At the time Robin was looking for a job there was an opening at Bonwit's."

In the early days it was easier to make a store to fit the children than to have the children fit the store. As the Gimbel family grew, so did the store. First it moved into larger quarters in Vincennes, Indiana, and became Gimbel & Sons Trade Palace. In 1887 a store was opened in Milwaukee and in 1894 one opened in Philadelphia. Sons were put in charge of each venture. By the time the Gimbel boys came into New York, they were not hicks from the boondocks (the Vincennes store was closed in 1887), but well-heeled, well-dressed gentlemen. The Milwaukee and Philadelphia stores were doing a combined business of $15 million a year. In its first year, the New York store far exceeded its hoped-for volume of $12 million.

Adam Gimbel's son Isaac was the dominant figure in the company's expansion until 1927 when he was forced to retire as a result of injuries sustained in a riding accident in Central Park. At this time, Isaac's son Bernard, known to his many friends as Bernie and to his family as Beanie, became the president of Gimbels New York. Bernard brought to his business career the same competitiveness and daring he had shown on the football field and in the boxing ring. This energetic man had, according to a friend, "a heart as big as all New York." He was also a brilliant merchant.

In Lyn Tornabene's 1971 *Cosmopolitan* article, "Peter Gimbel: How the Ultimate Jewish Prince Fights Fear," Gimbel said of his father:

> He was an enormously proud man who wouldn't take second-best anything. He was an extraordinarily fine businessman, smart, shrewd—extremely narrow in scope—read very few books but consumed all the media voluminously. His world was the world of athletes (boxers, especially), successful politicians—tycoons.

Bernard Gimbel's magnetic personality attracted friends from all walks of life. It also attracted sixteen-year-old Alva Bernheimer one evening at a small debutante dinner. The Bernheimers were part of New York's German-Jewish elite who regarded the Gimbels as "trade." When Bernard asked Alva's mother if he might pay a call on her daughter, he was informed firmly that he might not—certainly not until she made her debut. The tenacious Alva's reply to this was "Then I'll wait."

At Alva's debut, the couple met again, but the day after the party, the debutante fell ill. Recently, Alva Bernheimer Gimbel described her malady as "the longest case of scarlet fever in history."

To avoid what the Bernheimers considered a *mésalliance*, Alva was taken on the Grand Tour of Europe after her recovery. "But nothing could keep us apart," Mrs. Gimbel recalled. "I worked at the Henry Street Settlement after the trip the way young women did in my day. I was teaching knitting and needlework two afternoons a week." Since love will find a way, Miss Bernheimer purchased the wool for the settlement house at Gimbels. The shopping trips were also brief romantic interludes. "I wasn't such a good knitter," Mrs. Gimbel said, "but I did like buying the wool."

The twosome finally received parental approval and were married in 1912. With the wedding over, Mrs. Bernheimer set on a course to bring culture to Bernard, or at least Bernard to culture. She and her daughter for many years had regularly attended the opera together. So Mrs. Bernheimer made a concerted effort to secure an additional subscription seat for Bernard.

Mrs. Gimbel remembered this cultural power play with delight in the summer of 1977 as she sat in the cheery sunroom of her large stone house. The room was filled with plants, sculpture, paintings, and family photographs. The glass windows overlooked the grounds and gardens of her two-hundred-acre Connecticut estate, Chieftains. "Bernard had to put on a stiff collar and stiff shirt and he'd say, 'I don't know how I'll live through another Wagner.' Then one evening, a pair of opera glasses fell from one of the boxes into the orchestra seats and there was a brief commotion. After the performance, Bernard told my mother: 'This is the most dangerous place I've ever been in. I have too many responsibilities to risk being here, so I cannot come again.' He never went to another opera during his entire life."

Bernard Gimbel was a life-loving man who ate corned beef and cabbage and rode the subway. He was a runner, horseman, golfer, and boxer. He encouraged and promoted Gene Tunney all the way to Jack Dempsey's defeat and the world heavyweight boxing championship. Playing golf, he often turned exuberant somersaults on the fairway. He carried small toys—good-luck pieces—in his pocket and gave them away to children and to their parents alike. He was adored by his employees, customers, friends, children, and wife.

"It was an odd marriage," Peter Gimbel said. "My parents' worlds were about as far apart as any two worlds you can imagine."

"In his later years," Alva Gimbel said, "Bernard hoped he would live to celebrate his eightieth birthday and our fiftieth wedding anniversary. He did both."

In 1962 the mismatched couple celebrated their golden wedding anniversary. In 1965, Bernard F. Gimbel's friends and family celebrated his eightieth birthday with a springtime party at the Pierre Hotel in New York. He died in the fall of the following year.

"On my own birthday," Mrs. Gimbel said, holding several pages of paper, "he always wrote me a beautiful letter in longhand." She began to read, "Dearest Bebe—he always called me Bebe—As your birthday approaches, I've been thinking about you and the many contributions you've made to the children and to my happiness for more than fifty years. . . ." There was a catch in her voice. Mrs. Bernard F. Gimbel placed the letter on her desk. "Oh, well," she said, "it just goes on from there."

It was not a bad record for a *mésalliance*.

In 1957 Walter Rothschild, head of Abraham & Straus, presented the Tobé Award as Retailer of the Year to Bernard Gimbel. Like
many another merchant Mr. Rothschild had a penchant for the beat
of iambic pentameter. While Mr. Rothschild's lengthy poem was
hardly a literary prize-winner, it caught the spirit of Bernard Gimbel and, like Mr. Gimbel himself, it was full of heart.

Near the banks of the Wabash by Fort Vincennes
To the cries of the ox and mules and hens
On a peaceful April morn
Bernard F. Gimbel was obviously born. . . .

He bought some shoes and East went he
To Charter School and U. of P.
He learned to box and eat with a knife
And he found himself a lovely wife.
Friendship was the basic core
That brought all people to their door.
Alva with her charm and hustle
Bernie with his smile and muscle
Were known to be the finest pair
From Greenwich down to Greeley Square.
Bernie was no merchant mouse
When under the guns of Jesse Straus
The Macy lion began its roar
When Gimbels opened up their door.
It was considered mean and dirty
In any street that numbers thirty
To peddle merchandise for pay
Unless you had a Straus O.K.
Said Jesse to Herbert to Percy
"Show the fair-haired boy no mercy."
Quickly to poison Bernie's hash
Macy sold only for cash.
They weren't the ones to toss the sponge
Just cause Gimbels took the plunge.
Yet every year Price, Waterhouse
Would certify the Gimbel House
Had gone ahead instead of back
And had its figures in the black.
Just cross the street they said one day,
"Gimbels is really here to stay."

No one but no one figured that
The feather could grow in Bernie's hat.
Now Jack (Straus) and he sat side by side
Cheek by jowl on a subway ride. . . .

And though I could talk on at length
Of your kindness, warmth and strength
All these facts are but a symbol
Of the well-loved name of Bernard Gimbel.
Somewhere in the future time
If up into heaven's step we climb
Saying farewell to care and strife
Moving to a better life,
Whether by auto, train or bus
Bernard Gimbel will welcome us.

Bernard, I'm sure that I reflect the sentiments of all assembled when I say that I am delighted to present you with the Tobé Award for 1957.

When R. H. Macy & Co. arrived on Herald Square, it was firmly in the hands of Isidor and Nathan Straus, sons of another traveling peddler, Lazarus Straus. The patriarchs of the archrivals on nearby Greeley and Herald squares, Adam Gimbel and Lazarus Straus, both traveled long, twisting roads before their sons and grandsons ended up as gigantic mercantile neighbors, with Horace Sak's store serving as a buffer between them on Broadway in New York.

Lazarus Straus had been a landowner near his native town of Otterberg in the Bavarian Palatinate. Unlike the teenage peasant Gimbel, he had a wife and four children. He became involved in a political cause for freedom and when the movement failed in 1852, he fled to America. He traveled the peddler's paths through Georgia until he could open a store in Talbotton and send for his wife and children. The family moved north from Georgia to Philadelphia during the Civil War and in 1866 moved to New York. There L. Straus & Sons opened a small china and glassware store on Chambers Street. Isidor was the manager and Nathan was a traveling salesman who loathed traveling. To keep Nathan off the road, the Strauses opened glass and china departments in various stores on a lease basis. They had been selling their goods to R. H Macy and approached him in 1874 with their leasing proposition.

There was an agreement and L. Straus & Co. leased Macy's basement and expanded the glass and crockery departments.

For ten years after R. H. Macy's death there was a turnover in
Macy partners. Many factors contributed to these changes. For
one thing, when R. H. came to New York, his brother Robert, who
had backed many of his ill-fated ventures, refused to extend him
further credit. So Robert was not a partner in the Macy organization. Macy's early demise complicated the ownership problem. He
was fifty-four years old when he died in 1877 and left no suitable
heirs. Sadly, one son, Charles, had died in infancy. His other son,
Rowland H. Macy Junior, was a tragic, desperate young man
whom he disinherited. His daughter Florence married a store employee, James Sutton, but he was also a property owner in
Westchester County, New York, with tastes that were more sophisticated and expensive than Macy's. After a brief and unsatis-
factory stint in the store, Sutton took his wife to his several-hun-
dred-acre farm in Bedford, New York.

In the 1880s, the store's sole owner, Charles Webster, asked the
Strauses, father and sons, to join him. In 1893, Webster and
Macy's bought a half interest in a Brooklyn Store—it was called
Abraham & Straus. They later sold their interest, but the famous
A & S retains the Straus name to this day. When Webster retired,
the Strauses bought his interest and Macy's was theirs.

When the original R. H. Macy & Co. opened on Sixth Avenue
near Fourteenth Street in 1858, it was a small store even for those
times. It has been reported that Macy's was either eleven or seventeen feet across. Twenty feet was the customary store frontage.
Whatever the size, if the store didn't look too promising, neither
did its proprietor.

Rowland Hussey Macy was an irascible, flamboyant Yankee
Quaker given to outbursts and temper tantrums. He had roots that
went back to the earliest settlers in America and a diverse business
background. He had been a born loser. His Fourteenth Street store
"Grand Opening" was his fifth store inauguration. He had arrived
in New York from New England in a roundabout way and his credit rating was nil. He had closed his fourth store which had been located in Haverhill, Massachusetts, and had paid his creditors at a
rate of less than twenty-five cents on the dollar. Macy was an unlikely candidate to be the founder of what would become the larg-

est store in the world. Any present-day Macy's personnel director would more than likely toss R. H. Macy's résumé into a wastebasket and show him the door.

Rowland H. Macy was born on Nantucket Island in 1822. He was the fourth son of John and Eliza Macy. His father was a sea captain who retired at the age of thirty-one. His maternal grandfather had also been a ship's captain. The island was full of Macys at this time—there were over three hundred. Rowland was a sixth-generation descendant of Thomas Macy, a Baptist who had fled the religious persecution in England in the late 1630s and settled in Salisbury, Massachusetts. By 1650, religious freedom was more fancy than fact. The Puritans and Baptists considered the Society of Friends, or Quakers, heretics. Members of the Society were publicly humiliated, tortured, punished, and eventually banished from Massachusetts on the threat of death. Anyone associating with them was prosecuted and fined.

During a summer storm in 1659, Baptist Thomas Macy offered shelter to four Quaker gentlemen. The offense was discovered. Macy was called into court and fined 30 shillings. Two of the offending Quakers were caught. William Robinson, a merchant of London, and Marmaduke Stephenson of Yorkshire, England, were both hanged in Boston. The fate of the other two is unknown.

Earlier in that same year, Thomas Macy and nine other inhabitants of Salisbury had purchased Nantucket Island from William, the Earl of Sterling. After the unpleasant court experience and a reprimand by the Governor, Thomas Macy took his family and what goods he could carry and fled by boat to the island.

According to the *Genealogy of the Macy Family*, published in 1868 and written by Thomas Macy's great-great-grandson and Rowland Macy's grandfather, Silvanus J. Macy:

> He was driven from Massachusetts by the same persecuting spirit that drove the pilgrims from the shores of England. With unknown fear, with undaunted courage, and with an unfaltering trust in the guiding and guarding hand of Heaven, did he brave all dangers to secure a free altar and safe home, and thereby transmit to his descendants the seeds of liberty and pure religion.

Thomas's grandson, Richard, was the first Macy to join the society of Friends. The Macy Quaker tradition began in the early eighteenth century. Richard sired twelve children, ten of whom in turn begat and begat and begat and lived to ripe old ages. As Nantucket's population multiplied, it was becoming increasingly apparent that farming and fishing could no longer sustain the islanders. Fortunately, at this time a sperm whale was taken and the islanders discovered it produced a better quality of oil than other whales. The sperm whale migrated great distances, but the hardy Nantucketers, already men of the sea, took chase. For the next 150 years, whaling would be the island's major industry.

When R. H. was fifteen years old, he signed on to the whaler *Emily Morgan* as a foremast hand and sailed out of New Bedford. The voyage lasted four and a half years. The crew was paid in shares, or "lays," as they were called. The lay varied in proportion to the duty. Roland, at the bottom of the crew, received 1/160 percent of a cargo worth between $85,000 and $95,000, or a total of $550 for his four and a half years at sea.

R. H. Macy's only seafaring experience was working as the lowly hand on the *Emily Morgan*'s trip around the Horn, through the South Pacific to New Zealand, and back to Nantucket. In later years, however, he never discouraged people from calling him "Captain" Macy. It was said that when he became angry and his ferocious temper exploded, his language for a Quaker was as salty as that of the toughest first mate. A Macy trademark, the red star, is also said to harken back to his whaling days when he had had a red star tattooed on his arm as a reminder of a red star that appeared at sea and guided the *Emily Morgan* to safety. Although the experience at sea was memorable, it was lonely, dangerous, and hard work and R. H. Macy never went to sea again.

In the fifth-floor luggage department on Macy's Seventh Avenue side, there is a plaster frieze on the capital of one of the columns. It depicts the famous red star shining above a sailing ship. On the other side of the capital is another Macy's trademark—the crowing rooster. These logos were immortalized in the architecture when the area, designed by Robert D. Kohn, was completed in 1929, over fifty years after R. H. Macy's death.

There were several Nantucket Macy-family sailors. One, Captain Josiah Macy, wrote a lengthy, colorful letter to his grandson, genealogist Silvanus J. Macy, in 1867, describing his world travels and the cargoes of the day. *I Followed the Sea*, the letter, plus a foreword by Foster Macy Johnson, was published in a limited edition in 1960. Undoubtedly, as a young boy, R. H. knew his God-fearing, high-principled cousin Josiah whose grandparents had been Reuben Pinkham and Ann Starbuck, members of other stalwart Nantucket families. It is a pity R. H. could not have turned to his old seafaring relative in later years when he made desperate efforts to save his son. Captain Josiah had a knack for saving wayward youths.

In the foreword of *I Followed the Sea*, it is noted: "He has been the means of turning many from the paths of vice by his example, kind actions and advice. A much respected member of society who had yielded himself up to the gratification of all sorts of pleasures until wine had almost complete mastery of him and who had become a *vile drunkard*, recollected the Captain in his own words, 'Josiah Macy lifted me from the gutter a drunkard, took me to his hotel, and by his kind watchfulness and Christian care reformed me, and to him with devine [sic] assistance am I indebted for what I am today.'" There was no mention of what exactly the man was today. Also a Captain Benjamin Morrell was quoted in the foreword from his book, *Narrative of Four Voyages*: "I was justly considered a very 'wild youth.' How long I should have continued in this thoughtless [sic] career of folly is not easy to determine, had not Divine Providence raised up for me a faithful friend and advisor in the person of Capt. Josiah Macy, master of the ship *Edward* of New York, belonging to Samuel Hicks and himself."

But alas, where were you when they needed you, Captain Josiah Macy? In the years to come, there was no person, or "devine assistance," or "Divine Providence" that could shake the seeds of "folly" from Rowland Macy, Junior.

Whaling and island existence deeply influenced the character of Nantucket, the islanders, and Rowland Macy. Strange gothic overtones haunted Macy and his family throughout their lives. Nantucket was the women's island. With most of the men gone for long periods, only to return and go off again, or not to return at all, the women ran the shops and businesses. They spent long hours at work and raising their large families. During the desolate winter nights, they sought peace and release from the loneliness and isolation as they gathered to smoke the opium brought back to them from the Orient by their sailors. These God-fearing, austere, hardworking women filled the storm-tossed vacuums of their lives with hallucinations and the ghosts of their husbands and lovers. It may have been that some eerie specter—propagated in a far-off Eastern poppy field and nutured in a dark and smoky keeping room— attached its spirit to R. H. Macy, casting a spell over his life and the lives of his sons and daughter.

When young Rowland returned from the sea, he went to work in a shop. Today, a plaque designed by artist Glyn Lewis commemorates this early employment at the entrance of Murray's Toggery, 62 Main Street, Nantucket Island. This 6,000-square-foot store was opened in 1945 when new industries, tourism, and *summer people* brought economic vitality back to the island. The Toggery specializes in men's and women's clothing and is famous the world over for its Nantucket Red Pants. They are designed and manufactured by the shop's owner, Philip C. Murray.

While there is no discrimination today against the island's male merchants, in the 1840s it was considered "unmanly" among the rugged sea-oriented residents for a man to work in a "woman's business"—retailing. This undoubtedly brought about Macy's decision to leave for the mainland. He had served his years before the mast. He would not be ridiculed.

In 1842, Macy apprenticed to a printer in Boston. He remained in this position for only six months, but it is believed that this experience was reflected in his innovative use of type and layouts later in his extensive advertising. An example:

MACY!!!
Haverhill Cheap Store
Ever Onward!! Ever Upward!!

In 1843, the R. H. Macy Thread and Needle Store was opened in Boston. It was enlarged to include dry goods at a location on Hanover Street. This was not entirely satisfactory and another store was opened in Washington Street in 1848. This too closed.

By 1849, Macy was married and had a young son, Rowland, Junior, but he decided along with his brother, Charles, to follow their brother Andrew to the Golden West. The Macy brothers had contracted a violent case of "Gold Fever" along with thousands of other New Englanders. As the whaling industry was coming to a

standstill, plenty of ships waited to plow the waters to the Isthmus
of Panama or around the Horn all the way to California. In 1849,
the brothers sailed out of New York on the *Dr. Hitchcock*, an overcrowded brig with a conglomeration of passengers from every walk
and station in life.

Gold prospecting was difficult and unrewarding for the majority
of the Forty-niners. The Macy men were disappointed with their
mining efforts so they established themselves in the little town of
Marysville, fifty miles north of Sacramento, and opened Macy &
Co., selling general merchandise—miners' supplies, clothing, dry
goods—and acting as agents for the Hawley Company's express,
for whom they advertised "Letters, packages and Gold Dust for-
warded to all parts of the world."

California was not the promised El Dorado and Rowland Macy
returned to his wife and child. He salvaged a few thousand dollars
from the Marysville store and opened the Haverhill Cheap Store in
Haverhill, Massachusetts, in 1851. He never saw his two brothers
again. The Cheap Store flourished. Macy was ecstatic and reported
to his wife, Louisa, "This time *it's* working!" But *it* wasn't. He expanded and was hexed. He went bankrupt. His successful mer-
chant-brother and former backer, Robert, vowed never to lend him
another cent.

Macy tried his hand as a stockbroker and had an office at 18 Congress Street, Boston. He joined the Masons and for a while *it*
seemed to be working. He met Caleb Hunking, who financed
another Macy madcap scheme. Rowland thought there was a fortune to be made in land speculation in Wisconsin. There was. But
he got there too late. Early in 1857, he arrived in Superior City. He
made $8,000 and $2,000 in notes receivable before the Panic of
1857 sent land prices plummeting. He never received the receivable notes. There was also Hunking to be repaid.

Unable to return to Boston and go into business, he went to New
York and opened the store on Fourteenth Street. The "Grand
Opening" must have seemed more like the "Last Chance." With
no credit available, Macy was forced into a *cash only* situation.
The idea was heavily advertised and caught on. So did his one-
price policy and refusal to be undersold. *It* was finally working.
During the first year in business, the store did a $90,000 volume, al-
beit opening day was not too promising. Recorded: "First Day's
Sales, October 27, 1858—$11.06."

Much of the success Macy's enjoyed after 1860 must be credited to Margaret Getchell. Miss Getchell was a distant cousin, who was teaching school in Nantucket when she lost one eye in an accident. When it became too difficult for her to correct school papers in the dim light of the whale oil lamps, she wrote Macy seeking employment. She was hired as a cashier, moved up to bookkeeper, and finally became store "superintendent" or general manager.

Margaret Getchell was one of America's first women business executives. She was a brilliant innovative merchandiser with a talent for display and publicity. Her motto was "Be Everywhere, Do Everything, and Never Forget to Astonish the Customer." (Not unlike master merchant Walter Hoving's advice to P. G. Winnett, "Always *surprise* the customer.")

Macy's expanded constantly, adding new departments and grabbing up any leases available until it was a jumble of connected stores along Sixth Avenue and Fourteenth Street.

Margaret married Abiel La Forge, the lace and trimming buyer. During the Civil War, Abiel, a captain in the Union Army, had befriended Rowland Macy, Junior, who was assigned to his company after a court-martial for desertion. As a result, La Forge met Macy, Senior, and Margaret Getchell.

Rowland Macy, Junior, was a tragic disappointment to his father not only as a son, but also, considering the unwritten creed of stores, as a perspective heir to the business. Today young Rowland would probably be regarded as emotionally disturbed or mentally ill. In the nineteenth century, he had "wicked ways," and they required severe punishment. The boy was obstreperous in schools and at home. He was a trial to his mother and an exasperation to his father. At the age of fifteen, he ran away from home after a particularly ugly scene with his father and joined the Union Army under the assumed name of Charles Mitchell. Ten days after he enlisted, he ran away from camp. He was apprehended and with the war on, this was considered desertion, an offense which could be punishable by death. The boy's true identity was uncovered and his father was sent for. Pleas were made for young Rowland's life and were granted, but he was severely punished by restrictions, tours of duty, fines, and curtailment of his pay. He was assigned to Captain Abiel La Forge's company. Captain La Forge was compassionate and understanding toward the youth and worked to have Rowland's charges and sentences lessened. Under La

Forge's friendly wing, the boy's behavior seemed to improve. Macy's violent temper and his obvious disappointment in his son must have affected the unruly boy. Not surprisingly, the only two times in his life that the boy was befriended he responded with some responsibility and aptitude. Shortly after the young soldier mustered out of the army and returned home, however, he took up with low characters and caroused and drank heavily. He was barely eighteen years old. Attempts to have him work in the store failed. He was considered, according to most reports, a complete and utter wastrel. R. H. Macy's will, drawn in February 1877, was a heartbreaking document of parental confusion and concern. It read:

I am grieved to say in this solemn manner that my experience has been such with my son, Rowland H. Macy, Junior, that I cannot entrust him with the care of management of any property. He has never succeeded in supporting himself. On the contrary, though he is now twenty-nine years of age, he has been entirely supported and maintained by me, and although I have done everything in my power to aid him in establishing habits of temperance and sobriety yet I am compelled to acknowledge the failure of every effort made by me and others to that end. His passion for strong drink has not hitherto been controlled by him. In view of these facts, I have deemed it wise to make the following provision for his support and maintenance during his natural life. I direct that my said executresses or the survivor of them, do as soon after my decease as conveniently may be invest in United States Government Bonds, a sum the annual interest or income of which shall amount to one thousand dollars, and that they pay to my said son, the said interest or income when and as collected unless my said son shall contest this will, or undertake to defeat its provisions, in which case I direct that he have no part or portion of my estate.

After his father's death, the young man seemed to try again. He went to work in his uncle George Houghton's dry-goods store in Lebanon, New Hampshire, and took a solemn oath not to touch liquor again. For a while, he kept his promise, to the point where his uncle changed the name of the firm to Houghton & Macy. Things went well until he was sent alone on a buying trip to Boston. He went on a drinking bout and after causing a disturbance at the hotel, the Quincy House, he died alone in his room. The death certificate gave the cause of death as "Convultions [sic] and delirium tremens."

The Boston papers were somewhat kinder. The Boston Journal carried a small obituary, headlined:

SUDDEN DEATH OF A NEW HAMPSHIRE MERCHANT
Mr. R. H. Macy of the firm of Houghton and Macy Dry Goods Dealers in Lebanon, New Hampshire, died quite suddenly at the Quincy House in this city last evening of dropsy of the heart. He had been ill at the hotel for a couple of days. He was the son of a prominent New York merchant of the same name who died a few years since."

Rowland Hussey Macy, Junior, left no estate.

Macy, Senior, had died in 1877 at the age of fifty-four in Paris when he was on his way to Baden-Baden, Germany, for his health. He suffered from Bright's disease, but there is no doubt that the aggravation, frustration, and distress over the condition of his son contributed to his failing health.

Abiel La Forge had become a partner of R. H. Macy and La Forge now took into partnership a Macy nephew, Robert Macy Valentine. They bought out the Macy heirs, Mrs. Macy and her daughter, Florence Macy Sutton. It was announced that the name of the store would be changed to La Forge and Valentine in January 1879, but the Nantucket spirit finally gave R. H. Macy a break. Mr. La Forge died of tuberculosis in Florida in late 1878 and the Macy name remained. Valentine brought in a cousin, Charles Webster, as a partner and the following year Valentine died. Webster asked Jerome Wheeler to be a partner. Webster and Wheeler had clashing personalities and when Wheeler married Valentine's widow, it put additional tension on the not too successful partnership. Webster bought out Wheeler and asked the Straus brothers, Isidor and Nathan, to join the firm in 1888. The Straus-Webster management lasted until Charles Webster retired and sold his interest to the Strauses for $1.2 million.

An era began in which Macy's would become the most celebrated store in the world. It would be immortalized in songs, jingles, a play, a movie, a musical comedy, and a thousand jokes and cartoons. It would expand throughout the country. In 1978, Macy's New York and Hudson's Detroit tied as the nation's largest-volume department stores with an estimated $575 million in that calendar year, according to *Stores*, the magazine of the National Retail Merchants Association, Inc. R. H. Macy & Co., Inc., a corporation that conducts its department store business through 6 regional store divisions, operating 79 stores in 11 states, reported in July of 1978, net retail sales of $1,834,100,000.

Woodlawn Cemetery in the Bronx, New York, is something of a retail merchants association in itself. Franklin Simon, founder of Franklin Simon and Co., is there. So are F. W. Woolworth, Samuel H. Kress, and James Cash-Penney. William Sloane of W. & J. Sloane is there. There are store Sterns and store Hearns.

Along Myosotis Avenue, named after a family of herbs, a large pink block of granite is flanked by two low filligreed iron gates that open onto a courtyard surrounded by four mausoleums with grilled doors. Behind the doors are the tombs of Nathan, Jesse, Percy, and Herbert Straus and their wives. Carved into the granite block, facing the courtyard, is an Egyptian funeral bark. Seven oars are raised pulling against the crest of a giant wave. The inscription reads: "Many waters cannot quench love—Neither can the floods drown it."

    Isidor Straus—Born February 6, 1845
      Lost at sea April 15, 1912

    Ida Straus—Born February 13, 1849
      Lost at sea April 15, 1912

When the great ship went down, Ida and Isidor Straus refused to be separated or to take to the *Titanic*'s lifeboats. A survivor reported that they were last seen sitting in deck chairs, holding hands.

A basket of fresh chrysanthemums rested in front of the memorial. Dried fall leaves whirlpooled around the courtyard. Beyond the grilled glass door of Herbert Straus's crypt, a worn household broom was leaning against the sarcophagus.

There in the small rising hills of the Bronx memorial park among such New York giants as Oliver H. P. Belmont, who lies in an exact replica of the chapel of St. Hubert at Chateau Amboise in France, and Jules Bache, who rests in a mausoleum modeled after the Temple of Isis at Phylae, Egypt, and Herman Armour, Jay

Gould, Henry Westinghouse, Gail Borden, Collis P. Huntington, Victor Herbert, Vernon and Irene Castle, Joseph Pulitzer, and John "Bet-a-million" Gates, who organized Texaco along with the wire company that became part of United States Steel, Nantucket's righteous Captain Josiah Macy rests alongside family members with old-fashioned biblical names. The grassy plot is overgrown and full of weeds. It seems a pity that Captain Josiah is not a bit closer to Admiral David "Damn the torpedoes" Farragut and Herman Melville, who are up near the corner of 233rd Street and Webster Avenue. They would have gotten along together swimmingly.

West from the Captain, along Beech Avenue, set upon a grassy knoll overlooking the New York Central Railroad (Harlem Division) and the Bronx River Parkway, is a red stone obelisk. There are sculptured urns and wreaths and drapery—the Victorian trappings of grief. Foot-high *M*'s are carved into the sides of the monument. Here Rowland Hussey Macy, his wife, Louisa, his mother, Eliza, his brother, Robert, his infant son, Charles, and Rowland Hussey Macy, Junior (1847-1878) rest in peace—together. The inscription reads:

> The memory of the just is blessed
> In God have I put my trust
> The Lord is our judge
> He will save us.

The drooping branches of an ancient oak spread out mournfully and wrap the obelisk protectively. There is an empty headstone. Macy's beloved daughter, Florence Macy Sutton, lies miles to the north with the Sutton family in Valhalla, New York. She is there, close to the showplace estate she and James built in Bedford after she sold her interest in Macy's.

James Sutton was the son of a Bedford, New York, farmer, Aaron Sutton, and his wife, Mary. Sutton was a farmboy who longed for the good things in life. He went to New York and worked for Macy's. He married the boss's daughter. He was not, however, a fortune-hunter who lived off his wife's money. When they moved to the country, he worked hard as a gentleman farmer. He had a fine dairy herd and raised horses. He was generous to his wife. Atop the vast horse and cattle barn, he had a clock tower built in the manner of English barns. Since Florence was often lonesome in the country stillness for the hustle and bustle of New York City and the busy West Eleventh Street noises she had grown up with, he installed chimes in the clock that duplicated the sound of those in Grace Church, New York. Some years ago, the tower and clock were saved by a neighborhood committee and installed by the road at Sutton's Corner in Bedford. The clock keeps perfect time and the chimes ring out over the area—that is, when the committee members remember to wind it.

Along with farming, Sutton became an importer and dealer in fine art. He reputedly had several Monets, a fine collection of porcelains and Oriental objets d'art, furnishings, and carpets. Since nothing was too fine for his taste, he imported a French architect by the name of Charté to design and build him the finest house in the area.

He commissioned Frederick Law Olmsted, the designer of Central Park, to landscape acres of gardens and plant hundreds of maple, oak, elm, and pine trees in groves and along the gracious drives. Like many Victorian houses, the eaves and moldings were highly decorated with wood-carved gimcrackery but the trimmings on the Suttons' house were more along the lines of lacy chinoiserie. There was a pagoda-shaped porte-cochere. There were Oriental details on the gate house, the tool house, the ice house, and the wood and root sheds. Only the English cupola and clock on the barn and carriage house escaped the Oriental fillips.

Dorothy Hinitt of Bedford, who once owned the big house and now lives in the gate house of the former Sutton estate, described the interiors: "There was no plaster on the walls. They were covered with a heavy canvas that was welded at the seams and around the ceilings and the baseboards with intricately carved wood moldings. The mantels, door frames, and newel posts were Oriental fantasies. It was very Victorian, but it was not heavy like most Victorian. The details were very delicate and there were many details."

The house was an architectural masterpiece, but it seemed to take forever to build. There was all the hand carving to be done and the Suttons made constant changes and additions. James and Florence lived with James's parents and they were eager to move into their mansion. They constantly pressured M. Charté to finish the job. Then they would approach him and propose some new ideas.

One evening the architect arrived at the senior Suttons' down at the Corners. He presented the young couple with a key to the giant lock on the front door and announced, "Your house is now finished." There was joy and delight all around. Everyone wanted to go immediately, but the architect insisted not. "Come tomorrow morning between 9 and 10 o'clock and I shall be in the front hall to greet you."

Everyone acquiesced and retired immediately to be rested and ready for the next day and the long-awaited excitement. Promptly at nine o'clock the following morning, Florence and James Sutton climbed the hill up to their new house. The turrets and spires and gables silhouetted against the brilliant cloudless sky reached toward heaven above the freshly planted seedlings and saplings. The smell of clover filled the air as the morning sun drank the dew from the surrounding fields and mixed with the earthy scents drifting up from the cow barn. No monument, no cathedral ever stood more majestic than their house. They went up the broad steps, crossed the wide covered porch. Florence turned the key in the heavy brass lock and stepped into the wide gracious foyer with its sweeping staircase. James followed close behind her. M. Charté, the architect, was, as he had promised, waiting to greet them in the front hall. He was hanging by his neck in the stairwell.

Florence Macy Sutton and James Sutton lived out their lives in their Bedford house at Sutton's Corners. They had no children.

TWELVE

The One-The Only-The Fitz!

Wanamaker's, Macy's, Gimbels and Bernice Fitz-Gibbon

Bernice Fitz-Gibbon was born in Wisconsin and was raised on a farm. In 1915, having graduated from a convent school at the age of seventeen, she became the teacher in a one-room country schoolhouse complete with a potbellied stove. Bernice saved enough money from her meager salary to attend the University of Wisconsin. She graduated in three years. By her own admission in her book *Macy's, Gimbels, and Me*, which was published in 1951 and has been updated in six reprints, she was not chic and had a tendency toward "not fat—but certainly fattish." She wrote: "All the Hattie Carnegie originals and all the cosmetics at Elizabeth Arden couldn't have turned me into a femme skeletale."

Her employees, who were rather a unique group in themselves, have described her as "Marie Dressler in *Tugboat Annie*," "the Wicked Witch of the West disguised as an Irish leprechaun," and "like my grandmother, that is, if my grandmother had been Adolf Hitler." There was great camaraderie among the staffs of the advertising departments that Bernice Fitz-Gibbon tyrannized because, as an alumna explained, "There was one common enemy— FITZ!"

"Fabulous Fitz" was an image she herself helped to promote. For her eight-month teaching stint in 1915, she was paid $304. By the 1940s she was the "highest paid woman in advertising in the

250

country" and was commanding a salary of $90,000 a year as director of advertising at Gimbels.

Bernice Fitz-Gibbon revolutionized retail advertising. Store newspaper ads had traditionally been filled with facts and figures. They were also boring. Fitz made the ads spritely, entertaining, and literate. She trained several generations of aspiring ad men and women, who look back on those periods of their youthful nightmares with humor and on Fitz with affection, for in spite of her salary, the respect from top store executives, the awards—she was first and always a dedicated teacher.

At the time her trainees went through her rigors, they did not seem funny, nor did Fitz seem endearing. "Fitz" was a name that struck terror in college graduates' stout hearts, souls, and stomachs during the 1930s, '40s, and '50s. The phrase "Fitz wants you" or the sound of her buzzer could induce panic, tears, and nausea in a staff member and evoke sympathetic looks from co-workers. It meant only one thing—someone had goofed! There was always the threat of being "sent to the sign shop," which was a mysterious area in the bowels of the store where the *untalented*, the *stupid*, the people who loused up the king's English, used clichés or hackneyed ideas were sent to wither away, thinking up the simple phrases for signs that their limited brain power could handle. Or there was the ultimate insult of being told one should work in Nam's basement—a never-never-land in Brooklyn that surely must have been filled with the world's worst bores. To be *boring*, *un-witty*, *not-clever* was to be damned even by one's peers. For these were not graduates who had "squeaked through" assorted colleges, these were the cream of the crop, the BMOCs and BWOCs from top-drawer campuses. In today's parlance, they would be called "M-Q's"—"Most Qualified—instead of Big Man or Woman on Campus.

These were the *doers*, the *shakers*, the kids with the drive, the *smarts*, the ambition, who had been able to withstand the social and academic pressures and competition to emerge triumphant with the privilege and right to wear the Gold Key. Somewhere in their stud boxes and jewelry cases, they had tucked the $\frac{5}{8} \times \frac{7}{8}$-inch pendant with three tiny stars embossed in one corner and a hand in the other with a finger pointing to the Greek letters $\phi\beta\kappa$—Phi Beta Kappa. These young people were members of that elite scho-

lastic fraternity established on December 5, 1776, because Fitz
didn't interview candidates for her $35-a-week jobs who were not.
These graduates were not just "brains" or "bookworms"—they
were sharp and witty. They idolized E. B. White and envied the
group at the Algonquin Round Table. These *hotshots*, these *bullets*, held their diplomas sprinkled with *summa, magna* and *cum
laude* in one hand and the world by the tail in the other—or they
thought they did—until they met Fitz.

The *Fitz-minions* whose Gold Keys unlocked the doors to her
advertising departments at Wanamaker's, Macy's, and Gimbels,
who could take the heat in Fitz's kitchen and survive, moved on to
higher-paying jobs in advertising agencies, magazine and book
publishing, and merchandising. Her departments were constantly
raided, which was one reason for the fast turnover. It was a well-
known fact that through her portals lay a path to the glamour jobs
on Madison Avenue. It was the route to making it in the Big Apple,
which, of course, was not called the Big Apple in those days.

There were no politics involved in Fitz's departments. There
was only one head—*her*—nobody was angling. All one had to do
was produce. Fitz wrote in *Macy's, Gimbels and Me:*

> I was the perfect boss. Because I provided a climate where it was
> safe to make mistakes. Don't start any kind of writing career in any
> environment where it is not safe to make mistakes. Some advertising
> managers and copy chiefs and account executives are so scared of
> top brass that they discourage departures from the norm. They
> frown on any wild excesses of originality. Not me.
>
> I welcome wildness. There are always plenty of people around to
> tame things down. Taming is easy. If you must choose between a nut
> boss and a dolt boss—take the nut.

Few of her staff would have agreed with her at the time. The experience of working for Fitz was on a par with getting through the
Marine Corps wartime boot camp. But a former employee admits:
"She let us rip. She let us publish our secret thoughts. She had tremendous respect for the English language, grammar and imagination and *no* margin for error. It was like a childhood dream come
true for us to see our copy in a full page of *The New York Times*.
We were so young, so innocent, so full of ourselves!"

Those were the days of print—*The New York Times*, the *Herald Tribune*, the *Daily News*, the *Mirror*, and the *New York Post*—the days of *The Saturday Evening Post, Holiday, Collier's*, and the other weeklies and monthlies that devoured the written word. Those were the days before the tube bombarded the world with jingles and jangles and masses singing that they had "a lot to live and a lot to give" and that they'd "do it all for you." Those were the days when everything was in its place. Detroit made the cars, Hollywood made the films, and Madison Avenue sold everything.

Madison Avenue was a long liquid lunch of alphabet soup—BBD&O, Y & R, R & R, J. Walter. Floating among the letters were bits of glamour, pieces of the action, chunks of money, and strung out from the Madison Avenue bowl like a couple of strands of vermicelli were the New York, New Haven and Hartford Railroad tracks leading to Westport, Darien, New Canaan, the Greenwich Country Club, and the Stamford Yacht Club.

Many bright graduates, young men in gray flannel suits, pretty girls in swinging skirts, played the agency game well. They'd meet recent classmates at Tim Costello's or under the clock at the Biltmore and they'd "run it up the flagpole" with talk of *campaigns* and account *execs* and drink martinis and try to emulate the big kids of Mad Ave. In truth, most of them would walk daily through the golden portals of McCann and Benton and Bowles and go directly to the mail room or reception desk. Among themselves they'd wonder how they were ever going to learn the advertising business passing out envelopes and answering phones.

Meanwhile, over on the west side, the Gimbels gang in their grubby cubbyholes reeled under the pressures of turning out masses of retail copy under the sharp eye and ear of Teacher Fitz, who held the sign shop and Nam's basement over them like a ruler over knuckles. And they learned and they produced and they sold until they moved on to the Scrabble board of Madison Avenue, bypassing the mailrooms and the switchboards, for they became seasoned copywriters in short time—or they were lost in the sign shop or Brooklyn.

When a straightforward soap ad didn't move the product, Mark Dall, who had returned to Fitz after serving as a navigator in World War II, caught the tempo of the times, of Fitz, of Gimbels and cleared the shelves this way:

HELL BENT FOR LATHER

The cumulus is scattered, and we're over Biarritz,
But I'm not so scared of Jerry as I used to be of Fitz.
I'd rather meet a Stuka in a Hermann Goering rage
Than to hear the dread commandment: "Rewrite the *Tribune* page!"

Hardwater Soap is the only soap for me,
And I need soap terrifically.
It's silky as my parachute, it's flawless as a rivet.
One giant cake, they say, will purify a civet.

Hardwater Soap! Hardwater Soap!
Good old Gimbels will give you all the dope.
Sixteen flavors, fresh as all outdoors
To glamorize the debutantes, to sweeten all the pores.

Send your son a carton if he's fighting overseas.
One cake will bring a lassie from her high horse to her knees.
Send some soap to Iceland—it's too cold to wash the dirt,
But the Eskimos adore it—it's their favorite dessert.

Buy some soap for Malta and the prisoners at Crete,
The price is like the Allies—almighty hard to beat.
Send a box to Greenland (you know—where all the ice is).
And loudly shout hosanna for Gimbels' lower prices.

Hardwater Soap from the Suez to Gibraltar,
Dramatic at a burial, magnetic at the altar.
Hardwater Soap from Vine Street to Park Ave.
That's what the boys in the bathroom will have!

Hardwater Soap—lemon or gardenia?
For the mighty Army, Navy or Marine-ia.
Lave the tired ligament, suds the frontal lobe.
Hell-bent for lather right around the globe!

Now I see the Channel: a welcome, silver stream.
So I shall fly and fight again, and coming home I'll dream
Of precious jools and step-on stools—sic transit glorium—
Of objets Hearst and liverwurst at the Gimbel emporium.

Mothers, aunts, and girlfriends got the message and before long in
APOs throughout the land there were floods of hardwater suds.

Author Jeanne O'Neill had a love-hate relationship with Fitz which has turned more toward love over the years. To this day, however, she blanches when she thinks of her job interview. Jeanne was a Golden Girl out of William and Mary. She was brilliant, popular, beautiful, and a Campus Queen. She was also a Phi Bete. "I wasn't seriously looking for a job," she recalled, "but I saw an ad in *The New York Times* for a Gimbels' ad department copywriter which noted, 'only Phi Beta Kappas need apply.' I was amused. Gimbels—of all places! I answered it for a lark and met this sweet-faced Irish woman. I thought I was making quite an impression. I was confident and besides, who needed her lousy-paying job? I'm sure when I look back that I came across rather patronizing and snooty toward Gimbels and Fitz. She asked me, 'Are you Phi Beta Kappa?' And I answered, 'Of course,' implying that she was lucky to have the likes of me deign to be interviewed. Then this sweet-looking lady who reminded me of a dear aunt of mine let me have it. Whammo! She went right for the jugular—'A *Junior* Phi Bete?' she asked."

Jeanne O'Neill, under Fitz-Gibbon tutelage, became a top-notch fashion copywriter. She went on to write articles for the major national magazines and has authored *Flower Arranging Without Flowers* and *Make-It-Merry Christmas Book*. She lectures around the country on her creative designs. In Fitz's book Jeanne received an unheard-of accolade! "Thanks especially to Jeanne O'Neill without whose free-lance help my own business would have sagged badly."

Fitz spent her life in advertising. After starting as a clerk at Marshall Field in Chicago she went to New York and worked for Wanamaker's for one summer. She spent twelve years at Macy's, where she created the famous "*It's Smart to Be Thrifty*" slogan. She returned to Wanamaker's for three years and then became advertising director for Gimbels for fourteen years at the then unheard-of $90,000-a-year salary. She later headed her own agency until her retirement to her farm in Wisconsin in 1977.

"I was on the Marshall Field College Squad," Fitz reminisced recently. "They put us behind the counter selling and I was put into the ribbon business. The ribbon buyer tried to teach me to roll the circular ribbon rolls counter-clockwise. I couldn't because I have no digital dexterity. By the time the day was over, I was tangled from head to toe with grubby ribbon. I couldn't get out of the mess. I knew we all had to sell on the floor half of each day, so I suggested to the vice-president that they put me in selling large items that wouldn't tangle, like sofas or pianos. The old male furniture salesmen didn't want any females, but I insisted. I was a furniture success. In a month I was selling more than the men.''

The secret of Bernice Fitz-Gibbon's success was that she could sell *anything*—whether she was on the floor or putting words on paper. When she headed up advertising departments she pounded, browbeat, and humiliated her "bright young things" into using their brains, their wits, and their educations to produce words that would catch the public's eyes and ears and—*sell*. Gimbels' newspaper ads became "must" reading. "We were her little elves who thought things up. Of course the boss always took the credit," says a Fitz-ophile. "She was all emotion and old-fashioned, but underneath was sound merchandising."

Phyllis Condon, who worked for Fitz at Wanamaker's, went on to N. W. Ayer and later to Young and Rubicam. Speaking of Fitz's discipline she said: "It took me six days to write my first ad to her satisfaction. Six days! Can you imagine? She wouldn't let up until she got the best out of you. Her favorite was Mark Dall. We called him the 'sticky bun' writer. He wrote gustatory ads that made you want to rush to Wanamaker's tearoom. Then there were the poets like John Porter. We called them poets but they were really jingle-makers.

"I remember one time Fitz found hundreds of bird houses in the Wanamaker attic and she told us we were going to sell them. Someone came up with the headline 'House for Wren' and they sold like crazy. I think that was Mark's." Mark Dall, who according to Fitz was the best copywriter she ever had, later moved on to Dancer Fitzgerald.

"She also found flannel nightgowns that had been in that attic for at least twenty years. They were very *out*. These were the days when black chiffon nighties with spaghetti straps were *in*, but Fitz was determined. She said she was going to make every woman in New York a 'Bedtime Tory.' The ad ran with a sketch of a cute little Colonial dame in one of those monstrosities. She sold them!''

When Fitz became Gimbels' advertising director, she coined a slogan that became world famous and an expression that went into the American vernacular—*Nobody, but nobody undersells Gimbels*. The slogan was translated and at one time hung on signs around the Galleries Lafayette in Paris—*Ne personne, mais ne personne.* The origin of another of the great expressions of the Macy's-Gimbels feud has been lost in time. It is generally believed to have been born on a radio comedy show when Eddie Cantor was asked to disclose some secret and he answered, "Does Macy's tell Gimbels?"

Fitz not only delighted in creating slogans and selling the improbable like flannel nightgowns and bird houses; she welcomed the challenge of selling the impossible—of even creating the impossible as merchandise and then selling it. She personally regards as her number-one triumph her Christmas manure ad. Fred Gimbel had asked her to think up a feature gift for "the person who has everything." Fitz, remembering a garden lover who had once said, "What I want for Christmas is cow manure," decided that manure was to be the perfect Christmas gift. Selling cow manure by the ton in New York City would certainly seem the ultimate—like refrigerators to the Eskimos—selling test.

Fitz's young staff was shocked with the idea. The Gimbels Garden Department thought Fitz was going too far. Finally, fired by Fitz's enthusiasm, her elves began to give the ad the old college try. Rufus Bastion, the art director, came up with a layout— manure piles, shaped into a Christmas tree. He placed a rooster on top. The ad was designed for a full page in *The New York Times.* The headline was "No Bossy But No Bossy Has Finer Manure Than Gimbels."

The late Leslie Forester, who was to become editor of *Family Circle* magazine, wrote the copy which was lively and Christmas-y. The ad promoted the newly renovated street floor and the Gimbels Flower Shop. One bit of the copy said:

> . . . . We think it's a bright-eyed idea to give someone manure for Christmas. Tickle the earth, say we, and she'll laugh a harvest. And that's the very reason we've made contact with our bovine friends in Westchester, Long Island and New Jersey. We'll ship a magnificient 1-ton batch of Daisy's finest to your door (or to the rear door or the barn) for $19 (within 20 miles of Gimbels).

Other staffers contributed bits like the copy around a picture of a small cone-shaped package wrapped with a bow—"Gift wrap your package? Hardly."

The ad not only sold literally tons and tons of manure, it won prizes and over the years has become one of the great advertising classics.

"My manure ad caused the biggest indignant reaction of any store ad that ever ran," Fitz explained with glee.

The former Wisconsin farmgirl was constantly bringing bucolic touches into her ads for the giant department stores in major cities. But city people loved her cows and pigs and chickens and horses and proved it at the cash registers. A trade journal of the time was prompted to comment, "Even if Fitz became advertising head of Bergdorf Goodman, she'd drag in the barnyard."

It is doubtful that Fitz would have accepted being advertising director of Bergdorf's. This is not to say that Bernice Fitz-Gibbon was humble. Far from it! But she knew her customers and how best to reach them. When Carmel Snow, the famous *Harper's Bazaar* editor, wanted to take her to Paris to write up the openings for *Harper's Bazaar* in what Miss Snow called "Fitz's good blunt Gimbel manure English," Fitz refused. Fitz had great respect for fashion copy and advised young writers to use Eugenia Sheppard as a model and to "dig out her stuff in a library and study her word sorcery. She writes clearly, crisply and sensibly about fashion. Analyze her cool intelligent way of presenting fashion. And you'll never produce simpering silly stuff." For whatever Carmel Snow thought, Fitz knew that manure did not belong in the Paris salons.

Anyone in advertising today would think the hullabaloos over those ads of the 1940s were tempests in a coffee break, but they created talk and kept the store names before the public. Today ads, like window displays, sometimes border on the vulgar. They lean more toward porn than corn. Good taste might be found lacking if people sought good taste anymore. As stores reach out for the youth market, the swingers market, the homosexual market, ads are often designed to titillate and merchandise hints at assorted sexual gratifications. Young men are shown touching other young men and eyeing each other seductively. A Macy's men's cosmetic ad showed a photograph of a near-naked *male* behind. It was exposed where the towel around the model's waist did not meet. Bonwit Teller designed a lingerie ad with a drawing of a full frontal female nude. *The New York Times* not only drew the line, it drew shadows over the nipples and pubic hair. Writer Phyllis Tucker summed up the 1970s new look in department store newspaper advertising in *New York* magazine:

> It looks indeed as if New York department stores, long the home of life as it was, are *au courant*—reflecting current attitudes and lifestyles.

Today, in an effort to bring glamour and chic to their ads, retailers are turning more and more to advertising agencies. Ads are photographed on location, in real-life situations, by sophisticated photographers like Avedon and Scavullo. It is questionable whether anyone, with all the high-priced talent, has produced a more provocative ad than an unintentional *double entendre* in a Gimbels fashion spread of the 1950s. A naive (or was she?) fashion copywriter's headline was seen and passed by handfuls of people. In those innocent days, it was never questioned by anyone in art, layout, copy, or production. No one at *The New York Times* caught it. The finished ad winged its way from Gimbels to the *Times* and back again. No one batted an eye. It was not until a June Sunday when the full-page ad appeared in the *Times* that a few store sophisticates gasped. Gimbels executives held their breath through the next week waiting for the repercussions and accusations of vulgarity and obscenity from their customers. The ad was a large sketch of a pretty woman's head. On the head was a straw cartwheel picture hat. The headline: SMART GIRLS THIS SUMMER WILL BE FOUND UNDER A BIG BLACK SAILOR.

The chapeau sold like *hatcakes*. No one called to complain. In those bygone days, no one would have suspected or looked for innuendos in the rural, folksy, homey copy of a Gimbels ad.

Fitz's department abounded with the aura, enthusiasm, and rah-rah of the college-football films of the period. Fitz's team was alive with spirit. And the big drum major—the bear in the bearskin—in front, leading them over the fields of Greeley Square to victory, was Fitz! Fitz was Rudy Vallee—let's sing it for "dear old Maine!" and a chorus of "Far Above Cayuga's Waters!" It was *Good News* and the "Varsity Drag" all the way. Fitz was Knute Rockne giving a half-time locker room pep talk. Fitz was a Badger pom-pom girl, a Wiscon U. majorette dressed in red, stepping high in white boots, swinging her baton. Psyching up—hyping up—her verbal drummers who marched behind her in the background:

On Wisconsin
On Wisconsin
Plunge right through that line
Run the ball clean down the field boys
Touchdown sure this time

Rah! Rah! Rah!

On Wisconsin
On Wisconsin
Fight on for her fame
Fight, fellows. Fight! Fight! Fight!
We'll win this game.

Then:

Give me a G . . .
Give me a G . . .
Give me a G . . . I . . . M . . .

Give me a B . . .
Give me a B . . .
Give me a B . . . E . . . L . . .

GIMBELS! GIMBELS! GIMBELS! YEA!

The Big Game was played on Sunday when the big ads ran in the major city newspapers. The score was toted up on Monday morning when the ads pulled—or didn't. It was a jock atmosphere that many of the Phi Beta Kappas had never known with the old school tie and they loved it. For all the terrors, they knew it took guts to win and the message was clear. BEEEEAT MACY'S! FIGHT! TEAM! FIGHT!

There were fringe benefits in those days that had nothing to do with health insurance, overtime pay, or profit sharing. The Fitz followers, for all their word aptitudes, were young and human, and during the depression times at Wanamaker's, most of them lived at home with parents or in crowded all-boy or all-girl apartments. Most of them had little space or privacy. But love and youth will find a way. Wanamaker's advertising department was tucked into a far corner of an upper floor next to the "Start-a-Home" model rooms. The security force at the store was a few doddering night watchmen and their price was right. For fifty cents or a dollar, they were quite happy to look the other way. A young advertising department boy or girl with designs on a date would inform the partner that he or she had to work late. The date, impressed with the hardworking, eager companion, would be let into the store after hours and climb the half-lighted stairs to the copy department. There would be a subtle look at the Start-a-Home and more often than not one thing would lead to another. Later, the night watchmen would move through the vast floor filled with sofas, overstuffed chairs, and dining room suites. They would discreetly ignore the giggles, squeals, and sighs coming from the model rooms, except for switching off their flashlights. "I don't know if any of us really did start a home," said an old-time Wanamaker's copywriter, "but we did start a lot of something else." It sure beats Blue Cross.

Phyllis Condon used the Start-a-Home for a different purpose—survival. As Phyllis Smith, she had met and fallen in love with Eddie Condon. "I came to town with one thing in mind—to catch Eddie Condon—but I had to have a job and after a stint in Macy's book department, I went to work for Fitz at Wanamaker's." Phyllis led a double life, writing brilliant copy by day and at night following Eddie and his fellow musicians, Pee Wee Russell, Willie the Lion Smith, Wild Bill Davison, Jess Stacey, Hot Lips Page, Muggsy Spanier, Peanuts Hucko, and others around through a series of clubs—the Famous Door, the Hickory House, and the Red McKenzie Club. There would be early-dawn jam sessions which might include the Dorsey Brothers and Louis Armstrong. "I'd drag into work after being out all night and the only thing that could save me was Start-a-Home. I'd tell Fitz's secretary if she wanted me I was out getting pink sheets in the book or housewares department. These were the slips you wrote all the merchandise information on. Then I'd sneak off to the home for a nap. Everyone in Fitz's department tried to be clever—even the secretaries. I remember one time she winked and said, 'Maybe I should tell her you're in the mattress department.'"

Phyllis's exhaustion brought about part of the jazz revolution. "You've got to get this music out of the saloons and into the concert halls," she told Eddie Condon and his cohorts one night. Not too much later, the jazz concerts at Town Hall began and then later the music of Fats Waller, Benny Goodman, Artie Shaw, and Eddie Condon filled the sanctity of Carnegie Hall with "Muskrat Ramble," "Royal Garden Blues," and Condon group improvisations, "Carnegie Jump" and "Carnegie Drag."

And then there was Nick's in Greenwich Village. When Eddie's band was about to open there, they were nameless and Nick suggested they call themselves The Wildcats. Eddie was not happy with this name and, as he explained in his autobiography, *We Called It Music; a Generation of Jazz*, he called Phyllis.

"Give me a name for a jazz band composed of handpicked musicians," I said.

"Summa Cum Laude," she said.

"Don't talk with your mouth full of food," I said. "I'll wait until you finish."

"It means the very best, the tops," she said. "It's a Latin phrase in college if you win highest honors you are graduated summa cum laude. It's just right for your mob."

I told Nick. He nodded and said, "But who can pronounce it?"

"What difference does it make so long as they don't play it?" I said.

"Move in," Nick said.

And one of the great jazz combos of the era—Summa Cum Laude—had a touch of Fitz.

As in any department, there was a certain amount of buck-passing when someone made a boo-boo, but the important thing was to keep it away from Fitz. This was difficult since she was everywhere. But the great *swinging hammock fiasco* was handled masterfully until it reached the top.

One day an ad appeared with a hammock strung on a stand. In large block letters the headline said: HAMMOCK—$14.95. Below the copy promising Elysian fields of rest and relaxation, there was printed in very small type: STAND—$12.95. A woman from Brooklyn called customer service and said there had been some mistake. She had sent $14.95 and received the hammock, but no stand. The call was switched to the garden furniture department, where it was quickly detoured to advertising. Someone explained that the ad did say that the stand was extra and hung up. Again the call came through and the by now irate woman shouted that the picture implied that the hammock *and* stand were $14.95. The call was transferred to the art department. It was suggested that she string the hammock between two trees. The woman screamed that she lived in an apartment with a balcony. The call was switched back to the copy department, who knew nothing about it, and the woman was transferred back to customer service. There it was explained that she could return the hammock for a refund or send an additional $12.95 and receive the stand. The woman bellowed and yelled that the ad clearly pictured the hammock *with* the stand and said: HAMMOCK—$14.95. She would sue. It was false advertising. She'd call the Better Business Bureau. The call went back to advertising. Everyone was out to lunch. Between the cut-offs and transfers, the complaint went on for days. Finally, the woman called the president of Gimbels. The secretary was so undone by the hysterical woman that she put the call through to the top man and then she listened. The president suggested she return the merchandise for credit after he heard her story. The woman, now completely out of control and at the end of her rope, hollered that she wanted the hammock and the stand like the picture in the ad showed and she wanted them for $14.95 because—"Listen—you bastard—nobody, but nobody *screws* Louise Rosen!"

In the late 1960s, one of the Fitz Gimbels generation who had moved on to become an advertising agency success and then later had become a best-selling author discovered that he was to share the bill at a Book and Author Luncheon at G. Fox & Co. in Hartford, Connecticut, with his former boss, Bernice Fitz-Gibbon. He mentioned to his wife that he thought it would be nice if they offered to drive Fitz up there from New York. He called Fitz and she accepted. She had planned to take the bus. When the man hung up he said, "My God, I just hear that voice and I get the most awful butterflies in my stomach."

The ride north was pleasant and filled with witty conversation. At the luncheon Fitz talked little about her own book but extolled the man with the best seller. She was obviously the proud mother hen. She outlined their early association and quoted some of his long-ago headlines. She also managed to take a great deal of credit for his success.

On the return drive to New York, tired by the event, Fitz napped. While the tiger slept, the man whispered to his wife: "She's quite remarkable, isn't she? You know, I only worked for her for about eight months. I wonder why she frightened us all so terribly. I guess she's mellowed. After all, that was almost twenty years ago. I guess she's just gotten older."

"Haven't we all?" the wife asked.

Who taught you how to make clever quips?
Sophocles? Dewey? Or Mr. Chips?
No—
So—
Sound the drum and cut the ribbon
Six and a tiger for Bernice Fitz-Gibbon!
"WORDS are the diamonds as big as the Ritz,"
Said—the one—the only—Fabulous Fitz!

THIRTEEN

Ever Onward! Ever Upward!

Saks and other Fifth Avenue Fashionables

The giant game of store-checkers up and over the grid squares of Manhattan real estate turned into a game of chess when Saks & Co. planned a knight's move from Broadway and Thirty-fourth Street east to the Queen, B. Altman & Co. at Fifth Avenue and north to the Bishop at Fiftieth and Fifty-first, where St. Patrick's Cathedral was firmly ensconced. Since 1858, St. Patrick's American gothic steeples had looked down on the Kemp Farm and later loomed over the turrets, spires, and cupolas that topped the Vanderbilt, Astor, Huntington, and other fine mansions along the Avenue.

The stakes in the game were high. Horace Saks negotiated a 105-year ground lease for $300,000 annual rent for the property belonging to the Kemp family on Fifth Avenue between Fiftieth and Forty-ninth streets. Unfortunately, the Buckingham Hotel, a stubborn, well-placed rook, stood squarely in the center of the block. The rook was also the pawn of the Democratic Club, part owner and an occupant of the building. The rook/pawn refused to be checked for less than $1.2 million.

Although Horace Saks and Bernard Gimbel were competing merchants and neighbors at Greeley Square, they were also close friends. They toured Europe together, had summer homes near each other in Elberon, New Jersey, and played golf and commuted together.

One morning on the 8:20 train from Elberon, Horace and Bernard were unable to secure adjoining seats. According to Alva Gimbel: "They stepped into the baggage car and sat down on a coffin. Horace told Bernard that he was going to have to build his Fifth Avenue store in a *U* shape around the hotel and club since he was unable to meet the owner's price. Bernard said, 'You can't do *that*, Horace! Let me talk with our board of directors.' "

The Gimbel Bros.-Saks & Co. merger that resulted from their conversation was far from simple. A 1938 *Fortune* article, "Saks Is Very . . .," reported, "With the deal made on a dead man's chest, Gimbel-Saks became the biggest single department store organization of that time, with four big stores (Gimbels—New York, Philadelphia, and Milwaukee and Saks at 34th) having a combined net sales of nearly $100,000,000."

Prior to the 1924 opening, Saks Fifth Avenue advertised extensively, "apparel and accessories that are inexpensive but not cheap; exclusive, but not costly. Stocks of such volume, such vastness and variety as New York has never known."

Opening day was pandemonium. Mobs poured into the store and there was a near riot when the rumor spread that the Prince of Wales was there. He was not. Mayor Hylan was. And so was Jack Dempsey. This was two years before Bernard Gimbel's friend, sparring partner, and near-protégé Gene Tunney knocked Dempsey off the world championship pedestal in Philadelphia, in November 1926.

The first Saks delivery was a silk top hat in a leather case presented to President Coolidge. With typical Coolidge cool, the President remarked upon receiving the topper: "It's a perfect fit."

The first sellout item was every man's requisite during the prohibition era—a silver hip flask.

The new Saks had innovations such as "Tiny Town" on the second floor, where parents could register their children's names and receive a pamphlet entitled *Tiny Town News*. According to the *News*, the department was "a special section for baby boys where masculine vanity can get an early start and little girls aged 2 to 6 can learn the feminine art of loveliness."

While dressing up children was nothing new, Saks Fifth Avenue

advertising approach was. Early-day ads had been straightforward
and sincere-sounding. A Sunday *New York Times*, 1904, Best &
Co. Liliputian Bazaar ad said simply:

> We desire to remind parents that in the following lines of goods
> we carry the most complete and carefully chosen stocks, comprising
> every needful article, design, cut, style, weight and price from the
> lowest consistent with reliable goods, upwards:
> Infants' Wear and Furnishings.
> Millinery. Caps, Etc. for Infants and Nurses.
> Misses' Underwear, Shirt Waists, Etc.
> Boys' Kilts, Russian Blouses, Sailor Suits,
> Golf Suits, Jacket and Trousers Suits.
> Reefers, Overcoats and Raincoats.
> Etc.

As for shoes:

> Our Shoe Department has no equal for style, quality and specialties.
> The widest range of sizes, widths and special lasts assures our pa-
> trons of fit embodying health and comfort in the highest degree.

In the late 1930s, Saks Fifth Avenue juvenile department advertising made a pitch that went right to the core of tiny *male vanities*
and *female loveliness*—the parental egos and desires for status.
With a perking up in the post-Depression economy, who thought
about war? Who worried about the kiddies' health and comfort
when a Saks-labeled child's future held the promise of debutante
parties, membership in the Junior League or Skull and Bones,
evenings at The Stork and La Rue, perhaps a seat on the revitalized
New York Stock Exchange, a propitious marriage and glorious
wedding, outfitted by Saks' Bridal Salon, of course. Eventually a
new batch of little tweekers would appear to be barbered and
outfitted in blue suits and dainty dresses and thousands of miniature white cotton gloves that would be lost on the parquet floors of
Willie De Rham's or Mrs. Viola Wolff's dancing classes.

Saks ads spelled it all out for parents and the little ones, if they
could read. There were line drawings of pert youngsters and copy
written in a feigned, but legible, childish scrawl. A little girl with a
heavenly aura around her hair-bowed, curly head mused dreamily:

"Oh, I am not really PRETTY; it's just my Saks Fifth Avenue clothes!"

A tiny minx pointed to an astonished small fry: "She says YOUR clothes don't come from Saks Fifth Avenue!"

A dishevelled child looked enviously at a poised, well-groomed petite and said: "Some girls have all the luck—S.F.A. clothes since the day she was born."

And, heaven help me, there was a picture of a pensive little girl sitting in her underpanties on an ottoman, her chin on her fist. She said thoughtfully: "Now *how* can I wangle that coat?"

Saks seemed determined to reinforce parental insecurities about babies, young children, and the conventions of society, then to reassure everybody that there was no need for alarm. Saks was there, all-knowing, professional, and cool, like the sales personnel in the baby department, dressed in white nurse uniforms. Saks was a mercantile *arbiter elegantiae cum* Dr. Spock.

Starting with the obligatory haircut, "a happy event rather than an ordeal," a child could be maneuvered through and outfitted by the various departments. This enabled the youngsters to move on, poised and confident, through the stages of man. There was, of course, fierce competition from Best & Co., where secure New York and other eastern old guard had shopped or mail-ordered infants' and children's goods for years. These customers needed no reassurance about what was right. They knew. Often little boys graduated to the prestigious De Pinna boys' department; then as "preps" and college boys, went on to Brooks Brothers, Chipp, or Saks Fifth Avenue.

Young women sometimes defected to Bonwit's, Lord & Taylor, Peck & Peck, or Bendel. Some young women followed their mothers' shopping patterns. For others, a store switch was a statement of independence. Still others were lured by newly developed Campus Shops, college departments, or "College Board" advisors— sales personnel and peers who were up on the latest fads and fashion within the stores or as store "reps" on campuses.

When postwar air travel brought about student mobility, young staffs were recruited throughout the country by the stores to provide regional weather, fashion, and social activity information and—to make sales. How else was a Dobbs, Madeira, Miss Hewitt's, Ethel Walker, or Miss Porter's girl to know that silk hose were obligatory on the Stanford University Quad? That UCLA and USC students headed for Laguna Beach, Catalina Island, and Lake Arrowhead on weekends? That it seemed to rain *all the time* at the University of Oregon in Eugene. Ann Arbor? Where *was* that exactly? What did Los Angeles, Marlborough, Westlake, Beverly Hills, or Pasadena High students know about snow and boots and parkas? What did Bay Area, Anna Head, Branson, Dominican Convent, Sacred Heart, and Castalea girls or Miss Hamlin and Miss Burke girls or Galileo or Lowell High School bobby soxers in hilly San Francisco know about the appropriate dress for riding bikes around a Bennington or Sarah Lawrence campus? Or what went into a bag for an Amherst, Penn, or West Point weekend? And Colorado? What about Colorado? Forget it! Nobody went to school in Colorado.

Fashion magazines jumped on this marketing bandwagon. *Mademoiselle* and *Glamor* held national competitions and the winning editorial positions on their "College Boards" were as coveted as a Rhodes scholarship. The August issues of these magazines were guest-edited by the chosen few and were chock-a-block full of advertising, as thick and as well-thumbed as the New York Telephone book. *Vogue*, not to follow the pack, went a step ahead with the Prix de Paris contest aimed at the college market. The most famous winner of that prize was Vassar's Jacqueline Bouvier Kennedy Onassis.

The road of life was straight, narrow, and conventional. So was the ladder, rung by rung, up to success. All that was needed was the know-how, the accoutrements, and the wardrobe, which the stores were only too happy to provide.

In the dining halls of preparatory schools (boarding and city and country day schools—mostly in the east), youths in rep ties, blazers, and gray-flannel slacks (mini versions of Dad) stuffed their mouths with mounds of supposedly saltpetered food and stuffed their minds supposedly with learning. They read *The New Yorker* and dreamed of being Holden Caulfield. That was as far as anyone dared to revolt. They were too busy preparing for the tables down at Morey's, old Nassau Hall, the Yard where the Crimson in triumph flashed, and other *time-honored* institutions. Their time spent, their dues paid, they walked out of the ivy-covered walls in Cordovans and black Oxfords, leaving their white bucks behind. In gray-flannel suits, button-down collars, and narrow knit ties, they began the climb up to executive suites and board rooms. They made a quick stop along the way to scoop up the simply coiffed, well-scrubbed young ladies who wore tortoise-shell barrettes, single-strand pearls, and gold circle pins on their Peter Pan collars, before they jumped on the 5:27 for Larchmont and the good life—the American Dream—and began the cycle all over again.

There was the hiatus of World War II in which these stalwarts served God and country well on the battlefield, on the sea, and in the air. But the war only reinforced the desire for the *pie in the sky*, and the pie was apple and the sky was Scarsdale.

Some young women who had worked during the war, who had put their educations to use and tasted the sweet flavor of a paycheck, responsibility, and independence, were giving second thoughts to their answers to that old hen-session question, "Would you marry a man who wouldn't *let* you work?" It never occurred to even the staunchest supporters of the answer "No" that *he* (the man you married) had no God-given right to *let*, to *allow*, to *permit* this so-called breach of the system. That thought lay in the future and in the minds of their unborn daughters.

Of course there were a few young women who *had* to work and a few young men who did *let* their wives work, particularly if they were going to graduate school. Even tuition-paying fathers-in-law were willing to go along with *that* plan. It would be only a temporary arrangement until his son "got on his feet," so to speak. A whole generation of men seems to have gone through grad schools, internships, early low-paying jobs, and career setbacks on the flats of their backs because it was always said that someday they would "get on their feet!" A wife, long a reflection of her husband and a walking statement of his success, who brought home an occasional pork chop was still a reminder that her husband wasn't bringing home the bacon.

Being a "career girl" was regarded as a temporary situation until one "came to one's senses" or "settled down." Apparently when the men got on their feet, the women were supposed to get off theirs. These ladies in the dark could see where fighting the Pablum and the prune-juice system got Gertrude Lawrence. Right onto the psychiatrist's couch where Moss Hart and Kurt Weill put her. When Jenny did make up her mind, she did what was right because

everything, education, jobs, deb parties, travel, were all a dal-
liance, a stopgap, an amusement, until—the man. And when it
came down to the nitty-gritty between career and marriage, who
wanted to die a virgin anyway?—because that was what you were
supposed to be, in spite of that 1940s *Reader's Digest* survey, that
everyone knew about, with percentages of college females who
had had premarital—ahem—sex, and diaphragms, which everyone
didn't know about.

There were, of course, wives who were allowed to have their little jobs—until the kids came. That is, if they could also manage to
keep the house clean, market, and cook the meals, take the dry
cleaning, pick up the shirts, pay the household bills, meet the train,
give exciting parties, and be adorable, amusing, beautiful, and sexy
like Katherine Hepburn, Irene Dunne, and Rosalind Russell, the
movie "career girls"—and *never* talk about the "goddamned"
job—you didn't hear *them* talk about their jobs. Slowly things returned to normal because the 1940s-1950s wife either through exhaustion, social pressures, or the "kids coming," or the husband
getting on his feet, began to think that the *pie* in the sky was homemade and she had to make it and that the *sky* was Burlingame.

Out of the chaos of World War II, stores like Saks Fifth Avenue
helped bring about a sense of order. In postwar population shifts it
seemed important to have standards in cars, clothes, home furnishings, schools, and clubs. After all, who knew who your parents or
grandparents were? Who knew who you were, for that matter?
Then, suddenly, as if by some miracle, there appeared to the woman trapped in the suburbs, a Saks Fifth Avenue, Lord & Taylor,
Best & Co., Bonwit's, De Pinna—old friends you could count on
from childhood, school days, and college. The war was over and all
was right with the world. It was possible to recognize again a person of discriminating taste. A woman, no matter what part of the
country she came from or how funny she talked, in a Saks hostess
gown, serving rock cornish game hen, probably wouldn't cheat at
bridge or miss a hospital auxiliary meeting. A man in a Saks men's
department smoking jacket mixing dry martinis with Beefeater Gin
couldn't be *all* bad.

After the war, everyone needed order—the calm to get things
back into their proper perspective. During the late '40s and the
'50s, there were cocktail dresses for cocktails, evening gowns for

evening, day dresses for day. Slacks were for the garden or boats. Thrift shops were for the thrifty, not superstars or college girls. Bluejeans were for cowboys and overalls were for farmers, carpenters, plumbers, and electricians. And as any corporate executive knew that the "little woman" could be an asset, everybody knew that behind every great man there was a truly wonderful woman (Ha! Ha!), but she had just better be behind him and not pushing toward the front. The corporations could help, of course, with seminars conducted by store stylists and experts on fashion, home decoration, and entertaining to shape up the girl from Elkhart, Alpena, or Flagstaff. And then there were the clubs. Didn't everyone want to meet "their own kind"? Joining the right club could present problems. Some couples who couldn't make up their minds between golf or tennis or shore simply joined them all. One couple bought a speed boat and joined the American Yacht Club, only to discover that what had been good enough for the Michigan Lakes was called a "stink-pot"—American *Yacht* meant *sailing.* They quickly sold it. But it was wise to join a club so nobody would think you were Jewish. Not that some of everybody's best friends weren't Jewish, mind you. There were even those who had, through the service most likely, met some very nice—exceptional—colored people. But, of course, that had been during the war. No, people joined because it was important to join—to belong to the great WASP syndicate safe in the bedrooms in their bedroom communities. And because, if you didn't, life in the growing cities and burgeoning suburbs could be very lonely. Things were back in order—who wanted to be some kind of a weirdo, fer-godsakes?

Occasionally the road to acceptance was a bumpy one. How were the little tots who graduated out of their Merrymites into their Florence Eiseman's and Helen Lee's from the Saks Salon des Petits supposed to know the rules?

My daughter, Harriet, put a spanner in the works when she dropped out of the Barklay Dancing Classes for a year. Happy not to have to spend the $40 that was supposed to assure her future social success in our suburban community and all the world, I paid little heed. A year later, under pressure from her friends, she desperately wanted to return. It seemed a minor request in lieu of the riding, tennis, sailing, and golf lessons many of her friends were involved with.

I called the committee chairman only to discover that forty
bucks or no forty bucks, there seemed to be no way to get her rein-
stated. "There's a sequence to these things, Mrs. Birmingham,"
the woman said. "All the way up to coming out. Of course, the
dancing classes don't guarantee an invitation to the Cotillion, but a
consistency in attendance helps." There was hell to pay with Harriet, who bellowed and bawled because *everybody else* was going to
the parties, having all the fun. She couldn't see the "big picture."
The phone rang in the middle of her caterwauling. It was the chairman again, sounding chummy and syrupy. "I spoke to one of the
other gals on the committee and I think we can work something out
about your daughter. Is it Harriet? Yes, well, I understand that
Harriet has *two* brothers?"

Dancing and the process of learning to dance has long been the
cross that well-born boys and boys with upwardly mobile parents
have had to bear. The deal was made. It was quite clear—a "two-
fer"—two boys for one girl. After bargaining to get a fleet rate
failed, I sent my check for $120 to the Barklay Dancing School. We
trooped off to Saks White Plains to get everybody properly outfitted. Carey, thank God, could wear his brother's hand-me-down
blue suit. Unfortunately, my attempt to boil my old white cotton
gloves and shrink them down to size was as disastrous as my plea
for a discount.

As for dancing school, while there was a certain reluctance on
ten-year-old Mark's part, he did his sibling duty. Harriet and the
other eight-year-olds had a joyous time. But now that they had all
seen each others' new dresses, what were they going to wear to the
next class? Only my gentle, easygoing six-year old, Carey, seemed
distressed. This sweet boy, who *always* did what his big brother
did and he was told to do, was discovered, the evening of his dancing class, under the set tubs in the cellar. After an intensive interro-
gation and search for the blue suit, it was found wadded under his
mattress. He was then, as we say out west, *hog-tied*, stuffed into
the suit, and dragged bodily to the Apawamis Club. His refusal to
leave the car called for certain aggressive actions on my part, although I had not intended to meet the committee ladies at all, much
less in my sweatshirt, jeans, and sneakers (the ones with the toes
sticking out of the sides). The little shavers may have all been Very
Saks Fifth Avenue—their mother was Very *infra dig*!

We struggled up the steps, and inside the club I pushed him toward the receiving line. Confident that good breeding would take over when he faced the authoritative adults, I gave him one last shove in their direction and was pleased to see him extend his gloved hand when he regained his footing. A statuesque woman in a black cocktail dress, with pearls around her neck and marbles in her mouth, said with enthusiasm: "Hi! My, aren't you a handsome young man! You're a teensy bit late, but never mind *this* time. There are plenty of pretty little girls in there just waiting for a nice little boy like you."

I hid behind a pillar. She placed her hand on his shoulder and guided him toward the music and a voice that was calling, "step— step—step together—step." At the doorway, Carey stopped dead. "What's the matter, dear?" the lady asked.

"FUCK IT!" he said. And he ran past the woman, past me, and out the door of the club.

Through a variety of circumventions, such as changing the dates on my calendar, Carey never attended dancing school again. Harriet's "consistency in attendance" terminated the following year. As for the debutante Cotillion—named for an eighteenth-century French (a square-for-eight-figure) dance and song, *"Mon Cotillon (petticoat), quand je dance, va-t-il bien?"*—the musical gala marketing the virgins—by the late 1960s when Harriet and her friends were eighteen, their response to debs and debuts was like Carey's to the Barklay Classes. And what was that again about virgins?

Mark's new blue suit was torn to shreds in a snow fight during the Barklay Classes Christmas party. My Saks bill was $265.

Harriet did not exactly learn the *feminine art of loveliness* at Saks either. On the contrary, around the holidays there was a rather unfortunate and noisy sit-down strike over a red and white organdy. Later, buying underwear at Korvettes, we saw a dreadful fat child throwing a similar conniption fit. We both agreed that the little girl and her actions were very ugly. Seizing upon this opportunity to give one of *life's little lessons*, I pointed out how one could learn from such a disgusting scene how important it was to act like a lady, *behave* like a lady, particularly in public. I did perhaps belabor my point (as mothers are prone to do) and yammered on about the monstrous little girl, and behaving oneself and being a *nice* little girl and then, inspired, I said, "You wouldn't see Caroline Kennedy doing an awful thing like that. She's just a little girl, but always a perfect lady. She wouldn't kick and scream because *she* couldn't have some silly toy in Korvettes. We read about her and see her on television and everybody loves Caroline Kennedy because she is a little lady. It's very important, Harriet, do you understand? Harriet, do you understand?"

"Mommy?" Harriet asked.

"Yes, dear."

"There's something I don't understand."

"What is it, sweetheart?"

"What would Caroline Kennedy be doing in Korvettes?"

Last fall at the Neiman-Marcus Washington store opening, my son, Carey, handsome in his tuxedo, said, "Come on, Mom, let's dance!"

There has been a renewed interest in social graces among today's parents of small fry for a variety of reasons. For one thing, young couples want mobility. They want to travel, to ski and sail and backpack. Nannies, housekeepers, and sitters are at a premium. So are old-fashioned, ever-available grandparents, who are reluctant to be saddled with grandchildren for long weekends or weeks of vacation because they want their own mobility. Also, grandmother may be busy getting her MA or PhD or working. If grandparents are to be pressed into service, then they had better not be burdened with "little monsters." It is also advantageous to be regarded by the sitter syndicate as "low risk." In other words, "holy terrors" are no longer amusing or cute, they are *out. Nice* is once again becoming fashionable and it is wise for kids to know how to mind their manners. Also, the other alternative to child care is taking the child along and any fool knows that traveling with a well-behaved, polite youngster beats traveling with a brat.

It is also possible that today's young parents, having experienced the alienation, loneliness, and confusion of the "generation gap," are determined to communicate with their children, and communicating with a well-mannered child is more pleasant than conversing with an ill-mannered child. The rigors of discipline and child training being what they are, help is always welcome from any quarter and many department and specialty stores have been sponsoring etiquette courses for the young throughout the country.

These courses are the offshoot of three delightful books by Marjabelle Stewart and Ann Buchwald: *White Gloves and Party Manners, Stand Up, Shake Hands, Say "How Do You Do,"* and *What to Do, When and Why.* These books are textbooks for the programs, which consist of six or seven hourly sessions each week. The *White Gloves and Party Manners* course is for girls, the *Blue Blazers Spit 'N Polish* program is for boys; and there is a *Poise for Preteens* course. The courses have been held at Saks in Chicago and Skokie, at Carson Pirie Scott in Moline, Illinois, Gimbels in Milwaukee, and Ivey's in Florida, to name a few. They have been greeted with enthusiasm by parents and children alike.

Mrs. Stewart conducted etiquette classes in Washington, D.C., for fifteen years. Included in her groups were embassy, cabinet, and congressional offspring.

Ann Buchwald worked in merchandising, advertising, and fashion promotion in this country and was publicity director for Pierre Balmain in Paris for thirteen years.

Young college and graduate school "jocks" are instructors for the *Blue Blazers* course to emphasize the point that good manners are *manly.*

Mrs. Buchwald called upon her husband to write the foreword to *Stand Up, Shake Hands, Say "How Do You Do."*

> With this book you can avoid all the grave social blunders that I made in my youth because I didn't know any better.
>
> So study this book and see if it doesn't change your life.
>
> If, after three years, you don't see any difference in how people treat you, then I personally will give you your money back.
>
> ART BUCHWALD
> Husband of One of the Authors

Of course children traveling about and dining in chic restaurants also require proper wardrobes.

In a *Newsweek* report (December 12, 1977) on Life Style captioned *Kiddie Couture,* color photographs showed youngsters in designer suits, dresses, sleeping attire, and sportswear. Such fashionable names as Yves Saint Laurent, Louis Féraud, Jean-Charles de Castelbajac, and Jean Muir have jumped onto this lucrative kiddie-cart. Jean Strumpf, Bonwit Teller (New York,) buyer for the couturette department, is quoted: "Every mother has a fantasy about having her child look special because it's an extension of herself."

On the market are a Saint Laurent dress for $150, a Zingone boy's suit for $248; the Dior nightgown is a bargain at $29 when compared to the $785 Jean Muir cape for a young girl and the $200 Saint Laurent harem pants for her two-year-old sibling. The little darlings, in one New York shop, can get a Kenneth haircut for $50.

One mother tries to blame her extravagance on the kids: "Even your children can tell the difference between Saks and Sears."

With the exception of the quality of the photography and the size of the price tags, there is nothing different about today's dressing up of children from that of the nineteenth century. Considering today's traffic, it is easier to maneuver the kid in expensive Jag jeans into view than it is the Jag itself, or the Mercedes or the Rolls. And it is less dangerous than wearing jewels. Packaging the children in designer costumes broadcasts the same message bedecking them in ribbons and laces did in an earlier time. It is a way for a parent to tell the world, "I am very rich."

Fashion makes a *statement. Understated* elegance makes a quiet sound, but like a dog whistle, it is heard by the ears that are attuned and it speaks of wealth and good taste. When that bastion of assorted good tastes, Le Pavilion, was in operation under Stuart Levin, a woman who had been refused a table argued with Mr. Levin: "I read in a column that you allowed women here in pants suits." "Indeed we do," Levin said politely, "but you, madam, are wearing *slacks*."

If clothes make the man (or woman), they also say, soft or loud, but clear, who he (she) is, where he comes from, how much money he has and what kind of life he leads. The statement, like other verbal testimonies, may be true or false. The Pierre Hotel jewelry heist was not carried out by thugs in pinstriped suits and wide-brimmed hats or shabby hoodlums. The thieves were wolves dressed sheepishly (and properly for the Pierre lobby) in black tie and well-cut tuxedos.

And let us not forget Eliza Doolittle and Billie Dawn. First things first. They were dressed properly before their vocal cords or intellect were tampered with. First the body, *then* the mind.

Even the nonfashion of the 1960s and early 1970s worn by students and protesters was fashion in the sense that the mien was the message and the message was revolution. Long hair, jeans, and T-shirts said hippy, drugs, Commie, violence—bad. Jackets, ties, slacks, and haircuts spoke for the old values, "like father like son," the American way—good. Or did they?

At a fashionable Greenwich, Connecticut, cocktail party in the summer of 1969, the host, a corporate executive, proudly announced that there would be entertainment. The previous Christmas a neighbor had presented a son and his fellow Princeton Tiger Tones to sing Christmas songs at an open house. The appearance of the conservatively garbed young men had been reassuring and a wild success.

The host in the garden motioned to a teenager to step forward. He placed his arm around the boy and patted the shoulder of the youth's conservative sports jacket—the boy also sported a shirt, tie, and well-pressed slacks—"We mustn't get the idea that all kids are bad these days," he said as he rumpled the lad's short hair. Gentlemen in green or burnt-orange slacks, Navy-blue blazers, and Madras jackets and ladies in green or pink floral-print Lilly Pulitzer shifts and dainty Capezio sandals applauded enthusiastically. (Lime green and carnation pink in decor, dress, and accessories were and are *Greenwich*.)

An afternoon cloud drifted and the sun appeared. Its rays made contact with an electric eye that activated the awning across the rear of the house. There was a quiet whir as the giant striped canvas moved down electronically and shaded the terrace. The boy put his polished loafer up on a bench and strummed a chord on his guitar. A man said, "How did his folks *do* it? I tell that slob of mine . . ." A woman said, "I don't *mind* long hair—so long as it's *clean*." For a moment, all was right in Greenwich.

The boy began to sing:

> When the poor take over
> And the rich fall by the wayside . . .
> > by the wayside . . .
> > by the wayside . . .
> Then the world will be a better place
> When the . . .

As the meaning of the lyrics dawned on the crowd, the cocktail chatter rose to drown him out. Guests moved inside toward the bar. A few began to collect themselves to leave. The apoplectic host sputtered. A cloud appeared to darken the sun. A motor clicked on and the awning began to move, rolling up automatically on its track. Midway it stuck.

Today along Putnam and Greenwich avenues, on patios and decks in Greenwich, Connecticut, there are adults in well-cut and French-cut jeans. There are T-shirts with Calvin Klein written on the sleeve, or small *G*s for Givenchy, or little alligators, crossed tennis racquets, or olive branches on the chests. If you can't fight 'em, join 'em—properly labeled, of course. The revolution is over.

In the 1920s, Paris, not Seventh Avenue designer names or manufacturers' logos, was the spokesman for fashion. Adam Gimbel, vice-president of Saks Fifth Avenue, had gone to Paris to buy for the new store. In 1925, he had been there for the Paris Exposition and he had been influenced in the same way P. G. Winnett had been, but unlike Bullock's Wilshire, which was in the planning stage, Saks had been completed.

Horace Saks died in 1925, a little more than a year after Saks Fifth Avenue had opened. The Saks family relinquished their holdings, and Adam Long Gimbel, grandson of Gimbel founder, Adam, and cousin to Gimbel executive, Bernard, became president of the store. Adam Gimbel was young—barely thirty-two—full of ideas, and anxious to put his early architectural training to use. He had been a student at Yale School of Architecture but had left and entered the service during World War I. After the war, he had joined the Gimbel organization.

In 1926, Mr. Gimbel remodeled the year-and-a-half old store interiors in modernistic decor. He felt that the new society around Park and Fifth avenues during the easy-money twenties would be willing to pay well for things a cut above the ordinary and he bought the finest European merchandise and introduced exclusivity under the Saks labels. He wanted to sell luxury on a volume basis. He also wanted to establish a network of specialty stores on a nationwide scale. He followed his fashionable customers to their seasonal watering holes, as B. Altman had done when he dispatched his horses and wagons to the resorts to deliver Altman goods that arrived by train. Only Gimbel went a step further. He opened a store in Palm Beach and two years later another for the summer crowd at Southampton.

Barry Summerfield, former Saks vice-president, managed the

Southampton shop. He recalled living in an apartment in the store with his family. "It was like living in a fish bowl," he said. "My wife and kids had to troop through the store to go to the beach. We had to be careful what we cooked. The smell of onions or garlic didn't go with the elegant little shop. It was very strange. We came home one evening and found a man trying on dinner jackets. He wasn't the least bit flustered and went on posing and turning in front of the mirror. 'I have an account,' the man said. 'There is a black-tie dinner tomorrow evening and I'm sailing all day tomorrow. Your baby-sitter said it would be quite all right.' "

With the opening of a Chicago store in 1936 and a store in Beverly Hills in 1938, Adam Gimbel's dream of making Saks a "specialty store to the nation" began to come true. By the end of the thirties, there were an additional eleven resort and suburban stores. Today, there are over thirty Saks stores throughout the country and the projection is for forty stores by 1980.

According to M. Jean Bugin, director of the Gimbels-Saks Buying Office in Paris, one of Adam Gimbel's dreams did not come true. "He had a big ambition in 1950 to open a store in Paris. We looked carefully for a location, but the plan fell through. I'm sure it would have been successful with the French people—we had nothing like Saks in Paris—a large store with high-quality merchandise and service.

"Adam Gimbel was respected all over Europe. He spoke fluent French, German, and Spanish and had no difficulty dealing with designers, who can be very difficult. When he became president of Saks, he looked to Paris for the fashion. At the time French *prêt-à-porter* was a full industry compared to American ready-to-wear. He also installed a special barber shop in the New York store where customers could have the latest Parisian bob. He revolutionized hairdressing in the thirties when he introduced the Antoine de Paris salons into the Saks stores. He was always very drawn to Paris."

"Mr. Gimbel was a well-rounded man, a Renaissance man," said Helen O'Hagan, Saks Vice President and Director of Special Events and a close personal friend of Mr. and Mrs. Adam Gimbel. "He was a voracious reader and was knowledgeable on any number of subjects: art, fashion, history. He had fantastic taste and brilliant ideas, but he wasn't a workaholic. He was a sportsman and rode well. He was on the Rumson polo team and at one time owned twelve polo ponies and two hunters. He loved to shoot and he and Mrs. Gimbel would go to Cuba and later to Spain for the shoots. Mrs. Gimbel was an excellent golfer. They entertained beautifully and entertained everybody. They were a unique couple. You don't find people like that in business anymore.''

When Adam Gimbel took over the presidency of the store, there were rough days ahead for Saks. Not only did the stock market crash strike low blows to the luxury trade, but stiff competition had followed in Saks' wake up Fifth Avenue. Best & Co., which moved from farther downtown, not only had a firm grip on infants' and children's wear, it carried a line of quality fashions. Bergdorf Goodman moved from 616 Fifth Avenue into a full-line store on the Plaza, offering custom-made fashion and fine furs. Bonwit Teller flanked St. Patrick's on the uptown side. The store competed for the luxury market under the guidance of an extremely capable businesswoman, store president Hortense Odlum. Mrs. Odlum not only concentrated on quality and service, she invited her customers to join her for tea to discuss their personal fashion needs.

In 1932, Saks Fifth Avenue, with net sales amounting to $13,788,000 had a net loss of $595,000. The store's survival rested on Adam Gimbel's shoulders and he was not found wanting. He developed some of the most unique innovations and campaigns in the history of retailing.

Foreseeing the ski boom, he introduced ski merchandise and created a ski slide (consisting of borax snow) where ski enthusiasts could try out their equipment. Saks sponsored a snow boat cruise, chartering the liner *Paris* to Europe and a train to St. Moritz. There were sponsored ski trains to the Canadian Laurentians. Following the fast-growing interest in sports, a wind tunnel was constructed in the Juvenile Shop and a swivel-based 10-foot sloop was installed. An instructor was on hand to demonstrate the proper ways to set sail under varying wind conditions.

At Christmastime, the store opened to men only in the evenings to give them an opportunity for a Saks shopping spree and the slogan "Very Saks Fifth Avenue" became a password to chic, style, taste—to class.

In 1929, Adam Gimbel hired young Sophie Rossbach to counsel the buyers. She was called a "stylist." She was sent to Paris to buy

French models to be copied in the Saks workrooms and to be sold in the Salon Moderne. Sophie designed for the up-to-date 1940s Broadway shows like *The Women* and *Reunion in Vienna*, which featured witty and elegant stars. She had other designs made up in the Saks showrooms, and Broadway stars like Ina Claire, Lynn Fontanne, and Claudette Colbert, along with socialites, flocked to the Salon. In 1936 Sophie grossed $583,000. A line of ready-to-wear Sophie Originals was introduced that netted $1 million by the mid-1940s.

As Paris fought to regain her fashion supremacy after the war a fashion revolution took place. The "New Look" was launched by newcomer Christian Dior. Waistlines were squeezed, hips were padded, and skirt lengths were dropped. Fashion became a tent show with acres of fabric, and women, tired of the skimpy wartime costumes, joined the circus. Although the fashions were a sensation, they were uncomfortable and restricting.

In the fall of 1947, Sophie presented a collection avoiding the extremes of the Paris "New Look." That year, Sophie Gimbel was the first American fashion designer to appear on the cover of *Time* (September 15). The caption asked, "Who wants the New Look?"

In 1931, Sophie Rossbach had married Adam Gimbel. For sixteen years, she had been deeply involved with Saks Fifth Avenue, and according to the *Time* article:

> As Adam's wife, Sophie's abilities as a designer have not always been above suspicion in the skeptical dress industry. Her rivals try to belittle her by saying, "After all, she's the boss' wife." But no one who knows Adam really believes that that's the answer. Sophie has her job because she has earned it. And in the backbiting world of fashion, she is quite able to take care of herself.

Taking care of herself and her reputation as a designer was no simple task in 1964, when Sophie was asked to design Mrs. Lyndon Johnson's Inauguration Day costume.

Sitting in her New York town house, surrounded by eighteenth-century antiques, horse prints, and her collection of porcelain birds and flowers, the exquisite Sophie Gimbel recently recalled, with a certain amusement, the trial that accompanied that honor.

"My friend, Robin Duke, told me Mrs. Johnson wanted me to

design a dress and coat in cashmere the color of a dark American Beauty rose. We had sketches drawn. She selected one and we made the models according to her measurements. I flew to Washington with the dress and coat models and two fitters. Robin also told me that Mrs. Johnson wanted me for lunch. I was very excited since I was anxious to see Blair House.''

There was an ill omen when the trio arrived in the capital. "We were met," said Sophie Gimbel, "and I'd never seen such a car in my life. It must have been twenty years old and I have no idea what kind it was—a Dodge, maybe. We couldn't possibly get all the boxes in it.

"We finally got to the house and went through all that rigamarole to get inside, unpacked, and Mrs. Johnson came in and put on the dress. Now this was a *first* fitting, mind you, so it was all stitched on the outside. Anybody that knows *anything* knows that. Mrs. Johnson said, 'This is the worst-looking thing I've ever seen in my life.' And I said, 'Well, Mrs. Johnson, I'm terribly sorry that you think it's so bad. What would you like me to do about it?'

"Now, all of a sudden Linda Bird came in, looking like nothing you've ever seen, with black knee socks on and an old sweater— looking like *nothing* you'd think was very attractive. But she was adorable. She said, 'Mother, I think it's *lovely*, and you look *lovely* in it. You just don't understand because you aren't seeing it with the finishing touches.' And the maid said the same thing.

"It was now about one o'clock and we'd been there since ten-thirty. We'd left New York at dawn. Then Mrs. Johnson said, 'I'd like to show you the type of clothes that I like to wear.' And I said, 'I'd be very glad to look at them.' So she goes inside and puts on a dress and I said, 'Mrs. Johnson, if I had to make you a dress that fit that way, I would be so *ashamed* of myself. That is the worst-fitting dress I have ever seen in my entire life. I don't know how in the world you could possibly say that *that's* what you want to look like. If *that's* what you want to look like, you'll have to go to somebody else. I don't know how to make a dress like that.'

"So we go back in the other room. It is now two o'clock and we haven't even been offered so much as a drink of water. Then that *charming* secretary of her says, 'I don't understand you, Lady Bird. After all, you've got that beautiful mink coat. Why do you wear this coat? It can't compare with your beautiful mink coat.'

"I was sitting there controlling myself. I don't think I've ever been that mad in my whole life. I was boiling!

"Now it was about two-thirty and she offered us a demitasse of coffee, not a regular demitasse—a *half* a demitasse and not a *cracker*, not a *nut*—nothing!

"I asked to use the telephone. I called the Saks office and told them to send a limousine and have it wait for me. Mrs. Johnson said, 'But you don't have to do that, Mrs. Gimbel. I have a car waiting for you.' And I said, 'Well, yes, but *I'll* have a car waiting for me *too*.'

"It was after four o'clock when we left and we hadn't had anything to eat. So we all had to stop at some bar for a sandwich. Then I went to the office and I called Robin Duke.

"I said, 'Robin, I'm leaving the material with you with love and kisses and I want you to take care of it. And I am not going to finish the costume.'

"Robin said, 'You can't do that, Sophie. You just can't *do that*. You've got to finish it.'

"And I said, 'No *I don't*.'

"And Robin said, 'But she *loves* it.'

"I said, 'The *hell she does*. She loves it so much she thinks it's awful. I am not going to aggravate myself. You can send it down to Adele Simpson and get her to finish it.'"

Sophie Gimbel did finish it—only the next fittings took place in New York at the Carlyle Hotel, "which was like getting into a vault," Mrs. Gimbel said. "Finally she loved the dress; she loved the costume; sent me her picture in it and invited us to a party at the White House in honor of the President of Italy. Adolfo made the hat.

"I went to his collection this morning and his things were exquisite. But I don't understand women anymore. I wonder what some of those women are doing there. There was one woman in Turkish pants and a tunic—she looked like she belonged to one of those religious sects—she looked like the biggest damned fool I've ever seen in my life. I was awfully glad when they didn't take her picture.

"Oh, his clothes were lovely. He uses the most beautiful fabrics and Adolfo—Adolfo is the most adorable man you've ever met in your life."

Adolfo was born in Cuba. While the name and nationality conjure up an image of a suave, swarthy Latin, the truth is that Adolfo is blond and, with all due respect to this fiercely talented designer, he is as cute as a *button* and as sharp as a *pin*. He has the face of a cherub and his gentle speech is laced with his lyrical Spanish accent. "Behind all that is a steel-trap business mind and a computer brain," said an associate, but no matter, he is adorable Adolfo.

Adolfo left Cuba in the early 1950s and went to Paris for a year. "Everybody is misinformed," he said. "They say I work at Balenciaga: I did. I work at Balenciaga—collecting pins. Then I was taken to a salon in Rue de Cambon by Bettina Ballard and I work for six months as an apprentice. I came to New York when I was seventeen and work at Bergdorf Goodman designing hats. When I left Bergdorf, Halston took my job and I went with a company named Emme—in hats.

"I always wanted to make clothes—to start in New York is very difficult. I did have my conception of what I want to do and I did have to find my way and I thought making hats would be an easier way to enter the world of fashion in New York."

He credits a Cuban refugee, Anna Maria Borrero, with teaching him the architecture of fashion. "She was a fascinating lady who had been very honored in Cuba for her contribution to couture. She had developed a system of modern couture dedicated to measurements. It was all mathematics, trigonometry, construction—armholes, sleeves, body. She was a professor and very dedicated but she wanted to make functional things as well as beautiful things. She was nearly blind, but I learned more from that lady than from anybody. I learned practicability.

"I like things very lasting," he said. "and things that you can combine. It is the same with my men's fashions. Jacket and pants go from one suit to another. I don't want people to wear my things today and discard them tomorrow."

Recently Adolfo had an unheard-of coup in the world of high fashion. Enid Nemy, reporting in *The New York Times* (March 8, 1978), wrote:

> At one time, the embarrassment of it all would have sent even strong women into a decline. . . .
> Now, the ways of the rich being what they are, the ownership of

the dress of the season, or the dress of the year, is almost like membership in an exclusive club.

This season, on both coasts and most of the cities in between, the Cadillac of the fashion world is a three-piece Adolfo dress in gold and burgundy. . . .

To date, Adolfo has sold about 500 (at $750 each) of his three-piece evening outfits and although the design was one of his favorites, even he was somewhat surprised at the response.

Adolfo is sold exclusively at Saks Fifth Avenue, except in cities where there is no Saks. Then he is carried elsewhere, for example, at Neiman-Marcus in Texas.

"I work with the stores," he says, "and we have created something that is very close to custom-made. I find my work very challenging. I am much involved with my organization. I think that as long as there are beautiful fabrics and money to spend, people who have style will spend it. Of course, money changes hands," he added in his delightful accent, "but *still* it is to be spent."

The roster of Adolfo clients reads like a Who's Who in society and the entertainment and international set. Bernadine Morris reported his 1978 spring showing in *The New York Times* (January 5):

> There was a crescendo as the final group of dresses appeared. . . .
> "Adorable" is one of the words that could describe them.

My memorable *haute couture* experience was at Balenciaga in the Madrid—not Paris—salon, thus making it, in proper Castilian Spanish, a Bal-en-*thi*aga experience. I was introduced to the salon by Ava Gardner, with whom I had become friendly through a series of circumstances. It was a friendship that almost cost me my life.

Ava included me in her party for the benefit première of *The Night of the Iguana*. There was to be a supper in the foyer of Philharmonic Hall at Lincoln Center following the show. Between the film and the dinner, Ray Stark, the producer, was entertaining at a cocktail party for the stars and their guests in the Green Room. The night of the fete, Ava looked magnificent in an emerald green satin gown designed by the master himself, Balenciaga. When I complimented her she said: "When you come to Madrid, I'll take you

over there. His things are less expensive in Madrid than in Paris."
That taken care of, we settled down among the other luminaries
like Tennessee Williams and his aunt, to watch the film. A bottle of
Wild Turkey bourbon was passed around just as though we were
all in the bleachers at a Yale-Harvard game.

After the film there was wild applause and we moved down toward the stage of Philharmonic Hall in the direction of the Green
Room. We were going against the crowd. I didn't know who had
ended up with the bourbon. Ava took my elbow and whispered,
"Hon, do you know where the ladies room is?"

"I'll find it, just hang on," I said. We traveled up in an elevator
and through a labyrinth of halls. We made one false move into a
dressing room full of half-naked mariachis and finally found a small
sitting room connected to a lavatory and dressing room.

I said, "You first. You're the star," indicating the door. At this
point, I discovered that we had been accompanied by an
unidentified woman. I said, "I don't believe we've met—I'm Nan
Birmingham." And she said, "I'm Marion Javits." She ran a comb
through her hair and left. Ava reappeared and said with a nod,
"I'm not going in *there*." The cocktail party seemed to be going on
in the adjoining room. We sat down and since neither one of us had
ended up with the Wild Turkey, I stepped out into the party room
and returned to the little restroom with two drinks and Ava and I
relaxed.

There was a tap on the door and in came something fantastic in a
dark blue and silver sari fabric all flowing with a diamond tiara on
its head. Ava said, "Nan, have you met Mrs. Burton?" I said,
"No. How do you do, Mrs. Burton." Ava said, "This is Mrs. Birmingham," and Mrs. Burton said, "How do you do, Mrs. Birmingham." They went through whoops of "You were marvelous!" and
denials and "Oh, yes you were." And there was another tap on the
door. In bounded a vision in ballooning chiffon harem pants and
there were hugs and kisses and Ava said, "Hon, have you met
Mrs. Robards?" and I said, "How do you do, Mrs. Robards," and
Ava said, "This is Mrs. Birmingham." Mrs. Robards said in a
magnificent throaty voice, "How do you do, Mrs. Birmingham."
And Ava said, "You *know* Mrs. Burton," and Mrs. Robards said,
"Of course I *know* Mrs. Burton." And there were more squeals
and hugs and cheeky kisses. And then it all settled down and they

began to talk about how beautiful they were. As I sat there looking from one to another, I thought, All my life I've been trying to find my group, my pals, my chums, and I think at this moment I have found them—Ava Gardner, Elizabeth Taylor, Lauren Bacall—all here—in the *john* at Lincoln Center.

When the cocktail party dispersed, we moved down to the Philharmonic Hall foyer for dinner. I did not know at that time that soon my life would hang by a thread as fine as the steel wires that held the Richard Lippold ceiling sculpture. We were maneuvered toward Ava's table and the crowd crushed around us. The table seated eight. Ava sat opposite me and my dinner partner, Dr. Green, was a friend from her North Carolina home town. I had no sooner sat down than I was struck from the rear. My face was plunged forward, my arms were pinioned to my sides, as the mob surged. Arms and hands were pushing my head farther down; elbows rested, using my head, back, and shoulders for a tripod to photograph the star across from me. I gurgled and mumbled, saw my life pass in front of me, and tried to stave off panic. Dr. Green became cognizant that all was not well with me. He and security guards hauled the people off. I came up gasping for aid. I looked down and saw my face, bits of blue eye-shadow, dots of black mascara, and smudges of red lipstick, mushed into the first course of my dinner. I wiped my face and my remaining makeup came off in my napkin. I imagined the *Daily News*: "Unidentified woman drowned (or is it suffocated?) in an overripe casaba melon at chic star-studded gala." What a way to go!

Some months later I was in Madrid and I met Miss Adela, Ava's lady at the salon. Ava telephoned ahead and then sent me in her car, which was something of a happening in itself. It was probably the only Lincoln Continental in all of Spain. It certainly was the only Lincoln Continental with California license plates marked AG. All of Madrid recognized the car and little groups would chase it down the street and wave and call out, "Aba!"—"Aba!"—"Aba Gabney!"

I had gotten into the Lincoln and with a sweeping gesture had said, "Manolo—prim—ero—Bal—ennnn—thee—ah—ga!"

I was quite prepared as we drove down the Grand Via and stopped in front of the shop to let the crowd think I was Aba. I put on my dark glasses and readied myself for the fifteen-foot dash across the sidewalk. Manolo opened the door and before I could get out of the seat, a murmur went thought the people lining my path and they backed away—"Es nada! Es nada!"

Upstairs, Miss Adela greeted me and suddenly I was surrounded by the sales staff. They were all Principessas and Condesas, and Marquesas. I was gripped by a cold terror as they spoke in assorted languages not one of which was English. I explained that I was here to get a *Balenthiaga thuit*. Various models were brought out. I made a selection and now came the moment of truth as they all hovered around me in the dressing room. I said brilliant things like, "Gracias" and "Muy bien" as I removed my skirt and blouse. We were beginning to get on rather well, I thought. At least a smile or two had broken through. Then suddenly I looked at the assembled aristocracy, the cheeks had been sucked in, chins raised, and eyes widened—their looks were steely. I glanced into the mirror and caught a quick glimpse of something shining. A safety pin! Oh, my God! A safety pin at my slip strap. And not a little gold one. Not one of the tiny ones you have to take all the other pins off the loop to get to. No. This was a biggy. The *Biggest*. The kind I'd had around since I used them in the kids' diapers.

I selected the model and fabric and there were subsequent fittings, but things were never right between me and the *aristocratas* again. The fleeting second of warmth had passed with my shame. I was sustained by the garment itself. It was pink and white nubby French tweed—it was as delectable as Jordan almonds. The final tucks and little smoothings were made and I was to pick it up on the morning that I was leaving for Barcelona. I was almost beside myself with excitement.

The night before going to Barcelona I attended a reception at the Casteliano Hilton with some friends. Paul Hoffman, the then Madrid Bureau chief for *The New York Times*, was hosting the party in honor of the *Times* publisher, Arthur (Punch) Sulzberger, and his wife, and the *Times* Washington Bureau's Tom Wicker and his wife. There were rumors that Governor Nelson and Mrs. Rockefeller were in town and might attend. I dutifully went through the receiving line and suddenly there was a flurry at the ballroom entrance. The Governor and Happy *had* arrived, and as though a giant vacuum cleaner had been switched on, all the guests were sucked in that direction, except for Mrs. Sulzberger and Mrs.

Wicker. They remained in a receiving line with no one to receive. I said to my friends, "I'm going to talk to them. Then we will all look like three ladies in conversation rather than their looking like two ladies out in left field."

I had met Mrs. Sulzberger briefly at a parents' weekend when our sons attended the same boys' camp in the Adirondacks. I mentioned that for openers and we took it from there. "Are you touring?" I asked.

"Yes, we are going for about five days to Cordoba, Sevilla, Granada. And you?"

"Starting tomorrow,' I said, "I'm going to have ten days in Balenciaga."

"Really?" said Mrs. Wicker, with traces of a southern accent in her voice. "Ten *whole days*? What in the world are you going to do?"

"Oh, the usual thing," I said, "look around."

"How *absolutely fantastic*." And she called across the room, "Tom, come here, Tom, have you met Mrs. Birmingham?" Tom Wicker joined us. "She *really* knows how to do things. Why, starting tomorrow, she's going to have *ten whole days* at Balenciaga."

I heard her say it. I gathered my wits. I said, "Well, now, if you will pardon me." I started to move away.

Mrs. Wicker caught my arm. "Excuse me, Mrs. Birmingham, but since you know your way around, could I ask you something?"

"Of course," I said, flushed from the Balenciaga-Barcelona mix-up.

She dropped her voice. "I wonder if you could tell me where the ladies room is?"

"Mrs. Wicker," I said, "it is *very* simple. You go out past the Rockefellers and in the lobby turn either *derecho* or *izquierdo* until you come to a *puerta* marked '*damas*'—you can't miss it." And I fled.

So much for Spanish *haute couture*.

A store can have the finest merchandise in the world and display it in the most beautiful surroundings with all the ambience and music and lighting, but it it doesn't have someone to sell it, then it's not in business. There are legendary sales personnel in every store, people who "run big books," as they say in retailing, and who are adored by their customers. There are only a few, however, who are as legendary as Sara Middleman, if for no other reason than her three-base hit on the midtown Fifth Avenue playing Field. From De Pinna to Best to Saks.

Sara has spent most of her life in fashion. She was born in Pittsburgh and started as a model at Kaufman's in that city. She became a buyer and then moved to De Pinna in New York, where she was a top buyer for twenty-five years, until she moved with her staff of eight saleswomen and three fitters to Best & Co. to head its newly decorated Designers Shop.

"I had twelve of the most beautiful fitting rooms in the world. Each was decorated in a different period and had large windows facing the Cathedral," Miss Middleman recalled.

The rooms contained Aubusson rugs, crystal chandeliers. There were brown velvet sofas and yellow and black accents of French Criel porcelains. Five years later, when Best & Co. closed in 1970, Miss Middleman and her staff, which by then numbered fifteen, including her devoted assistant, Miss Lee, moved bag and baggage down the block, past St. Patrick's, and up into the Connoisseur Suite at Saks Fifth Avenue, where Sara became the director and buyer in a complicated arrangement that did not deprive other Saks personnel of their particular bailiwicks.

In Europe Sara moves through the back streets and in and out of ateliers as mysteriously as a CIA undercover agent. Her sources are secret. Many designs are exclusive and made to her specifications. There is a Sara classic—a silk hand-painted overblouse and skirt, long or short, or both, that comes in a rainbow of colors and combinations that is made in France. The costume is adapted and changed slightly each year. Each year it sells in the *thousands*. "It is what we call our bread and butter dress," Miss Lee said casually. The ponchos are a Sara trademark and the women who wear them are *Sara's ladies.* "Somewhere in France," said an associate, "there is a cave, like they have for Roquefort cheeses or fine wines—only for years this one has been filled with little Frenchmen painting giant flowers on silk and hand-rolling hems. Somewhere in France. And only Sara Middleman knows *where.*" There are other glories in the Connoisseur Suite from Paris, Rome, Florence, London, and heaven-knows-wherever else the enigmatic Sara stalks.

Beyond having the knack of buying, there is the selling. It is said that hell hath no wrath like Sara Middleman when she discovers a credit. "Why?" she will question her staff, "Why would you *sell* something to someone that they would want to *return?*"

"There is a right way and a wrong way to sell," Sara said. The statuesque silver-haired woman moved quickly into the back room. She returned holding a confection in front of her. She moved, turned, dipped with the grace of a prima ballerina. The fabric fell within reach. There was the softness, the silkiness, and the gossamer flew away. Like the old bells ringing for Pavlov's dog, there were suddenly visions of sweeping staircases, Cary Grant, Robert Redford—in that gown, *anything* could happen. A small voice inside whispered first, then shouted, "I *want* that." There was a quick check in the wallet for the credit card. The seduction went on. There were Sacher tortes and Debussy and evening mists across a mountain lake. "You have to romance a dress," Sara Middleman said.

There are international differences in sales techniques and they sometimes seem like no techniques at all. I had a close call with British undersell that could have been an expensive disaster in December of 1977 when I stopped in London on my return from India. Given the season, I deemed it appropriate to purchase Christmas puddings and crocks of Stilton cheese at Fortnum & Mason.

This delectable store was not the outgrowth of a dry-goods or piece-goods shop like so many establishments. Fortnum's began in the pantry of the Royal Household of Queen Anne, where William Fortnum served as a footman in 1707. As a perquisite William received the used candles that he took from the candlesticks when he refilled them nightly. These he sold to the ladies of the Household. The "perks" paid off. It could be said that William "candlelighted" on the side by becoming a candle and grocery merchant in his spare time. Upon his retirement from the Royal Household he and his friend, Hugh Mason, opened a grocery shop.

By the time William's grandson, Charles entered the service of Queen Charlotte, inflation being what it was in 1761, the "perks" included, in addition to candles, handsome quantities of food, coals, house linen, and wine. Charles was able to introduce further business into the family concern. The Palace staff was somewhat akin in size and structure to that of the General Foods Corporation. It was simply a question of semantics. Instead of vice-presidents and assistant vice-presidents there were Gentlemen, Yeomen, and Grooms of the Pantry, the Buttery, and the Cellar. There were a Clerk, an Assistant, and a Porter of the Spicery. The pastry department had its Yeoman and Groom. Charles Fortnum, upon receiving his "perks," sold them back to the Royal Household.

I stood coatless on that December morning in the chill on Piccadilly and waited for the monumental Fortnum & Mason clock to chime. The structure, comprised of two pavilions cast in solid bronze which support the main clock face in an elegant center ornament, chimes on the hour. Delicate eighteenth-century airs ring out on seventeen bells as Mr. Fortnum and Mr. Mason, each about four feet high, appear and bow to each other. The automated figures turn and bow again and move back into their pavilions and the doors close behind them until the next hour. These eighteenth-century gentlemen were as colorful as the sales personnel in their red cutaway coats inside the store during the holiday season.

With McDonaldization spreading throughout the world, it is particularly delightful to relish the Britishness of Fortnum's. The restaurants throughout the store measure all spirits at a "sixth of a gill." One can have an Apple Savoury, Scrambling Savoury, Fortnum & Mason's Special Game Pie, or a Chicken and Bacon Stack—an English version of a BLT with the B and the T served on a bed of the L with chopped chicken.

The department arrangements seem singularly disorganized and senseless to an American. On the Lower Ground Floor (Basement—U.S.) there are available China and Glass and Antique Silver and Shooting Sticks. The provisions, groceries, teas and coffees, fresh fruit and flowers, wines and spirits and candles are located on the Ground Floor, along with the Spanish Bar and Fortnum & Mason's Restaurant and Soda Bar. There is a Mezzanine Restaurant on the mezzanine.

On the First Floor (Second Floor—U.S.) hard by perfume and cosmetics are chocolates and confectionery. There are music boxes, television, radios, ladies shoes, and a ladies hairdressing salon on the Second Floor, along with Fine Blue Porcelain. Gentlemen's furnishings and a barber shop lodge on the Third Floor with writing table furnishings, electrical appliances and kitchen equipment, and greeting cards. The Fourth-Floor St. James Restaurant is a jolly place for tea beside the Fine Antiques Department.

I curbed my desire to try one of the sundaes, a Chicago Buster, a Knickerbocker Glory, or an onomatopoetic concoction that would put an American restaurateur and menu-writer on the Anti-Defamation League's boycott list—a Piccaninny Poppet [sic]—coffee ice cream with chocolate sauce, macaroons, and cream. In spite of a pot of Fortnum's own blend Darjeeling tea, I still was suffering from a chill brought on by my clock watching. Having come from the desert of Rajastan, I was not clothed for London in December and so I decided to buy a coat.

In Ladies Fashions, a soft-spoken woman understood my need. She selected a honey-colored cashmere polo coat. Wrapped in the coat, I began to thaw. "It is, madam, a *coe—zy* coat," the very Fortnum & Mason saleslady said. And indeed she was right. I pulled the collar around my ears. "*Toe*—sty," she added. Yes. Cozy—toasty—it was a very British coat. It called for sturdy gillies and pink cheeks. "Cuddly, ach—ly," the woman said. It was very biscuits and scones and crumpets and tea, but something was wrong. We calculated the pounds into dollars and I was about to reach for my traveler's checks when I looked into the mirror again. In a nick of time I came to my senses. For $585.00, cuddly or no, I did not need to look like Winnie the Pooh.

Not all the "big-book" ladies in the world can show a profit if the goods don't get through and that is called service. At Saks Fifth Avenue, service goes far beyond the book, the eight-hour day, the tissue paper, and the packaging department. Merve Retchin, the snappy manager of the Saks White Plains Designer Salon would swim upstream clutching an Ungaro, Halston, or Bill Blass in her teeth if she had to in order to ensure a customer of a delivery—and she almost has.

One evening at closing time, Mrs. Retchin discovered a $1,500 Chloe hanging in the alteration department, dated for delivery that afternoon. She telephoned the customer and guaranteed delivery by 7 o'clock. Fortunately Mrs. Retchin was attending a dinner party in the neighborhood. She drove home, bathed, changed into her own flowing Oscar de la Renta. Mrs. Retchin's husband was ready in black tie. As they prepared to leave, she picked up the suit box. Her husband said, "What are you going to do with that?" "I have to deliver it," she said. "We'll drop it off on our way."

"Oh, my God, Merve," he said, "I had no idea. I let Peter take the car. I thought we'd go over to our party on his scooter."

In a few minutes heads were turning in car windows along the New England Thruway as the little gray Vespa swished past. Underneath one crash helmet was a gentleman in a tuxedo. On the rear of the bike, under another crash helmet, was a vision clutching a Saks Fifth Avenue box. Swirls of chiffon sailed across the highway like multicolored snow flurries.

The Saks customer stood in her bathrobe behind her maid in the hallway as Merve Retchin, her helmet cosseted under one arm, handed the package through the door. Somewhere in the hall a clock chimed seven.

"It wasn't that it was an expensive Chloe," said Mrs. Retchin after she had risked life and limb, "It was a purchase from Saks Fifth Avenue."

Saks offers other services besides delivery. Harry J. Beethoven found he not only could get alterations on a robe he had bought from Saks, he could get them years after the purchase. In 1926 Mr. Beethoven's fiancée spent two weeks of her pay, or $28.00, on a gift bathrobe for her future husband. The following correspondence between Mr. Beethoven and Saks tells the tale that led to the celebration of the robe's fiftieth anniversary.

> Harry J. Beethoven
> 65 East 76th Street
> New York City
>
> September 20, 1967

Saks Fifth Avenue
5th Avenue at 49th St.
New York, N. Y.

Attention: Complaint Department

GENTLEMEN:

This camel hair robe was purchased from you during your Grand Opening in 1926. It was bought for me as an engagement present by my wife. At the time, your salesman said that a robe of this kind would last 50 years.

I have worn this robe for only 41 years, and I am rather fond of it. However, it has become somewhat frayed and worn on the sleeves and collar.

I feel that a robe from Saks Fifth should last at least 50 years, and this one still has 9 years to go in accordance with your salesman's guarantee.

I must in all fairness inform you that in our travels to Europe and around the world, my wife has tried, without success, to duplicate this robe. Since I am sure that you too will not be able to replace it . . . will you kindly repair it.

Very truly yours,

Harry J. Beethoven

SAKS FIFTH AVENUE

EXECUTIVE OFFICES
611 FIFTH AVENUE
NEW YORK, N.Y. 10022

October 9, 1967

Mr. Harry J. Beethoven
65 East 76th Street
New York, N. Y. 10021

Dear Mr. Beethoven:

I delayed answering your letter until I ascertained what our workroom could do toward repairing your robe. They advised me that they will replace the worn piping, but their only solution to repairing the worn sleeve cuffs would be to shorten them slightly. The material and pattern of which the cuffs are made is no longer available, and it is their considered opinion that to replace the fabric with that of another quality and design would detract from the beauty of the garment.

We regret that the wearing quality of the robe did not live up to your expectations, and since it shows signs of wear after only forty-one years, we beg to have the privilege of making the repairs without charge to you. It is a handsome garment, and we are pleased that you had these years of pleasure wearing it.

May I hear from you relative to shortening the cuffs? If convenient to you, it might be best to visit our Custom Department for a fitting before any work is done.

Sincerely yours,

ADAM L. GIMBEL
President
October 23, 1967

Mr. Adam L. Gimbel, President
Saks Fifth Ave.
New York, N. Y. 10022

Re: 41 Year Old Robe

DEAR MR. GIMBEL:

I appreciate your kind letter of October 9th and your offer to repair my robe, after only 41 years of wear. Nobody can ever say that Saks Fifth does not guarantee its merchandise unconditionally.

As you must have gathered, my sending back the robe was certainly not in the nature of an ordinary complaint, but to bring to your attention that a garment which you sold 41 years ago was still in use and was as much admired now as it was when first purchased in 1926.

I thank you for your genial reply and your generous offer to make the repair without charge, but it would be my pleasure to pay any charge you chose to make.

I shall contact your custom department and get on with the repair of this handsome garment. I expect it to last another 50 years and it is quite likely that some time in A.D. 2017 some great-grandson of mine will write Saks Fifth referring to your letter of October 9, 1967.

Cordially yours,

H. J. BEETHOVEN

HJB:hw

February 28, 1968

Mr. Adam L. Gimbel,President
Saks Fifth Ave.
611 Fifth Ave.
New York, N. Y. 10022

DEAR MR. GIMBEL:

    I have just returned from the West Coast and find my precious
41 year old robe, which you so graciously and generously restored to
almost new condition. Mere words of thanks seem inadequate so
(with apologies to Hans Christian Andersen, Frank Loesser and
Danny Kaye), I'm moved to the following:

Isn't it grand isn't it fine, look at the
    cut, the style, the line
Isn't it great isn't it rich, look at the
    charm of every stitch. . . .
My robe is back and it's all together
And altogether, but altogether
It's the most remarkable kind of robe that
    I have ever seen
Its braid is bright and blue and golden
And to Saks Fifth, I am beholdin'
For this raimant fine, the nicest robe,
    that ever made the scene . . .
It's a truly remarkable thing
It's even too fit for a king!!

Again, I thank you.

                                 H. J. BEETHOVEN

HJB:hw

To Celebrate the

50th Anniversary

of

H. J. B's Bathrobe

There will be open House at the

H.J. Beethoven's
1401 So. Flagler Drive
West Palm Beach
on Sunday, November 7, 1976
(from 2 p.m. until 5 p.m.)

YOU ARE CORDIALLY INVITED TO ATTEND

and also

to view a private showing of miniatures

sculptured by "H. J. B."

Dress: Very informal, or
your favorite kimono, or
dressing gown.

In the August 1974 issue of *Vogue*, Blair Sabol wrote:

> So Saks Fifth Avenue turns a golden-oldie fifty on September 15. And here I thought it had been around for at least two hundred years. . . .
>
> Saks seems larger than life, more of an institution than a specialty department store. How else can you look at it when everywhere you go in almost every major American city (look out, Anchorage) there sits a stately Saks Fifth?

She concluded:

> No matter how you feel about shopping . . . you can't beat Saks.
>
> I guess you could call that *"the Joy of Saks."*

FOURTEEN

Via Condotti Comes to Via Fifth

Gucci and Other Italians

Not all Fifth Avenue elegance has come from the tip of lower Manhattan, the Ladies Mile, or Paris. Recently there's been Rome.

If, indeed, all roads lead to Rome, then when in Rome it would seem that all roads lead to Gucci. Along the Via Condotti, up and down the Spanish Steps, in the Excelsior lobby, the Hassler garden, and on the cafe tables flanking Via Veneto, the mottled brown shopping bags, each with a red and green stripe, gold horse bit, heraldic seal, and GUCCI are more prevalent than summer tourists.

Gucci, a family-owned business, manufactures and distributes from its home base and factory in Florence, luggage, leather goods, shoes, gift items, accessories, jewelry, men's and women's ready-to-wear, and recently a limited line of furniture. The goods are sold exclusively through fourteen Gucci specialty stores and a handful of franchises in Italy, France, England, the United States, Japan, and Hong Kong. A Gucci shopping spree is a "must" on a visit to affluent watering holes like Palm Beach and Montecatine as well as a dozen world capitals. Although prices on Gucci items are lower in Italy where there are no duties and freight costs are minimal, there is no such thing as a Gucci bargain. Gucci means expensive the world over.

In Rome during the summer, more than 2,000 customers a day pour in and out of the Via Condotti store, across from the prestigious Knights of Malta palace. When the crush becomes too great (four and five deep at counters), the uniformed doorman turns traffic cop and limits the number who can enter the elegant portals. There is a similar frenzy in Firenze and madness in Milano, where a Gucci visit is as obligatory as a walk across the Ponte Vecchio and through the Duomo.

This does not mean that Gucci is a tourist trap. Far from it. Numbered among Gucci customers through the world are millionaires, aristocrats, potentates, and presidents. Socialites and superstars are regular clients. Gucci customers come in every race, color, creed, and size and shape.

At a counter in Milan, a bronzed teenager in cut-off jeans scrounged in his pockets for enough 1000-lire notes to pay for a key ring. Nearby, a man in flowing robes waved ancient, ring-covered fingers over a mountain of merchandise and spoke Arabic. His companion translated, "Charge it!" Gucci is a mecca for pauper and prince.

What is the magic formula that makes people empty piggy banks and Swiss bank accounts for coveted Gucci purchases? Loyalists say it is quality in design, materials, and workmanship. They emphasize long wear and fashion timelessness. But Gucci also has detractors. They brush off Gucci as a fad, a put-on, the nadir of the status-snob con job. And yet, in 1975, when a national magazine headlined an article on Gucci "The Rudest Store in New York," people flocked into the Fifth Avenue shop to experience for themselves the "drop-dead put-down" attributed to the sales staff. It was rumored that Dr. Aldo Gucci, president and chairman of the board of Guccio Gucci Soc. R.L., and patriarch of the family, acknowledged the vicious attack by sending the author an enormous bouquet of flowers. Others say a lawsuit was threatened. Whichever is the case, Gucci has a way of creating a stir.

Attempting to explain the Gucci phenomenon, one twentieth-century cocktail-party philosopher turned medieval alchemist: "They mix a secret alloy into the brass trimmings that gives off magnetic gas which physically attracts people into the shops." *Magnetic gas?*

A certain giddiness does seem to grip people once they are inside the paneled Gucci walls. For example, on a recent visit to the Florence shop on Via Tornabuoni, a delicate Japanese scooped up a fistful of scarves and gave them to the saleswoman in the Gucci uniform—a blue shirtwaist. The fifteen scarves, at 38,000 lire or about $45 per scarf, totaled over $700, but the scarves were only a small part of her purchase. The customer adjusted her obi, giggled, and said, "Tonight I cable Yokohama—'Sen' more yen!' "

A block from Rome's Piazza di Spagna the buses arrive mid-day from their morning excursions to the Borghese Gardens, the Trevi Fountain, and Vatican City. Passengers relegate the glories of Rome to memory and rush around the corner to inundate #8 Via Condotti before the Gucci door is closed at one o'clock and the metal blinds drop like sleepy eyelids over the display windows, not to open again until four in the afternoon. This three-hour mid-day closing is an Italian practice that drives foreigners up the Roman Walls.

"Frankly," explains forty-five-year-old Roberto Gucci, executive vice-president of Gucci and director of the Florence store, "we would like to open from nine to six." He had been mobbed as he left the locked store. A woman, grabbing, demanded, "When do they open? *When?*" Unruffled, he removed her hands, glanced at his paper-thin gold Gucci watch, and said in lightly accented English, "*They*, madame, will open in a moment."

This impeccable gentleman kept the same cool head in 1966 when he slogged through waist-deep water to reach his store during the disastrous flood of the Arno River. "We were caught when the Lungarno walls broke. There were no lights and the merchandise was floating all around. It was horrible." At three in the morning when the water receded, he was able to make his way out. Exhausted and heartsick over the devastation, not only to his store but to his beloved Florence, he walked the twenty-five miles to his country home.

Moving along the narrow streets and pointing to the still-visible watermarks on the ancient buildings, he reverted to the topic of working hours. "Many of our staff live some distance away. They go home and return at four to work until eight o'clock. It's a long day, but when we suggest a change the labor people say we cater to our rich clientele and don't consider the workers. The three-hour closing is an Italian tradition and traditions die hard in Italy. If the lunch was one hour, people wouldn't be able to go home and there would be only *two* traffic jams a day instead of *four!*" His eyes, the color of the Tuscan sky, roll up in mock helplessness as he shrugs his shoulders.

In the United States, where people are accustomed to stores staying open into the evening, sometimes even all night and on Sundays, Gucci's 12:30 to 1:30 closing is regarded as a personal affront. "They want to keep out office workers," a secretary believes. "Who do they think they are? My money is as good as anyone's." A Gucci spokesman contends the closing is an American version of the Italian tradition only in part. The real reason is service. "When we're open, we operate with a full staff. It takes getting used to, but remember the fuss when Broadway changed the curtain times? No matter—people who want to shop Gucci will shop Gucci."

One evening I was walking along Via Ludovisi in Rome. Gucci Parfum #1 wafted behind me and the silk of my new silk scarf brushed my neck. I felt tall, thin, cool, and elegant. Something happens to a woman in Rome. I was Audrey Hepburn on a Roman holiday about to meet Gregory Peck, or was it Rossano Brazzi? I was humming "Volari" when three women accosted me, shouting, "Gucci? Gucci?" They were desperately pointing to their watches. It was 7:30. With the instincts of a Piedmont truffle hound sniffing out his treasure, I can get to Via Condotti from any direction. "Follow me," I said.

Breathlessly they explained they were from the Philippine Islands on a tour of the Holy Places. They had been to Fatima, Lourdes. On this day their bus was late bringing them from Assisi. Early next morning they would go to Castelgandolfo, the Pope's summer residence, for an audience. In the evening they would fly on to the Holy Land. This was their only chance for Gucci and they had panicked not knowing where it was. When we reached the open store, I was hugged and called a saint. Our Lady of Gucci? They disappeared inside.

When I mentioned this pilgrimage to Roberto Gucci, suggesting Gucci was like the shrines, he said modestly, "Ah, no. The *G* stands for Gucci, not God!"

His father, Dr. Aldo Gucci, is notoriously less humble. "I want to be like the Holy Father," he said. "The Pope always speaks in plural." Dr. Aldo Gucci was sitting in his Rome office behind a marquetry desk and in front of a portrait of Guccio Gucci, his father and the founder of the company. The walls are covered with burnt-umber velour and hung with seventeenth- and eighteenth-century paintings, a key to the city of San Francisco (a gift from Mayor Joseph Alioto in 1971), and the Gucci heraldic seal. The high vaulted ceiling is painted with eighteenth-century trompe l'oeil frescoes. On the antique desk, a clear plastic lamp base holds seeds forming waves of terra cotta, ocher, olive green, and siena. It blends with the room, which, like the lamp base, is in the colors of the Tuscan landscape.

"We, Gucci family, are Florentine. We go back to 1240," he says, gesturing extravagantly. His energy and mien belie his seventy-two years. "We have lived here before the Renaissance and through the evolution historic and artistic of Florence. We cannot disassociate ourselves with Florence because Florence is in our spirit, in our minds, in our education, and in our creativeness. This artistic sense is in the background of anything we want to realize, to make, to create." His voice drops to a whisper. "The spirit of Florence is *here!*" he says, pounding his heart as he reveals an impeccable baby-blue shirtsleeve beneath his white silk suit. His cuff is fastened with gold double *G*s. There is a red-orange African daisy in his lapel. One must keep in mind that it was Dr. Gucci's brother, Rudolpho, who was the actor. Dr. Gucci holds an advanced degree in economics from Florence's San Marco College. Thus, according to Italian custom, he is addressed as "Doctor."

"We are not businessmen." He shakes his head and thunders. "We are *poets!*"

The Wharton School of Finance (University of Pennsylvania) disagrees. At a recent seminar for executives on "Fundamentals of Finance," Dr. Gucci was cited as a "marketing wizard." There was a lot of talk about profits in this fast-growing luxury-goods company that operates contrary to general merchandising practices but there was not *one word about poetry.*

One old-fashioned basic accounts at least in part for the Gucci success. In fourteenth-century Florence, births were recorded by dropping beans into a box; a black bean for a boy and a white bean for a girl. For the last three generations there has been a preponderance of Gucci black beans. Chauvinism aside, this is an important factor in founding dynasties and retail stores. Guccio Gucci had three sons, who in turn had four sons, who have had six sons. As for the women, Dr. Aldo's daughter-in-law is in the family business as is the oldest of four granddaughters. His fifteen-year-old daughter, Patricia, and the other three granddaughters are considered too young, at the moment, to work.

The company growth has been closely related to the family talent available and, as in a chess game, Gucci has played with the skill of a master, making the right moves with the right man or woman at the right time.

The company structure is simple. They design, manufacture, and sell the merchandise. *They* are Gucci and with the exception of a few franchise holders, no one else has a finger in their pizza pie.

The leather-goods business had its beginning at the turn of the century when a successful straw merchant, Gabriele Gucci and his wife, Elina, decided the time had come for their son, Guccio, to go to work. Until that time, Guccio, according to his grandson, Roberto, "had been doing the happy life. I don't say playboy, you must understand." Perhaps sensing that hats and therefore, straw, might not always be big business, Guccio Gucci, in 1906, started a saddle factory with four workmen. He expanded into saddlery, accessories for the horse, such as canvas feedbags and leather saddlebags. These articles were marked with his initials, GG, to provide their owners with identification. Surcingles and girths to hold blankets and saddles were made of webbing woven in red and green stripes, the colors in the Gucci coat of arms. It was a short evolution from saddlebags to handbags.

The modern handbag came into fashion after the turn of the century. Prior to that time, voluminous skirts had concealed pockets for carrying essentials. Dainty reticules and little pouches were sufficient for women's few effects and were worn on their wrists. When narrow styles and hobble skirts revealed every bulge, handbags grew in popularity. As World War I dragged on and more women took on men's jobs in England and France a bigger pouch became a necessity for the working woman. In another way the handbag became an early symbol of a kind of liberation. "Ladies," who always had been accompanied in public, began to move about unescorted and more freely. This necessitated carrying money and a latchkey. The use of makeup which began to gather momentum after 1912 was squelched by the war. In the early 1920s, as cosmetics became popular, there was a need for a place to carry a vanity and lip rouge along with that shocking new symbol of the free woman—cigarettes.

From handbags, it was only a small step to valises. The Guccis used fine leather then, as they do today, in their bags and luggage. They were stitched with the two-handed *sardo* stitching then, as now, and trimmed with facsimiles of horse hardware. The leather came from the large Tuscan cattle, Val di Chiano, that are raised in stalls which protect both the surrounding cultivated fields and the animals' hides.

Guccio and his wife, Aida, had three sons, Aldo, Vasco, and Rudolpho. From "doing the happy life," Guccio became a demanding employer and exacting parent. Maria Elina Angelotti recalls her early days as Mr. Guccio's secretary: "I was very young and he was a perfectionist. For months, I would go home and cry. But I learned very much." Twenty-seven years later, Miss Angelotti is administrative director and general export manager. She has great admiration for her bosses. "Dr. Aldo—such energy! He makes you feel, how you say, like you can jump through the circle of fire—do the impossible. He is an inspiration. Mr. Vasco, who died a few years ago, was a merchandising genius. He knew exactly what would sell from a collection. They all have an eye. They see beauty and recreate it. One day, Mr. Rudolpho was walking in a park and he picked some wildflowers. He brought them to one of the artists to draw. The design became 'Botanica,' one of our most famous scarves. This year, we do the flowers on umbrellas. They are beautiful. These Gucci men are fantastic!"

After Guccio Gucci's death in 1953, Dr. Aldo became the company commander. He says of his father: "He was formal, but not ostentatious. Always with the walking stick and patent-leather shoes. We would never have slapped him on the back and said, 'Ciao Dad!—Hi Dad!—Whoopee!' "

It is doubtful whether any Gucci offspring would slap his father on the back. "Roberto's children stand like soldiers when he enters a room," says their grandfather. "It is beautiful to see the respect. Social manners reflect the education, the good taste, and a way of life."

According to Roberto Gucci, "The question is simply—to be or not to be ladies and gentlemen."

For all the discipline and strict social standards, Gucci heirs have been free to choose their life work. At the time Aldo and Vasco went into the leather business with their father, Rudolpho went into the movies. Today, the six Guccis over sixteen-years-old either already work or plan to work for the company. But they have not been pressured. According to Dr. Aldo, "They *ask* to work. I confess, with not a little pride, that when they start to smell the leather and come to know the grandpa—the plate comes very tasty." He speaks with a touch of the chef as well as the poet. "We are like a *trattoria* and the whole family is in the kitchen."

During the 1920s and '30s, the company grew as the reputation of Gucci fine leather goods spread throughout Italy and Europe, but it was a twist of fate, coupled with ingenuity, that was to make Gucci a household word. With the war on, only scraps of leather were available and it was necessary to adapt or go out of business. Gucci returned to using canvas with a minimum of leather for strength, as they had done with feedbags. To add distinction, the fabric was stamped with reverse double *G*s and trimmed with woven red and green webbing. *Attenzione!* The "Gucci bag" was born and the rest is fashion history. With the advent of postwar air travel, Gucci was ready with stylish lightweight luggage—quite by accident.

On the other hand, the Gucci moccasin, a fashion classic that is immortalized in the Costume Institute of the Metropolitan Museum of Art, was painstakingly developed. "We wanted to create in the proper way, the Gucci way, a moccasin, which had nothing to do with the origin of the word, the Indian moccasin," said Roberto Gucci. "We felt women after the war would be mobile and want comfort they hadn't had in high heels and style they hadn't had in heavy low heels." A soft leather shoe was made with a stacked heel, arch support, and brass horse bit or chain trim. It was the first fashionable low-heeled woman's shoe and the death of ugly ground-grippers. A similar shoe was later introduced for men and the red and green web trim was used. The word *Guccis* went into several languages. In fiction, film, and television, wearing or referring to *Guccis* implied chic, wealth, status, and/or snobbism. Then, as happens in the fashion world, "Everyone, like the mosquitos, followed." Figures, both profit and production, are "very personal," says Roberto Gucci, "but I can say there doesn't exist at our level—no, I don't mean a $5 dollar shoe—a manufacturer who sells as many shoes as we sell." The level is far removed from five dollars. Gucci shoes and boots range from $75 to $300.

As production increased and new merchandise was developed, the factory moved, first to a building on the Lungarno, then into a fifteenth-century palazzo, and six years ago into a newly built factory-office complex in Scandicci, thirty miles outside of Florence. Before the war, Vasco was the director of the factory and the Florence store. In 1938, Dr. Aldo had opened a store in Rome. After the war, with the Cinecittà film studios destroyed and little work for actors, Aldo said, "Rudolpho, why the *h-e*-double *l*, don't you join us?" When the Milan store opened in 1947, Rudolpho became the director. As the company grew, so did Dr. Aldo's sons, Giorgio, Paolo, and Roberto. Vasco had no children and Rudolpho's son, Maurizio, was a baby.

By the 1950s, with three third-generation Gucci males ready for business, "It was time to put our nose out of the country," said Mr. Roberto. "First to London, then Paris, and then in 1953, Roberto Gucci, who is myself, opened the first Gucci Boutique in New York at East Fifty-eighth Street, where used to be the Savoy Plaza Hotel and now is the General Motors Building. I had my best life experience when I was twenty-one years old, going to the States to open the store." And to his delight, this very young Italian businessman discovered, "Across the street was Reubens!"

Today, as surely as if they were covered with double G canvas, the bases are loaded with Gucci. People, who, according to Giorgio Gucci, director of the Rome store, "try to speak the same language—in family and business tradition."

They seem to be everywhere. Rudolpho in Milan or at his house in Switzerland. Rudolpho's son, Maurizio, a recent law school graduate, has also joined the firm. He is a one-man flying squadron commuting between the United States and Italy. He has a beautiful Milanese wife, Patricia, a baby daughter, Alexandra, and an apartment in the Olympic Towers. The couple, when they take time out to socialize in New York or at Swiss ski recorts, are greatly in demand.

Giorgio has 100 percent family participation in the business. While he is upstairs in his Rome office, his sons, Alessandro, twenty, and Guccio, eighteen, are downstairs working as salesmen during school vacations. The young men are alert about business and often make merchandising suggestions as to what might appeal to the younger generation. They are also, according to a customer, "Charming and beautiful—like *putti*—the cherubs you see in sculpture."

A block away, on Via Borgognona, Giorgio's second wife, Maria Pia, is the *direttrice* of the Gucci Boutique. A pretty woman in her thirties, she has worked for Gucci since she was fifteen. "After I marry Giorgio," she says, "we worked in this little shop, and when he went into the main store, they left me here alone. Via Borgognona is not so well known as Via Condotti, but it is an elegant little street. The Romans come here to avoid the crowds at the main store. But now everybody knows this shop." The only white bean among the male Gucci management, Maria Pia is pleased with her success. "Every time my father-in-law, Dr. Aldo, comes to Rome, he visits the shop and he says, 'Brava, Pia! Brava!' It makes me feel very proud; very happy."

In Florence, Mr. Roberto not only minds the store, but as the director of exports, he travels to the Gucci stores around the world. Occasionally, when time allows, he and his wife, Drucilla, and their six children, sail on his boat to Mediterranean ports like St. Tropez. He is an avid student of art, history, Florence, and of course, Gucci. He recently acquired an antique carved marble slab commemorating an ancestor, Joseph Guccius, who, in 1630, restored a convent in Macerata. "These Gucci people still have the manic idea of restoring," he says, referring to the fifteenth-century palazzo and former factory at 7 Via Caldaie which has been renovated and modernized to house the export and perfume offices and showrooms. Work was delayed for months while paint was carefully peeled away from the fifteenth-century frescoes discovered beneath it. The 80×40-foot palazzo ballroom with its resplendent floral ceilings and walls now provides a dramatic background for shows for the trade—the holders of Gucci franchises. These Gucci people also have a flair for showmanship.

Mr. Roberto's oldest sons, Cosimo, twenty-two, and Filippo, twenty-one, are also preparing to enter the family business and have plans to study in the United States. "I'm doing for my sons as was done for me," he said. "I believe that America is the best experience, personal, business, and professional, that a young man can receive." Meanwhile, Roberto's other soldiers, Umberto, seventeen, Olimpia, fifteen, Domitilla, thirteen, and Francesco, nine, are waiting in the loggia as fourth-generation Gucci move into line.

Dr. Aldo's son, Paolo, the chief designer, became director of the factory when his uncle died. Working in Scandicci, out of the public eye, he is the least well known of the Guccis. But his fame as a fashion designer has been growing since luxury ready-to-wear was introduced by Gucci eleven years ago. The line was developed to ease Mr. Paolo's frustration with being limited to designing handbags. Since then both the collection and his talent have expanded. The 1978-79 fall-winter show was presented during the July "Alta Moda Italiana" fashion week in Rome at the Casina Valadier in the Borghese Gardens. The collection for men and women in leather, boucle, jacquard silk and knitwear inserted with velour suede was shown in futuristically named colors—"Cosmic Red," "Space Blue," "Sun Glow," "Night Flight," and "Neptune Green." It is proof that Mr. Paolo continues to create a classic sportive line that is imaginative, elegant and very "Gucci."

At the luncheon that followed on the terrace overlooking the gardens and the rooftops of Rome, the guests were seated at tables set with white linen Gucci tablecloths and napkins trimmed with the red and green stripe and gold-colored horsebit. The members of the press drank wine and dined on *crespelle alla Fiorentina, filetto di bue allo Toscana*, and *semifreddo Valadier*. Dr. Gucci was heaped with compliments and it was generally agreed that the collection was a triumph. "You are a great *Signor!*" someone cried.

There was a slight disturbance at the end of the elegant party and consternation among the Gucci staff members when an American fashion writer, not content with her booty of eight napkins ($5 each—retail), demanded two *fresh* tablecloths ($29 each—retail), promising "They will be great publicity for Gucci when I entertain." Upon refusal she barked, "You can hardly expect me to take them off the tables! Those are soiled!"

It was perhaps wise that the sensitive Mr. Paolo had remained at the factory. He let his father bask in the limelight and cope with the fracas, which Dr. Gucci rose above by delighting his other guests with titillating bits of information about his soon-to-be-launched Gucci (and here confusion set in as some thought he said *catalogue* and others thought he said *Cadillac*). It later proved to be the Gucci-Cadillac with interiors covered in double-G-fabric and trimming of assorted Gucci brass fittings.

The Scandicci factory and headquarters are surrounded by landscaped acreage. "Mr. Paolo, like all the Guccis, loves flowers," said Miss Burgoni, his secretary. Outside was the scent of summer roses; inside, the heavy smell of leather.

Swatches of suedes and silks were draped over the brown tweed couch in Paolo Gucci's office. Photographs of the collection were stacked on his desk among the red Gucci desk equipment. The view from the window behind his desk was like a picture postcard: cabbage fields across the road, rolling Tuscan countryside dotted with villas and poplar trees, and on a far-off hill, the church and village of S. Martino alla Palma. The side walls of the office are glass. To the right, looking through the order department, one sees large clocks on the end wall, giving the time in the Gucci shops around the world. Beyond the other window-wall are the desks of the purchasing staff who order ostrich and crocodile skins from Indonesia and North Africa, boar and pigskin from Poland, cashmere from Scotland, and bolts of GG canvas from Ohio, where the fabric is sent to Firestone for a secret waterproofing process. Beyond, in the distance, are the Apennines.

Seventy employees work in these offices and across the hall in the design studios. The walls and drawing boards in these rooms are kaleidoscopes of color and fabric samples. There are sketches of handbags, buckles, watches, cachepots, table linen, and china. An artist sketching and shading dozens of circles said, "Buttons. They take a lot of time."

Downstairs at ground level, General Director R. E. "Rocky" Kirkpatrick manages the leather-goods factory and its 150 workers. An American, Mr. Kirkpatrick spent 19 of his 29 years in Italy with U.S. Steel. "It's different from steel. It's cleaner and quieter, but business is business," he said. In the vast, well-lit room of the factory, there is the thump of cutting tools, the whir of sewing machines and the fans that remove glue fumes. Buggies like multilayered shopping carts are filled with goods in production and rolled from cutting to sewing, to glueing, back to sewing, to trimming and hardware. Mr. Kirkpatrick explained: "There are as many as 130 pieces in some bags, and in spite of the machines, there is a lot of handwork. These people are Florentines. They are artists."

In the shipping room, each piece of goods is inspected and slipped into a little white flannel wrapper. Walking among the shelves laden with Guccis—handbags, suitcases, makeup cases, and totes—is simply *too* much. The clothing is manufactured in a nearby villa; shoes and ceramic gift items are made elsewhere. The orders are shipped through Italy by truck, to Paris and London by rail, and to the rest of the world by air.

In the Florence store, one of the young women handling newly arrived merchandise was Elisabetta Gucci, Mr. Paolo's daughter, who was working prior to her marriage. Her seventeen-year-old sister, Patricia, will be able to work in two years.

Through this network of family, people, and places, Dr. Aldo Gucci moves with ease and enthusiasm, offering encouragement and advice. He might be found in his office in Rome or New York or at his house in Palm Beach. His energy is boundless, whether he is being interviewed on Tokyo television or overseeing his newest project, the Beverly Hills Gucci Galleria. "To see my father sit in a chair in Acapulco would be a sad day," said Roberto Gucci. But he need not worry—it seems an unlikely sight. Dr. Aldo says. "We have to sweat, as we say in Italian, the tradition of seven shirts." He looks cool, well pressed, and elegant.

Something may be said for a poetic philosophy in a high-pressure competitive business. The Guccis, different from one another in temperament and talents, all have a relaxed manner and look younger than their years. If Rome wasn't built in a day, well, neither was Florence. "Why *Florence?*" Dr. Gucci asks. "Couldn't we be from another part of Italy?" He roars with laughter at the thought. "Why don't you ask why the Chianti is in Chianti Tuscany and not in Lombardia?" Then, appalled at the stupidity of such a question, he bellows, "*It won't be Chianti anymore—like Gucci won't be Gucci!*" He flings his arms wide, "*How* could we not be Florentine if we are what we are?"

One must glance back over seven hundred years to understand the pride of being Florentine and a merchant. In 1293, the Ordinances of Justice defined Florence as an independent republic. The city was governed by the *arti*, twenty-one merchant and artisan guilds. Gregorio Dati, a Renaissance silk merchant wrote: "A Florentine who is not a merchant, who has not traveled through the world, seeing the foreign nations and peoples and then returned to

Florence with some wealth, enjoys no esteem whatsoever." To the Florence merchant, to be rich was to be honorable, and with riches went obligations: to finance city buildings and churches, to live in a grand palazzo with glorious gardens, and to be a patron to painters, sculptors, poets, and musicians. This was the seed of the Renaissance. It sprouted and spread throughout Europe.

The spirit of Florence—the love of beauty and pride in creating it, in spite of war, plague, flood, and politics—has never died. From Giotto to Della Robbia to Michelangelo, to nineteenth-century transplanted poets Elizabeth and Robert Browning to 20th- Century craftsmen in their workshops today, the fruits and flowers of the arts, propagated by merchants, have flourished. "We are like we are," Dr. Gucci says, "because we exercise a certain performance. I don't say charm. People—they say charm—I don't. We cannot conceive of anything we do for fun or for business that doesn't reflect the good taste. Good taste is irreversible. Good taste has a precise form."

It is the good taste that keeps a battery of lawyers prosecuting manufacturers of Gucci knock-offs, thirty-four lawsuits in six months. It is more than the good taste that keeps *carabinieri* on the lookout for trucks smuggling imitations—"hot" Guccis—through the Alps to Switzerland since copyright infringement is a public offense in Italy.

In Roberto Gucci's Florence office, an overhead grill serves to lower the lofty ceiling in the Renaissance building and to camouflage the air-conditioning apparatus. The room is white and airy. One wall is filled with art and history books. On another is a black and white painting by Luciano Guardineri, a modern Florentine, whose portrait of Drucilla hangs in the Gucci villa. The furniture in the office is low, white, and modern. There are touches of chrome. Roberto Gucci stands behind his desk, a variegated slab, the color of honey and caramel, cut from the root of the *pioppo* tree. He is tan and slim, a fine athlete; fencing, skiing, and tennis. He is soft-spoken for the most part. His powder-blue shirt is set off by a darker blue *G*-dotted tie and the vibrant blue Gucci eyes, said to turn green with rage. Mr. Roberto begins to raise his voice: "Thieves! We confiscated 82,000 belts last week! *82,000!*" He becomes a knight charging into battle: "I tell you—it is a war!" More is involved in fake Guccis than money. The shoddy merchandise is an insult to craftsmanship, the good taste, the honor of the Gucci name. "And I am going to *destroy* them!" His eyes narrow, chameleonlike. They no longer match his shirt.

It was certainly a matter of the good taste when Gucci sued Federated Department Stores for $1 million after a young woman of the Picture Pie Company decorated loaves of bread at Bloomingdale's with "Gucci Gucci Goo." The same can be said about the action taken against the manufacturer and distributor of toilet paper embossed with the Gucci diagonal pattern and double *G*s and packaged in clear plastic with the surcingle stripe. The status bathroom tissue retailed for $5.00 per two rolls. There was no lawsuit over tote bags printed "Goochy." Their creator, Mrs. Anthony Drexel Duke, said, "It was all a joke."

The Guccis are not without humor, but if jokes are to be made, they will make them. In the Florence store, the leather-lined elevator is trimmed with the red and green webbing and brass chain. Mr. Roberto remarked, "Rather like riding around inside a suitcase, don't you think?" He added, "A friend asked, 'Roberto, do you have the stripe around your bedroom?' 'No, no, no, I say, that would be *too* much.'" One subtle joke is the heraldic seal. "In the middle of the shield, the *armigero* [knight in armor] holds in his hands one handbag and one valise," Dr. Gucci points out. "The rose in the corner is the symbol of the poetic spirit, the wheel is a symbol of leadership—our destiny." Gucci ancestors served as the standard-bearers during the Republic, the honored custodians of the *gonfalone*, the red fleur-de-lis on the field of white.

These Italians delight in the trappings of chivalry and a few years ago had a joust with the French tricolor during the battle of the banners on Fifth Avenue. Gucci and Cartier both left their flags flying long after the parade had passed by. Each refused to be the first to lower his pennant, until New York City police, more in tune with city ordinances than the romantic spirit, stepped in. The Gucci guidon now hangs in the store. But no matter, there is more than one way to fly a flag. Since that incident, Gucci has purchased the nine-story Inland Building on Fifty-fourth Street. High on the side of the building is an enormous painted sign—GUCCI—and the heraldic seal.

Like their forefathers carrying the *gonfalone*, the Guccis hold their heads high. Dr. Aldo says: "In our operation, our projection, we don't look down. We look up. Because from up, you can go up and from up, you can go down. From down, you *never* go up.''

The Guccis continue to go up. Next to their building on Fifty-fourth Street, they have purchased a fourteen-story building that fronts on Fifth Avenue, the former office of Air France. They have bought property in Palm Beach and there's the palazzo renovated in Florence. Their most exciting project, however, is not real estate but merchandising. The Gucci Galleria on Rodeo Drive in Beverly Hills.

The Galleria on the Gucci second floor, built at a cost of nearly $2 million, is reached by an "inside-a-suitcase" decorated elevator. When the Galleria opened in the fall of 1977 a new status symbol appeared—the tiny gold key in a flat leather case that unlocks the magnificent store within a store. A limited number of keys were issued to special customers. There is talk that only customers who regularly charge more than $10,000 a year at Gucci receive the keys. This is untrue. However, the who, why, and how many information about the keys is a carefully guarded secret. Another vicious rumor is talk that you must pay $250 for a membership card to look at the Galleria. If you are serious about visiting the second floor, a proper salesperson-escort will accompany you and remain by your side. Key-carriers have free access.

While other designers and manufacturers reach for a mass market by putting their names or initials on T-shirts made in Taiwan, sheets made in South America, Tiffany and Cartier have stocked relatively inexpensive gift items to attract young customers. Meanwhile, Dr. Gucci strikes another blow for exclusivity. The treasures in the jewel-like Galleria setting are "the best of the best," one-of-a-kind gowns, an 18-karat gold desk set, lizard luggage, and a much-publicized handbag for $11,000. Actually, $11,000 is a going price for several items. There is an 18-karat gold belt, for instance. Here in "Sock-it-to-me" land, nothing so gauche as money, credit cards, or price tags appears in the Galleria. Tawdry details are worked out in a small, elegant salon over a glass of champagne or whatever you desire. Around the room are a few well-placed "second thought" gifts. "God forbid," says a key-holder, "you should want anything as simple as a $350 picture frame, maybe for your maid? But if you should, they will add it to your bill without embarrassment."

This wizard of merchandising who keeps locking his customers out of his store only to have them pound down the doors says: "We are offering the finest merchandise in the world to people with the taste and education to appreciate it."

Gallerias are planned for New York and Palm Beach, but is there a better place to reach for the stars than Beverly Hills?

There is a delicious story of a Florentine envoy sent to France in the sixteenth-century that says it all for Italian elegance, artistry, and grand style. The Queen of France, Catherine de' Medici, was a Florentine whose ancestors (probably once apothecaries, as the name implies) became the richest and most powerful family in Europe. The diplomat presented a gift—two superbly crafted watches attached by a single delicate chain—toward the Queen. As she reached forward, he withdrew it. Breaking the chain in half, he then gave one watch to Her Highness and placed the other in his doublet. He said, "Now, Your Majesty, for you it will always be the same time in France as it is in Florence."

The row of clocks on the wall in the Gucci headquarters tells the time in the Gucci stores around the globe. The clock in the middle tells the time in Florence. Linked together by family, business, spirit, and good taste, it would seem that for the Guccis, wherever they may be in the world, it is always the same time in Florence.

FIFTEEN

India-The Ultimate Promotion
The Twain Meet at Bloomingdale's

From the day in 1852 when Madame and Monsieur Astride Bou-çicaut opened the doors of their Parisian shop, Bon Marché, and welcomed customers to browse and, they hoped, to buy, other techniques, more subtle and less annoying than the street "pullers-in" have developed to lure the public inside stores. In the begin-ning, curiosity and the novelty of commercial hospitality were en-ticements. As the uniqueness of moving freely in and out and through stores wore thin, the merchandise itself became bait, and lavish interior displays were created. During the last half of the nineteenth century, store architecture and interiors became part of the attraction. At street level, the cast-iron and marble structures consisted of large areas of glass divided by solid piers and gave rise to extravagant window displays to whet customers' appetites. Ele-gant tearooms brought an element of sociability to shopping. Mod-el furniture showrooms and later fashion shows were diversions and appetizing "soft" selling methods.

As stores became massive institutions, design and color were used in interiors, wrapping papers, delivery wagons, and store uni-forms to coordinate a well-defined public image of a commercial establishment. B. Altman & Company's signature and use of ma-roon were early-twentieth-century prestigious symbols. To further create a store "personality," institutional advertisements came into being. Store policy, personnel, and far-flung buying adventures were touted. Stores became romantic places where the mysteries of foreign lands unfolded along with the exotic merchandise. A walk through Field's rug department was as thrilling for midwesterner as a tour through a pasha's harem.

In the great mercantile palaces, pipe organ music often resounded through the rotundas and employees were organized into choral groups to present musicales. Entertainment became an integral part of merchandising. The components of a store—space, creative personnel, colorful merchandise, and advertising and publicity that could attract designers, socialites, and celebrities—were also the essentials of show business and meant that sets, stagehands, lighting, costumes, and a cast were readily available. A new theatrical phenomenon—the store promotion—was born.

Although this aspect of merchandising is primarily American, one of the most elaborate twentieth-century promotions took place around 1910 in a Cuban store, El Encanto (The Charm). Planning the re-creation of Paris in Havana took more than a year. Trees and shrubs were planted in the store gardens to simulate a mini Bois de Boulogne. Models of clothes from Poiret, Worth, and Robert Piquet were imported. There were hats by Reboux and perfumes by Guerlain. The ball that marked the opening of this extravaganza was catered by chefs brought from Maxim's. The opening-night party was the highlight of the Havana social season. During the weeks following the gala, measurements of the elegant Cuban haut monde were taken and orders were sent to Paris, where the clothes were made. The finished products were returned across the Atlantic Ocean to Cuba. The event was a wild success.

Although European stores are less given to razzle-dazzle than American stores, a promotional event took place in 1977 on the roof of Le Printemps department store that set Paris agog. During the seven months following the opening of "La Maison sur le toît," over half a million people made their way into Le Printemps and up to the store's rooftop terrace to parade through the three-bedroom house. The house was set in the middle of a garden filled with azaleas and unusual yellow and orange rhododendrons—"extrêmement rares," according to press reports. The rooms were furnished and decorated by Le Printemps. The house featured two bathrooms (2 salles de bains avec WC), a laundry, an outdoor patio, and a two-car garage. The *pièce de résistance* was a red Citroën parked in the garage. *La voiture*, the latest LN Citroën model, had been hoisted to the roof by a crane. "La Maison sur le toît," in full view of the Eiffel Tower, had overtones of America suburbia. It was built by an American company, Kaufman and' Broad, which had been constructing single-family houses in village developments outside Paris since 1968. According to *Elle* magazine, Kaufman and Broad and its young president, Bruce Karatz, who had been raised in Minneapolis and Phoenix, had given the French an opportunity to satisfy their wishes to live, *"le rêve americain"*—the American dream. "La Maison sur le toit" was the sensation of Paris. While it made Parisians aware of the housing developments built by Kaufman and Broad to the east and west of the city—La Closerie à Claye-Souilly and Le Parc de Port-Royal à Voisins-le-Bretonneux—it also accomplished the main purpose of any promotion whether it be Santa Claus or cooking classes. It attracted large numbers of customers into the store.

Until recently, European merchants have never been as promotion-minded as Americans. It is impossible, for instance, to imagine the Macy's Thanksgiving Day Parade floating and bouncing and tumbling down the Champs-Elysées. Whoopla promotions and merchandising techniques are as singularly American as turkey and pumpkin pie and, like Thanksgiving, they are difficult to explain to foreigners. But it was a European store that inspired Stanley Marcus, who is as much a showman as he is a merchant, to create the superstar among American foreign promotions, the Fortnight. In his autobiography *Minding the Store*, Mr. Marcus explained:

> In 1956 I made my first visit to Scandinavia, and while in Stockholm I saw something which gave birth to a merchandising idea that has had a great effect on our business and on the many other retail enterprises that have copied us. The Nordiska store was having a promotion of French goods, with their windows filled with French merchandise and the tricolor decorating their escalator well. I learned from the management that they had received assistance from the French government through its Comité des Foires. On my return to Paris, I met with officials of the agency and told them I wanted to do something similar, but on a much larger scale.

In 1957 Neiman-Marcus launched its first salute to a foreign country—France. The Fortnight, held the last two weeks in October in the downtown Dallas store, has become an annual event. In addition to the honored country's fashions, foods, and furnishings being displayed and sold within the store, the customs and cultural life of the country are featured in schools, universities, museums, libraries, and theaters with programs and exhibitions. The proceeds from the Fortnight ball that launches the two-week promotion benefits a local charity and the event attracts celebrities and socialites from all over the world. Diplomats, film stars, and royalty have represented the various foreign countries and even "non-countries" as guests of honor over the past twenty years.

In 1971 when Australia withdrew from its planned Fortnight participation, Neiman-Marcus created the mythical kingdom of Ruritania to be the host country. The store commissioned a national anthem, designed a postage stamp, and had coins of the realm struck in chocolate in Holland. At the gala ball, Victor Borge played the part of the prime minister and Gloria Vanderbilt Cooper and her husband, the late Wyatt Cooper, appeared as the king and queen. There was an operetta quality to the decor used to create the make-believe country and merchandise from all over Europe was promoted.

The following year, the Fête des Fleurs Fortnight was a great flower show and merchandise was developed with flower themes and colors. The guests of honor were Prince Rainier and Princess Grace of Monaco.

Neiman-Marcus has honored France four times in its Fortnights; Britain—three; Italy—three. There have been two Far Eastern galas and one collective South American promotion. The United States, Switzerland, Denmark, Austria, Ireland, and Japan have each been honored once, along with Ruritania. The Fortnight has become a national institution. It is the old guard among promotions. It has been copied but never duplicated. It stands alone—the Grande Dame of store and merchandising ballyhoo.

In the fall of 1977, Bloomingdale's and Air India announced that a promotion of Indian merchandise would take place the following spring. It would be a six-week store-wide program in fourteen

Nan Tillson Birmingham

Bloomingdale's stores. The concept, considering the number of stores and space to be decorated and filled with merchandise, and the logistics, considering the distance from the source (India is halfway around the world from New York, give or take a few thousand miles), were staggering. Right off the bat, the diversified personalities of the major participants would seem to spell *impossible*. How could the whiz-kid of department stores, the store that can "spin on a dime" to follow trends (or better yet, to be there first), and Air India, which represents a country that measures its past not in decades or centuries, but in thousands of years, cooperate? How could India, with traditions and a past that recede far back beyond the beginning of recorded time, and an organization that represents the "Saturday Generation" do business together? How could a store that thinks of itself as "the sizzle" on the consumer's steak and a country where the steaks walk around on all fours through the streets because they are sacred possibly communicate?

In the spring of 1978, "India—the Ultimate Fantasy" opened with fourteen separate galas in fourteen eastern cities. The multi-million-dollar project was an instant success. It was the talk of the public, of Seventh Avenue, and of retailers throughout the country who readied themselves to jump on the Indian bandwagon with their own promotions. "India—the Ultimate Fantasy" was extended for two extra weeks by popular demand and to allow Bloomingdale's and Air India to play host to India's Prime Minister Morarji Desai. "India—the Ultimate Fantasy" went down in retailing history as the *ultimate* promotion. "How in God's name did they pull it off?" a Bloomingdale's competitor asked. The answer from Bloomingdale's and Air India officials was, "It wasn't easy!" For a more conclusive answer one must look at both of the participants.

What exactly *is* Bloomingdale's? Other than being a department store that covers a full block of Manhattan's east side, with branch stores in east coast cities and suburbs, what makes Bloomingdale's different from any other large department store? What is this mystique, this magic, and how and when did it all come about?

There was nothing unusual about the beginning of Bloomingdale's. It was started in 1872 by Lyman and Joseph Bloomingdale as a dry-goods store at 938 Third Avenue and it was called the Great East Side Bazaar. The 20×75-foot store and its stock of ribbons, laces, and fabrics were much the same as the other little dry-goods stores. The Bloomingdale brothers did not go into business setting fashion but because of the demise of a fashion. Lyman, who had worked in assorted shops from the age of eleven, had joined his father in opening a hoopskirt factory. During the 1860s, the hoopskirt, which had been invented to conceal the Empress Eugénie's pregnancy, became the rage. It lingered on after the Empress gave birth, but by the 1870s was on the wane as the fashionable look. The Bloomingdale boys closed the factory and opened the store. The first day's sales totaled $3.68.

The store grew with the neighborhood and by the late 1870s, when the El moved along Third Avenue, it was a full-fledged department store. The store later moved up Third Avenue from Fifty-sixth Street to Fifty-ninth and gradually found itself at the hub of east side transportation. There were the El and the Fifty-ninth Street Bridge, which had been completed, and eventually the Lexington Avenue subway stop. Eventually, Lyman's son Samuel became president and the store continued to grow along with the middle-and upper-middle-class neighborhood. By the end of the twenties, Bloomingdale's had a sales record of $24 million and before the new decade began, it joined the Federated Department Stores, Inc. This affiliation carried the store through the dark days of the Depression. By the thirties and forties, the El, which had originally been a boon to the store, had become decrepit and outmoded. The El rendered Third Avenue dirty, dark, and noisy and the area around it deteriorated. Bloomingdale's expanded into the suburbs during the forties and fifties and its home furnishings departments flourished with the postwar boom. Bloomingdale's had none of the cachet or chic of the Fifth Avenue stores—nor did it have the loyal following of a Macy's or Gimbels. Bloomingdale's was, quite simply, a conservative middle-class department store— the *only* department store on the upper east side, which was probably its biggest asset. So what happened over the next twenty years that could bring about an ad in *the New York Times* on September 19, 1976, headlined "Why is Bloomingdale's Today's Cultural Phenomenon?" It went on to say: "Morley Safer reports on the very unique and always newsworthy reasons why people turn into Bloomie's addicts. Watch this cultural phenomenon in action this Sunday on 60 Minutes—CBS 10 PM."

On *60 Minutes*, Morley Safer said: "The idea that intelligent adults would go to a department store to get spiritually refreshed as others would go to a museum or opera takes a little getting used to.''

A woman answers, "There's this love-hate thing. I love coming here, but I hate the addiction to it. Why has this store so much power? What is this thing?"

"It's probably the most successful store in the country," Safer reported.

"Bloomie's knows what's hip. It knows what's 'in,' " said another *60 Minutes* interviewee, "and I want to get hip with the trip."

Actually, Bloomie's knows a lot more than that. It knows, for instance, that as long as people keep asking "What is this thing?" curiosity will eventually reach the unreachable stars like Queen Elizabeth. Appearances in the store by those who are not associated with the "hype" stimulate appearances in the store by those who are and everybody gets into the act. The end result is that Bloomie's is the darling department store of celebrities and the press which further *hypes the hip*.

In *New York* magazine (March 5, 1973) Lois Gould wrote in "Confessions of a Bloomingdale's Addict":

> Where else could you find—in a single recent week—Antony Armstrong-Jones stocking up on no-iron sheets; Marietta Tree stripping in public to try on a sequined pants suit; Mrs. Jacob Javits clutching a bulging United States Senate folder and confessing that Bloomingdale's takes her a whole day to 'do.' (She starts at the top and works down, like a tourist covering the Louvre.)

Time (December 1, 1975) featured a crowd of shoppers on its cover and headlined *U.S. Shopping Surge—Trendy Bloomingdale's*. The lead of the Economy & Business section story:

> On any given day, Dr. Spock might be glimpsed there selecting towels; Walter Matthau trying on suits; Jacqueline Kennedy Onassis recently passed through to order presents to be sent to Caroline in London. Singer Diana Ross outfits herself and her children there— by long distance from California. Basketball star, Earl Monroe, may drop in to pick up some after-shave lotion—and, he says, to "see how people with money act."

A *Ford Times* (August 1977) article, "The Party at Blooming-dale's" by Frances Koltun, named a few more biggies in the first paragraph:

> Bloomingdale's is the quintessential New York experience . . .
> the biggest free party in town . . . the place where you are likely to
> run into Robert Redford, Jackie O., Liza Minnelli, the Paul New-
> mans . . . eight floors, one mezzanine, three basement levels and
> various nooks and crannies, all of them bursting with marvelous
> merchandise like a fantastic horn of plenty.

The article advises:

> Sail all the way to the eighth floor and make your way down (as
> New Yorkers will, taking the whole of a Saturday to 'do' Blooming-
> dale's) and the store's magic charms you.

The celebrity chase is part of the fun of "doing" Blooming-dale's. Rumors float through the air like Muzak. Almost anyone who moves through the aisles in dark glasses with an air of self-confidence or sporting an outrageous outfit can provoke a whis-pered, "*Who* is that?" from customer to clerk, clerk to customer, or customer to customer. When any one of three great names drifts through the atmosphere of Bloomie's main floor, like the mist from all the spray colognes, "Garbo!"—"Dietrich!"—or "Hep-burn!"—business is apt to come to a halt. Anyone who has not cir-cumvented counters, run up or down the wrong way on escalators in hopes of glimpsing one of the Big Three under a floppy hat, has not, in truth, "done" the *total* Bloomingdale's experience. Odds are that the *personage* in the chapeau will turn out to be a suburban housewife or someone in drag.

The food is part of the fun at Bloomingdale's and culinary expert Mimi Sheraton would seem to have had the most fun of anybody. For *New York* (October 16, 1972) she researched and wrote the article titled "I Tasted Everything in Bloomingdale's Food Shop." Elin Schoen's "Cookie Chic: The Great Chocolate-Chip Contro-versy," also in *New York* (August 15, 1977) was prompted by the Bloomingdale's–Famous Amos fracas.

As for the city press, *The New York Times* has a veritable on-going love affair with Bloomingdale's.

"Face it," said a journalist, "Bloomingdale's makes good copy. It's an easy assignment because there is so much going on that's new and daring and—it's fun."

Love or the promise of it is part of the Bloomingdale's myth. Although executives discreetly attempt to play down their store as "New York's number-one pick-up place" for boy-girl, boy-boy, girl-girl liaisons, sex keeps rearing its straight or gay head. In a touching scene from the hit film *An Unmarried Woman*, the husband tearfully announces to his wife that he is in love with another woman and chokes out, "I met her in Bloomingdale's."

But just how did all this come to be in a massive, almost dowdy department store?

It began twenty years ago in the mid 1950s, when the Third Avenue El was torn down. As the area around the store became cleaner, lighter, and quieter, prime real estate, high-rise apartments were built and a new, postwar generation of East Siders moved in. They were young. They wanted to be swinging and "with it," and they had the money in their pockets to be both. The area became consumer country *par excellence*, and Bloomingdale's was the heart of it. Executives Jed Davidson and James Schoff, Sr., spruced up the store and turned to two bright young men, Lawrence Lachman and Marvin Traub, to find out what the new, affluent customers wanted. The team of Lachman and Traub worked together for over twenty-five years. They moved up the corporate ladder together until the spring of 1978 when chairman of the board Lachman retired and president Traub moved into his place as chairman.

Marvin Traub was a handsome, soft-spoken graduate of Harvard Business School when he went to work for Bloomingdale's in the early 1950s. Besides his business training, he had the eye and instinct of a merchant. These he had inherited, along with good taste, from his mother, Bonwit Teller's famous personal shopper, Bea Traub. He also had an uncanny ability for finding talent and bringing out the best in people.

A chapter in Bloomingdale's growth might well be entitled "Marvin and the Redheads," for two of Mr. Traub's finds, his wife, Lee, and Bloomingdale's vice-president and director of merchandise presentation, Barbara D'Arcy, both have flaming red hair and they are both keys to the Bloomingdale's success story.

Being the wife of a great merchant is extremely demanding. She is a public figure who must participate in her community. She is also a showcase. She must endure the loneliness of a doctor's wife, have the stamina of a campaigning politician, and display the tact of a diplomat. She must be more than supportive, for she is the consumer and her taste and ideas are not only welcome, they are required. The wives who have filled these bills are themselves legends. Jeanne Magnin, Alva Gimbel, Nena Goodman, Sophie Gimbel, Minnie Marcus, and Lee Traub of Bloomingdale's have played a part in the history of retailing along with their merchant husbands.

The ambience of Bloomingdale's, which is part of the mystique, might be different had the other redhead, while a young student at the College of New Rochelle, not been queasy. Barbara D'Arcy was majoring in art. When she decided to become a medical artist, a science minor was necessary.

"We were required," Miss D'Arcy said, "to view an autopsy at New Rochelle Hospital. I did and I threw up. Then, in anatomy class, I had to dissect a cat. It turned out to be pregnant and that just about finished me. Finally, when I had to stun a frog with a very long needle, it jumped out of my hand. I screamed, ran out of the room, and the good sisters suspended me. Right then I decided that medical art was for the birds!" Such are the events that change retailing history.

Miss D'Arcy worked briefly for a carpet company that had a mail-order floor plan promotion. "I think I drew over a quarter of all the floor plans in the United States, but as a result, I have never had to use a ruler. I was fired because the company was on the verge of bankruptcy. An employment agency sent me to Bloomingdale's, but I had been raised near the store and didn't think I wanted to work there. The agency woman told my mother and she had a fit since she was tired of having me around the house umemployed. So, I went to work for Bloomingdale's on May 5, 1952. Because of my floor plan experience, I was made a junior decorator in the fabric department on the fourth floor. This was at the time when mattress ticking was very popular."

Again fate stepped into Miss D'Arcy's and Bloomingdale's future. "One day a snazzy South American couple came in to order ticking slipcovers. I thought they looked much too chic for that and before I knew it, I had sold them a whole room of furniture and had arranged to have it shipped to Argentina.'' Word of this transaction reached upstairs and Miss D'Arcy was made a fashion coordinator for home furnishings.

"Bloomingdale's had been a wonderful store for modern furniture, but we were becoming aware that people wanted to get away from the hardness and the sharp corners. We felt there was going to be a swing toward traditional. We had every kind of Early American traditional. We must have had ninety million bunk beds and cobblers' benches, but we knew we were groping for something else. I'd been raised around the Third Avenue antique shops and I suddenly said, 'country French.'''

On his next trip to Europe, Marvin Traub scouted for what he thought might be "country French." He returned with two Italian olive burl chairs. "That was the look!" Miss D'Arcy said. "Rustic, but traditional. And then we discovered armoires. The only thing we didn't know was where to get these things. We had an American cabinetmaker make samples, but the prices were astronomical. We wanted to create a line in a price range to appeal to young married and single people.''

In 1959, drawings were sent to Europe and samples were made and the price was right. Small furniture factories sprang up in French and Italian villages. "We had a terrible time getting the workmen to understand the antique look we wanted. 'Why do you want new furniture to look old?' they'd ask. We had to teach them how to 'distress' the furniture, beat it with a hammer, chains, rub it on the edge with files and make it look fly-specked. They were horrified.''

In 1960, the armoire and one hundred other pieces of "country French" furniture were introduced. The "Bloomingdale's style"— comfortable, warm, informal but elegant—was born. The prophetic Italian chairs grace Marvin Traub's office to this day.

Barbara D'Arcy became the coordinator and creator of the model rooms. "Not having had formal decorating training, I didn't know there were rules, so I could break them all." Model rooms had been used to display furniture for years, but under Miss D'Arcy's direction, they reached new heights in originality and showmanship. It did not matter that the most often heard comment was "I couldn't live in a room like that!" Thousands flocked to see them and over the years Bloomingdale's model rooms have become as much a part of the New York scene as the Empire State Building. Miss D'Arcy's personal favorite was The Cave Room, a free-form molded room that was created by spraying urethane foam over a lath and wood frame. "I remember the Saturday night when we were constructing the room. I was working in coveralls and wearing an Army surplus gas mask because of the toxic fumes, when Mr. and Mrs. Traub arrived from a formal dinner party. You can't imagine the chaos and mess because we didn't really know what we were doing or if it would work. I'm sure they were appalled, but they never said anything. Mr. Traub will always support one's flights of fancy. Only once when I was on a color kick, he said, 'Barbara, if I don't watch you, this whole store is going to be orange.'"

Today, Miss D'Arcy is responsible for tying the whole atmosphere of the store together—the model rooms, the displays, the advertising—everything that creates a total effect. Designer Richard Knapple is in charge of the model rooms and his creations for the Indian fantasy were breathtaking. Each room was created around the mood of an Indian city—Chandigar, Bombay, Delhi, Jaipur, Udaipur, Srinagar—and there was a colorful, cozy, exotic beach house in the spirit of the state of Goa. One show-stopper was the white room of Udaipur, in the fashion of the famous Lake Palace Hotel that seems to float in the middle of Lake Pichola. The walls and ceiling were covered with carved white sheesham wood panels, inlaid with mirror. The white tile floor was inset with silver-plated studs. The low, carved Rajastani chairs were painted white and covered with silk embroidered with mica mirrors. It was a dazzling spectacle and a long way from Early American bunk beds.

In the early sixties, as home furnishings, housewares, and linens caught on as a "look"—a "style"—Bloomingdale's took giant steps into the fashion market. Young designers were encouraged and established designers were courted. Fashion departments were remodeled to create an atmosphere of boutique shopping and the famous "Saturday Generation" hip image came into being as a Bloomingdale's "look" evolved in men's and women's wear.

In the fall of 1961, Bloomingdale's held its first major "import show," which was called "L'Esprit de France." An artist was commissioned to design a shopping bag appropriate to the theme and the now-famous Tarot card bag was created. Eugenia Sheppard wrote in her "Inside Fashion" column in the *Herald Tribune* (October 4, 1963) under the heading "The Highbrow Shopping Bag":

> That the shopping bag is no longer a completely frumpy item linked with the cook's day out can be credited mostly to Bloomingdale's. By eliminating the store name for identification, the bag lost its commercial look and became a thing of beauty and a bit of art. The store's first supply of playing card bags hardly lasted out the press-preview for L'Esprit de France. A genuine Bloomingdale's playing card shopping bag was hard to come by that season. It became a fad, a status symbol—whatever you like to call it.

Other famous bags have featured the commedia dell'arte figures and the Epinal prints of the soldiers of the nineteenth-century Royal French Guard.

To select the design for the India promotion, Bloomingdale's and Air India jointly sponsored a poster contest in India and the United States. The winning artwork, a fanciful "Flying Elephant," was created by Anand Zaveri of Ahmadabad, India. It appeared on a half-million shopping bags. Various elements of the design appeared in the 650,000 special catalogues created and distributed for the "Ultimate Fantasy." The catalogues were filled with photographs of models and merchandise, filmed on locations throughout India. The design was used in posters, advertising, 500,000 inserts mailed to charge customers, and millions of hang tags and labels. The graphics were a major part of the enormous promotion.

As Bloomingdale's "new look" emerged through the sixties, the store also became a frontrunner in the gourmet food and cooking revolution that was beginning to take place. The Delicacies Department reputedly stocks over 7,000 items, which include 146 varieties of bread and 300 kinds of cheese. As competition has challenged Bloomingdale's lead in this department (most notably, Macy's highly touted "Cellar"), a renovation of the Bloomingdale's sixth floor has taken place. In September 1978, the Main Course, an interior street of food and housewares, opened, along with a skylighted terrace café. A test kitchen was installed. Cooking classes are held for children, teenagers, beginning cooks, and advanced gourmets who want to concentrate on foreign cuisine. A special feature has been an evening lesson designed for twenty couples. After the food preparation, the couples dine. They also dance to live music. The program is called "Saturday Night Flavor."

Keeping all this excitement going is a continuing challenge to Bloomingdale's executives and personnel.

"I guess if there is any key to what makes Bloomingdale's what it is, it's that we have all been around for years," Barbara D'Arcy said. "Mr. Lachman, Mr. Traub, myself, and two or three other vice-presidents have worked together from a time when the store wasn't so big. We knew each other socially. We grew up together and grew up with the store. We all have built-in antennas that reach out to get any new spark in the air. There are six of us that if you asked the same question, you would get almost the same answer. You could almost say we are brainwashed into thinking alike. We know what works. We know how to go about making it work. *And* we know what doesn't work. We have very strong feelings for things and we have very strong feelings for Bloomingdale's."

Marvin Traub's answer to the secret of Bloomingdale's success: "We are all highly professional."

Lawrence Lachman said: "The same top management has worked together for twenty-five years. We work well as a team. There's a continuity. This doesn't mean we're set in our ways. We have young executives and we listen to them and we can make decisions very quickly."

The idea for an Indian promotion was not acted upon quickly. It first came into being in 1966. "We were encouraged by designers Boris Kroll and Adele Simpson to go to India to see what we could buy," Marvin Traub said. "We organized a research team and twelve of us went to India. We have been buying rugs, gifts, jewelry, textiles, and furnishing accessories on a regular basis ever since. (Sales of Indian-made goods, according to *The New York Times*, run about $1 million a year.) At that time, however, we never felt that there was enough merchandise available for the kind of promotion we would want to do.

"I must give Lee a lot of credit for keeping the idea alive. As a dancer, she became fascinated with the classical Indian dance, Bharat Natyam, and studied it. She also became the best non-Indian Indian cook in New York. Over the years, we've made Indian friends and our son, James, taught English at the university in Aurangabad. Lee and I became deeply involved with India on a personal level and made several return trips after 1966. I kept feeling there'd come a time when Bloomingdale's and India could be involved on a bigger business level."

If Mr. Traub was the head behind the Indian promotion, Mrs. Traub was the heart. "Lee Traub was very sensitive to our country," said Chota Chudasama, director of public relations for Air India. His sentiments have been echoed by many others both in New York and India.

"From our first trip, I related to everything in India so easily," Mrs. Traub said. "Something must have been left over from a childhood Indian fantasy. I found the people so kind, so hospitable and easy to be with. I came home and studied the classical dance. I wish I had been exposed to it as a youngster. I had such a feeling for it. There is so much about India that Americans don't understand—the music, the art and handicrafts, the incredible history. And there's such beauty. You'd think that I had discovered India, but it's the way I feel. It's my place. It's a very strong feeling. I also loved the food and learned to cook Indian. I'm sure I'm the only person in Scarsdale who makes her own ghee."

Over the years, Marvin Traub watched the quantity of Indian merchandise increase and the quality improve, and early in 1977, another Bloomingdale's team visited the country to investigate the possibilities of doing the promotion. "Eight of the twelve who had gone in '66 were along and they were astounded by the progress," Mr. Traub said. "The design and decor people were thrilled and inspired. So were the buyers. We made the decision to go ahead with a promotion on an emormous scale, but we had to have support of some kind from India. We approached Air India about making it a joint venture."

Air India is unique among international airlines. For one thing, although it is government owned, it does not operate on subsidies. On the contrary, with the exception of the year when there was a strike, the airline has consistently made a profit. "Air India is a spot of black ink among the red on India's balance sheet," an Indian businessman said.

To accomplish this, the airline has used two of the country's greatest assets—its artistic creativity and its gracious people. The interiors of the planes and waiting rooms, the flight attendants' saris and other uniforms, the company's graphics and advertising, all reflect in color and design—India. Even more important is the spirit of hospitality that is extended by the personnel. The Indian concept of hospitality is far removed from the western idea of give and take or "you scratch my back I'll scratch yours." It is deep-rooted and steeped in mythology, religion, and tradition. Indians are raised on the ancient tales of the stranger who, passing by and receiving food and warmth, turns into a god. They know the virtues of hospitality. It is the giver who is blessed. According to an Indian saying, "The guest is as a god. To serve is to love. To love, divine." The airline personnel are imbued with this idea and passengers are to be treated as one would treat a guest in one's home.

"Air India's contribution was tremendous help. Not only in the travel plans for the sixty-five buyers we sent on over a hundred trips, but they knew where to find bazaars and craftsmen and remote marketplaces. They were invaluable in helping work out our special events program and finding the artists," Mr. Traub said.

Pallavi Shah of Air India (New York) and Peggy Healy, vice-president of public relations for Bloomingdale's, scouted India for talent for the various programs. It was like mounting a full-scale Broadway production. Twenty-eight artists, craftsmen, dancers, and musicians were selected to come and perform in the United States.

During the "Ultimate Fantasy," the events featured displays and demonstrations of Rangoli, the ancient art of floor decoration created by an artist hand-sifting powdered glass to create a colorful welcome mat, and Mehndi, the delicate art of hand and foot painting that has been handed down for centuries.

There were art exhibitions of Pichwais, paintings depicting the Hindu god Krishna. Ten-foot-high paintings on fabric of the great emperors, commissioned by Bloomingdale's, decorated the stores, and there were displays of Indian miniatures. A master painter demonstrated the techniques used in this centuries-old art. There was an exhibition of Kathakali Dance miniature dolls presented by the prize-winning artist who makes them. There was a demonstration of crafting the lost blue pottery of Jaipur.

During the promotion, there were shows galore. A group of Kathak dancers performed the classical dance of north India accompanied by sitar, tabla, and voice. The celebrated dancer Mrinalini Sarabhai and her daughter Mallika from Ahmadabad performed the classical Bharat Natyam dances. A troup performed with their Shadow Puppets of Andrha, and a man and his wife entertained with the complicated Rajastani String Puppets.

There were demonstrations of ancient and modern musical instruments, a gift from the government of the State of Tamil Nadu in south India to the people of the City of New York, and the instruments were later presented to the Metropolitan Museum of Art's Musical Instrument Wing. There was an astrologist-palmist-face reader whom Bloomingdale's customers could consult.

As the plans for the promotions were moving along, Bloomingdale's buyers and additional Indian agents were roaming India in search of exotic merchandise and ordering textiles and accessories and furnishings to be made to their specifications. Traditional Indian designs, materials, and products were adapted to the American market. Hundreds of brass water jugs, for instance, were polished and fitted with electrical fixtures and simple modern shades—a Bloomingdale's exclusive. "Those jugs have been around for centuries, but it took Bloomingdale's to envision them as lamps," an Indian merchant said. It is this ability to find and adapt merchandise that is one of Bloomingdale's fortes.

Indian clothing was purchased and European, American, and Indian designers were asked to create special collections of ready-to-wear using Indian fabrics and design inspirations. Perfume manufacturers created exotic scents.

Barbara D'Arcy of merchandise presentation and Candy Pratts of display were having a creative heyday buying statues, artifacts, doors, window frames, ceiling panels, and even the façade of an entire building. "We needed things on a large scale if we were to create the effect we wanted," Miss D'Arcy said. "We decided to take a traditional and classic approach to the presentation of the merchandise and play on India's cultural assets—the art, architecture, sculpture, and design. My job was to romance what everyone else was buying. I wanted to buy a life-sized carved wood elephant. Then, in the Folk Art Museum in Ahmadabad, we found fantastic life-sized canvas animals all in ceremonial dress. So I bought *two* elephants, five camels, four horses, two buffalo. We bought a bullock cart right off the street. I must say the Indians were rather bewildered.''

Ruth Eshel, Bloomingdale's delicacies department buyer-manager, began her Indian experience by becoming a regular in New York's Indian restaurants early in the year. She haunted New York's Indian markets, read Indian cookbooks, and consulted with Madhur Jaffrey, the well-known Indian cookbook author. But Ms. Eshel's real discovery came in India. ''I found things that were not to be believed—saffron-flavored honey from Kashmir, Assam honey with a flavor from tea flower blossoms. And chutney! One morning I tasted thirty-five chutneys. And cocoanut crunch candy and cookies! And mango squash! Oh, the markets—Crawford market, the Bengali Market, and the Chowpathy Beach stalls! Fantastic!'' Ruth Eshel's enthusiasm about food comes from her belief that ''food isn't shelves of groceries; it's alive. It's terribly exciting.''

Miss Eshel is a handsome woman who was born thirty-two years ago in Israel. Her father served as Israeli Ambassador in posts all over the world and eventually as Ambassador to the United Nations. When Miss Eshel's mother died, she found herself, at the age of thirteen, running the Israeli Embassy kitchen in foreign countries with help from a small staff and a limited budget. ''I planned the menus, supervised the marketing, and helped cook. I loved to cook and I learned that it was nothing to have 125 people for lunch on short notice.''

Upon receiving her BA in political science from the Hebrew University in Jerusalem, she decided she wanted to work with food. ''I went to the school of Hotel Administration at Cornell for a year of graduate studies and then worked for an airline, coordinating the china, glassware, and linen. I left to go into food and worked for Joe Baum, the genius director of the mammoth food operation at the World Trade Center. I came to Bloomingdale's in January 1977, and I love it. I have so many ideas and I want to *celebrate* food. The India promotion was an incredible experience. It was another step in what I want to do—which is to make Bloomingdale's the best delicacies store in the world!''

In the early fall of 1977, western-style news conferences were scheduled in Bombay and Delhi to announce the Bloomingdale's-Air India almost $10 million promotion and a basic problem of east-west differences arose. Some western institutions do not relate to the subcontinent, and a department store, much less a hip store like Bloomingdale's, is one of them. India is a country of open markets, shops, and bazaars. It seemed highly unlikely that India's relatively unsophisticated press corps would comprehend what the conference was about.

The Air India Indians involved did not want to offend the Bloomingdale's people by saying that not many people in India knew about Bloomingdale's. Nor did they want to point out the naivete of their countrymen. And yet, they wanted to save Bloomingdale's any embarrassment. Suddenly, they came up with a very simple solution. Some Indians had been to London and shopped in the big stores there. Others could at least relate to the stores from the years before Independence when goods poured into the country in boxes marked Harrods, Fortnum & Mason, and Selfridges. If Bloomingdale's would explain briefly that it was a large organization like Harrods, then everything would be fairly clear. End of problem.

The Americans were struck dumb by the Indians' suggestion. Like *Harrods*? Why in the world would Bloomingdale's ever say such a thing? Bloomingdale's was BLOOMINGDALE'S. Their ads said: *Bloomingdale's, it's like* NO *other store in the world*. Why would they say it was *like* Harrods?

The Indians discreetly suggested then, if not Harrods, what about Selfridges? Yes, that would be better. Selfridges had been founded by an American.

Well, there was simply *no way*. Wherever did these Indians come up with such a crazy idea?

A Bloomingdale employee said: "Can you imagine what the *Times* would do with that story? Bloomingdale's says New York's beloved Bloomie's is *like* Harrods! My God!"

The press conference was held in Bombay and the announcement was made about the Bloomingdale's and Air India poster contest and the Indians did what Indians do when they are confused or bored. They bobbed their heads and they drifted into deep meditation while making vague gestures of taking notes.

"We had to face it," said a member of the Bloomingdale's team, "Bloomingdale's wasn't exactly a household word in India. You might say, 'We bombed in Bombay.'"

Before the Delhi press conference, Telexes flew across the oceans and continents and a film was sent for. When it arrived, it was a video tape. It would show some of Bloomingdale's greatest triumphs. It would give an idea of the store. It would be very impressive. After great difficulties in locating a video machine, the press conference at the Oberoi-Intercontinental Hotel got under way. The tape rolled and there were clips from the CBS *60 Minutes* program and clips from the day when Bloomingdale's got Lexington Avenue turned around. And then a woman appeared on the screen. She was strolling down the store aisles like any other middle-aged shopper with her husband in tow. She was Queen Elizabeth II of England.

An American correspondent overheard an exchange between two Indian newsmen:

"Those are the Brits," one Indian said to another.

"I know," said the other, unimpressed by the Queen.

"And *that* is Harrods," announced the more worldly of the two.

India has a vast network of communications that has nothing to do with press conferences, video tapes, or Telexes. As the word spread before long, everyone knew what Bloomingdale's was—or almost.

In January 1978, a letter arrived at Air India's New Delhi office. It was written in what Indians call "Hinglish," a stilted form of English that is used by many Indians—one of the end products of the formal British school system.

To
The General Manager
Air-India
New Delhi.

Most Respected Sir,

Sub: Booming Sales—Exhibition to be conducted at New York in April 1978—by Air-India—regarding.

It is learnt that the Air-India is going to conduct a Booming Sales Exhibition at New York in April 1978. In this regard I would like to introduce myself as an eminent artisan.

As such I very kindly request your goodself to consider my case favourably for demonstration and sales for the ensuing Booming Sales

Exhibition to be conducted by Air-India at New York in April 1978.
I very earnestly request your goodself to include my name in the list
and arrange to take me as one of the exhibitor for the exhibition.
            Yours faithfully,

There were, of course, minor mishaps along the way, as there
had to be with any project of this size. One freighter filled with
containers of Bloomingdale's merchandise docked in California.
The story was that the Bombay shipping company, having heard
about the snow and ice blanketing the east coast, hauled the goods
overland to Calcutta and shipped it to the warmer shores on the
west coast. It is an unlikely explanation since another cargo for
Bloomingdale's landed in Anchorage, Alaska.

Miss D'Arcy's menagerie simply vanished from the face of the
ocean. Only after a frantic search did it turn up in the hold of a Caribbean cruise ship. Miss D'Arcy's building façade arrived
"knocked down" with not a clue in the carload how to reassemble
it. "I spent hours in the warehouse," she said, "and over the years
I've been able to put back large structures from Portugal, Spain, Italy, almost anywhere—but this was truly one of the mysteries of
the east. We finally had to use the carved pieces individually.
There was simply no way to put them together."

There were problems for the visiting Indian artists, too. The Rajastani puppeteers, who spoke no English, were lost for most of
one day in Boston and the psychic had problems with his vibrations. "He said that the loud speakers jumped his heartbeat and
threw him into the wrong wave length," Peggy Healy said. "He
claimed some of his powers came from having lived for a period of
time in a burial ground where he absorbed 1,268 different blood
types. There were times when his vibes didn't function that I
thought it would be better if we just turned him over to the Red
Cross."

I personally found the gentleman's vibrations functioning on a
very fine frequency at the party that opened the "Ultimate Fantasy" in Boston. In the quiet corner of one of the model rooms he
touched my hand and then looking into the beyond, or more accu-
rately into the outdoor furniture department, he revealed my past
with uncanny and frightening accuracy. He told me I was a writer,
which I knew, of course, and that I had come to the party in con-

junction with a project that I was about to finish. This I also knew. He then disclosed something I did not know. In 1979 he said I would find *glory*. I have never given much thought to glory, so it is amusing to think about. He also warned me that I would have trouble with my gall bladder in 1992.

Somewhat shaken by the experience, I headed for the bar. As I was moving through the crowd in the modular furniture area a quotation came to mind: "The paths of glory lead but to the grave." I hesitated for a moment. Then with total disregard for my gall bladder, I sallied up to the bar and ordered a Scotch. Somehow in the magic of Bloomingdale's surrounded by the mystery of India with the orchestra playing and the Bennington College Alumnae, who were sponsoring the benefit gala, circulating, 1992 seemed very far away.

By the early part of June 1978 various Bloomingdale's personel were off to France to scour the country for fine food and cooking equipment for their sixth-floor gourmet department to be opened in the fall.

As for India, it took the whole affair in its stride and added to the long succession of invaders—Persian, Greek, Parthian, Scythian, Hun, Turk, Afghan, Arab, Mongol, Brits—the Bloomies.

SIXTEEN

"Wrap It Up!"

A store is a place where goods are bought and sold. A store is also a treasure and the coffers are filled with essentials, luxuries, and even bits of stuff-and-nonsense.

For over 125 years there have been stores, large and small, in the north, south, east, and west of the United States that have been more than purveyors of goods. For the goods have been bought, displayed, promoted, and sold with a special kind of attention—a special kind of magic. These stores distribute, along with the merchandise, moments of wonder and joy.

The moment when paper is clawed and torn away by excited pudgy fingers is special. The moment is heightened when the lid is lifted and out of the box comes a glorious delight—Teddy Bear—Winnie the Pooh—Paddington Bear—warm and cuddly—to be snuggled and fondled. Or an elegant princess or a soft baby—doll—to be dressed up and hugged. There is the moment of squeals and coos and smiles all around. It's Christmas—a birthday—a remembrance—it's love.

The quiet moment of anticipation before the ribbon is pulled and a bow is untied is followed by the noisy moment when crisp tissue paper crackles like a blazing fire. There is the breathless moment relieved by a gasp when slender manicured fingers raise a gossamer to shoulder height. Then comes the exalted moment of admiration as swirls of fabric envelop space with a colorful tornado of beauty. A body twirls and a voice cries out, "Oh, I love it! I love it!"

There is the thrilling moment when a truck arrives and a burly giant asks, "Okay, where do you want this?" There are the tense moments of grunts and groans and sweating and straining until the heavy carton is set down. There are the nervous moments when a hand writes a signature across the bill of lading and trembling grown-up fingers tear away the cardboard and butcher paper and a sofa—a table—a chair—is unveiled. Rattan or wicker from a far-off land? Antique walnut or mahogany shaped and polished years ago? Or chrome and glass as futuristic as tomorrow? No matter—it is the moment when a heretofore empty room becomes a home.

Oh, "the world is so full of a number of things. . . ."

And then there are the moments of remembering other moments—the cold marble of the pink and gold ladies room. A gentle mother driven to exasperation by a stubborn little girl wanting to grow up too fast. The warmth and mystery of a Chinatown shop and the silky feel of a pair of furry slippers and the acceptance of the remaining years of childhood. The memory of the admiration and indulgence of loving grandparents, the jealousy and envy of siblings, the patience of a mother who knows "what's right," and the anxiety of a shopping father who's "not quite sure." Shopping ties a parent to a child—temporarily, like a Christmas ribbon—they are wrapped in the shared excitement of "discovery" or "something new." There is the memory of fear—the awesomeness of the vast emporiums and the terror of being lost, never to be found. And there is the security of tightly held hands and the remorse over a lost glove. There are the grown-up memories of extended courtesies and extra thoughtfulness or the coldness of a haughty salesperson, or the embarrassing remembrance of pinned-together *underpinnings*.

Memories of a morning, a day, a shopping trip trigger memories of the events that followed—the christenings—the graduations—the weddings. And then again—the christenings—the graduations—the weddings—the cycle of life's productions. The costumes, the scenery, the makeup, the props—the show business that livens up our lives.

And the people. The Miss Roses offering guidance to what is "proper." The Sara Middlemans taking from a hanger a dress that holds the promise of romance. The Ruth Eshels offering new and exotic taste experiences—fiery curries and chutneys—sweet prize-winning homemade relishes discovered at an Iowa State Fair—sticky honeys from Kashmir—Assam—odoriferous cheeses from France. A store is the people.

Top management hires "the people" and through them sets the tone, the style. It also controls the budget. Top management is less visible today than it was when stores were one-man operations. More than likely it comes out of Harvard Business School than up through the ranks. Handling the complexities of today's behemoth organizations requires intensive training. Most management operates in a partnership, a tandem team with the chief executive in charge of planning, financing, and operations, and the president overseeing merchandising and promotion.

Unlike the faithful Gimbel brothers, only a handful of sons follow their father's footsteps into retailing. Those who have tend to detour from home base. Richard Marcus, the son of Stanley Marcus, spent a year in the executive training program at Bloomingdale's and was offered a permanent job. He declined. He also spent several months working at Saks Fifth Avenue before returning home to Dallas and the family store Neiman-Marcus. He is currently the store president although Neiman-Marcus is owned by Carter Hawley Hale Stores, Inc. A recent Harvard Business School graduate, Andy Traub, although emulating his dynamo merchant father, Marvin Traub of Bloomingdale's, has entered Bloomie's enemy camp. Young Andy is a member of the R. H. Macy & Co. training squad. Marvin Traub's own situation was unique. He followed in his mother's footsteps—almost. When he became a merchant like the famous Bea Traub of Bonwit Teller he did so six blocks away at Bloomingdale's.

But there have been shattered hopes and broken dreams of family continuity along the way.

On the night of October 16, 1951, when Bergdorf Goodman celebrated with a Golden Anniversary Ball in the Grand Ballroom of the Plaza Hotel, all seemed right with the world. Edwin Goodman, the store founder, took pride in his son, Andrew, who had proved himself to be a superb and imaginative merchant. In his book, *Bergdorf's On the Plaza*, Booton Herndon wrote of that night.

Edwin Goodman had lived to see the institution he had fashioned honored on its golden anniversary, a celebration the like of which New York had seldom seen before, had lived to pass the reins of leadership down firmly to his son, Andrew, had lived to see his grandchild Edwin take an early but sincere interest in enhancing the natural beauty of women through clothes.

Edwin died in 1953. The following year young Edwin accompanied his father on a European buying trip. At fourteen years of age he showed the instincts and taste of a merchant. His older sister, Vivien, when she graduated from Wellesley, showed an interest in working in the store. The two younger Goodman daughters, Mary Ann and Pamela, were too young to have made up their minds. The hopes were hinged on Edwin according to Booton Herndon, in 1956.

And so the future of Bergdorf Goodman was set, to continue under the tasteful guidance of the family of the founder.

In 1972 Carter Hawley Hale (then Broadway-Hale) purchased the glamorous glory of Fifth Avenue—Bergdorf's on the Plaza. Young Edwin Goodman and two of his brothers-in-law, having served as store executives, had departed voluntarily to follow their own pursuits. The family affair was over.

Andrew Goodman remains as chairman of the board of Bergdorf Goodman. He and his wife, Nena, continue to live over the store. In the days when Bergdorf's featured custom-made clothes, Edwin Goodman had been designated janitor of the building in keeping with a city ordinance which allowed only a superintendent to reside where manufacturing was taking place. The sixteen-room penthouse high atop Bergdorf Goodman is a far cry from the average super's quarters.

Bergdorf's top-top management, Carter Hawley Hale, is far removed from the elegant store on the Plaza at Fifth Avenue. It is located in Los Angeles, California. And so it goes, with Federated Department Stores, Inc., overseeing Bloomingdale's in New York, Rich's in Atlanta, Bullock's and Magnin's in California, from its headquarters in Cincinnati, Ohio. The giant Amfac conglomerate guides the policies of its retail operations from Hawaii, along with agricultural, food processing, real estate, and hospitality divisions. The bigness has enabled many stores to survive as downtowns decay or real estate values soar, as volume buying in the highly competitive business has become a necessity that requires masses of working capital. But with it goes the risk that the bigness might defuse the regional qualities that are part of the store's "personality."

It is the people in the local management who fight to hang on to those elusive qualities that make a store unique and a civic pride. "We must keep the *Texas-ish-ness* in Neiman-Marcus," said vice-president Tom Alexander. "Saks anywhere must be Very Fifth Avenue," said an executive. In Chicago the outrage was swift when Carter Hawley Hale threatened to take over Marshall Field & Co. "It's unconscionable for some *foreign* company that probably doesn't even know Chicago to run Field's," a customer told *The New York Times*. The article that appeared on Christmas Day, 1977, said that the threat was received by Chicagoans "as warmly as might be a bid by New Jersey to take over New York City's Broadway or an effort by the Grinch to steal Christmas."

Surprisingly, Field's chairman of the board, Angelo Arena, who had recently come from Carter Hawley Hale's Neiman-Marcus, and who was not a Chicagoan, went to battle against his former employers to keep the tradition that "Field's *is* Chicago."

It mattered little to Chicagoans in early 1978 that the next round went to Carter Hawley Hale when it outbid Field's for Philadelphia's Wanamaker's. Let Philadelphia take care of itself. What mattered was that, for the time being at least, Chicago's beloved Marshall Field's was saved from a *foreign* takeover.

Sometimes during a takeover the "baton of management" is dropped as it is being passed along or it is picked up and run with a different pace. The changes are apt to catch the customers off guard, like expecting to hear a string quartet and tuning in on a rock concert.

At a recent charity benefit held in Bergdorf Goodman things seemed much the same. A few ribbons tied into the chandeliers, nothing raucous. Elegant and luxurious Bergdorf's had in the past a slightly racey undertone—there had been discreet and whispered innuendoes involving such bygone characters as "kept" women and "sugar daddies"—but over the past few years the store had taken on the air of a lavender-haired grande dame. The 1978 spring party seemed traditional enough. Uniformed maids and butlers passed champagne and hors d'oeuvres. Mr. Andrew Goodman gave a welcoming and spoke with enthusiasm about their designer's collection. People readied themselves for the old solid fashion-show beat—"A Pretty Girl Is Like a Melody." The lights dimmed and then—KAPOW! It was a zippy disco-y rhythm and there were flashes of color, fabric, skin, sparkling teeth, frizzed hair—as long-legged young men and women zinged across the platform, spun and disappeared, leaving the audience struck by brilliant flashing thunderbolts. It was a new jet-speed fashion show. The crowd gasped, picked up the beat, and loved it. A wide-eyed young woman said, "*This* is Bergdorf Goodman? WOW!" In a corner Ira Neimark, Bergdorf's new, young president, smiled. His eyes darted around the room, watching the audience and the lightning-fast show. Upstairs he was readying another surprise. In a few weeks he would reopen the second floor with individual boutiques offering the elegant fashions of Saint Laurent, Givenchy, Fendi, Mila Schön, Chanel, Geoffrey Beene, and a designer new to America, Muriel Grateau. This would be the *new* Bergdorf's—marching to the up beat of today's drummers.

For all the IBM read-outs and computer operations it is the people who, while making the change, must keep the personality, the magic, the adventure, the excitement, the tradition, and the faith—those elusive qualities that have made the great stores great. It is the buyers who know the markets and the territory and race across the crowded jet streams to Europe, the Orient, Africa, and the sub-continent of India, who comb the markets of the United States looking for the new, the exotic, the "something special." It is the sellers behind the counters and in the salons who must entice the customer and "make the sale." In between are hundreds of others: people in display and store design; in advertising; shipping and receiving; the alterationists and bookkeepers. It is the people in publicity and promotion who hoist the *gonfalone*, sound the drum, and ring the bells to create the big parade—the razzmatazz—the theater—the fun. They are today's "pullers-in." And there are the service crews and a few remaining doormen.

Henri Bendel's has a special flair all the way from the executive suite of president Geraldine Stutz down to the street where "Buster" of Bendel's, in his snappy brown pillbox and double-breasted brass-buttoned coat, opens doors and hails cabs. "Buster," as James Jarrett is known to the chic world of New York's Fifty-seventh Street, at the age of fourteen answered a Bendel's window ad for "Boy Wanted." That was in the early 1900s, when the store was located on Fifth Avenue. The store recently celebrated his eighty-third birthday. For over sixty-five years Buster has seen the changes from fashionable horse-drawn carriages to limousines to today's customers, most of whom arrive by foot or taxicab. He has seen a steady flow of the rich and the beautiful—Vanderbilts, Astors, DuPonts—and some things that don't change much. "The rich aren't different today," Buster said. "Some are big tippers—and some aren't." At 4:30 daily a Bendel car arrives at the Fifty-seventh Street entrance. Buster opens the door. He then steps inside and is chauffeur-driven home.

A store is a place—a building—like the great marble palaces of the Ladies Mile or the towered *modern* Bullock's Wilshire. Often it's a group of buildings strung together over the years, like Marshall Field's. A store may be a place within a place, like the sprawling malls scattered throughout the nation's suburbs or the latest downtown multilevel shopping centers: Chicago's Water Tower Place; Philadelphia's Gallery; Kansas City's Crown Center, and Los Angeles's Broadway Plaza. A store may be a mix of the old and new, like Philip Johnson's plan for San Francisco's Neiman-Marcus which is designed to contain the turn-of-the-century City of Paris rotunda and stained-glass dome within a modern block-long structure. Architects who build stores know that they are more than buildings. John Portman calls his Peachtree Center in Atlanta, Embarcadero Center in San Francisco, Renaissance Center in Detroit—"people places." Arthur Novak of Copeland, Novak and Israel, architects for stores and shopping centers throughout the world, said, "A store is a center for a festive occasion."

A great store is a collection of all the tangibles—the building, the people, the merchandise, the whoopla—combined with a special spirit. "It must have a soul," said Walter Hoving. "It's show business," said Milton Hofflin, a Copeland, Novak consultant. "It's excitement," said Saks's Helen O'Hagan. "It's romance," said Sara Middleman. "It must be fun!" said Mildred Custin. "It's change," said Lawrence Lachman. "It's a celebration," said Peggy Healy. Bergdorf's Jo Hughes said at the Top of the Fifth, "Retailing! It's not the same old ball game!" But then even the "old ball game" isn't the *same* old ball game.

No one knows how trade began. Perhaps one hairy fellow saw another turning over a bright pebble in his hand and thought he'd like that pebble for himself. It may have been the discovery that a bearskin was warmer than a fig leaf. Trade has taken people across deserts, oceans, mountains, and up and down rivers by camel, horse, muleback, clipper ship, steamship, "bungo," stagecoach, train, bus, car, and foot and high into the air lanes. Searching for that something to buy and sell to make food taste better, to make men and women look more beautiful, to make homes more comfortable, to delight the eye and lift the spirit and warm the heart, so that someone—somewhere—at some age—can have that moment—that thrill that comes when the wrapping comes off and there is a cry of, "Oh, don't you *love* it!"

And so the beat goes on. The searching and finding, the buying and selling, the remodeling and the building, the expansion. The store—the reflection of our country's differences, our pride, our life-styles, ourselves—the tempo of our times. The rhythm may slacken, the pace may quicken, the beat may change—but the beat goes on.

Bibliography

Adburgham, Alison. *Shops and Shopping 1800–1914, Where and in What Manner, the Well-Dressed Englishwoman Bought Her Clothes*. London: George Allen & Unwin Ltd., 1964.

Arnason, H. H. *History of Modern Art*. Englewood Cliffs, N.J.: Prentice-Hall, 1977.

Artley, Alexandra. *The Golden Age of Shop Design, European Shop Interiors 1880–1939*. London: The Architectural Press, 1975.

Banham, Reyner. *The Architecture of the Well-Tempered Environment*. London: The Architectural Press, 1969.

Batterberry, Ariane and Michael. *The Bloomingdale's Book of Entertaining*. New York: Random House, 1976.

Battersby, Martin. *Art Deco Fashion—French Designers 1908–1925*. Academy Edition. London and New York: St. Martin's Press, 1974.

Bayer, Herbert, and Walter Gropius, eds. *Bauhaus*. New York: Museum of Modern Art, 1938.

Bennett, George. *Mannequins*. New York: Knopf, 1977.

Bloomingdale's 100—Perspectives on a New York Tradition. New York: Bloomingdale's, 1972.

Caro, Ruth; Patricia Gerbie; and Judith Telinger. *The Lake is Always East*. Evanston, Ill.: Chicago Chauvinists, 1977.

349

Chase, Edna Woolman, and Ilka Chase. *Always in Vogue*. Garden City, N. Y.: Doubleday, 1954.

Condon, Eddie. *We Called It Music—A Generation of Jazz*. London: Peter Davies, 1948.

Corbitt, Helen. *Helen Corbitt's Cookbook*. Boston: Houghton Mifflin, 1957.

D'Arcy, Barbara. *Bloomingdale's Book of Home Decorating*. New York: Harper & Row, 1973.

Edwards, Richard, Jr. *Tales of the Observer*. Boston: Jordan Marsh Co., 1950.

Emory, Michael. *Windows*. Chicago: Contemporary Books, 1977.

Ewing, Elizabeth. *History of 20th Century Fashion*. New York: Scribner's, 1974.

Fairchild's Financial Manual of Retail Stores. New York: Fairchild Books, 1977.

Fitz-Gibbon, Bernice. *Macy's, Gimbels and Me*. New York: Simon and Schuster, 1967.

Flanner, Janet. *Paris Was Yesterday*. New York: Viking, 1972.

Gillon, Gayle, Margot, and Edmund V., Jr. *Cast-Iron Architecture in New York*. New York: Dover Publications, 1974.

Goldstone, Harmon, and Martha Dalrymple. *History Preserved—A Guide to New York City Landmarks and Historic Districts*. New York: Simon and Schuster, 1974.

Gottlieb, Robert, and Irene Wolt. *Thinking Big*. New York: Putnam, 1977.

Greenfield, Howard. *They Came to Paris*. New York: Crown, 1975.

Harriman, Margaret Case. *And the Price is Right—The R. H. Macy Story*. New York: World, 1958.

Herndon, Booton. *Bergdorf's on the Plaza*. New York: Knopf, 1956.

Johnson, Curtiss S. *The Indomitable R. H. Macy*. New York: Vantage Press, 1964.

Johnson, Philip. *Architecture: 1946–1965*. New York: Holt, Rinehart & Winston, 1966.

Kirby, Gustavus T. *I Wonder Why?* New York: Coward McCann, 1954.

Klein, Jerome, and Norman Reader. *Great Shops of Europe*. New York: National Retail Merchants Association, 1969.

Lief, Alfred. *Family Business—A Century in the Life and Times of Strawbridge & Clothier*. New York: McGraw-Hill, 1968.

Maccoby, Michael. *The Gamesman—The New Corporate Leaders*. New York: Simon and Schuster, 1976.

Macy, Josiah. *I Followed the Sea*. Meriden, Conn.: Bayberry Hill Press, 1960.

Macy, Silvanus J. *Genealogy of the Macy Family from 1635–1868*.

Mahoney, Tom, and Leonard Sloane. *The Great Merchants*. New York: Harper & Row, 1974.

Maino, Jeannette Gould. *One Hundred Years—Modesto, California, 1870–1970*. Modesto, Calif.: Belt Printing & Lithograph, 1970.

Marcus, Stanley. *Minding the Store*. Boston: Little, Brown, 1974.

Mark, Norman. *Norman Mark's Chicago—Walking, Bicycling and Driving Tours of the City*. Chicago: Chicago Review Press, 1977.

Mayer, Harold M., and Richard Wade. *Chicago—Growth of a Metropolis*. Chicago: University of Chicago Press, 1969.

Miller, Merle. *Plain Speaking—An Oral Biography of Harry S Truman*. New York: Putnam, 1974.

Morris, Bernadine, and Barbra Walz. *The Fashion Makers*. New York: Random House, 1978.

Nasatir, A. P., ed. *The Letters of Etienne Derbec, A French Journalist in the California Gold Rush*.

New York City Guide. American Guide Series. Boston: Houghton Mifflin, 1939.

Nordstrom, John. *The Immigrant in 1887*. Seattle: Dogwood Press, 1950.

Portman, John, and Jonathan Barnett. *The Architect as Developer*. New York: McGraw-Hill, 1976.

Reed, Henry Hope, and Sophia Duckworth. *Central Park—A History and a Guide*. New York: Clarkson N. Potter, 1967.

Sakol, Jeannie. *New Year's Eve*. Philadelphia: Lippincott, 1974.

Sandburg, Carl. *Chicago Poems*. New York: Henry Holt, 1916.

Scully, Vincent. *American Architecture and Urbanism.* New York: Praeger, 1969.

Sen, Gertrude Emerson. *The Pageant of India's History.* London: Longmans, Green, 1948.

Sibley, Celestine. *Dear Store—An Affectionate Portrait of Rich's.* New York: Doubleday, 1967.

Stewart, Marjabelle Young, and Ann Buchwald. *What to Do—When and Why.* New York: David McKay, 1975.

Stewart, Marjabelle Young, and Ann Buchwald. *Stand Up, Shake Hands, Say "How Do You Do."* New York: David McKay, 1977.

Tolbert, Frank X. *Neiman-Marcus.* New York: Henry Holt, 1953.

Trahey, Jane. *Jane Trahey on Women & Power.* New York: Rawson Associates, 1977.

Vogue Poster Book: A Collection of Magazine Covers from Vogue (1911-1927). Introduction by Diana Vreeland. New York: Harmony, 1975.

Wendt, Lloyd. *Give the Lady What She Wants—The Story of Marshall Field & Co.* Chicago: Rand McNally, 1952.

White, Norval, and Elliot Willensky, eds. *AIA Guide to New York City.* New York: Macmillan, 1968.

Index

355